# The *Sexual* Organization of the City

# The

# *Sexual*

# Organization

# of the City

Edited by

Edward O. Laumann,
Stephen Ellingson,
Jenna Mahay,
Anthony Paik,
and Yoosik Youm

The University of Chicago Press
*Chicago and London*

EDWARD O. LAUMANN is the George Herbert Mead
Distinguished Service Professor of Sociology at the University
of Chicago. He is coauthor of *The Social Organization of
Sexuality* and coeditor of *Sex, Love, and Health in America*, both
published by the University of Chicago Press. STEPHEN
ELLINGSON is assistant professor of sociology at the Pacific
Lutheran Theological Seminary. JENNA MAHAY is a
postdoctoral fellow in the Population Research Center at the
University of Chicago. ANTHONY PAIK is a doctoral student
in the Department of Sociology at the University of Chicago.
YOOSIK YOUM is assistant professor of sociology at the
University of Illinois at Chicago.

The University of Chicago Press, Chicago 60637
The University of Chicago Press, Ltd., London
© 2004 by The University of Chicago
All rights reserved. Published 2004
Printed in the United States of America

13  12  11  10  09  08  07  06  05  04          1  2  3  4  5

ISBN: 0-226-47031-8 (cloth)

Library of Congress Cataloging-in-Publication Data

The sexual organization of the city / edited by Edward O.
   Laumann . . . [et al.].
      p. cm.
   Includes bibliographical references and index.
   ISBN 0-226-47031-8 (cloth : alk. paper)
   1. Sex customs—Illinois—Chicago.   I.  Laumann,
Edward O.
HQ18.U5 S495 2004
306.7'09773'11

                                             2003017586

# Contents

# Illustrations and Tables

## Map

## Figures

Tables

# *Preface*

The Chicago Health and Social Life Survey (CHSLS) has had a long and complex project life over the past twelve years, with many people and institutions playing critically important supportive roles at key points in its development. Here, we would like to share some of the CHSLS story in the modest hope of acknowledging and expressing our deeply felt gratitude for the intellectual, financial, and technical assistance from which we have greatly benefited over the years.

The CHSLS's intellectual gestation was in 1991, after Edward O. Laumann, John Gagnon, Robert T. Michael, and Stuart Michaels had endured a three-year delay in initiating the survey phase of the National Health and Social Life Survey (NHSLS) (see Laumann, Gagnon, Michael, & Michaels, 1994). Recall that this period was near the height of the AIDS epidemic in the United States, and many in scientific and medical circles were fearful that we would not get the desperately needed information on American sexual practices quickly enough to aid in the design of more effective public-health interventions to stop the spread of HIV. The NHSLS's survey instrument was reviewed by the White House's Office of Management and the Budget (OMB) in the Reagan/Bush administrations because it was an official government survey and, therefore, subject to such a review. This review provided the first opportunity (in 1989) to stall work on the national survey by those who vehemently opposed it. Subsequently, congressional opponents, under the leadership of Representative William Dannemeyer (California) and Senator Jesse Helms (North Carolina), succeeded in stalling the funding for the national survey for several years.

The NHSLS coprincipal investigators decided that it might be possible to avoid such political maneuvering, and, thereby, avoid delay, if a regular grant proposal to conduct a community-based sex survey were submitted to the National Institute of Child Health and Human Development (NICHD). If such a grant proposal successfully passed National Institutes of Health (NIH) scientific peer review and was recommended for funding, the survey instrument would be treated as a research tool for which the scientific team itself was wholly responsible—in short, the survey instrument would have no official government status and, therefore, would not be subject to the regulatory oversight in which the NHSLS was embroiled. While the data to be gathered by the grant would not meet all the goals that a national survey could achieve, it would at least provide some critically needed information. Moreover, there was a compelling rationale for undertaking a community-based as opposed to a national survey of sexual practices, namely, that sexual transactions are fundamentally local phenomena, occurring in locally organized markets, embedded in locally organized social networks, and so on. Locally contextualized phenomena are simply beyond the reach of national surveys.

A high-priority score was, in fact, achieved for the proposal, rather pusillanimously entitled "The Social Demography of Interpersonal Attraction," to avoid the dreaded word *sex* in public listings of federally funded projects, which, as experience with the NHSLS had made clear, would inevitably attract unwanted attention in the highly confrontational atmosphere of the time. It was announced in June 1991 that the proposal had passed the higher-level review by an NICHD public oversight panel and that funding would begin in October. On 6 September 1991, the first day of the hearings on the appointment of Clarence Thomas to the Supreme Court—a matter that had drawn the undivided attention of liberal and conservative senators alike—Senator Helms, in a precisely timed political move, introduced an amendment to the NIH funding bill that transferred the funding for the national sex survey to funding for a "say no to sex" public initiative that Helms had been advocating for years. In a sixty-six to thirty-four Senate vote that evening, Helms's amendment carried. Shortly thereafter, NIH officials decided that, in the light of the Senate vote, it was not feasible to proceed with funding of the grant at that time. Happily, however, the vote did precipitate the resolve of a number of private foundations to fund a much scaled down version of the national sex survey, which was conducted in the following year.

Shortly after the election of President Bill Clinton in November 1992, the NIH announced that the grant would be funded after all. But the data-analysis and write-up phases of the national survey were by that time in full swing. So work on the grant had to be deferred until mid-1994, when study and questionnaire design could begin in earnest.

When work on the project began in earnest, project staff quickly decided that the recently developed technology of computer-assisted program interviewing (CAPI) would greatly enhance the sense of privacy and confidentiality in answering highly sensitive questions (and would, thus, improve the candor of the respondents on socially sensitive questions) as well as facilitate negotiating the complex skip patterns that were needed to refer to different sex partners and their relationships with the respondent. While the CAPI technology ultimately lived up to its billing as a methodological advance (Newman et al. 2002), in employing it we did, of course, incur all the pitfalls and challenges associated with untried technologies, including lengthy delays and cost overruns in the design phase of the project. The unavoidable delay in starting the project had also imposed unexpected costs because of the "across-the board" cutbacks in federal funding, in several years on the order of 10 percent or more per year, that were imposed as a result of declining tax revenues during the period. It was a constant struggle to secure sufficient funding to cover field costs, and our fieldwork had to be interrupted on several occasions because of funding shortfalls.

Throughout this period, we had the full support of the National Opinion Research Center (NORC) and its panoply of institutional resources. The NORC staff created an intricate design for the five sampling frames (i.e., the Cook County cross section and the four neighborhood oversamples), hired and trained a highly motivated interview team of over fifty people, made certain that, during the interview phase of the study, we would be able to match respondent and interviewer in terms of race and ethnicity, and prepared a cleaned data tape ready for analysis. A public-use tape containing all the interview data, and stripped of all personal identifiers, is available in the NORC data archive for the use of interested researchers. (The data are also on deposit in the Inter-University Consortium of Political and Social Research at the University of Michigan, Ann Arbor.)

Throughout this challenging period, we were greatly assisted by the ready advice and support of NICHD project officers, including Wendy Baldwin (now deputy director of the NIH), Virginia Cain (deputy director, Office of Behavioral and Social Science Research, NIH), Susan Newcomer (program officer, Demographic and Behavioral Sciences Branch, NICHD), and Christine Bachrach (section chief, Demographic and Behavioral Sciences Branch, NICHD). We also gratefully acknowledge the financial support of the NICHD through grants RO1 HD28356 and RO1 HD 36963.

Several supplementary grants were secured to field surveys in additional Chicago neighborhoods and, thus, obtain better coverage of selected minority populations, especially Puerto Ricans and Mexicans. Noteworthy here were the two broad-based grants (940-1417 and 970-0155) from the Ford Foundation that supported the addition of another neighborhood to the study design, the distinctive institutional ethnographic component of the study, and an outreach effort to feed information back to the communities under study.

Looking back over this lengthy study period, we must recognize the superb contributions of a number of research assistants at different critical junctures.

In the questionnaire- and study-design phase (about 1994 to 1997), we want to thank Christopher Browning, Stephen Ellingson, James Farrer, Joel Feinleib, Kara Joyner, Nora Leibowitz, Kristen Olsen, Philip Schumm, and Ezra Zuckerman. Stuart Michaels and Martha Van Haitsma, serving as senior research managers during much of this period, deserve special recognition for their unstinting service to advancing the goals of the constantly evolving project. They were ably succeeded by Jenna Mahay and Anthony Paik, who served as co–project administrators for the balance of the project period.

Special thanks are also due to the eight-person team that conducted in-depth interviews with the 160 institutional leaders in the several neighborhoods—Kimberly Driggins, Matthew Hill, Amanda Nothaft, Greta Rensenbrink, Mark Sawyer, Michael Shaver, Clare Sullivan, and Nelson Tebbe. Finally, in the most recent period, we have been ably assisted by a hardworking group of quantitative analysts, including Jennifer Buntin, Marianna Gatzeva, Geoffry Guy, Kang Jeong-han, Zohar Lechtman, Jenna Mahay, Anthony Paik, Kirby Schroeder, Arnout Van de Rijt, and Yoosik Youm. John Blandford, an economist holding a Social Science Research Council Postdoctoral Fellowship in Sexuality Research at the University of Chicago, has consulted with us on a number of conceptual issues involved in the study of markets.

We also are very much in the intellectual debt of a number of faculty colleagues here and elsewhere, in particular Robert T. Michael, who has always been there to give us invaluable advice and counsel at every phase of the project, as well as Sevgi Aral (associate director of science, STD Division, Centers for Disease Control), Dr. John Bancroft (director, Kinsey Institute), Diane DiMauro (program officer, Social Science Research Council), John Gagnon, Patrick Heuveline, William Parish, Robert Sampson, Dr. Mark Siegler, Ross Stolzenberg, Linda Waite, Kazuo Yamaguchi, and Dingxin Zhao.

Of course, with an enterprise of this scale and complexity, we would surely have failed were it not for the unstinting administrative support that we have had from Isabel Garcia, Adelle Hinojosa, Kathleen Parks, Gail Spann, and Brian Whiteley. We especially want to acknowledge the key role that Ray Weathers has played in coordinating, seemingly without conscious effort, the multitude of meetings, exchanges of papers, and administrative paperwork (like IRB submissions, annual reports, filings) that inevitably flow in the wake of such endeavors.

Last, but certainly not least, we want to extend our sincere thanks to our respondents, who gave up their time to answer our questions. Because we maintain the confidentiality of respondents as a condition of proper research, we cannot name our many benefactors—public officials, community leaders, and everyday folks without whose cooperation no study of this sort could ever be done. In a world with increasing demands for information, people are beset with requests to complete surveys of one sort or another at every turn. This makes it ever more difficult for survey researchers to convince potential respondents that study participation is worthwhile. We truly appreciate the fact that our respondents trusted us to use the information that they freely provided to make useful scientific advances. We hope that they see value in the products of this research.

*Edward O. Laumann*
*Principal Investigator*
*Chicago Health and Social Life Survey*

# Part One )

## *Introduction*

1 )

# The Theory of Sex Markets

Stephen Ellingson,
Edward O. Laumann,
Anthony Paik,
and Jenna Mahay

Aurelia Salinas is a parish counselor at Saint Paul of the Cross Catholic Church in the Westside neighborhood of Chicago.[1] Ms. Salinas is formally trained in psychotherapy, is skilled in the arts of traditional herbal medicine and witchcraft of her native Peru, and was raised in the Catholic Church. She

1. *Westside* is the pseudonym that we have given to the neighborhood on the West Side of Chicago on which, along with three other neighborhoods, we focus in this study. The other three (also pseudonymous) neighborhoods are *Shoreland* (on the North Side), *Southtown* (on the South Side), and *Erlinda* (on the Northwest Side). For a detailed description of these neighborhoods, see Van Haitsma, Paik, and Laumann (chapter 2 in this volume). For a schematic rendering, see map 3.1 in Mahay and Laumann (chapter 3 in this volume).

All informants have been given pseudonyms as well.

uses all three "points of view" as she tries to help individuals, couples, and families deal with their relational problems. The main sexual problem that she encounters—and she encounters it all the time—is that women dislike sex, viewing it as a burden of marriage. There seems to be a widespread belief among men that women who have experienced the sexual pleasure of kissing or being caressed will no longer be receptive to penetration with the penis. Men therefore resist any form of sexual activity other than penetration. Ms. Salinas's problem has been to find a way to challenge this belief, but the traditional remedies do not help.

Barbara Boyer is a therapist whose clients are gay men and lesbians. When asked about gender and age differences among the two groups, she responded as one would expect—until she turned her attention to the post-AIDS generation:

> As a group, lesbians who are over thirty or thirty-five tend to be looking for relationships. Younger women tend to move through relationships quickly. Men of all ages tend to move through relationships quickly. Young women tend to think that it is OK to sleep around more than older women do. Moral or religious values do not tend to curtail activities; fear of AIDS does. Women still tend to think they're immune, and they shouldn't. For men, AIDS is a big issue in terms of getting into a relationship. They are mostly afraid that they are getting involved with someone only to lose him. There are two ways that men deal with the crisis. There are those who try to hold on to whoever they have left and those who don't want to make close attachments. Young men are fatalistic; they assume that they will get infected with HIV regardless of what precautions they take. Because of this there has been a loss of ground—people are not being as safe as they used to be. In a strange way, AIDS is influencing the "in" and "out" crowds within the adult community. Those who were "in" are HIV positive. I think it has to do with all of the attention that is given to men who are infected. There is a sense that they are waiting for the other shoe to drop. Friends and the community want to help, and they make those infected the focus of attention. More and more services are being directed at dealing with [AIDS], like all the support groups for men with HIV. HIV/AIDS is what people connect over.

Derek is a bisexual African American man from the city's South Side. Following his usual routine of looking for a straight, Hispanic gang-banger, Derek visits a public park in Chicago's Northwest Side neighborhood of Erlinda—the scene of a curious interracial détente that brings together unlikely buyers and sellers. Gay white and African American men looking for "drive-up" sex (i.e., a quick blow job) cruise the park to trade cash or drugs for sex with drug addicts, Hispanic gang-bangers, and other straight-identified Hispanic men looking to make a quick buck. At the park Derek meets Juan, forty-something, straight, married, and Hispanic. The initial encounter is a simple transaction: oral sex for a few dollars. On subsequent visits to the park, Derek keeps coming back to Juan. The two become friends, and the casual sex becomes something more than casual. The relationship ends when Derek decides to be exclusively heterosexual. Juan, however, decides to become exclusively homosexual, takes a new lover, and is dumped by his wife.

Father Gately serves a large Latino parish in the predominately Mexican neighborhood of Westside. When asked how residents of the neighborhood meet their partners, he gives a response that reveals the central role that family and immigrant networks play in partner choice: "Among the rural immigrants, where machismo is especially strong, women aren't really allowed out to parties or public places to meet guys. People often meet through family events such as *quinceañeras*.[2] Many people I marry are from the same town in Mexico, even though they met here, because they meet at these sorts of events." When asked whether single men go back to Mexico to find wives, Father Gately says that some do, especially those men who have come to the United States alone. When pressed, he explains that, even though men who were farmers in Mexico get factory jobs in the States, they remain part of the rancho culture and, therefore, prefer to marry women from the same background, women who will be familiar with and maintain their religious and cultural traditions. More cynically, women fresh off the farm will likely be more subservient than immigrant women, who will have been exposed to urban American culture and more egalitarian gender roles and, thus, will likely be more self-assertive.

Robert Park ([1929] 1967, 18) once noted that, in the city, "all suppressed desires find somewhere an expression," and these four vignettes illustrate some of the possibilities for and some of the outcomes of sexual expression that we discovered in our study of sex in Chicago.[3] As are we, Park was interested in the social ordering of urban processes. Specifically, we seek to explain why the choice of sex partner and the outcome of the resultant relationship are consistently patterned within and organized by particular com-

2. A *quinceañera* is a party held when a girl turns fifteen, the age at which she is eligible to be married.
3. The vignettes are drawn from three key informant interviews that are part of the Chicago Health and Social Life Survey (CHSLS). For a description of the survey, see Van Haitsma, Paik, and Laumann (chapter 2 in this volume).

munities, social networks, organizations, and meaning systems. These vignettes highlight some of the themes of this book:

- the constructed, highly organized venues in which individuals search for sex partners;
- the role that group cultures and community norms play in structuring sexual relationships and behavioral repertoires;
- the limited efforts of institutional actors, like churches or social-service agencies, to regulate relationships and behaviors as well as the limited effects of those efforts;
- the importance of urban space as a facilitator of sexual transactions; and
- the social, family, and health consequences of sexual decisionmaking.

Thus, the animating questions of the book are, How is the process of sexual partnering organized within local settings in a large metropolitan center, and what are the consequences of the resultant sexual relationships? We are interested in explaining recurrent patterns of partner selection and relationship formation in different urban subpopulations (e.g., single heterosexual African American women, gay white men) and the unintended outcomes of different patterns of sexuality. From this general interest we begin to generate more specific questions that will guide the analyses presented in subsequent chapters: Why do sexual partnerships rarely cross racial and ethnic lines even where the lack of available partners—the usual situation for, for example, African American women—should motivate individuals to seek out partners of a different race or ethnicity? What accounts for the cases in which racial or ethnic lines are crossed, as with Derek and Juan? Why do public-health/safe-sex campaigns seem to alter the behaviors of some groups but go consistently unheeded by others? Why do gay men and lesbians have few public or commercial meeting spots in some neighborhoods and a wide variety in others? Why do some populations rely on personal networks to find partners and other populations on bars and dance clubs?

## The Social Organization of Sexual Partnering and Sexual Relationships

Sexual partnerships are fundamental elements of adult social life and have important social outcomes, such as health, marriage, fertility, and social stratification. Yet people must routinely solve the problem of finding sex partners in order for sexual partnering to occur. The way in which sexual partnering is organized is not random, genetically predetermined, or uniform. Depending on the communities in which they live, the networks in which they are embedded, and the institutions with which they come into contact, people solve the problem of finding sex partners in different ways; nevertheless, the problem of "matching" is a universal feature of human societies.

National surveys of sexuality, such as the National Health and Social Life Survey (NHSLS), allow for the examination of broad patterns of sexual behavior. The NHSLS, for example, demonstrated that sexual behavior was organized by "master-status" categories, such as marital status, race/ethnicity, education, age, and religion. In an analysis of the NHSLS data, *The Social Organization of Sexuality* (Laumann, Gagnon, Michael, & Michaels, 1994) found that the vast majority of sexual partnerships originate within tightly circumscribed social settings, producing many partnerships between persons with similar characteristics and few partnerships between people with dissimilar characteristics. This study made new inroads into our understanding of the basic organization of sexual partnering in the United States.

However, sexual partnering is fundamentally a *local* process; typically, two people must live within reasonable geographic proximity to initiate and develop a sexual relationship.[4] People often meet because they are members of the same social network, belong to the same organization, live in the same neighborhood, etc. The social forces that make relationships easy to initiate and sustain with certain people and difficult to initiate and sustain with others are amplified, muted, and reconfigured according to the confluence of important social variables, such as group culture, religious affiliation, sex ratios, age, marital status, class stratification, and racial/ethnic segregation. Thus, sexual-partnering opportunities are heavily structured by the local organization of social life, the local population mix, and the shared norms guiding the types of relationships that are sanctioned or supported.

A brief example illustrates this claim. While there is a widely held social and cultural preference for heterosexual over homosexual relationships in the United States, there are local variations. For example, a young man living in San Francisco will be more likely to consider pursuing a male sex partner than will, say, a young man living in Wyoming. Also, should these young men choose to pursue male sex partners, the opportunities for finding social support for that choice will be quite different for each.

These local differences in the manner in which and the degree to which general social expectations are enforced are not captured by national surveys. It is difficult to investigate in any detail the various aspects of social context relevant to the NHSLS data because survey respondents are spread too widely among locales with different norms, opportunities, and supports for various

---

4. While it is possible for two geographically distant people to establish a personal relationship over the telephone or via the Internet, they must be in close geographic proximity in order to establish a physical, sexual relationship.

sorts of sexual partnerships and practices. In an effort to better understand the local context that informs and shapes decisions regarding sexual practices and sexual relationships as they actually occur, the Chicago Health and Social Life Survey (CHSLS) was conducted from 1995 through 1997. This book, which is based on the data collected by this survey, represents our attempt to understand the significance of local context.

One metaphor with considerable power is, we believe, the idea of the *sex market*. Opposed to the black-box, economic notion of autonomous markets, the notion of the sex market places the explanatory focus on local social and cultural structures that limit or channel sexual behavior. In other words, we emphasize the way in which actors' social embeddedness in personal networks, meaning systems and sexual scripts, local organizations, and urban spaces leads to different patterns of sexual partnering, sexual behaviors, and sexual-relationship outcomes. Thus, the sex market is the spatially and culturally bounded arena in which searches for sex partners and a variety of exchanges or transactions are conducted. Readers should note that, throughout this study, we distinguish between *sex markets* generally (i.e., the general social/relational structure in which the search for a sex partner takes place) and particular *sexual marketplaces* (i.e., the specific places where one goes to find a sex partner). In the remainder of this section we give a general overview of the model. In subsequent sections we discuss its constitutive elements in more detail.

We start with the premise that an interrelated set of social forces organizes sex markets and influences the outcomes of the partnerships that are formed and the exchanges that occur within them. Hypothetically, everyone in a given population (e.g., the entire adult population of Chicago) is a potential sex partner for everyone else, but, in reality, the population is divided into highly differentiated pools of buyers and sellers. Networks, local sexual meaning systems, institutional legitimators of particular sexual identities and sex practices, and the designation of space for sexual activity shape how individuals construct and maintain different types of sex markets and organize different types of sexual relationships.

A brief example will make this claim more concrete. Residents of neighborhood A believe that homosexual identity and behavior are immoral and that heterosexual marriage is the only moral way in which to express one's sexuality. These beliefs are conveyed through the socializing practices of an individual's family and work networks, and they are reinforced by the public messages of salient and powerful institutional actors, such as religious organizations and social-service providers. In turn, the lack of cultural and institutional support for same-sex sexuality will discourage individuals from creating social spaces that serve a lesbian and gay population (e.g., bars and clubs, businesses that cater to a lesbian or gay clientele). Under such conditions, we expect that the same-sex market in this type of neighborhood will be forced underground, created in private spaces, or that the search for same-sex sex partners will have to be conducted outside the neighborhood. In short, different configurations of these broad social forces will lead to the construction of different types of sex markets, each with a particular set of legitimated search practices and a range of sanctioned transactions.

In earlier studies (e.g., Laumann, Gagnon, Michael, & Michaels, 1994), we explained sexual partnerships and sex events by examining how they were differentially organized across the life course and by master status (e.g., race, gender, age). Master status and life course are, of course, still important explanatory variables, but, here, we attempt to contextualize both. That is, instead of treating a particular master status as uniform in meaning or effect, we argue that a particular status (e.g., white male) is associated with particular outcomes (e.g., concurrent hetero- and homosexual partners) because that status is embedded within a set of social networks and local sexual norms that proscribe some market activities and encourage others. For example, an African American woman born and raised in the African American neighborhood of Southtown but now living in the predominately white neighborhood of Shoreland will have a different market experience than will an African American woman born and raised and still living in Southtown. The former is less likely to have family and church in close proximity, and her dominant reference group may no longer be African American. Under such conditions, she may be less tied to the sexual norms and institutional surveillance governing sexual activity in Southtown and, thus, be freer to pursue relationships with white men or other women.

Thus, in our approach, we place the individual in a mutually constitutive relation with the sex market. Individuals, having particular profiles of master statuses as well as sexual interests, tastes, and preferences, must negotiate the social networks and the operative institutional actors of their social world. For example, a middle-class white male from suburban Chicago most likely will have had his sexual interests formed by his particular life experiences: the socialization processes peculiar to his family, religion, school, and work and the images of beauty and messages about sexual desire and behavior absorbed through media exposure. While he initially relies on these extant tastes, interests, and preferences when he enters the sexual marketplaces of a city neighborhood like Shoreland, his interaction within those marketplaces may subsequently alter them. He may change his interests when he realizes that professional women in the city dress or wear their hair differently than women in the suburbs do (thus altering his notions of sexual attractiveness), that certain types of women are not available in these city marketplaces, or that in these marketplaces he can find partners who are willing to engage in sex practices that potential partners in his suburban home wish to avoid.

Sex markets, and especially particular marketplaces, are organized to facilitate or hinder the formation of specific types of partnerships. For example, some markets are structured to help individuals develop long-term relationships (social networks acting to discourage one-night stands), while others are set up to allow for short-term sexual exchanges or transactions. As argued above, markets are shaped and constrained by a variety of institutionalized forces, but they also operate according to an internal logic and set of rules. The use of clothing in gay bars to signal one's preferences in partners and activities is one such example. The partnerships that are formed and the interactions that occur within markets also lead to different sexual outcomes, which in turn may alter market behavior or the norms of a market. Sexually transmitted infections (STIs) may be more likely to result from short-term, anonymous sexual partnerships formed in same-sex marketplaces than from long-term, dating partnerships (either heterosexual or homosexual) established through family or friend networks. Thus, individuals who contract an STI via a short-term exchange may alter their partner preferences or behaviors or switch from a "transactional" to a "relational" marketplace. At the same time, outcomes may be more directly shaped by their embeddedness within group cultures and particular institutional spheres. For example, the sexual jealousy that emerges from a cohabitational relationship may be derived from double standards about sex roles in a group's culture. Institutional control over sexual outcomes is most evident in the efforts of public-health agents to inculcate a belief in the practice of safe sex in targeted populations.

## Conceptualizing Sex Markets

The idea of treating the search for sex partners as taking place in a market is not novel. As in many other areas of social life, in the sexual arena market metaphors are commonly used to describe how partners find and evaluate one another. For example, certain meeting places, typically bars, are commonly known as *meat markets,* and those lucky enough to acquire a sex partner in such places frequently compare notes with friends to assess the quality of their *catch.* However, despite the fact that the market metaphor is nearly ubiquitous in public discourse about the search for sex or marriage partners, because its meaning varies from one place to another it is sufficiently ambiguous to raise the question whether the concept has been adequately specified in sociological research. Are markets made up of people or institutions or both? How do personal traits, such as race, ethnicity, education, religion, and age, factor into the dynamics of markets: are they goods to be exchanged, are they ways of signaling quality, or do they constitute the boundaries of the markets themselves? Indeed, it is our belief that conceptual ambiguity over what actually constitutes a *sex market* or a *marriage market* currently hinders the study of the formation, organization, and dissolution of partnerships.

From the economic perspective, the answers to these questions are clear. Defined analogously to the term *product market,* the term *marriage market,* or *matching market,* refers to a collection of women and men seeking marriage partners among the opposite gender. In other words, a matching market consists of two populations—men and women—that together compose the market and involves individuals offering themselves as bundles of traits in all-or-nothing exchanges (Mortensen, 1988). This also makes matching markets unique from product markets in the sense that the goods to be exchanged are both heterogeneous and indivisible. Thus, the matching market involves a set of individuals with differentiating characteristics that allow for subjective rankings according to individual preferences. One should note that this leaves two important issues unspecified: (1) the processes through which the pool of market participants is identified and, therefore, the compositional characteristics (e.g., wealth, education, gender, and racial composition) of market participants determined and (2) the processes through which preferences are formed.

Nevertheless, the power of the economic perspective derives from its focus on the dynamics and properties of matching markets once the population has been specified. An important advance in this area was the integration of theoretical work on marriage markets with matching algorithms (see, e.g., Gale & Shapley, 1962; Becker, 1973, 1981; Mortensen, 1988). According to Mortensen (1988), a stable match order is generated when no matched individual prefers to be single and no one prefers another match over his or her current partner. However, economists have long been aware that actual matching conditions radically depart from an efficient marriage market (Becker, Landes, & Michael, 1977; Becker, 1981; Mortensen, 1988; Frey & Eichenberger, 1996). To explain this gap, researchers have incorporated search-theoretic concepts into their models to account for the high transaction costs and uncertainty. Since search can be costly, the optimality of a matching market is characterized primarily by its efficiency, with higher search costs generating more mismatches. An important factor making search costly for individuals seeking a match on similar characteristics (e.g., ethnicity, race, class), especially when such a match is rare, is that average characteristics are more readily encountered in the market (Becker, Landes, & Michael, 1977). Overall, economists would argue that individuals frequently search for partners in school and at work because search costs are reduced there and information about prospective partners tends to be better.

The primary issue with the economic approach to matching markets is its exclusive focus on individual-level characteristics and dynamics. We suggest that this perspective overstates the role of individuals at the expense of that of institutional forces. For example, is it more useful to think about preferences as exogenous to market dynamics or as endogenously generated? This is an old debate between sociologists and economists, and we do not propose to solve it here. Instead, we focus in this study on the processes, both individual and institutional, that constitute the boundaries in which market-like dynamics occur. Specifically, we intend to analyze the unique contribution of each in relation to a number of market dimensions, including what determines the pool of eligible market participants, the sources of preferences, and the environments in which individuals locate one another.

We are also building on the work of those sociologists who have already investigated how social structure affects the organization of marriage markets. For the most part, sociological critiques of matching markets have focused on the two areas, noted above, that economists left unspecified: the nature of preference formation and the structural constraints of the marriage market. Research on the sociological nature of preference formation has focused on comparing cultural and socioeconomic statuses (DiMaggio & Mohr, 1985; Kalmijn, 1991b, 1994) as well as on investigating the importance of gender and economic roles (England & Farkas, 1986; England & Kilbourne, 1990). Other researchers have focused on specifying the structural constraints of the marriage market with regard to age and sex ratios (Oppenheimer, 1988), education (Mare, 1991), and propinquity (Kalmijn, 1991b; Lichter, LeClere, & McLaughlin, 1991; South & Lloyd, 1995). There has also been some work done on how social characteristics, such as occupation, act as signals for quality (Kalmijn, 1994). Taken together, most of this literature has sought to demonstrate how traditional sociological variables, such as education, occupational status, or gender, influence the economist's purely individual-level model. Few of these extensions, however, directly challenge the black-box conceptualization of the market itself, even though Oppenheimer (1988) noted that there is substantial ambiguity about what market behavior is in the first place.

The central theoretical focus of our work highlights markets as social structures. We believe that studies of matching markets can benefit from the insights of economic sociology, which recognized early on that markets are socially constructed (see, e.g., White, 1981; Faulkner & Anderson, 1987; Podolny, 1993; Baker, Faulkner, & Fisher, 1998). In this study, we argue that individuals searching for partners are involved in the joint social construction of matching markets. Drawing on Harrison White's (1981) now-classic statement on product markets, we propose that orthodox economic and sociological theorizing about matching be embedded within this sociological view of markets. The basic unit organizing our analysis is the *sex market,* defined as a subsystem of a community whose participants are mutually relevant to one another and generally share some common orientation by observing each other's strategies and evaluative criteria regarding sexual part-nering.[5] (Readers should be aware that, as noted earlier, *sex markets* are dis-tinct from *sexual marketplaces,* defined as specific places within the city where one goes to meet potential sex partners.) One important feature of a sex mar-ket is that the actions and strategies of the participants serve a feedback role, confirming each individual's "rational" expectations of what are effective and appropriate strategies (White, 1981). The central problem facing partici-pants, then, is not comparing alternatives but, rather, finding out what the alternatives are in the first place (Geertz, 1992). In short, we seek to provide the reader with a series of discussions about various structural aspects of sex markets.

What, then, are the relevant structural features of markets? In the sections of this chapter that follow, we characterize three kinds of structural features, features that are not necessarily mutually exclusive but that capture the notion that there are micro- and macroaspects of markets. These are the structuring of individual sexual choices by roles and positions, by local brokers, and by the social and cultural embeddedness of sex markets. Structuring by roles and positions emphasizes the ways in which individuals create and re-create mar-kets through their choices of partners, relationship types, and search venues. Structuring by local brokers emphasizes the ways in which individuals, net-works, clubs, voluntary associations, formal organizations, and other social institutions facilitate partnering within and, quite often, between sex mar-kets. Structuring by the social and cultural embeddedness of sex markets em-phasizes how those markets are constrained by particular social networks, sexual cultures, and institutions.

## Structuring by Roles and Positions

There are two fundamental dimensions characterizing sex-market transac-tions: the quality and the form of sexual relationships. The former focuses on how sex markets designate quality among the pool of eligible partners, the latter on how sex markets organize expectations about sexual interactions themselves. Economists argue that the quality of the sexual relationship is de-termined by the quality of the individuals involved as well as by their prefer-ences. We suggest that quality is unknown, that, instead, market participants rely on the status ordering of potential partners as a proxy or, in essence, a signal for quality. An important difference between the economic theory of signals and the one presented here is that we follow Podolny (1993), who sug-gested a loose linkage, mediated by other actors, between signal and quality. Specifically, social networks and organizations, embedded within a particu-

5. This concept is quite similar to Knoke and Laumann's (1982) *policy domain.*

lar local social space and sexual culture, bias subjective evaluations as well as rendering these biased evaluations consistent over time. We expect that individuals associated with high-status others or prestigious institutions receive positively biased evaluations of their own status position, evaluations that are independent of actual quality.

Sex markets are distinct from one another to the extent that there is a well-defined status order among them. Individuals can, therefore, occupy different status positions, depending on the sex market in which they find themselves participating and where they are in their sexual careers. The institutional level of social organization, which again includes the larger cultural scenarios, social networks, physical space, and local organizations, is particularly important because it provides the boundaries of a sex market with a taken-for-granted quality as well as serving as an important segregating mechanism. For example, we have collected data on a white-male, same-sex market concentrated in a neighborhood that we call *Shoreland*. This market is widely recognized, regardless of sexual orientation, as a gay neighborhood and features extensive organizational support for same-sex lifestyles, including bars, voluntary associations, and extensive social networks as well as public gatherings. Indeed, this sex market operates cheek by jowl with an almost equally vibrant opposite-sex market, but the boundaries are so distinct that the partnering strategies of one market are rarely mistakenly applied in the other. Nevertheless, when an individual participates in multiple sex markets, his or her status is likely to change accordingly.

Figure 1.1 presents a conceptual diagram of the organization of sex markets in Chicago. In much of this book, we assume that the boundaries of sex markets are defined by two important status characteristics: sexual orientation and ethnicity or race. Thus, in figure 1.1, the ovals represent distinct sex markets, while the crosses indicate specific sexual marketplaces. Note that some sexual marketplaces act as bridges, facilitating interaction between participants from different sex markets. Crosses located at the intersection of two or more sex markets indicate these bridges.

Regarding expectations about the form of sexual interaction, we argue that sex markets are composed of a varying distribution of role structures for men and women. By *role structures* we mean the distinct symbolic codes operative in a given market concerning the rules of exchange and interaction between participants. Market participants commonly hold important expectations regarding the exclusivity of sexual partnering and the form of sexual interaction. These expectations emphasize the role that social structure plays in defining appropriate behavior. For example, certain social situations, such as the search for a partner in a public park, are organized to encourage casual sexual partnerships characterized by transactional sexual behaviors and little expectation of exclusivity. Others, however, such as the search for a partner

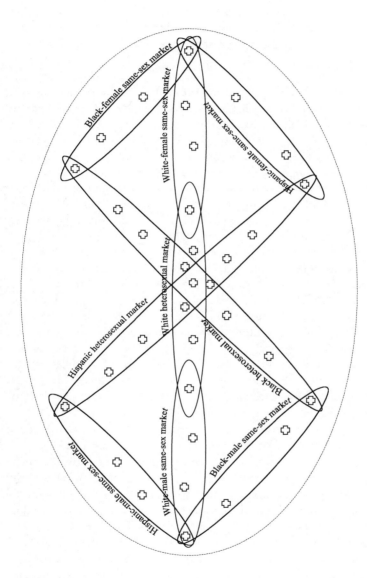

Figure 1.1. Chicago sex markets.

*Note:* Ovals indicate specific sex markets; crosses indicate specific sexual marketplaces.

through one's social network, are organized to encourage the formation of more enduring and exclusive relationships and discourage transactional sexual behaviors.

In the literature on marriage markets, marriages are seen as implicit, long-term contracts (England & Farkas, 1986). In contrast, sexual relationships can be of two types: one-time encounters (spot transactions) or dating situations. We refer to the former relationship type as *transactional* and to the latter as *relational*. Since both types are subject to moral hazards and uncertainty (i.e., actors are unsure of the intentions of potential partners), there is a strong tendency to embed relationships. That is, just as status and quality are linked, the rules of exchange, which are distinct for each sex market, are linked (albeit loosely) with relationship form (e.g., transactional or relational, monogamous or nonmonogamous). Here, again, social institutions play an important mediating role by trying to establish distinct codes of conduct.

Up to this point, we have focused solely on the internal organization of sex markets with respect to status positions and roles. This raises the analytically prior question of the nature of the external organization of sex markets, the question, in other words, of how sex-market boundaries are constituted. Since sex markets are distinct collective systems organizing sexual behavior, each market constitutes a kind of niche, being characterized by its own institutionalized boundaries and internal processes (Hannan & Freeman, 1977; McPherson, 1983). Our perspective is agnostic about what distinguishes different populations and, thus, markets; we make no assertions about the centrality of one status over another (e.g., cultural vs. economic). Instead, we focus on the local segregating and blending processes that create distinct boundaries between populations. That sex markets are distinct collective systems also suggests that they go through developmental stages, the early stages marked by less institutionalized boundaries, role structures, and status orders, the later by more objective social structures.

The fact that there are distinct sex markets accounts for the importance of competition both within and between different populations/markets and, thus, the importance of the actual composition of the pool of eligible partners. For example, competition within an opposite-sex market will be affected by the relative ratio of men to women. Any imbalance places individuals of the less well represented gender in a superior market position, one that enables them to select higher-quality partners. An imbalance may also cause members of the more well represented gender to search in other sex markets. However, the search process is also guided by group norms as to the qualities—younger or older, taller or shorter, black or white—distinguishing preferred partners.

The power of group norms is evident in the case of heterosexual African American women, who face a market situation characterized by a lack of status–equal black men. They have, however, few other options since white and Hispanic men continue to value "whiteness" in their sex partners. This preference for whiteness results, in part, because white and Hispanic men are embedded within social networks that discourage interracial relationships and are, further, closed to black women. Thus, the combination of population dynamics and the institutionalization of role structures and status orders creates substantial coordination problems for the process of matching appropriate individuals.

The significance of the internal structuring and population dynamics of sex markets is that these are the bases on which individuals make their choices about markets in which to participate. Thus, a fundamental question that we seek to answer is how individuals in the CHSLS interface with sex markets. Our interest here is in search behavior and the patterning of sexual networks as well as in the socioemotional consequences of these behaviors (e.g., the social distribution of sexual jealousy).

## Structuring by Local Brokers

Because of their relative permanence, or inertia, relative to individuals, brokers provide the basis for the continuing social construction for both individuals and organizational actors and, thus, coordinate partnering strategies. In our study, the term *local brokers* refer to networks or organizations that act as coordinators for individuals within the same sex market or as liaisons between different sex markets. Moreover, local brokers frequently act as gatekeepers, discouraging classes of individuals from participating in a particular sex market.[6] A public park is one example of a social space that serves as a local broker coordinating individuals located in different sex markets.

However, even if local brokers facilitate partnering, the goal of matching sex partners does not necessarily coincide with brokers' own social organizational goals. For example, the primary purpose of most networks of friends is not to match partners. Rather, matching partners is usually a secondary, unintended consequence of other activities. Further, not all a broker's activities can accommodate matching behavior, as evinced by the practice common among religious institutions of setting aside singles' nights for just this purpose. Thus, brokers can be conceptualized as varying as to the degree in which searching for partners is expected and actively encouraged, or, simply, the degree of *marketization*.

Brokers vary according to the degree to which matching is coupled with other organizational goals. Coupling can, for example, be quite loose, as in the

---

6. We should note that our definition of *local broker* combines several of the ideal-typical brokerage types laid out by Fernandez and Gould (1994).

case of a religious institution attended primarily by singles, where matching is not the primary purpose and is, therefore, likely to conflict with other, more important activities. Or it can be direct, as in the case of a gay bathhouse, whose primary purpose is matching sex partners. We term those networks or institutions that are primarily oriented toward matching sex partners, or that are highly marketized, *direct sexual marketplaces.* Typical examples of direct sexual marketplaces include bars and dance clubs, bathhouses, personal ads, and such informal settings as private parties and public parks. Health clubs and voluntary organizations also occasionally fall into this category. We term those networks or institutions that are not primarily oriented toward matching sex partners but that occasionally facilitate search, or that are moderately marketized, *mediated sexual marketplaces.* Typical examples of mediated sexual marketplaces include churches' singles' nights and blind dates set up by friends. We expect direct sexual marketplaces and mediated sexual marketplaces to encourage different types of sexual partnerships and behaviors, with the former focused more on transactional partnerships (e.g., one-night stands) and the latter more on relational ones (e.g., long-term dating relationships).

## *Structuring by the Social and Cultural Embeddedness of Sex Markets*

As suggested above, sex markets do not exist in isolation but are embedded within a local social system that powerfully constrains or channels the market activities of individuals. Like Granovetter (1985), we argue that individuals neither make choices about sexual partnering outside the network of social relations in which they find themselves, as suggested by the economic approaches to matching markets, nor slavishly follow behavioral scripts, as suggested by pure constructivist accounts.[7] Rather, explaining sexual partnering and the various outcomes that follow from it (e.g., marriage, disease) rests on understanding how type and degree of social embeddedness limit opportunities, narrow sexual choices, and, more generally, push individuals to search for certain types of partners, follow certain sexual scripts, and engage in certain sexual behaviors. We argue that four interrelated social constraints—social networks of market participants, space, sexual culture, and organizations within different institutional spheres—structure and regulate sex markets in a number of ways. First, they may define normative frameworks that code some partners, behaviors, and relationships as legitimate, moral, or safe and

---

7. In the now-classic statement on social embeddedness, Granovetter (1985, 487) notes: "Actors do not behave or decide as atoms outside a social context, nor do they adhere slavishly to a script written for them by the particular intersection of social categories that they happen to occupy. Their attempts at purposive action are instead embedded in concrete, ongoing systems of social relations."

others as illegitimate, immoral, or unsafe. Second, these constraints may provide opportunities for individuals to meet potential partners. Finally, sex markets may be constrained by the sanctioning and surveillance activities of the networks and institutions in which individuals are embedded. We devote the rest of this section to detailing the operations of these four factors.

SOCIAL NETWORKS. Social networks have distinct effects on sexual partnering through two major mechanisms: information and control. As for information, because social networks tend to be composed of people with similar characteristics and, therefore, structure contact between members, information of necessity circulates among members. This information includes where to go, whom to approach for introductions, and proper manners once introduced. For example, because the lesbian sexual marketplaces are widely dispersed and not easily identified, one of the most important functions of lesbian social networks is the dissemination of information about which bars or clubs are the most likely places in which to meet other lesbians. Social networks also convey information about the intentions of potential partners. For example, potential partners may be more likely to trust one another if they are introduced by a mutual friend than if they meet through a personal ad.

As for control, third parties—parents, children, close friends, colleagues—often act as stakeholders, influencing the kind of person one chooses as a sex partner and interfering with relationships of which they disapprove. Moreover, attached to one's roles within given networks are normative expectations regarding sexual behaviors and relationships. Parents, for example, may pressure children to seek potential marriage partners with certain preferred characteristics (e.g., churchgoing, college educated). Or they may pressure a son to marry his pregnant girlfriend if she is the daughter of a family friend more strongly than they would if she is an outsider. The more firmly embedded individuals are in a network, the more likely other network members are to influence their sex-market choices. For example, individuals who live far from their families face few constraints on partner choice and relationship organization because family expectations are, if not less salient, then certainly less easily enforced. In all these ways social networks can act as arbiters of sexual relationships, setting boundaries for their members (Eggert & Parks, 1987; Parks, Stan, & Eggert, 1983; Johnson & Milardo, 1984).

Given that these information and control mechanisms structure sexual partnering, we therefore expect network embeddedness to constrain the pool of potential partners. For example, a middle-class, twenty-something white woman who socializes primarily with twenty-something white men and women from work or school in the white neighborhood of Shoreland is unlikely to develop sexual partnerships with persons of color or those from lower-class backgrounds. We also expect networks to affect the nature or quality of sexual partnerships. For example, people with few social ties are more likely both to conduct their partner searches in direct sexual market-places (e.g., in singles bars or through personal ads) and, because of a lack of social support and monitoring, to end up in short-term relationships. Conversely, people with strong social ties are more likely to conduct their partner searches in mediated sexual marketplaces and to end up in long-term relationships. We further expect the decision of whether to embed a relationship in one's social network to be a conscious one. For example, individuals who are seeking casual relationships will avoid embedding those relationships in their social networks, just as those who are seeking serious relationships will work to embed those relationships in their social networks.

SPACE. Physical space plays two roles in the structure of sex markets. It both delimits the geographic boundaries of sex markets generally and organizes specific sexual marketplaces.

First, space delimits sex markets in that, realistically, people can search for a partner and initiate and develop a sexual relationship only within a reasonable geographic proximity.[8] Since most people do not travel extensively in the course of their daily lives, few, if any, find long-distance relationships to be feasible—owing to the time and monetary costs involved. Thus, sexual partnering is essentially a local activity.

While physical propinquity has been recognized as a factor in mate selection for some time (e.g., Burgess, 1943; Ramsoy, 1966; Peach, 1974), most studies of mate selection ignore the role of physical space, often treating the entire nation as one large marriage market in which everyone theoretically has access to everyone else (Mare, 1991; Kalmijn, 1991a, 1991b, 1994; Qian, 1998; Smits, Ultee, & Lammers, 1998; Spanier, 1980). These analyses lose sight of the fact that mate selection occurs within a geographically bounded area and is, therefore, limited by that area's demographics, social networks, cultural understandings, and institutions.

Even studies of mate selection on the city level (Blau, Blum, & Schwartz, 1982; Blau, Beeker, & Fitzpatrick, 1984) or the labor-market-area level (Lichter, McLaughlin, Kephart, & Landry, 1992) mask neighborhood differences in sexual-partnering opportunities. For example, a woman living in a Mexican American neighborhood who does not have a car and conducts most of her routine activities (e.g., shopping and socializing) in that neighborhood is unlikely to meet potential partners from other areas of the city. High levels of residential segregation mean that racial and ethnic groups are

8. On geographic proximity, see n. 4 above.

isolated from each other even within the same city (Massey & Denton, 1993). Owing to both physical boundaries (i.e., railroads, highways, rivers) and social boundaries (race, language, culture), the city is divided into distinct communities with distinct demographic characteristics, institutions, social-network patterns, and normative orientations, all of which affect sexual partnering.

In addition, how public and private spaces are regulated by institutional actors may influence the way in which different markets operate. The lack of private space within the family home in the Mexican neighborhood of Westside—the result of large families and small houses as well as cultural norms strictly regulating female sexuality—leads young, single residents to make public spaces such as schools, street corners, and parks primary venues for conducting partner searches. Thus, distinct neighborhood contexts may foster different sexual-partnering processes and sexual marketplaces.

Second, within particular geographic spaces, individuals organize their social relations around activities that take place within specific locations, such as workplaces, parks, and churches, and are more likely to form ties with the people they meet there (Feld, 1981; McPherson, 1982; Wasserman & Faust, 1994). Urban spaces thus become meeting places for people in search of particular types of partners or particular types of sexual activities. Some urban spaces are publicly known or designated as direct sexual marketplaces, such as red-light districts, while other spaces whose primary purpose is not sexual (e.g., workplaces) may operate secondarily as mediated sexual marketplaces. Some marketplaces attract individuals from across the city, while others are created for and used by only groups within one neighborhood (e.g., the weekend dance parties held at small clubs in Chicago's African American neighborhood of Southtown).

Moreover, space and sexual culture are often related. Some marketplaces are tied to particular interpersonal scripts that further help coordinate market activities (see Duyves, 1994). For example, an eight-block area of Erlinda is used as a sexual marketplace for men interested in oral sex with prostitutes, especially Hispanic and African American prostitutes. Or gay men involved in bondage and other forms of sadomasochism frequent certain bars in Shoreland.

Sexual space is not restricted to marketplace institutions that are organized to coordinate searches and transactions efficiently (e.g., bars, dance clubs). Space in more diffuse relational markets may also be constructed as a site for partnering activity. Perhaps the best illustration of this is the city women's softball league. The park space is set up primarily for softball games, but, over time, it has been defined secondarily as a place where lesbians from the Chicagoland area can come to meet friends, socialize, and possibly develop sexual relationships. Health clubs, volunteer organizations, and churches may come to be coded by particular groups as places in which to conduct searches for potential partners. Co-opting space not primarily defined as a sexual marketplace is an important way of making partner search in more diffuse sex markets more efficient, as suggested in the following comment by a pastor of a Metropolitan Community Church (MCC) congregation in Shoreland:

> The MCC also serves as a social place because you can assume that others there are also gay. It's like a gay bar in that sense, but a better environment for people not comfortable with bars. How do people find lovers and establish monogamous relationships? There are rules for this among heterosexual couples, but how do you do this when you're gay? It requires that you be out to your potential partner and they to you. The MCC is a safe place to assume this of other members. Also, what better place to meet than at church? I feel that a big problem faced by couples is coming from different religious backgrounds. Meeting in the same church reduces the possibility of this happening.

In short, when space is collectively defined as sexual, it improves market coordination because it signals the type of partner, sexual activities, and possible relationships that one can expect to find there.

SEXUAL CULTURE.  While understanding the geographic boundaries of sex markets generally and the ways in which particular sexual marketplaces are organized is relatively easy, understanding how to negotiate a given market is more difficult. This requires a familiarity with and, in many ways, a mastery of the system of meanings, that is, the sexual culture, of a market.

A sex market is governed both by an internal sexual culture and by an external sexual culture.

The term *internal sexual culture* refers to the set of scripts that inform and guide sexual behaviors, preferences, and identities within a given market. These scripts provide information about how and where to search for partners, roles to adopt (e.g., top or bottom in male same-sex markets), behavioral expectations (e.g., no intercourse before the third date or mutual orgasm as the ideal outcome), and the relative values of potential partners. Internal sexual cultures may be heavily influenced by a specific group culture surrounding a market. For example, many of our Hispanic informants discussed how machismo and gender roles that privilege men structure sex markets and sexual relationships and lead to specific outcomes—from male same-sex transactions that are not stigmatized, to sexual jealousy that erupts into domestic violence, to high expectations about female virginity (see Almaguer, 1991; Alonso & Koreck, 1993).[9] Or internal sexual cultures may develop their own rules. For example, prostitutes expect their johns to follow a certain behavioral script (e.g., no kissing), and deviations are not permitted.

The term *external sexual culture* refers to sets of meanings that help individuals organize sex markets. It can best be understood by reference to Simon and Gagnon's (1987, 364) notion of *cultural scenarios*—or "paradigmatic assemblies of the social norms that impinge on sexual behavior." These widely shared ideas and images about appropriate sexual objects, aims, and activities define the boundaries of sex markets and inform how individuals and institutional actors value sexual relationships, partner preferences, and behavioral repertoires. These scenarios, often conveyed through popular song lyrics and music videos, films, and magazines like *Cosmopolitan* and *Playboy,* define broad ideals about sexual orientations (heterosexual), gender roles (male dominance or equality), and relationships (marriage or monogamy) that undergird interaction within sex markets. Market participants take their cues about what constitutes the erotic and desirable, the safe and the risky, from cultural scenarios. For example, the notion that large-breasted, thin-waisted women are more desirable than small breasted, wide-hipped women—as conveyed through fashion magazines, Barbie dolls, and animated figures in cartoons and video games—may lead an individual to search for potential partners who have these physical characteristics and avoid those who do not.

Thus, sexual cultures—both internal and external—provide the criteria according to which individuals construct their partner preferences and rank order market participants.

Sexual cultures will be powerful and binding to the degree that they are carried by institutional actors who have a stake in the processes and outcomes of

9. One reviewer noted that, in places, our approach to culture approximates a "culture-of-poverty" explanation. While we argue that the sexual cultures of particular ethnic or racial groups sometimes channel individuals toward greater, and often riskier, sexual activity, we are not making strong causal claims linking culture to social pathology. Our understanding of culture is more closely aligned with approaches that see culture as scripts or repertoires that shape action (see Lamont, 1999, xi). Moreover, our approach differs from the culture-of-poverty approach in three respects. First, our use of culture is not essentialist or reductionistic. Culture is just one of several explanatory variables, not the universal key to understanding the sex acts and sexual relationships of the different social groups encompassed by our study. Second, we highlight the ways in which a group's norms, values, and beliefs about sexuality and gender have positive outcomes. Third, the claims about sexual pathology are voiced by our key informants, and, as noted by Buntin, Lechtman, and Laumann (chapter 8 in this volume) and Ellingson, Van Haitsma, Laumann, and Tebbe (chapter 11), we do not accept these claims uncritically.

market participation and who also exert control over individuals. The meaning systems and scripts that guide sexual behaviors and relationships do not
exist independently of institutional actors. Key stakeholders—for example,
members of one's family or one's church—devise and reinforce messages
about appropriate and inappropriate potential partners (e.g., must be a practicing Catholic) or partnerships (e.g., cohabitation forbidden) and threaten
to punish deviations from cultural expectations. Individuals who are more
tightly linked to these stakeholders (e.g., those who attend church regularly)
are more likely to follow the normative prescriptions about sexuality that
they advance (see Sherkat & Ellison, 1997; Cochran & Beeghley, 1991; Thornton & Camburn, 1989; Hertel & Hughes, 1987). Some stakeholders, like
schools and public-health agencies, may attempt to regulate sex markets
by devising and reinforcing messages about sex practices (e.g., always use a
condom, "just say no!") and the moral status of behaviors and their outcomes
within different cultural scenarios (Nathanson, 1991; Markova & Wilkie,
1987; Herdt, 1992b).

INSTITUTIONS.  Institutional control of sexual identity and behavior is
a common theme in histories and contemporary accounts of sexuality. Some
accounts suggest that institutional actors exert strong control over sexuality by
outlawing certain practices and identities, restricting access to potential partners or at least raising the costs of access, and, more generally, defining what
kinds of partners and search practices are legitimate. According to Foucault
(1990), for example, medicine, education, religion, the police, and the family
powerfully channel sexual behavior and identity into particular forms (e.g.,
heterosexual, monogamous marriage) through stigmatization, socialization,
and surveillance (see also Chauncey, 1994; D'Emilio, 1983; DeLamater, 1981).
Institutional control continues indirectly as individuals internalize norms regarding sexuality and, thus, become self-regulating. Academic and popular
treatments of the medicalization of AIDS and the rise of safe-sex interventions suggest that the efforts of public-health organizations to slow or stop the
disease have changed the structure of some gay sex markets by altering search
processes, partnering choices, and behavioral repertoires (see Murray 1996,
99–142; Aveline, 1995; Ostrow, Beltran, & Joseph, 1994; Davidson, 1991;
Shilts, 1987).

At the same time, many accounts identify the inefficiencies of institutional
control and suggest that individuals and groups often circumvent the norms
and restrictions that are intended to govern sexual activities. This is evinced
in the literature on gay and lesbian communities, especially gay resistance to
the safe-sex paradigm (Murray, 1996; Sadownick, 1996), in work on adolescent sexuality (e.g., Nathanson, 1991), and in accounts of the Sexual Revolution and its consequences (D'Emilio & Freedman, 1988). Consistently high

rates of premarital sexual activity and the liberalization of attitudes toward sexuality as documented in the NHSLS, the CHSLS, and the GSS (General Social Survey) suggest that the surveillance and socialization powers of religion and family have declined (see Joyner & Laumann, 2001). Thus, the empirical work on sexuality suggests that organizations in different institutional spheres exercise direct and indirect, strong and weak control over market activities. But how and why control is exercised (or not) has not been an explicit object of inquiry or theorization. Surprisingly, even the "new institutionalism" literature provides little help.[10] However, both literatures provide enough clues to piece together a nascent theory of how institutional actors influence sex markets.

A common premise in recent work on institutions is that each institutional order (e.g., family, politics, medicine) has a central logic, framework, or organizing principle that orders reality, "defines ends, and shapes the means by which interests are determined and pursued" (DiMaggio & Powell, 1991, 10; see also Friedland & Alford, 1991; Haveman & Rao, 1997). In other words, each institutional sphere has a primary goal or goals and a set of rules and practices by which to realize those goals. Moreover, these frameworks serve as lenses through which institutional actors see the world—helping them identify social problems and their causes—and as guides for acting in the world. For example, the central framework within medicine is to preserve and prolong health, and actors follow a biomedical model of disease and treatment. This leads health-care practitioners to minimize or ignore the social, cultural, and economic causes of disease (e.g., poverty) and focus their attention on treating the immediate biological symptoms. Thus, institutional actors have a model for "how to do something," but that model constrains opportunity and action because it focuses attention on a narrowly defined imperative (see Clemens & Cook, 1999, 445). Areas of social life that fall outside the mandate of an institutional sphere likely will be treated as an externality—something that demands attention only when it begins to impinge on the resources of a particular institutional actor.

Sexuality is one of those areas. There is no one institutional sphere primarily concerned with sexuality (the family may be the closest), nor do most institutional actors make strong claims for ownership. As a result, sexuality is an institutional stepchild, tending to be acted on when it threatens to disrupt the institutional order or when participants in a particular sex market bring

10. This literature generally focuses on explaining how institutions emerge and how institutions and organizations within them change, grow, and die, but little attention has been given to explaining how institutions affect various aspects of the social world that may lie outside the explicit mandate of a particular institution (see Zucker, 1988; Powell & DiMaggio, 1991; Brinton & Nee, 1998).

sexual concerns to institutional actors. Once sexuality is placed on the agenda of some organization, that organization becomes a stakeholder with a set of interests and goals to protect or to advance and deals with sexuality according to its institutionally specific framework. Institutional actors then draw on a preexisting set of symbolic resources by which they articulate a specific normative understanding of sexuality and identify what constitutes a sexual problem, who or what is to blame, and how to resolve it.[11] Health-care organizations address sexuality in terms of how sexual behavior affects personal and public health and attempt to organize the sex market to minimize the health risks of sexual activity (e.g., by promoting safe-sex campaigns). From the perspective of the police, sexual expression becomes problematic only when it threatens to upset the social order or to violate the law. The logic and practices of policing limit market interventions to conflict resolution or incarceration, as with domestic violence, and the institutional framework of policing excludes more general efforts to influence an individual's partner preferences, behavioral repertoires, or understandings of valuable sexual capital.

An important tool of institutional stakeholders is the causal stories used to make sense of the sex market and justify institutional action. Causal stories are accounts that "describe harms and difficulties, attribute them to the action of other individuals and organizations, and thereby claim the right to invoke governmental [or some other institutionally based] power to stop the harm" (Stone, 1989, 282). The import of causal stories is illustrated in Nathanson's (1991) work on adolescent sexuality. Nathanson identifies three causal models of teen pregnancy: one model considers pregnancy to be the outcome of social, political, and medical barriers that limit teenagers' access to contraception and abortion services; a second sees it as the outcome of the state's legitimization of sexual permissiveness through the subsidization of family-planning services; and the third views it as the outcome of deeply rooted cultural and social problems (e.g., the culture of poverty). She goes on to note how the causal stories inform and justify particular interventions or solutions on the part of different institutional actors. For example, some health-care organizations rely on the first model to advocate for federal funding of family-planning services, condom distribution in public schools, and safe-sex education campaigns, while some political actors promote abstinence as the appropriate solution and work to end federal or state funding of family planning.

Causal stories become a key means of constructing particular normative definitions of moral (read: safe vs. risky, legal vs. illegal, functional vs. dysfunctional) sexual expression. These stories often draw on and reinforce widely held cultural scenarios about sexuality in the United States and, thus, indi-

---

11. This conceptualization of how institutions work draws on Gusfield's (1981) work on the drinking-and-driving problem.

rectly shape sex markets by setting standards for appropriate behaviors, partners, and venues for search. As illustrated in the example given above, conservative political actors' causal story about teen pregnancy defines heterosexual
marriage as the only legitimate relationship in which sexual behavior can be
expressed, upholds, at least implicitly, the sexual double standard that marks
virgins as *good girls,* and delegitimates a set of behaviors (e.g., extramarital intercourse) and relationships (nonmarital unions).

Organizations within different institutional orders may exert both direct
and indirect control over sex markets. Direct control may be seen in behavioral changes that follow from sex-education programs or in the incarceration of individuals who abuse family members. We expect direct control to
be less common as most institutional actors consider sexuality to be a secondary or tertiary concern and address it in a compartmentalized rather than
a holistic manner. In addition, the widespread suspicion of organizations and
institutions in U.S. society and the weakening of institutional surveillance
and regulatory power make direct control less likely.[12] We expect that indirect control will be the more common pattern of institutional constraint on
sex markets. Indirect control may take a variety of forms. For example, organizations in various spheres that advance or support a particular relationship (e.g., heterosexual marriage) as normative may increase the power and
salience of the script and, thus, shape the preferences and search patterns of
some market participants. Alternatively, a safe-sex ideology articulated by
health-care providers may not persuade people to use condoms until peers or
potential partners also validate this message through their actions (e.g., de-
manding that a condom be worn during intercourse or talking about the
virtues of practicing safe sex [see Kendall, 1994, 250–51]).

Brief overviews of two institutions—health care and social services—that
we target in our study of sexuality in Chicago illustrate how institutional actors constrain and shape sex markets.

Organizations within health care (e.g., STD [sexually transmitted disease]
clinics, public-health departments, or hospitals) approach sexuality from the
perspective of the biomedical model, with the goals of restoring an individual to health and preventing the spread of disease to larger populations. The
biomedical model starts with the notion that disease is fundamentally bio-

---

12. For example, Christianity in the United States has an increasingly loose hold
over the sexual beliefs and practices of its adherents, especially among moderate and
liberal Protestants and Roman Catholics. For example, while many Christian groups
officially disapprove of extramarital sexuality and abortion, large numbers of adherents hold attitudes at odds with the official positions or engage in the disapproved-of
behavior (see Hertel & Hughes, 1987; Cochran & Beeghley, 1991; Greeley, 1994;
Miller, 1996; Dillon, 1999).

logical and that the social, psychological, and behavioral dimensions of illness are irrelevant or, at best, secondary to understanding its causes and treatment (see Engel, 1977). Cassell (1997, 48–49) notes:

> Working within the scientific model of medicine, the social, psychological, and personal elements found in *all* illnesses do not logically follow from considerations of disease because of a fundamental assumption of the medical system: since diseases are biological entities, they are part of nature. From this assumption, it follows that they can be understood and investigated as material things—matter—just like the rest of nature. . . . Medical science, therefore, can examine the diseased body as a mechanism gone wrong. From this perspective, pathophysiology is independent of culture, consciousness, the meaning of things, morality, or spirit. This notion excludes thinking logically about social, psychological, ethical or personal issues within the same system—at the same time—as the mechanistic elements of disease.

Viewed through this framework, sexuality is problematized as an illness, and practitioners aim to treat the symptoms (e.g., prescribing penicillin for gonorrhea) or induce behavioral changes through education (e.g., sponsoring safe-sex campaigns). Even when health-care workers understand that social causes underlie sexual diseases and their transmission, the social is considered to be outside the scope or the reach of the organization. Thus, a health educator who works with Hispanic youths despaired that her efforts to teach her clients about safe sex and pass out condoms represented nothing more than "adding band aids to the surface"; the real causes of high rates of disease transmission—such social conditions as poverty, abusive families, and gang violence—remained unchanged. She noted that "the core issues facing youth in the neighborhood are not ultimately about HIV/AIDS"—which limits the interventions' effectiveness. Similarly, a clinician at a public STD clinic noted how difficult it is to convince individuals to change their sex practices and take care of their health when "the day-to-day priorities of their lives are not preventing STDs and HIV but finding work, food, and housing." When asked how the clinic could change behaviors, he framed his answers in the discourse of medicine: what could be done would be to help people "see that they need to care about their health status" and to develop "'stealth protection' for women—a gel that women could use to protect themselves from STDs, HIV, and pregnancy, without talking to the man about it. This way women would not have to negotiate condom use, and it would empower them in sexual situations."

Health-care organizations try to shape the market through problem definition and education. First, they create a set of sexual problems framed in terms of the biomedical model (i.e., sexual problems are conceptualized as conditions that are biological in nature and lead to personal and social harm, e.g., STDs, unintended pregnancy) and identify the "risky" behaviors and environments that are associated with these problems (e.g., unprotected sex, sex while under the influence of drugs or alcohol). Second, they aim to educate patients and the general public about the risks and methods of protection (see Kendall, 1994). The goal is to change individuals' preferences for potential partners (e.g., avoid prostitutes) and sexual repertoires (e.g., stop having anal intercourse), and even the boundaries of sex markets, in order to minimize exposure to risk.

Organizations within the sphere of social service also rely on education as a means to control market activities, but they reach that intervention strategy from a different starting point. Social-service providers take on the mandate of "regulating social dependence" (Reid, 1992, 35). That is, they aim to move individuals from a state of being unproductive members of society to one in which they have a useful and self-sustaining role in family, work, and/or community. At a minimum, the social-service mandate aims to protect individuals from the consequences of dependence. The institutional framework advances the values of autonomy, empowerment, self-determination, and self-improvement, while institutional action to realize those values focuses on reform, rehabilitation, and reintegration (see Hartman, 1994, 15).

Sexuality and the sex market are placed in an explanatory frame that emphasizes risky behavior arising from the social or community context (e.g., gangs, a sense of fatalism arising from poverty, high rates of alcohol or substance abuse). Decisions to engage in unprotected sex as part of gang initiations or to trade sex for drug money are coded as *bad* or *dysfunctional* because they threaten to undercut individuals' independence and ability to function in society as well as their future life chances (e.g., the teen who becomes pregnant may be forced to drop out of school, a decision that, in turn, affects her occupational opportunities and may even affect her ability to care for her child). Educational interventions focus on teaching individuals how to recognize the contexts or situations that will lead them to make bad decisions and how to escape from them (e.g., counseling a woman to leave an abusive relationship and go to a women's shelter).

Social-service organizations also utilize a second type of intervention strategy—the provision of some sort of service. Such services can range from psychological or family-planning counseling, to health care, to condom-distribution or needle-exchange programs. Again, the goal is to empower individuals to avoid making sexual choices (e.g., partners, markets, or behaviors) that will place them in a state of social dependency. As in medicine, the effect on a sex market tends to be indirect.

An often-reported causal story among social workers in Erlinda and West-side (the two Hispanic neighborhoods in the study) illustrates how institutional actors in this sphere construct sexuality as a problem and attempt to alter market behavior. According to this causal story, the fundamental cause of sexual problems in these neighborhoods is the "culture of silence" surrounding sexuality that pervades Hispanic communities. This collective unwillingness or inability to speak about issues of sexuality with one's partner creates a social context in which individuals, especially girls and women, lack the basic biological facts about conception and disease transmission. Individuals are, therefore, unaware of what constitutes high- and low-risk behaviors or relationships. This causal story leads social workers to create basic sex-education programs to teach young people such things as how conception and disease transmission occur and how to put on a condom. The goal is to help them make better decisions and, thus, avoid the dependency problems that can arise from the unintended effects of sexual activity.

## Relationship Maintenance

The maintenance and the internal dynamics of relationships are also significantly influenced by sex markets. After individuals have solved the problem of meeting partners, relationships must be either maintained or dissolved. Relationship maintenance has much to do with the dynamics of the sex market and the way in which the partners met. For example, bargaining power within relationships is a product, not only of one's contributions to the relationship, but also of one's alternatives outside the relationship (England & Farkas, 1986; Lennon & Rosenfield, 1994). The costs and benefits of staying in a relationship must be weighed against the opportunity costs of partnerships with other people. Thus, the availability of potential other partners may play a role in the maintenance of a current relationship.

However, aspects of the sex market other than the availability of other partners are also important for relationship maintenance. Perhaps most important, one's social network—acting as a stakeholder—may play an active role in maintaining or dissolving a relationship. Generally speaking, if the partner is accepted by the social network, social-network embeddedness can help build trust between partners, create shared norms and understandings between them, and provide them with information and other resources. On the other hand, if the partner is not accepted by the social network, social-network embeddedness can make it difficult to maintain the relationship. For example, Youm and Paik (chapter 6 in this volume) describe how the lack of social-network embeddedness can be used to explain part of the difference between the marriage rates of African Americans and those of whites. Whites tend to have more social-network support for their partnerships, and this means that they are more likely to get married.

Institutions also have a stake, and thus play a role, in the maintenance of some types of relationships and the dissolution of others. Some institutional actors simply work to end relationships that they see as destructive. For example, organizations that lobby for the incarceration of men who beat their wives make it harder to maintain abusive relationships. Other institutional actors consciously promote certain types of relationships over others. Religious organizations, for example, define certain sexual expressions as moral and others as immoral, thus helping to maintain the former (e.g., providing counseling to heterosexual married couples) and to disrupt the latter (e.g., refusing to recognize a homosexual cohabitational relationship as legitimate and attempting to break it up). Still other institutional actors unintentionally promote certain types of relationships. For example, when the police treat domestic-violence situations as "matters to be worked out between husband and wife," they are making it easier to maintain abusive relationships.

The characteristics of the relationship that is maintained, and the alternatives to maintaining it, are also influenced by the particular culture, or the expectations and norms, of a given sex market. For example, in a very conservative cultural context, cohabitation and divorce may simply not be considered options. This is typically the case among Mexican Americans, who tend to adhere to traditional Catholic norms. Ethnographic studies have also found that a sexual double standard exists among Mexican Americans whereby a husband's extramarital affair is not considered a threat to the marriage as long as he comes home to his wife and continues to support his family financially (see Horowitz, 1983). In other sex markets, however, such a partnership configuration would not be considered stable.

Finally, as it does in the sexual-partnering process, physical space also plays a role in relationship maintenance. Not only is one not likely to meet people who live far away, but, even if one does and, moreover, manages to establish a relationship, that relationship is more costly to maintain given the distance that the partners must travel in order to spend time together. Space can also be used in order to maintain concurrent relationships. For example, partners can be chosen who live far away from each other, keeping them from finding out about one another.

## Limitations of the Market Approach

With the decline of marriage, the rise of cohabitation and divorce, and the decoupling of much of sexual expression from family life, the metaphor of the *sex market* is, as we have suggested above, apt for describing new patterns of adult singlehood and multiple partnering. In addition, the strength of the market approach is that it treats markets as social structures, thereby integrating insights from a variety of theoretical perspectives (i.e., economic, network, constructivist, demographic). Thus, the theory of the sex market has the potential of offering a comprehensive, robust explanation of sexual activity. Nevertheless, no one approach is sufficient in and of itself, and our approach has three limitations that stem from misfits between our empirical data and the predictions of more general market theories.

First, the sex-market metaphor appears to favor utilitarian thinking when, in fact, much of our research actually suggests the importance of nonexchange, value orientations. In a few cases (e.g., prostitution), sex acts are exchanged for money, but most sexual relationships are created on the basis of nonmonetary values. Sex may be exchanged for security or belonging, as is the case with, for example, homeless young men in Shoreland, who work the gay transactional market, oddly hoping to become HIV positive in order to find a group that they can consider family. On the other hand, sexual relationships may be formed to fulfill family obligations or to express love. None of these examples fit comfortably within a utilitarian framework, nor do sex markets work like the product markets for steel, groceries, or legal advice. However, we are persuaded that, for better or for worse, sexual expression is organized like a market and shares many of the same features of traditional matching markets (e.g., transaction costs, search behaviors, exchanges of one sort or another).

Second, unlike theorists working with economic markets, we do not conceptualize humans as atomistic individuals free to make exchange decisions that solely serve their economic self-interest, nor do we see individuals as wholly constrained by social and cultural structures. Rather, we see individuals' sexual choices as channeled by the social networks, organizations, cultures, and spaces within which they act. We advocate a bounded, highly contextualized notion of human agency that does not rest comfortably with economic approaches. While this may create problems with predictability and modeling, it may more closely resemble the empirical reality of how individuals search for and create sexual partnerships. Thus, our approach does not fully address the issue of motives for action. Unlike economic theories of sexual and marriage markets, which rest on the assumption that self-interest motivates decisions and actions, our theory can only suggest how possible sexual motivations are constructed and shaped by the nature of individuals' social embeddedness in group cultures, social and familial networks, and social space.

Finally, some sexual activity involves the use of force, a social fact that does not fit comfortably with the idea of autonomous, voluntary market participation. Indeed, forced sex and domestic violence, both appalling features of intimate relations, are common enough to suggest that the notion of freely negotiated sexual relationships is a strong assumption. While we offer no explicit theory of the role of force in markets, several chapters of the book address the role of violence and force in the dynamics of sexual relationships.

## Outline of the Book

All the chapters in this volume use the data gathered by the CHSLS. This unifying fact of a shared database provides the opportunity to examine the interrelatedness of sexual expression and its regulation from different points of view. Thus, while each chapter can be read as a freestanding discussion, all the chapters were written with an eye toward mutually informing and enriching one another, thereby yielding a whole that is, we hope, greater than the sum of its parts.

### Part One: Introduction

In chapter 2, the second chapter in this introductory part, Van Haitsma, Paik, and Laumann lay out the rationale and design of this endeavor. The CHSLS, the follow-up study to the 1992 NHSLS, was designed to better assess the local processes through which individuals meet their partners and organize their sexual relationships. The chapter provides readers with an overview of the study, including details about the design of the survey, the qualitative and quantitative components of the data, and descriptions of the neighborhood samples. Briefly, in addition to a metropolitan-area sampling design, data were collected on four distinctive (and pseudonymous) neighborhoods: Shoreland, on the city's North Side (an affluent, mostly white area with a concentration of men who have sex with men); Southtown, on the South Side (a black, lower- to middle-class area); Westside, on the West Side (a predominately Mexican American, lower- to middle-class area); and Erlinda, on the Northwest Side (a mixed-Hispanic area with a concentration of Puerto Ricans). The chapter also examines some of the distinctive features of sexual expression in the CHSLS data as well as the rationale for, and advantages of, studying sexuality in an urban setting.

### Part Two: The Structure of Urban Sex Markets

In chapter 3, Mahay and Laumann examine the spatial organization of sex markets, conceptualizing the four neighborhoods in the CHSLS as socially bounded sex markets. Each market is distinguished by four organizing features: the character of its spatial location and attributes vis-à-vis other neighborhoods in the city; its mix of local institutions, including churches, health clinics, and the police; its locally operative cultural norms regarding sexual behaviors and beliefs; and the ramifying social ties in which residents are embedded. These four dimensions combine to produce distinctive neighborhood-based patterns of sexuality, including the prevalence of STIs, children, domestic violence, and partnership durability.

In chapter 4, Ellingson and Schroeder examine the social construction of same-sex markets for men and women in the four neighborhoods. They show how different combinations of sexual culture, institutional and social-network support (or the lack thereof), and social space create two types of same-sex markets: transactional and relational. The male same-sex markets for both whites and racial/ethnic minorities are predominantly transactional, but for different reasons. For white men, the sexual culture of the gay community and the availability of social space create a public market and encourage short-term sexual relationships, whereas, for Hispanic and African American men, the lack of public space for same-sex encounters, the culture of machismo, and embeddedness within tight kinship networks create a private market while encouraging short-term sexual relationships. Same-sex markets for women, regardless of racial/ethnic identity, tend to be relational. The sexual cultures of the female same-sex markets in the neighborhoods define monogamous, committed relationships as the ideal, and market space is constructed to facilitate the building of relationships and community rather than the finding of casual sex partners. The facts that, in the African American and Hispanic neighborhoods, lesbianism has little legitimacy, limited public space is devoted to same-sex partnering activities, and the residents are strongly embedded in family networks have led to the creation of a privatized sex market for African American women and forced Latinas out of their neighborhoods to search for potential partners.

## Part Three: Sexual and Social Consequences of Sexual Marketplaces

In chapter 5, Mahay and Laumann examine how an individual's market position, or "value," in sex markets changes over the life course and how men and women adapt their sexual-partnering strategies in response. As the average age at marriage and the divorce rate both increase, greater numbers of men and women find themselves participating in sex markets at later stages of the life course. However, one's position in the sex market changes with age, and it changes for men and women differently. With age, women's market position becomes weaker, men's stronger. This is a result of several factors: unfavorable sex ratios for older women; cultural definitions of beauty; and the fact that women are more likely to be caretakers of their children. Mahay and Laumann show that many older single women have responded by changing their sexual-partnering strategies. They are more likely than are their younger counterparts to meet their sex partners at bars, clubs, and restaurants, go outside their existing social network to meet partners, and have sex outside a dating or more serious relationship. These data show that, although older single women have more traditional sexual attitudes and values, they have less traditional sexual-partnering strategies.

In chapter 6, Youm and Paik examine the link between sex markets and marriage markets, a link that helps explain why some groups are less likely to marry than are others. They first differentiate between marriage and sexual-matching markets and show how patterns of behavior in both markets in Chicago are related. Specifically, they investigate how the existence of sex-market opportunities outside a relationship reduces the likelihood of entering marriage. They show that the mutual trust needed for committing to marriage exists with few sex-market opportunities, high expectations of future marriage benefits, and strong embeddedness with mutual friends and acquaintances. They then examine whether these differences in sex-market conditions account for the racial differences in marriage rates.

In chapter 7, Paik, Laumann, and Van Haitsma investigate the social-psychological dynamics that result from participation in sex markets, focusing on the quality-of-life consequences of different types of sexual networks. Building on the insights of chapter 6, they first examine how concurrency and the kinds of commitments that people make to their sex partners produce sexual jealousy, which is conceptualized as a perceived breach of the commitment of sexual exclusivity. Next, they argue that sexual jealousy is the key social-psychological mechanism affecting relationship quality and examine how it conditions the dynamics between commitments and aspects of relationship quality, such as intimate-partner violence and relationship satisfaction. In general, they find that, when there is no jealousy, having extensive commitments tends to protect individuals from concurrency and sexual jealousy and to produce higher levels of relationship satisfaction and less violence. However, in the event that jealousy occurs, having extensive commitments has negative consequences, increasing the likelihood of intimate-partner violence and lowering relationship satisfaction. The broad implication of this research is that commitments confer risks as well as rewards.

In chapter 8, Buntin, Lechtman, and Laumann examine criminality in sexual interactions and address how intimate-partner violence and forced sex are interrelated phenomena yet, at the same time, involve different forms and mechanisms. Their discussion of violence between intimate partners begins with an analysis of the prevalence of violent acts toward an intimate partner, as reported differentially by men and women. They then look at patterns of intimate-partner violence among different social groups (racial/ethnic, same sex, neighborhood, etc.) and discuss explanations of patterns among genders and their implications. Finally, they examine patterns of help-seeking behavior: What percentage of those who have experienced intimate-partner violence seek help, and to whom do they typically turn? They then turn their attention to forced sex, beginning with the prevalence of forced sex among men and women and among different social groups. They examine the patterns and characteristics of a forced-sex event and the meaning of forced sex and its implications for sexuality. Specifically, what percentage of those who said that they experienced forced sex defined it as rape or a crime? How many sought help after the experience? And how does the event affect the victim's life in terms of overall well-being and intimacy with others? Finally, they examine these two types of violations of sexuality and intimacy in terms of the sex market. How do they affect sexual partnering and behavior in the sex market?

In chapter 9, Youm and Laumann examine how the organization of social networks affects the transmission of STDs. They provide empirical evidence that social networks can lower STD rates as a result of "third-party embeddedness," which can provide critical information about sex partners or can exert social control over the person's partner choice and sexual activities, thereby reducing or enhancing the risk of STD transmission.

## Part Four: Institutional Responses and Silences

In chapter 10, Ellingson examines how organizations within the institutional spheres of health care, social service, and law enforcement attempt to control sexuality and ameliorate sex-related health problems. Relying on in-depth interviews with service providers in the four neighborhoods, he analyzes the causal stories that institutional actors construct and deploy as they attempt to understand how and why clients are at risk and to justify their own interventions. He found that the five causal stories used by providers stress the complex cultural and structural features of each neighborhood's population that go beyond the expected institutionally driven interpretive models. However, the intervention strategies rely more heavily on institutionally based understandings of sexual problems and solutions. He argues, contra Foucault and Bourdieu, that institutional control of sexual norms, relationships, and activities is limited and not terribly strong because the causal stories draw contradictory moral boundaries and rely on contradictory understandings of moral agency. As a result, the discourses that we expect to strengthen social control undercut institutional efforts to change unhealthy or risky sexuality.

In chapter 11, Ellingson, Van Haitsma, Laumann, and Tebbe observe that questions about sexuality are at the very center of recent intradenominational conflicts within American Christianity. At the level of the congregation, clergy must contend, not only with the policies and doctrines handed down by regional and national bodies, but also with the pressures of the local religious market, the local institutional context, and the culture and the needs of the local population. Drawing on case studies from three of the neighborhoods (Shoreland, Southtown, and Westside), they illustrate the ways in which congregations' policies and practices in matters related to human sexuality are not simple translations of denominational traditions and doctrine but, rather, the outcomes of complex negotiations by congregations' leaders faced with organizational, demographic, and institutional constraints and resources. They argue that these constraints and resources lead clergy to construct normative frameworks that provide them with the interpretive lenses and action scripts with which to address specific sexuality issues facing their congregations and communities.

In chapter 12, Ellingson, Mahay, Paik, and Laumann provide a summary description of the sexual world that we have uncovered. This world does not look like Foucault's world of strong institutional control over sexual identities and behaviors. Chicago's institutions simply do not exercise extensive or authoritative power over sexuality; instead, their control is partial, driven by restrictive institutional logics and institutions' reluctance to take ownership or become stakeholders.[13] Thus, institutional solutions to sex-market problems are incomplete and ineffective. A culture of individual choice has come to permeate all social life. One of the consequences of the institutional disembeddedness of sexuality is that it gives rise to a kind of moral heterogeneity: there is no overarching moral framework to guide sex-market activity. Each institution offers its own definitions of good/safe sex, identities, and relationships, definitions that exist alongside specific cultural norms/scripts about sexuality, thereby creating a smorgasbord of sexual norms from which individuals in the market select. And there is no dominant institution providing the means to adjudicate between competing normative frameworks. To be sure, individuals' sexual choices are constrained and channeled, but, in particular, by local forces—familial and friendship networks, local cultural scripts, and locally organized social and physical spaces. The dominant American myth about sexuality has been decoupled from actual behavior. The story

---

13. For example, the police tend to intervene in sexual issues only when a law is broken (e.g., cases of child or spouse abuse) and then quickly hand over the alleged perpetrator to the court system. Police interventions usually do not include efforts to ameliorate, fix, or eradicate sexual problems (except by way of arrest), nor do they attempt to address sexual risk taking or the health consequences of sexual behaviors. In these ways, the police avoid taking public ownership of sex-related social problems.

about how boy meets girl and they fall in love, get married, have children, and then atrophy sexually with age is by no means the only story that we see in our data. There are many different sexual life histories and partnering sequences and, perhaps, the emergent new story of long periods of singleness, the commonplace nature of cohabitation, and the ways in which the myth cannot function for some populations, such as the African American.

# 2 )

# The Chicago Health and Social Life Survey Design

Martha Van Haitsma,
Anthony Paik,
and Edward O. Laumann

In 1992, researchers at the University of Chicago fielded the National Health and Social Life Survey (NHSLS), a national probability survey documenting how individual sexual expression, attitudes, and behaviors varied systematically across major social categories (gender, age, religion, education, marital status, race/ethnicity) of American society. The core findings of that survey were reported originally in two studies—*The Social Organization of Sexuality* (Laumann, Gagnon, Michael, & Michaels, 1994) and *Sex in America* (Michael, Gagnon, Laumann, & Kolata, 1994)—published at a time when the last, comprehensive scientific study of American sexuality to have been conducted was the two-volume Kinsey Report (Kinsey, Pomeroy, & Martin, 1948; Kinsey, Pomeroy, Martin, & Gebhard, 1953) and when the threat of HIV/AIDS was a mounting public health concern. A follow-up volume, *Sex, Love, and Health in America* (Laumann & Michael, 2001), presented a more detailed exploration of the NHSLS data set, focusing on the social and cultural contexts that frame such disparate topics as abortion, adult–child sexuality, circumcision, sexual dysfunction, modes of sexual expression, and changes in America's sexual mores in the wake of the Sexual Revolution of the late 1960s.

The NHSLS, and other studies also released in the 1990s (e.g., Catania et al., 1995; Tanfer & Schoon, 1992), provided critically needed baseline information about adult sexuality: who does what with whom, how often, and why. However, meeting and mating are fundamentally local processes, not activities that occur at the level of abstract, analytic demographic characteristics. The 1995–97 Chicago Health and Social Life Survey (CHSLS), the follow-up study to the NHSLS that provided the data on which *The Sexual Organization of the City* is based, was designed to better assess how people meet partners and organize their sexual relationships. This chapter provides an overview of our research strategies, describes the CHSLS data, and highlights some of the distinctive features of sexual expression in Chicago.

It is our immodest, wishful aspiration that the picture of urban sexuality presented by *The Sexual Organization of the City* replace that presented by such media representations as the television show *Sex and the City,* which portrays the sexual adventures of four professional, white women living in Manhattan. While the world of *Sex and the City* is decidedly narrow, it is at the center of several demographic trends (which no doubt have been thoroughly assessed by market researchers): upwardly mobile white women marry later, divorce more frequently, and have fewer children than do other women. In contrast, our study looks at sexuality as it is expressed across an entire city population. Many of our respondents are poor, are members of racial/ethnic minorities, and are unlikely to come into contact with the rarefied world portrayed in *Sex and the City. The Social Organization of the City* is about the diversity of sexual expression found in an American metropolis.

Cities are important places to study because they are at the locus of major societal patterns. Georg Simmel ([1903] 1971), and Robert Park ([1929] 1967) afterward, argued that the city was at the heart of modern life. Economic restructuring and racial/ethnic segregation are social processes affecting the whole United States throughout the twentieth century and into the twenty-first (Wilson, 1987; Massey & Denton, 1993), but they are considerably more dynamic in cities than in rural and suburban settings. Cities are demographically heterogeneous. They are the ports of entry for immigrants; they have high concentrations of racial and ethnic minorities. Indeed, in some cities, such as Los Angeles, white Americans are no longer the majority ethnic group. Young people, the nonmarried, and individuals with same-sex orientations tend to congregate in cities, making urban areas the most vibrant of all settings in which people search for sex partners. Because cities are also the unfortunate hosts to many social problems—poverty, homelessness, out-of-wedlock fertility, violence, drug abuse, etc.—they are important places to study if we are to understand the regulatory role of collective processes (e.g., social capital) and local institutions (Sampson, 2002). In short, cities are where the action is, and, given its variegated urban social processes, Chicago in particular is an exemplar.[1]

Sex in the city, then, takes place in an environment where search activities are heightened and potential opportunities are stunningly diverse. Sex is an important activity of many city dwellers, especially those who are not married. A considerable amount of socializing among urbanites is oriented toward meeting potential sex partners. The demographic heterogeneity and density of the city also allow for diverse sexual lifestyles and the possibility of mixing with socially distant others, both alternatives that are largely unavailable to many rural populations. At the same time, many people have crystallized views of whom they want as a sex partner and tend to share their preferences with those who are socially similar, creating ecological niches of sexual matching patterns in the city. In part because of their large concentrations of men who have sex with men, American cities are also at the heart of one of the key social problems associated with sexuality: the transmission of HIV/AIDs and other sexually transmitted infections (STIs). Finally, there are many collective-level actors and institutions that must deal, directly or indirectly, with sexual expression and its concomitant problems. Ultimately, then, while a study of urban sexuality cannot claim to be representative of the sexuality of a nation as a whole, it does allow us to study sexual expression in an environment of diverse social contexts.

To capture these multiple urban social processes, we designed the CHSLS to be representative yet comparative and to have individual- and institution-level components. We began with the premise that sexual partnering occurs within real social groups and networks, not within analytic social categories. Sex partners meet each other because they attend the same church, belong to the same professional organization, live in the same neighborhood, work at the same firm, patronize the same bar, have mutual friends, or somehow share social and physical space at some point in time. In other words, sexual-partnering opportunities are heavily structured by the local organization of social life, the local population mix, and the local norms guiding the types of relationships that are sanctioned or supported. Thus, we adopted a multi-sample strategy to facilitate comparative analyses and a mixed-methods approach to capture both individual and organizational aspects of local communities. In the next section, we go into greater detail regarding the study

1. For a contrary perspective as well as responses, see the debate over the "Chicago school" of urban sociology in the March 2002, inaugural issue of *City and Community*.

design of the CHSLS, how we fielded the survey and key-informant interviews, and the design of the questionnaire.

## Study Design

In a national survey, it is impossible to investigate detailed aspects of social context because respondents are spread too widely among locales with different norms, opportunities, and supports for sexual partnering and expression. The CHSLS looks at local communities with distinctive institutional configurations, local histories, and networks of social interaction. It emphasizes the social processes that produce intergroup differences as well as intragroup variation. What sexual behaviors occur, between whom, and how often are channeled by the social pressures and opportunities of the immediate social environment in which people live. The CHSLS was designed to uncover these social forces.

The research design itself consisted of two components: a household survey and key-informant interviews. The probability data are based on a representative, face-to-face household survey, conducted in five samples of persons aged eighteen to fifty-nine. The CHSLS utilized a similar methodology as the NHSLS in terms of mode of administration and target population. However, unlike the NHSLS, interviews were conducted in Spanish when necessary, and interviewers used programmed laptops rather than printed questionnaires to allow for complex skip patterns and self-answered questions. In total, we collected 2,114 cases. One sample, which included the city of Chicago as well as the inner suburban ring, was based on a two-stage survey representative of residents of Cook County. The remaining four samples were each household surveys representative of a community area within the city of Chicago.[2] We also conducted key-informant interviews with institutional actors within each sampled community area. We completed a total of 160 interviews with community leaders and service providers within the four community areas. A limited amount of general observation of community life and events was also undertaken in each neighborhood in order to better characterize the local social milieu. The various types of interviews and samples were intended to produce results that would both stand alone and shed light on each other.

2. Our community areas largely overlapped with official community areas, but in no case did they coincide exactly. As we discuss at greater length below, the city is divided into seventy-seven contiguous clusters of census tracts, each known as a *community area*. Our areas always included at least one census tract contiguous to the community area but outside it and, further, did not include every tract in the area.

## Choosing the Oversample Neighborhoods

Four focal communities were selected to provide a set of comparative case studies. These communities were chosen to represent various points along a continuum of perceived cohesiveness and insularity as well as to provide samples of different racial, ethnic, and sexual-orientation populations. The selection process involved three stages: choosing target neighborhood types; identifying general community areas that represent those types; and finalizing the choice of community areas to be studied.

As ours was a study of sexual expression and health, we focused on populations relevant for public-health policy: gay men; African Americans; and Hispanics. Gay men, African Americans, and Puerto Ricans have disproportionately high rates of HIV and other STIs. The Mexican American population in Chicago is also of special interest to public-health providers. This rapidly growing population includes many needing Spanish-language services as well as a subgroup of illegal immigrants who are often reluctant to access government programs.

Furthermore, Chicago is one of the few urban areas where sizable Puerto Rican and Mexican populations reside, allowing separate studies of both groups. Other studies have shown the obfuscation that results when Hispanics of different national origins are lumped together, particularly when they live in different parts of the country. Thus, it seemed important to take advantage of Chicago's population mix by selecting two different Hispanic groups for comparison.

The choice of community areas rested on several factors. The primary criterion was the relative degree of group concentration. An area characterized by its gay-male concentration was selected first because there is only one such neighborhood in Chicago. This neighborhood is interesting because it is also a singles' scene, drawing people from around the metropolitan area to its restaurants, clubs, theaters, and other social venues. There are a few community areas with a predominance of Mexicans, several contiguous neighborhoods where Puerto Ricans are concentrated, and numerous neighborhoods that are more than 95 percent African American. According to the 1990 census, the two most concentrated community areas of Mexican residence are each about 85 percent Mexican, but the most concentrated area of Puerto Rican residence is only 33 percent Puerto Rican.

The second and third criteria were avoiding areas of extreme poverty and attaining some degree of class comparability among the Mexican, Puerto Rican, and African American neighborhoods. The CHSLS was not meant to be a study of poverty. Although health and poverty are related, we anticipated that the effects of severe-poverty concentrations would dominate other local factors that would be of general interest and have policy relevance for sexual expression. We also hoped to avoid confounding race/ethnicity with class. The preselected area of gay concentration is one of high income and high levels of education, but there are no comparable neighborhoods with Puerto Rican or Mexican concentrations. There are middle-class black neighborhoods in the city, but these are not typical of the black urban population as a whole. We thus chose to look for working-class black and Hispanic areas. Class matching proved difficult in the case of blacks and Hispanics, however, because class markers are distributed so differently within each group. In the heavily immigrant Mexican neighborhoods, incomes are clustered around the poverty line, and education levels range from extremely low to average, but employment is high, and welfare use is low. In black neighborhoods with similar median-income levels, the dispersion of income is much wider, and education levels are higher, but unemployment and welfare reliance are greater as well. Puerto Rican neighborhoods are similar to African American neighborhoods in some respects and to Mexican neighborhoods in others. Because statistical measures of class are not entirely comparable between black and Hispanic areas, we relied on observation as well as census figures to locate suitable neighborhoods. We looked for areas with some on-the-ground similarity in terms of street life, local business activity, and residential housing stock.

Finally, we wanted neighborhoods that had some sense of boundedness as communities apart from Chicago in general. Again, it was not possible to do this in a strictly comparable way for both the Hispanic and the black communities. Chicago has historically been highly segregated by race, and this pattern continues today (see Massey & Denton, 1993). The black community is, thus, more commonly thought of in terms of large contiguous areas on the West and South Sides of the city—the traditional Black Belts—than in terms of smaller, neighborhood areas. Mexicans and Puerto Ricans are more widely dispersed throughout the residential areas of the city as a whole, although there are a few identifiable areas of higher concentrations.

Chicago is formally divided into seventy-seven community areas. These areas are useful designations because they refer to spaces that typically have real social meanings. These areas are made up of groups of census tracts and have been used by numerous city and social-service agencies as catchment areas. We thus began with census data for these defined areas and narrowed the choices to about twelve communities. We sent field-workers out to walk the main streets of several areas and spoke to service providers and residents of these communities, inquiring about the geographic boundaries as defined by local residents. Our final choices of areas do not correspond exactly to any of the seventy-seven officially designated community areas. Rather, we included most, but not all, tracts in chosen areas as well as a few tracts outside the community boundaries. Pseudonyms were assigned to final choices to reinforce the fact that areas do not strictly conform to official community-area boundaries. The general location of each pseudonymous area—"Shoreland" on the North Side (a neighborhood dominated by affluent young white singles and gay men), "Southtown" on the South Side (an African American neighborhood), "Westside" on the West Side (a predominantly Mexican neighborhood), and "Erlinda" on the Northwest Side (a mixed-Hispanic neighborhood)—will be clear to anyone familiar with Chicago. However, our choices of contiguous tracts distinct from the contiguous tracts that constitute the official community areas make it impossible to know with certainty whether any given census tract falls within one of our sample areas. Maps in later chapters indicate the general areas of the city in which interviews were conducted but do not accurately outline the sample areas.

## Fielding the Study

The CHSLS fieldwork was conducted during two separate field periods. Data were collected on the first four samples—the Cook Country cross-sectional sample and the Shoreland, Southtown, and Westside oversamples—in 1995. The initial study was not fully funded, resulting in a delay while additional monies were secured to complete the neighborhood samples. Subsequent cost overruns truncated the first field period early so that resources were also needed to boost initial samples. Funding was obtained to collect data on the Erlinda oversample and to collect additional data on the Cook County cross-sectional and the Shoreland and Westside samples in 1997.

Table 2.1 shows final numbers of cases and response rates for each sample. The CHSLS produced five probability samples derived from the household-survey instrument and over eleven hundred pages of field notes from open-ended, key-informant interviews. The Cook County sample consists of 890 completed cases and the Shoreland, Southtown, Westside, and Erlinda oversamples of 358, 307, 349, and 210 completed cases, respectively.

Table 2.1 Numbers of Cases and Response Rates for CHSLS Survey Samples

|  | Cook County Cross Section | Shoreland | Westside | Erlinda | Southtown |
|---|---|---|---|---|---|
| Men (N) | 377 | 176 | 140 | 82 | 117 |
| Women (N) | 513 | 182 | 209 | 128 | 190 |
| Total cases (N) | 890 | 358 | 349 | 210 | 307 |
| Response rate (%) | 71 | 66 | 70 | 78 | 60 |

Note: A description of each of the four pseudonymous neighborhoods can be found earlier in this chapter, in the section "Choosing the Oversample Neighborhoods."

Response rates ranged from 60 to 78 percent across the samples. Readers may wonder whether low response rates were due to survey content. We do not believe this to be the case. The initial, 1995 field period ran into unanticipated, costly household-listing expenditures when the purchased sample proved to be of lower quality than expected. This led to cost overruns and a sudden, premature closing of the first field phase. Specifically, the low response rate in Southtown was due to the abrupt termination of field operations that resulted in many "in-process" interview prospects not being successfully pursued to completed interviews. However, no special difficulties were encountered in the field, and interviewers did not have problems gaining cooperation from Southtown respondents. Similar truncated field operations in the other samples were offset by reopening cases in 1997. During this second field period, additional cases were collected in a new sample area—Erlinda—and in three of the four original samples—the Cook County cross section, Shoreland, and Westside—but not in Southtown. This meant that low response rates from the shortened first field period could be remedied somewhat in all but the Southtown samples. Because limited funds precluded collecting more cases in all the neighborhoods and the number of completed African American cases in both the cross section and Southtown was sufficient to sustain independent analysis, the decision was made to spend what limited funding was available on collecting cases from areas where two other minority populations of interest—Hispanics and gay men—were more prevalent.

Shoreland, unlike Southtown, did provide some special field difficulties. These were due to contact rather than cooperation problems, however. Shoreland is characterized by many locked, high-rise buildings and gated developments as well as a population that works long hours and is also highly socially active and, therefore, seldom at home. The high response rate from Erlinda, which area was fielded entirely after the listing and contact problems that plagued the Shoreland collection process were resolved, demonstrates that survey content did not preclude high response rates.

The National Opinion Research Center (NORC) fielded the close-coded CHSLS survey. Interviewers were provided with written "Q-by-Q's"—question-by-question explanations of the purpose of questions, acceptable probes, and definitions. They were also required to attend an intensive all-day training session and a series of mock interview sessions. The all-day training included presentations by the principal investigators about the purpose and importance of the research and "desensitivity" sessions to help interviewers maintain a professional and neutral demeanor when asking respondents about sensitive topics. In addition, trainers gave interviewers practical advice and demonstrations of acceptable and unacceptable ways in which to obtain cooperation, probe for clarity and completeness of responses, and so forth. Mock interviews gave interviewers a chance to practice reading the questionnaire aloud and permitted supervisors to observe interviewing style and to correct any problems. Highly experienced operations staff supervised interviewers, providing them with ongoing oversight and direction throughout the field period.

Interviews in the neighborhood samples were conducted mostly by matched-race interviewers. Most interviewers in Southtown were African American, virtually all those in Westside and Erlinda were Hispanic and bilingual, and most interviewers in Shoreland were white. The countywide sample was more mixed in terms of the match between respondent and interviewers. Most of the interviewing staff were women, but NORC found that men were more successful in Shoreland and, thus, moved as many of the male interviewers as possible to that area. NORC also found that it was best not to send Puerto Rican interviewers to Mexican households but that sending Mexican interviewers to Puerto Rican households was usually not a problem.

People are often suspicious of the responses that interviewees provide to socially sensitive questions, and rightly so. Research into honesty in survey response consistently shows that, the more socially undesirable (desirable) the behavior, the more it will be underreported (overreported) (Sudman & Bradburn, 1982). While such social-desirability effects cannot be overcome entirely, there are techniques that can be employed to reduce the degree to which over- or underreporting occurs, including normalizing sensitive questions and providing greater privacy in which to respond to the most sensitive questions (Tourangeau, Rips, & Rasinski, 2000).

Interviewers for the CHSLS were carefully trained to conduct interviews in a professional manner and in private. In cases where spouses or partners insisted on being present during an interview, interviewers reported creative means of preventing the intruder from overhearing responses to questions most likely to be influenced by the presence of a second party. For example, interviewers reported asking a partner sitting within earshot of the interview for a glass of water at critical junctures and quickly running through the most sensitive questions while the partner was out of the room. Interviewers also reported utilizing seating arrangements that allowed interviewees but not others to view the computer screen and asking for responses by number. The use of hand cards—a technique to reduce social-desirability effects more generally—facilitated such practices. A self-administered portion of the questionnaire allowed interviewees to answer some of the most sensitive questions in a completely private manner.

In short, while it is impossible to know just how honest self-reports about sensitive and private behavior are, this study used available means to reduce this source of bias as much as possible in the context of an interviewer-administered questionnaire. Interviewers were carefully instructed in how to comport themselves so as to reduce bias, questions were worded in ways that normalized behaviors as much as possible, and some sections of the questionnaire were self-administered.

## Key-Informant Interviews

To better understand the institutional regulation of sexual expression, the CHSLS conducted 160 interviews with community leaders and service providers in four institutional domains—medical, religious, legal, and social services. These domains were selected to cover the ways in which sex is most often framed in public discourse—as a health issue, as a moral issue, as an issue of social control, and as an issue affecting individual, family, or community well-being. Those interviewed were asked about community norms and behavior with regard to AIDS, other STIs, domestic violence, homosexuality, family formation, and the like. Interviews lasted between thirty minutes and four hours, with most taking about an hour and a half. Table 2.2 provides the number of interviews in each institutional domain in each of the five samples.

To ensure that we captured as much data as possible in these interviews, we adopted a unique, interviewer-assignment process in which two interviewers attended and independently wrote up each interview. In addition to ensuring greater completeness and reliability, this strategy allowed interviewers to specialize either in one community or in one institutional domain, with the result that most interviews were conducted by both a community specialist and an institution specialist. Eight research assistants in total were assigned to the key-informant interviews. The person responsible for a community area at-

Table 2.2 Distribution of CHSLS Key Informants by Institutional Arena and Neighborhood Service Area

| | Whole City or County | Shoreland | Westside | Erlinda | Southtown | Total |
|---|---|---|---|---|---|---|
| General[a] | 9 | 2 | 3 | 5 | 1 | 20 |
| Religious | 3 | 7 | 11 | 10 | 10 | 41 |
| Social Service | 6 | 14 | 6 | 10 | 8 | 46 |
| Legal | 7 | 2 | 2 | 1 | 2 | 14 |
| Medical | 11 | 12 | 5 | 7 | 6 | 38 |
| Total | 36 | 37 | 27 | 33 | 27 | 160 |

[a]*General* respondents were aldermen, community organizers, and other local leaders who were not attached to an organization in one of our four targeted institutional domains. These persons were often key gatekeepers and sources of information about the local structure of institutions more generally.

tempted to attend all interviews with local service providers, while the person responsible for an institutional domain tried to attend all interviews with relevant organizations. The eight interviewers were four men and four women— two African Americans (one man, one woman), one gay man, one lesbian, and two persons conversant in Spanish (one fluently). At times, we varied from the prescribed community/institution-specialist pairing and matched interviewer and informant characteristics (i.e., race, language, or sexual orientation) in order to gain informants' cooperation or put them at their ease.

## The CHSLS Questionnaire

The survey instrument was administered to all respondents in each of the five probability samples—the Cook County sample and the four Chicago community areas. The CHSLS questionnaire was designed specifically to complement the NHSLS questionnaire. In order to facilitate comparison between the samples, basic questions from the NHSLS, such as those about frequency of sex and numbers of sex partners, were worded so as to mirror the NHSLS versions as closely as possible. Because the NHSLS already provided a baseline distribution of sexual behaviors, lifetime numbers of partners, and demographic characteristics for all partners, we deemed it unnecessary to collect this information in detail again. At the same time, we wanted to be able to compare the CHSLS distributions with the NHSLS distributions. Thus, numbers of partners in the last year and important lifetime facts such as age at first sexual experience, number of marriages, number of cohabitations, and total number of partners were collected again. Questions about sex practices, on the other hand, such as frequency of particular sex acts over the life course, were restricted to only the two most recent partnerships. Likewise, detailed social and demographic characteristics of partners were also limited to the two most recent sex partners.

To take maximal advantage of the local character of the CHSLS, we added several new sections and made modifications to the basic NHSLS questionnaire. Whereas the NHSLS was intended to provide representative statistics for a national sample, the strength of the CHSLS was that the survey focused on local sex markets.[3] Persons interviewed could potentially partner with each other. Thus, patterns of partnering and nonpartnering would represent actual network cleavages rather than artifacts of the research design. In a national survey, it is impossible to control for local availability when looking at

3. On the terms *sex market* and *sexual marketplace* as they are used in this study, see the section "The Social Organization of Sexual Partnering and Sexual Relationships" in Ellingson, Laumann, Paik, and Mahay (chapter 1 in this volume).

intergroup partnerships. So, for example, perhaps Hispanics married to non-Hispanics captured by a national study are those persons living in areas with few or no coethnics. In Chicago, we know that Mexicans are within reach of Mexican, Puerto Rican, black, white, and Asian partners so that matched partnering represents a positive choice. We wanted to use this fact to document how sexual partnering is socially structured on the ground.

We therefore decided that the questionnaire should focus on current rather than lifetime partnerships. We wanted to be able to ask about the actual physical locations where the partners met, which would permit us to geocode the neighborhoods where dating partners resided. We also wanted to ask respondents about their social networks more generally and about connections between their social and their sexual relationships. This, too, argued for focusing on current relationships, as it is difficult to report retrospectively about the characteristics of network ties. Thus, we added new questions about social networks, neighborhood characteristics, and the geographic parameters of respondents' sexual, social, and work lives.

Another modification—the heart of the CHSLS questionnaire—was a section designed to collect detailed information about the characteristics of respondents' two most recent sex partners. The NHSLS data documented the fact that most people's sex lives follow the pattern of periods of stable, long-term relationships punctuated by periods of numerous short-term relationships. That is, at any given point in time, most people are in the midst of long-term relationships; thus, cross-sectional data underrepresent more transient partnerships. By collecting information on the two most recent partners, we were typically able to capture the current primary partnerships of our respondents as well as a past short-term relationship. Details about relationship characteristics, as well as network and neighborhood information, allow us to specify the social contexts surrounding sexual partnerships.

The questionnaire was pretested in a paper-and-pencil format. This strategy was adopted because of the high costs associated with reprogramming laptops as the questionnaire was continually revised. That is, whereas the paper-and-pencil format was easily revised (by altering a computer file stored on a word processor and printing the results), the process by which the computerized format was revised was much more complicated. Since the software employed to program the laptops utilized linked screens, each change to the questionnaire required considerable work to ensure that skip patterns remained logical. Thus, it made sense to accumulate revisions using the paper-and-pencil format and to reprogram the CAPI instrument (the computerized format) only after accumulating a large number of revisions.

Using flyers, we recruited pretest respondents from a variety of demographic categories—men and women, young and old, gay and straight, minority and white. We paid pretest respondents for their participation and informed them that their interviews were pretests and were being observed. The questionnaire was administered to pretest respondents in a room with a two-way mirror, allowing members of the questionnaire-design team to observe. The questionnaire was revised when questions did not function as envisioned or when wording proved inappropriate for some respondents.

The programmed version of the questionnaire was tested by project staff rather than by actual respondents. Staff acted as respondents to test the limits of skip patterns when there were no partners, numerous partners, or unusual situations. Further, testers refused to answer critical screening questions or answered inconsistently to make sure that built-in cross-checks worked properly.

The final questionnaire was long, taking an average of ninety minutes to administer, and included complex skip patterns. However, CAPI automatically managed skips and text substitutions for gender and tense. A relatively lengthy self-administered section was included in the questionnaire to improve response rates on especially sensitive topics, such as sexual orientation, same-sex sexual experiences, domestic violence, and drug use. Because two of our oversample neighborhoods included large numbers of Spanish-speaking residents, the entire questionnaire was translated into Spanish (the Spanish-language version was available only in a paper-and-pencil format), and bilingual interviewers were used in these neighborhoods.

## Describing the Samples and the Communities

Table 2.3 compares NHSLS and CHSLS data for various subsets of respondents—those in the top twelve metropolitan areas of the United States, Cook County, the city of Chicago, and the four community areas (Shoreland, Southtown, Westside, and Erlinda)—in terms of basic demographic categories. We see that Cook County has a somewhat higher proportion of minority residents than do the top twelve metropolitan areas generally. Marital-status distributions are reasonably similar between Cook County and the top twelve metropolitan areas, particularly for men. However, fewer Cook County women than women in the twelve-metropolitan-area aggregation are currently married. Age distributions are very close across the Cook County and the top-twelve-metropolitan-area samples for both genders. Large differences in marital-status and age distributions appear between communities within Chicago, however, highlighting the spatial organization of social groups by life-course stage and race/ethnicity.

Tables 2.4A and 2.4B summarize the basic demographic characteristics of the four community areas in comparison with the city of Chicago as a whole

Table 2.3 Comparison of Racial/Ethnic, Age, and Marital-Status Composition of NHSLS and CHSLS Samples by Gender

| | Top 12 Metro | | Cook County | | City of Chicago | | Shoreland | | Westside | | Erlinda | | Southtown | |
|---|---|---|---|---|---|---|---|---|---|---|---|---|---|---|
| | Men | Women | Men | Women | Men | Women | Men | Women | Men | Women | Men | Women | Men | Women |
| Cases (N) | 266 | 365 | 377 | 513 | 210 | 292 | 176 | 182 | 140 | 209 | 82 | 128 | 117 | 190 |
| Non-Hispanic white[b] | 60.0 | 62.1 | 53.6 | 46.8 | 44.8 | 31.2 | 81.3 | 84.6 | 10.0 | 8.6 | 8.5 | 9.4 | .9 | .5 |
| Non-Hispanic black[b] | 20.8 | 20.8 | 23.3 | 31.2 | 30.5 | 43.8 | 6.8 | 7.1 | .7 | .5 | .0 | 4.7 | 96.6 | 99.9 |
| Total Hispanic[b] | 12.5 | 12.7 | 19.6 | 17.5 | 21.8 | 23.3 | 6.3 | 5.0 | 87.9 | 90.4 | 89.0 | 85.9 | .9 | .5 |
| Mexican descent[c] | 8.7 | 3.3 | 14.6 | 11.5 | 13.3 | 14.4 | 3.4 | 1.7 | 81.4 | 84.7 | 57.3 | 39.1 | .0 | .0 |
| Puerto Rican[c] | 1.5 | 4.7 | 3.5 | 4.3 | 5.7 | 7.2 | .6 | 1.7 | 1.4 | 1.9 | 20.7 | 37.5 | .0 | .5 |
| Other Hispanic[c] | 2.3 | 4.7 | 1.6 | 1.8 | 2.9 | 1.7 | 2.3 | 1.7 | 5.0 | 3.8 | 11.0 | 9.4 | .9 | .0 |
| Non-Hispanic other | 6.8 | 4.4 | 3.5 | 4.5 | 2.9 | 1.7 | 5.7 | 3.3 | 1.4 | .5 | 2.4 | .0 | 1.7 | .0 |
| Age 18–29 | 28.7 | 26.1 | 30.5 | 26.5 | 33.3 | 29.8 | 48.9 | 55.5 | 40.0 | 42.1 | 39.0 | 35.9 | 32.5 | 30.0 |
| Age 30–39 | 36.6 | 33.2 | 33.7 | 33.5 | 35.2 | 29.8 | 34.1 | 24.2 | 31.4 | 31.6 | 31.7 | 34.4 | 30.8 | 31.1 |
| Age 40–49 | 20.0 | 26.4 | 20.7 | 23.6 | 17.1 | 21.9 | 13.1 | 12.6 | 15.7 | 16.3 | 23.2 | 16.4 | 17.1 | 20.0 |
| Age 50–59 | 14.7 | 14.3 | 15.1 | 16.4 | 14.3 | 18.5 | 4.0 | 7.7 | 12.9 | 10.1 | 6.1 | 13.3 | 19.7 | 19.0 |
| Married | 43.9 | 50.3 | 45.4 | 42.1 | 31.9 | 30.5 | 15.3 | 19.2 | 49.3 | 52.6 | 43.9 | 42.2 | 28.2 | 27.9 |
| Noncohabitants: | | | | | | | | | | | | | | |
|   Never married | 33.6 | 26.4 | 34.8 | 27.9 | 43.8 | 32.5 | 65.9 | 63.7 | 30.0 | 15.3 | 36.6 | 25.0 | 45.3 | 37.9 |
|   Divorced, separated, widowed | 15.7 | 16.4 | 11.4 | 20.1 | 13.3 | 23.3 | 4.6 | 8.8 | 8.6 | 12.9 | 6.1 | 17.2 | 14.5 | 27.4 |
| Cohabitants: | | | | | | | | | | | | | | |
|   Never married | 5.0 | 3.6 | 5.3 | 7.0 | 7.6 | 10.6 | 13.1 | 5.5 | 8.6 | 13.4 | 9.8 | 9.4 | 9.4 | 5.3 |
|   Divorced, separated, widowed | 1.9 | 3.3 | 3.2 | 2.9 | 3.3 | 3.1 | 1.1 | 2.8 | 3.6 | 5.7 | 3.7 | 6.3 | 2.6 | 1.6 |

[a]The twelve most populous metropolitan areas in the United States in 1990, drawn from the NHSLS (1992).

[b]This table excludes the NHSLS oversamples of African-Americans and Hispanics to show representative proportions.

[c]The numbers are percentages of the total population; together they sum to total Hispanic.

Table 2.4A 1990 Census Data for Suburban Cook County,[a] the City of Chicago, and Four Neighborhood Areas within Chicago Selected by the CHSLS

| | Suburban Cook County | City of Chicago | Shoreland | Westside | Erlinda | Southtown |
|---|---|---|---|---|---|---|
| **Age:** | | | | | | |
| 0–11 | 15.7 | 16.9 | 5 | 24 | 23 | 19 |
| 12–17 | 7.3 | 7.8 | 1 | 11 | 11 | 10 |
| 18–29 | 21.5 | 25.1 | 43 | 30 | 25 | 25 |
| 30–39 | 16.3 | 16.1 | 22 | 15 | 16 | 14 |
| 40–59 | 22.2 | 18.8 | 16 | 14 | 16 | 22 |
| 60+ | 17.0 | 15.2 | 14 | 8 | 9 | 11 |
| **Households:** | | | | | | |
| Nonfamily households | 27.4 | 37.5 | 77 | 23 | 18 | 17 |
| Man alone[b] | 8.7 | 13.1 | 27 | 11 | 6 | 6 |
| Woman alone[b] | 14.7 | 18.6 | 35 | 8 | 8 | 8 |
| Family households | 72.6 | 62.5 | 23 | 77 | 82 | 83 |
| Husband, wife only[b] | 32.3 | 20.9 | 13 | 13 | 17 | 23 |
| Husband, wife, children[b] | 27.4 | 17.9 | 5 | 39 | 34 | 19 |
| Family head, children[b] | 4.6 | 10.6 | 2 | 9 | 17 | 17 |
| Mean persons per household | . . . | 2.7 | 1.4 | 3.3 | 3.3 | 3.2 |
| **Race/ethnicity:** | | | | | | |
| Non–Hispanic white | 80.3 | 38.8 | 78 | 11 | 19 | 1 |
| Non–Hispanic black | 9.9 | 38.3 | 8 | 1 | 5 | 99 |
| Total Hispanic | 6.0 | 19.3 | 9 | 88 | 74 | 1 |
| Mexican[b] | 4.7 | 12.6 | 4 | 83 | 26 | . . . |
| Puerto Rican[b] | .3 | 4.3 | 2 | 2 | 41 | . . . |
| Other Hispanic[b] | 1.0 | 2.4 | 3 | 3 | 7 | . . . |
| Asian | . . . | . . . | 5 | . . . | . . . | . . . |
| **Education (age 18+):** | | | | | | |
| Less than high school | 18.1 | 33.4 | 9 | 64 | 51 | 32 |
| High school degree only | 50.8 | 44.0 | 28 | 28 | 39 | 53 |
| Associates degree | 5.9 | 4.6 | 4 | 2 | 4 | 6 |
| Bachelor's degree | 16.8 | 11.7 | 38 | 3 | 4 | 6 |
| Advanced/professional | 8.3 | 6.4 | 20 | 2 | 2 | 3 |

*Source:* 1990 Census.

[a]Suburban Cook County is that part of the county outside the city limits and includes roughly the first ring of suburban communities around the city.

[b]Numbers are percentages of the entire population but subsets of the categories they appear under. In the case of household types, the percentages do not add up to the base category because not all subtypes are shown. Thus, there are more types of nonfamily household than men and women living alone, but only these are broken out here. In the case of Hispanics, the different origin group percentages do add to the total Hispanic percentage.

Table 2.4B 1990 Census Data for Suburban Cook County,[a] the City of Chicago, and Four Neighborhood Areas within Chicago Selected by the CHSLS

| | Suburban Cook County | City of Chicago | Shoreland | Westside | Erlinda | Southtown |
|---|---|---|---|---|---|---|
| **Employment (%):** | | | | | | |
| Men 16+ employed | 75.8 | 63.9 | 85 | 71 | 68 | 52 |
| Men 16+ unemployed | 3.8 | 8.4 | 3 | 10 | 9 | 16 |
| Women 16+ employed | 57.6 | 50.4 | 73 | 43 | 45 | 50 |
| Women 16+ unemployed | 2.6 | 6.0 | 3 | 6 | 7 | 10 |
| % white collar | . . . | 58.0 | 80 | 27 | 37 | 56 |
| **Income (%):** | | | | | | |
| Household in poverty | 5.2 | 21.2 | 10 | 28 | 25 | 21 |
| Household with income: | | | | | | |
| $0–$9,999 | 7.6 | 20.6 | 13 | 24 | 25 | 19 |
| $10,000–$19,999 | 11.3 | 17.9 | 15 | 25 | 19 | 18 |
| $20,000–$29,999 | 14.1 | 16.7 | 19 | 20 | 19 | 16 |
| $30,000–$39,999 | 15.1 | 14.1 | 15 | 14 | 15 | 14 |
| $40,000–$59,999 | 24.7 | 17.0 | 17 | 13 | 16 | 20 |
| $60,000+ | 27.3 | 13.7 | 21 | 4 | 6 | 13 |
| **Housing stock (%):** | | | | | | |
| Median rent | . . . | 445 | 490 | 324 | 330 | 472 |
| Median value, homes occupied by owners | . . . | 77,576 | 247,963 | 42,526 | 71,589 | 56,593 |
| **Stability (%):** | | | | | | |
| Owner occupied | . . . | 41 | 23 | 25 | 36 | 61 |
| Foreign born | . . . | 16.9 | 15 | 49 | 23 | 0 |
| Foreign-born adults | . . . | 19.1 | 14 | 59 | 29 | 1 |
| Different residence 5 years ago | . . . | 45 | 66 | 45 | 53 | 30 |

*Source:* 1990 Census.

[a]Suburban Cook County is that part of the county outside the city limits and includes roughly the first ring of suburban communities around the city.

and with suburban Cook County. We see great differences among respondents in each sample, differences that reflect neighborhood character. These are elaborated below.

## Shoreland

Shoreland is an affluent, mostly white area with trendy retail stores, restaurants, bars, and clubs drawing daytime shopping and nighttime leisure traffic from around the city. High-rise apartment buildings, town homes, and condominiums predominate. Streets are lined with late-model cars; parking is difficult. Many residents are young adults (i.e., between eighteen and twenty-nine): 43 percent, compared to only one-quarter for the city as a whole. Fully three-quarters of the locals live in nonfamily households, an astounding 62 percent living alone. There are few children, fewer teenagers. Two-thirds of the population lived in a different residence five years earlier. These percentages correspond to key-informant descriptions of Shoreland as a transitional neighborhood: singles meet there, marry, and then leave, particularly once a child is born or reaches school age.

In terms of status characteristics, Shoreland residents are upwardly mobile. Income and education-attainment levels are high. Over half the residents have a bachelor's degree, a fifth an advanced degree. Although the poverty rate in Shoreland is higher than it is in suburban areas, it is half that of the city as a whole. The residents—most with high-paying jobs, and few with children—have considerable disposable income, a fact reflected by the luxury goods and services offered by local businesses.

Shoreland is also a highly secular community, with roughly 25 percent of the population professing no religious affiliation. About 30 percent are Catholic and 30 percent Protestant, with a slight majority of the Protestants attending liberal, mainline churches. The last 14 percent are split between Jewish and other religious affiliations. Attendance at weekly services is, however, low.

A distinctive feature of Shoreland is its visible concentration of businesses, from bars to bookstores, geared toward gay men and lesbians. The preeminent social-service agency for gays and lesbians in Chicago is located in this area, and the annual gay and lesbian pride parade is routed through the neighborhood. It is not unusual to see same-sex couples walking down the street holding hands, and such behavior does not draw public attention.

## Westside

Westside is a port of entry for Mexican immigrants, both legal and illegal. Roughly half the population is foreign born, a fifth of these individuals having immigrated to the United States in the last five years. Westside was formerly an Eastern European enclave. One-tenth of the local population is non-Hispanic white, mostly elderly homeowners whose grown children have left the neighborhood. The local culture is firmly, palpably Mexican. Signs in stores are in Spanish. There are Aztec-themed murals on the walls. Radios blare *ranchero* music. Restaurants offer Mexican cuisine. A lively street trade in fresh fruit and vegetables is geared toward Mexican cooking. Shop windows display paraphernalia associated with the many church- and family-centered ritual occasions that organize community life—baptisms, first communions, confirmations, *quinceañeras*,[4] graduations, and weddings.

Westside is poor, a working-class neighborhood. Although the business strip is thriving, barred windows are common. Most Westside immigrants hail from rural areas of Mexico; many lack even a secondary education. Men are employable but earn little for their labor. Indeed, household incomes are clustered around the poverty line, although welfare dependence is quite low, as would be expected in an immigrant neighborhood. Reflecting the traditional division of labor preferred by most Westside families, women work at rates below those of women in Chicago generally. In keeping with their Mexican origins, most Westsiders are Catholic—over 80 percent. The remainder are mostly Protestant. Westside has an unusually high proportion of Catholics who claim to have been born again. This pattern likely reflects the expressive character of Mexican Catholicism in contrast to that of the Catholicism of European immigrant groups. Westsiders also attend church more frequently than do residents of Shoreland, Southtown, or Erlinda or residents of Cook County generally.

Westside houses are mostly two-flats or three-flats, with some three- and four-story walk-up apartment buildings. Houses are often built one in front of the other on narrow lots, and residences are among the most crowded in the city. The overall age profile is very young, with a quarter of the residents under age twelve. Nuclear families predominate, with almost two-fifths of households composed of a married couple and their children. Owing to the presence of unattached immigrant men, nonfamily households are more common here than they are in Erlinda or Southtown. Gangs are also prevalent, and their graffiti is liberally applied to garage doors and park benches.

## Erlinda

Erlinda, another community area in which the population is predominantly Hispanic, mirrors Westside in many respects. However, Erlinda is more racially and ethnically diverse than is Westside and houses fewer immigrants and more later-generation Hispanics. The area is commonly thought of as a Puerto Rican neighborhood—and it is, in fact, 40 percent Puerto Rican—but Mexicans and other Central and South Americans make up a third of the population. One-fifth of the population is non-Hispanic white, and 5 percent is African American.

The Erlinda area is a somewhat more desirable section of the larger Puerto Rican/Hispanic Northwest Side, a place where relatively better off residents

4. On *quinceañeras*, see Ellingson, Laumann, Paik, and Mahay (chapter 1 in this volume, n. 2).

have moved as gentrification has squeezed them westward and as upward mobility has allowed them to purchase modest homes. Houses are small but well kept. Despite the fact that the household incomes of a quarter of the population are below the poverty line, there is a local sense of progress, of having "moved up" from the more dangerous and poorer parts of the neighborhood.

Like both Westside and Southtown, Erlinda is dominated by families. Fully 80 percent of the residents live in family households. But only one-third of all households in Erlinda are nuclear-family households, 5 percentage points fewer than in Westside, and 17 percent are female-headed households, contrasting with Westside's 10 percent, and identical to Southtown's 17 percent. As is also true in Westside, one-third of Erlinda's population is under the age of eighteen.

Education-attainment levels in Erlinda are very low, although more Erlinda residents than Westside residents have completed high school. Employment is relatively high given poverty rates, indicating that many of the poor are working rather than unemployed. Like Westside, Erlinda is heavily Catholic, and rates of church attendance are high. In contrast to Westside, however, Erlinda has a larger group claiming no religious affiliation and a larger group of Type II Protestants—Baptists, conservative fundamentalists, and members of Pentecostal sects. This is consistent with trends in Puerto Rico, where many have become disaffected with the Catholic Church and proselytizing Protestants have won many converts.

## Southtown

Southtown is an African American neighborhood that has seen better days. The large industries in the surrounding neighborhoods that once provided Southtowners with good, blue-collar jobs have downsized or shut down entirely. Now, only half the men and women are employed. Once home to a shopping district with national chain stores serving the entire South Side of the city, Southtown is left mostly with liquor stores and miscellaneous dry-goods stores (advertising wigs, jewelry, and gym shoes)—all heavily barred. Many shop owners are Korean or Arab and live outside the area. There is also a red-light district located on the main street. Drug activity and gang activity are both concerns along the main street.

At the height of factory closings in the 1970s, over nine hundred mortgages were foreclosed in the surrounding area, and vacant homes and commercial buildings remain a concern in some parts of the neighborhood. The housing stock is mostly single-family homes, well-constructed one- and two-story brick bungalows on lots with yards. Many of these homes are occupied by older couples with grown children and by white-collar workers who have retained their jobs. However, a growing proportion of the homes are shared by multigenerational, female-headed families (e.g., mother, daughter, and daughter's children) or by single mothers doubling up with one another. Seventeen percent of household heads are women with minor children. The poverty rate for Southtown is right at the city average—a fifth of the households are under the poverty line—but a third of the households earn upward of $40,000. Persons interviewed described the area as mixed income, crediting the single-family homes with retaining the better-educated, employed segment of the population.

Southtown is also known as a community of churches. The black church is the social center of the black community. There are at least two or three churches to be found on every block of the main street. There are large churches with high-profile ministers that pull congregants from all over the South Side as well as many small churches, including numerous storefront churches. There is, however, little interaction between the two.

There is a great deal of activity on the main street during the day. Many people hang out there. Most are between sixteen and thirty, and most are men, but some are young women, often teenagers with infants and/or toddlers. Residents of this neighborhood have attained higher levels of education than have Hispanics in Westside or Erlinda; still, 18 percent of the residents never graduated from high school, and only 11 percent have a college degree. The majority of Southtown residents are single (72 percent), but the average age of singles in Southtown is somewhat older than that of singles in other neighborhoods. And Southtown is highly segregated; 98 percent of Southtown residents are African American.

## Sexual Expression in the CHSLS Communities

As mentioned earlier, a central objective of the CHSLS was to capture the diversity of sexual expression in urban life. Tables 2.5A and 2.5B present respondents' reports regarding selected aspects of sexual expression—such as attitudes, behavior, and health—broken down by sample and by gender. Comparing these two tables, we note two striking patterns: substantial variation across the samples and important gender differences in sexual expression. We discuss these patterns in greater detail below.

### Sexual Attitudes and Sexual Identity

There is substantial variation across the samples and between men and women with respect to sexual attitudes. In general, many of the respondents in the CHSLS exhibit nonpermissive attitudes toward extramarital sex, homosexuality, pornography, and abortion. Overwhelming majorities of the respon-

Table 2.5A Features of Sex Markets in the Five CHSLS Samples, Male Respondents

| Variable | Cook County | Westside | Southtown | Shoreland | Erlinda |
|---|---|---|---|---|---|
| Number of sex partners last 12 months: | | | | | |
| None (%) | 12 | 14 | 6 | 5 | 12 |
| One (%) | 59 | 72 | 47 | 46 | 70 |
| Two (%) | 13 | 11 | 23 | 12 | 6 |
| Three to five (%) | 11 | 3 | 18 | 19 | 9 |
| Six or more (%) | 6 | 0 | 6 | 18 | 2 |
| N | 374 | 139 | 117 | 175 | 81 |
| Number of one night stands ever: | | | | | |
| None (%) | 25 | 56 | 15 | 12 | 51 |
| One (%) | 18 | 18 | 24 | 10 | 23 |
| Two or three (%) | 20 | 13 | 30 | 29 | 11 |
| Four to ten (%) | 20 | 6 | 14 | 23 | 7 |
| Eleven or more (%) | 16 | 6 | 17 | 26 | 8 |
| N | 352 | 124 | 113 | 174 | 74 |
| Participated partly to meet partners (nonmarried only): | | | | | |
| Gym, health club, or fitness program (%) | 10 | 0 | 9 | 21 | 2 |
| Sports team, club, or organization (%) | 11 | 3 | 8 | 24 | 5 |
| Church or religious organization (%) | 7 | 7 | 6 | 6 | 2 |
| Class (%) | 4 | 2 | 3 | 7 | 0 |
| Bar, nightclub, or dance club (%) | 40 | 22 | 35 | 60 | 12 |
| Placed/answered personal ad (%) | 3 | 2 | 0 | 3 | 0 |
| Private party/dance (%) | 24 | 19 | 19 | 46 | 12 |
| Set up for a date (%) | 18 | 7 | 21 | 25 | 7 |
| N | 189 | 58 | 80 | 149 | 42 |
| Did the following in last 12 months: | | | | | |
| Went to a nightclub with nudity (%) | 25 | 13 | 16 | 48 | 12 |
| Watched porn at a theater/arcade (%) | 15 | 14 | 8 | 13 | 11 |
| Watched porn on video (%) | 40 | 29 | 33 | 65 | 27 |
| Paid someone for sex (%) | 2 | 4 | 4 | 2 | 2 |
| N | 375 | 140 | 117 | 176 | 82 |

*continued*

Table 2.5A *continued*

| Variable | Cook County | Westside | Southtown | Shoreland | Erlinda |
|---|---|---|---|---|---|
| Sexual attitudes: | | | | | |
| Extramarital sex is | | | | | |
| always wrong (%) | 67 | 74 | 68 | 57 | 83 |
| Homosexuality is | | | | | |
| always wrong (%) | 59 | 76 | 80 | 20 | 88 |
| Should be law against sale | | | | | |
| of porn (agree) (%) | 34 | 57 | 38 | 15 | 54 |
| Against allowing abortion | | | | | |
| for any reason (%) | 44 | 70 | 51 | 25 | 73 |
| N | 375 | 140 | 117 | 176 | 82 |
| | | | | | |
| Sexual identity: | | | | | |
| Attracted to opposite | | | | | |
| gender only (%) | 93 | 96 | 91 | 64 | 99 |
| Friends are heterosexual | | | | | |
| only (%) | 72 | 83 | 82 | 24 | 87 |
| N[a] | 368 | 139 | 116 | 175 | 81 |
| | | | | | |
| Health issues (N varies): | | | | | |
| Respondent has been | | | | | |
| forced sexually (%) | 6 | 6 | 9 | 16 | 7 |
| Respondent has used | | | | | |
| crack or cocaine (%) | 13 | 11 | 16 | 33 | 5 |
| Respondent has had | | | | | |
| an STI (%) | 17 | 9 | 35 | 26 | 7 |
| Respondent has traded | | | | | |
| sex for drugs (%) | 6 | 5 | 13 | 7 | 9 |
| Respondent had sexual | | | | | |
| problems in last | | | | | |
| 12 months (%) | 32 | 22 | 35 | 37 | 15 |
| | | | | | |
| Most recent partner: | | | | | |
| Very/extremely physically | | | | | |
| satisfying (%) | 82 | 79 | 73 | 83 | 74 |
| Very/extremely emotionally | | | | | |
| satisfying (%) | 71 | 82 | 68 | 63 | 66 |
| N[a] | 357 | 124 | 113 | 175 | 77 |

[a]N's vary slightly from question to question because of non-response.

Table 2.5B Features of Sex Markets in the Five CHSLS Samples, Female Respondents

| Variable | Cook County | Westside | Southtown | Shoreland | Erlinda |
|---|---|---|---|---|---|
| Number of sex partners last 12 months: | | | | | |
| None (%) | 18 | 15 | 17 | 13 | 18 |
| One (%) | 69 | 81 | 63 | 62 | 77 |
| Two (%) | 8 | 3 | 12 | 14 | 6 |
| Three to five (%) | 5 | 0 | 7 | 10 | 0 |
| Six or more (%) | 1 | 0 | 1 | 1 | 0 |
| N | 511 | 208 | 189 | 178 | 125 |
| | | | | | |
| Number of one night stands ever: | | | | | |
| None (%) | 54 | 72 | 45 | 31 | 81 |
| One (%) | 22 | 20 | 31 | 21 | 10 |
| Two or three (%) | 12 | 5 | 21 | 25 | 4 |
| Four to ten (%) | 8 | 2 | 3 | 18 | 5 |
| Eleven or more (%) | 4 | 2 | 1 | 6 | 0 |
| N | 489 | 199 | 189 | 179 | 121 |
| | | | | | |
| Participated partly to meet partners (nonmarried only): | | | | | |
| Gym, health club, or fitness program (%) | 4 | 0 | 2 | 20 | 4 |
| Sports team, club, or organization (%) | 5 | 0 | 2 | 15 | 1 |
| Church or religious organization (%) | 7 | 4 | 12 | 11 | 9 |
| Class (%) | 5 | 1 | 1 | 17 | 1 |
| Bar, nightclub, or dance club (%) | 13 | 7 | 15 | 44 | 6 |
| Placed/answered personal ad (%) | 1 | 0 | 1 | 7 | 0 |
| Private party/dance (%) | 10 | 2 | 8 | 40 | 4 |
| Set up for a date (%) | 9 | 2 | 9 | 26 | 1 |
| N | 273 | 90 | 137 | 144 | 68 |
| | | | | | |
| Did the following in last 12 months: | | | | | |
| Went to a nightclub with nudity (%) | 6 | 2 | 11 | 5 | 3 |
| Watched porn at a theater/arcade (%) | 5 | 2 | 3 | 1 | 2 |
| Watched porn on video (%) | 17 | 7 | 15 | 25 | 4 |
| Paid someone for sex (%) | 0 | 0 | 0 | 0 | 0 |
| N | 513 | 207 | 190 | 182 | 127 |

*continued*

Table 2.5B *continued*

| Variable | Cook County | Westside | Southtown | Shoreland | Erlinda |
|---|---|---|---|---|---|
| Sexual attitudes: | | | | | |
| Extramarital sex is | | | | | |
| always wrong (%) | 75 | 81 | 83 | 62 | 91 |
| Homosexuality is | | | | | |
| always wrong (%) | 54 | 72 | 74 | 14 | 75 |
| Should be law against sale | | | | | |
| of porn (agree) (%) | 44 | 82 | 46 | 30 | 72 |
| Against allowing abortion | | | | | |
| for any reason (%) | 38 | 76 | 39 | 15 | 69 |
| N | 513 | 207 | 190 | 182 | 127 |
| Sexual identity: | | | | | |
| Attracted to opposite | | | | | |
| gender only (%) | 86 | 89 | 91 | 70 | 98 |
| Friends are heterosexual | | | | | |
| only (%) | 68 | 86 | 75 | 32 | 81 |
| $N^a$ | 507 | 205 | 190 | 178 | 126 |
| Health issues (N varies): | | | | | |
| Respondent has been | | | | | |
| forced sexually (%) | 20 | 6 | 20 | 29 | 15 |
| Respondent has used | | | | | |
| crack or cocaine (%) | 10 | 4 | 12 | 23 | 4 |
| Respondent has had | | | | | |
| an STI (%) | 21 | 8 | 36 | 25 | 8 |
| Respondent has traded | | | | | |
| sex for drugs (%) | 6 | 3 | 10 | 4 | 6 |
| Respondent had sexual | | | | | |
| problems in last | | | | | |
| 12 months (%) | 43 | 43 | 47 | 51 | 26 |
| Most recent partner: | | | | | |
| Very/extremely physically | | | | | |
| satisfying (%) | 77 | 72 | 74 | 83 | 73 |
| Very/extremely emotionally | | | | | |
| satisfying (%) | 72 | 71 | 67 | 69 | 69 |
| $N^a$ | 489 | 198 | 189 | 179 | 121 |

[a]N's vary slightly from question to question because of nonresponse.

dents in Westside, for example, believe that extramarital sex is always wrong (74 percent of men, 81 percent of women), that sex with a same-sex partner is always wrong (76 percent of men, 72 percent of women), that the sale of pornography should be illegal (57 percent of men, 82 percent of women), and that abortion for any reason should be illegal (70 percent of men, 76 percent of women). Respondents in Shoreland, by contrast, exhibit much more permissive attitudes. There are interesting gender differences as well. Men in all the samples tend to have more permissive attitudes toward pornography and extramarital sex, which is interesting considering the fact that they are more likely than women to cheat on their spouses and to purchase pornography (Laumann, Gagnon, Michael, & Michaels, 1994). Women, in contrast, are more tolerant of homosexuality and are more likely to hold proabortion views than are men.

One implication of these differences for sex markets is the importance of local context. For example, individuals with an interest in forms of sexuality considered taboo in their neighborhoods will be forced to pursue those interests in other parts of the city. Social disapproval can also result in the strict segregation of certain sex markets, even forcing some underground. The subject of the importance for sex markets of local context generally is taken up by Mahay and Laumann (chapter 3 in this volume). An extended discussion of the construction of same-sex sex markets specifically can be found in Ellingson and Schroeder (chapter 4 in this volume).

Another implication of these differences is the resulting differential management of or response to sexual issues as public-health issues. Ellingson (chapter 10 in this volume) discusses institutional approaches to sexual problems generally. Ellingson, Van Haitsma, Laumann, and Tebbe (chapter 11 in this volume) discuss the religious response specifically.

## Sexual Behavior, Search, and Commercial Sex

Closely connected to sexual attitudes, sexual behavior exhibits similar patterns. Respondents in Southtown and Shoreland are more oriented toward multiple partnering strategies. About half the men in each sample reported having had at least two sex partners during the twelve months prior to being interviewed; 61 percent of the Southtown men and 78 percent of the Shoreland men have had more than two one-night stands during their lifetime. In Westside and Erlinda, vast majorities of the men and women are monogamous, and few have ever engaged in a one-night stand. Overall, men tend to have more partners than do women.

Shoreland respondents are distinctive in that they are the most likely to engage in active searches for potential sex partners. For example, during the year prior to being interviewed, 20 and 21 percent of unmarried women and

men, respectively, went to the gym partly with the hope of meeting someone. The comparable figure for Cook County is 4 percent of women and 10
percent of men. Indeed, Shoreland respondents are the most likely of all our
respondents to engage in search behavior, from joining sports teams to taking classes, from going to bars to being set up with dates.

Overall, the majority of CHSLS respondents do not engage in public
commercial sexual activities, such as going to a "gentlemen's" club, watching
pornographic movies in public theaters, or hiring a prostitute. That is not to
say that no one in Chicago engages in such behavior. Indeed, substantial
numbers of Chicagoans, particularly among the men, appear to participate in
the commercial sex market. The most popular form of commercial sex is
watching a pornographic video at a private residence. Forty percent of the
men in Cook County did so during the year prior to being interviewed; the
comparable figure in Shoreland is even higher (65 percent). In contrast, prostitution is quite rare. Only 2–4 percent of men, and essentially no women,
hired a prostitute in the previous twelve months.

These patterns raise certain issues. One is the question of what leads men
and women to engage in search behavior, a topic taken up by Mahay and Laumann (chapter 5 in this volume). Another is the fact that the prevalence of
multiple partnering strategies in Shoreland and Southtown suggests that sexual partnering is organized differently among different racial/ethnic groups.
Aspects of this issue are discussed by Youm and Paik (chapter 6 in this volume) and by Paik, Laumann, and Van Haitsma (chapter 7 in this volume).

## Health and Well-Being

Finally, tables 2.5A and 2.5B present data regarding health issues. Overall, exchanging sex for drugs is relatively rare, although we note that this practice
is significantly more common among respondents in Southtown than among
those in the other samples. On the other hand, drug use generally is quite
common, especially in Shoreland, where one-third of the men and one-
quarter of the women have used either crack or cocaine in the past.

One striking feature is the prevalence of forced sex, particularly among
women. Twenty percent of Cook County women and nearly a third of the
Shoreland women report ever having been forced to have sex. These statistics are significant for our argument since an economic view of sex markets
would imply negotiated transactions without force or fraud. Clearly, the use
of force, primarily by men against women, is an important feature of sex markets. This topic is taken up by Buntin, Lechtman, and Laumann (chapter 8
in this volume).

Reported experience with STIs varies across the samples, although men and women appear to be equally at risk. This topic is discussed by Youm and Laumann (chapter 9 in this volume).

We stress, however, that sexual expression involves more than negative outcomes. Indeed, most men and women in the CHSLS samples find their sexual relationships to be very satisfying, both physically and emotionally. Thus, while sexual activity involves certain risks, it certainly has its rewards as well. The following chapters touch on these issues as well as others.

*The Sexual Organization of the City* cuts across several sexual scenes, each distinctly marked by the types of people and the sexual attitudes and behaviors found there. It is able to do so because it is based on a unique data set, one that allows us to tell a story about sexual expression in Chicago that is representative and general as well as site specific and contextual. Thus, we capture both the diversity and the broad patterns of sexual partnering in Chicago.

Part Two )

# The Structure of Urban Sexual Markets

# 3 )

# Neighborhoods as Sex Markets

Jenna Mahay
and Edward O. Laumann

This chapter describes the organization of four sex markets in Chicago. Ellingson, Laumann, Paik, and Mahay (chapter 1 in this volume) characterized sex markets as the spatially and culturally bounded arenas in which searches for sex partners and a variety of sexual transactions take place.[1] Here, we focus on how local organizations, social networks, culture, and space in-

A version of this chapter was presented as "The Sexual Organization of the City: Space, Networks, Culture, and Institutions in Urban Sexual Marketplaces" at the annual meeting of the American Sociological Association, Anaheim, California, 21 August 2001.

1. On the terms *sex market* and *sexual marketplace* as they are used in this study, see the section "The Social Organization of Sexual Partnering and Sexual Relationships" in Ellingson, Laumann, Paik, and Mahay (chapter 1 in this volume).

teract on the ground to create the sex markets found in the four neighbor-hoods. Our interest in the organization of sex in the city follows from the early Chicago school's interest in the patterns of urban life. Although the di-versity, mobility, and lack of institutional surveillance typically associated with large cities such as Chicago might lead us to expect chaos in sexual part-nering, we find that the sex lives of the people living in the four neighbor-hoods on which our study focuses are highly organized—and organized in particular ways—by the nature of the social networks in which they are em-bedded, local norms and institutions, and the constraints of geographic space. All these elements interact in a given sex market to structure the sexual be-havior of its participants in patterned and predictable ways, but they can often also have unintended consequences. In this chapter, we focus on heterosex-ual sex markets. Homosexual sex markets, which operate under very differ-ent rules, are discussed by Ellingson and Schroeder (chapter 4 in this volume). We do, however, discuss the overlap between heterosexual and homosexual sex markets.

## The Sexual Organization of the City

Let us look first at the spatial organization of sexual partnering in the four neighborhoods in the context of the city as a whole. Map 3.1 underscores how the four neighborhoods form distinct sex markets both because there are few sexual ties between them and because residents most often choose partners who live in or around their own neighborhood. The solid lines rep-resent the ties between the four communities and those communities in which more than 5 percent of residents' sex partners live, while the dotted lines represent ties between the four communities and those areas in which between 3 and 5 percent of residents' sex partners live. These percentages are based only on the single respondents (unmarried and noncohabiting) in the four neighborhoods and use data on the two most recent sex partners in the last five years.

   Map 3.1 shows us that residents of Shoreland predominantly choose sex partners living in the North Side, white upper-middle-class communities along the shore of Lake Michigan. About one-quarter (24 percent) choose sex partners living in their own neighborhood. Almost no residents of Shore-land choose partners living on the city's South Side. While a few residents have sex partners in the adjacent community areas to the west, which have some Hispanic populations, almost none have sex partners on the Far West Side of the city, which is predominantly African American.

   Both the Erlinda and the Westside sex markets are fairly isolated. For ex-ample, the majority of Erlinda residents choose sex partners who live in their

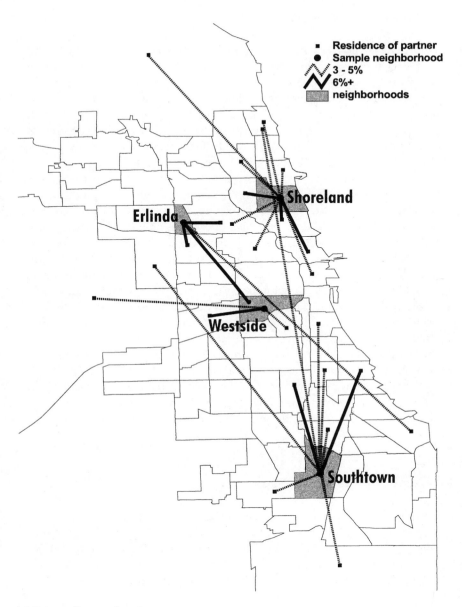

Map 3.1. Sex-market ties.

*Note:* Each of the four communities is represented by a shaded area. Circles indicate respondents' neighborhood, squares the partners' neighborhood. The solid lines represent the ties between the four communities and those communities in which more than 5 percent of residents' sex partners live, the dotted lines ties between the four communities and those areas in which between 3 and 5 percent of residents' sex partners live.

own neighborhood or in the two neighborhoods directly east and south, both of which, like Erlinda, have large Puerto Rican and Mexican American populations. And 50 percent of Westside residents choose sex partners who live in the same neighborhood, although the Westside sex market also extends into two adjacent community areas (west and south), both of which have significant Mexican American populations. Nevertheless, despite the geographic distance between them, the Erlinda and the Westside sex markets do overlap somewhat. Westside, which is predominantly Hispanic, is the location for a significant percentage of Erlinda respondents' sex partners.

In contrast to the sex markets in the other three neighborhoods, that in Southtown is more dispersed. Southtown residents choose sex partners from throughout Chicago's South Side neighborhoods. Almost the entire South Side is predominantly African American, and key informants reported that, although Southtown itself is an identifiable subcommunity, residents identify with the entire South Side on many social and political issues. Thus, while the Southtown sex market is geographically dispersed, it is still racially segregated from the rest of the city. Interestingly, the Southtown sex market has little to do with the West Side of the city, even though that too is predominantly African American. Clearly, these separate and distinct sexual networks *within* the broad racial category *African American* are lost in national and regional surveys that group respondents on the basis of broad categories like *race.*

What explains these patterns in the city's sexual partnering? How are Chicago's sex markets internally organized, and what are the dynamics among space, culture, institutions, and social networks that determine their specific forms?

## Neighborhoods as Sex Markets

Turning to the internal dynamics of Chicago markets, table 3.1 presents data on the demographic characteristics, table 3.2 on the spatial characteristics, table 3.3 on the social-network characteristics, and table 3.4 on the cultural and institutional characteristics of the city as a whole and the four target neighborhoods. We discuss each of the four neighborhoods in turn.[2]

2. All sex-market descriptions are informed by or adapted from three sources: the statistics calculated from the survey section of the study; the field notes kept by those researchers who conducted the qualitative in-depth interviews and the ethnographic observation in the community; and the study summary written by Martha Van Haitsma, which was used to orient new research assistants brought on to analyze project data and to inform those writing papers and reports (see Van Haitsma, 1999).

Table 3.1 Percentage Distributions of Sex-Market Demographic
Characteristics: Chicago Adults, Aged 18–59, CHSLS, 1995–97

| | Cook County Cross Section | Westside | Southtown | Shoreland | Erlinda |
|---|---|---|---|---|---|
| **Age:** | | | | | |
| 18–29 | 28.2 | 41.3 | 30.9 | 52.2 | 37.1 |
| 30–39 | 33.6 | 31.5 | 30.9 | 29.1 | 33.3 |
| 40–49 | 22.4 | 16.1 | 18.9 | 12.9 | 19.1 |
| 50–59 | 15.8 | 11.2 | 19.2 | 5.9 | 10.5 |
| **Race/ethnicity:** | | | | | |
| White | 49.8 | 9.2 | .7 | 83.0 | 9.1 |
| African American | 27.9 | .6 | 98.1 | 7.0 | 2.9 |
| Mexican | 12.8 | 83.4 | .0 | 2.5 | 46.2 |
| Puerto Rican | 3.9 | 1.7 | .3 | 1.1 | 31.0 |
| Other Hispanic | 1.7 | 4.3 | .3 | 2.0 | 10.0 |
| Other race/ethnicity | 3.9 | .9 | .7 | 4.5 | 1.0 |
| **Education:** | | | | | |
| Less than high school | 15.4 | 55.6 | 17.9 | 1.1 | 48.1 |
| High school degree | 34.6 | 28.4 | 52.4 | 16.8 | 31.4 |
| Vocational degree | 5.6 | 3.2 | 3.6 | 2.2 | 5.2 |
| Associate's/vocational degree | 12.9 | 6.0 | 15.6 | 5.0 | 9.1 |
| Bachelor's degree | 21.5 | 6.0 | 8.5 | 51.1 | 5.2 |
| Advanced/professional degree | 10.0 | .9 | 2.0 | 23.7 | 1.0 |
| **Marital status:** | | | | | |
| Never married | 37.2 | 33.5 | 48.2 | 74.3 | 39.5 |
| Currently married | 43.5 | 51.3 | 28.0 | 17.3 | 42.9 |
| Divorced/separated | 16.9 | 13.5 | 19.2 | 7.3 | 14.8 |
| Widowed | 2.5 | 1.7 | 4.6 | 1.1 | 2.9 |
| **Religion:** | | | | | |
| None | 8.3 | 6.0 | 8.1 | 26.0 | 8.1 |
| Mainline Protestant | 12.6 | 2.3 | 6.8 | 17.3 | 2.4 |
| Fundamentalist Protestant | 28.8 | 6.0 | 73.6 | 12.0 | 14.8 |
| Roman Catholic/Orthodox | 44.5 | 81.4 | 6.8 | 30.5 | 70.8 |
| Other religion | 5.8 | 4.3 | 4.6 | 14.3 | 3.8 |
| *N* | 890 | 349 | 307 | 358 | 210 |

*Note:* A description of each of the four pseudonymous neighborhoods can be found in Van Haitsma, Paik, and Laumann (chapter 2 in this volume), in the section "Choosing the Oversample Neighborhood."

Table 3.2 Percentage Distributions of Sex–Market Spatial Characteristics: Chicago Adults, Aged 18–59, CHSLS, 1995–97

| | Cook County Cross Section | | Westside | | Southtown | | Shoreland | | Erlinda | |
|---|---|---|---|---|---|---|---|---|---|---|
| | Men | Women | Men | Women | Men | Women | Men | Women | Men | Women |
| Mean distance to sex partner[a] | 9.2 | 10.3 | 4.3 | 3.2 | 10.1 | 8.4 | 7.8 | 7.9 | 8.2 | 6.2 |
| N | 120 | 118 | 30 | 26 | 71 | 84 | 56 | 84 | 21 | 23 |
| Type of place met most recent partner[b] | | | | | | | | | | |
| School | 18.6 | 23.4 | 9.3 | 18.0 | 16.7 | 16.9 | 31.0 | 29.2 | 10.7 | 19.4 |
| Work | 7.1 | 10.8 | 5.6 | 6.6 | 16.7 | 3.9 | 14.9 | 12.4 | 7.1 | 8.3 |
| Church | 1.3 | 1.3 | 7.4 | .0 | 3.7 | 2.6 | .0 | .9 | .0 | 5.6 |
| Bars/dance clubs/nightclubs | 12.8 | 17.7 | 18.5 | 23.0 | 18.5 | 9.1 | 14.9 | 18.6 | 10.7 | 5.6 |
| Family member's home | 6.4 | 2.5 | 16.7 | 18.0 | .0 | 9.1 | 1.2 | .0 | 10.7 | 11.1 |
| Friend's home | 23.7 | 19.6 | 13.0 | 8.2 | 14.8 | 15.6 | 16.1 | 14.2 | 25.0 | 22.2 |
| Public place | 16.0 | 11.4 | 20.4 | 16.4 | 22.2 | 27.3 | 6.9 | 13.3 | 25.0 | 13.9 |
| Other | 14.1 | 13.3 | 9.3 | 9.8 | 7.4 | 15.6 | 14.9 | 11.5 | 10.7 | 13.9 |
| N | 156 | 158 | 54 | 61 | 54 | 77 | 87 | 113 | 28 | 36 |

| | | | | | | | | | |
|---|---|---|---|---|---|---|---|---|---|
| Goes outside neighborhood to meet partners[c] | 38.4 | 18.9 | 13.8 | 5.6 | 39.0 | 17.2 | 43.2 | 38.9 | 9.8 | 6.0 |
| N | 177 | 264 | 58 | 89 | 77 | 134 | 95 | 139 | 41 | 67 |
| Goes to parties mostly outside neighborhood[c] | d | d | 40.0 | 25.8 | 42.0 | 45.2 | 37.9 | 40.1 | 40.0 | 32.9 |
| Goes to dances mostly outside neighborhood[c] | d | d | 38.6 | 23.7 | 49.4 | 27.5 | 42.1 | 27.5 | 35.6 | 23.3 |
| Goes to bars mostly outside neighborhood[c] | d | d | 18.6 | 16.5 | 35.8 | 26.7 | 40.0 | 26.8 | 11.0 | 16.4 |
| Has access to a car[c] | 72.9 | 64.3 | 58.6 | 30.9 | 58.0 | 57.0 | 74.7 | 60.6 | 68.9 | 48.0 |
| N | 192 | 286 | 70 | 97 | 81 | 135 | 95 | 142 | 45 | 73 |

[a] Distances were calculated only for those who were not living with their partner and whose partner was of the opposite gender. Calculations are based on distance between the place of residence of the respondent and his or her most recent partner from the last five years. If respondent's partner lived outside Cook County, then the distance to the second most recent partner was used instead, if this partnership was within the last five years, the partner was of the opposite sex, and the respondent was not living with the partner. For more information on this variable, see Kang and Mahay (2001).

[b] Percentages based only on those who self-identified as heterosexual and met their partner in the last five years.

[c] Percentages based only on those who self-identified as heterosexual and are currently single (not currently married).

[d] These questions were not asked of respondents in the cross-sectional sample.

Table 3.3 Percentage Distributions of Sex-Market Social-Network Characteristics: Chicago Adults, Aged 18–59, CHSLS, 1995–97

| | Cook County Cross Section | | Westside | | Southtown | | Shoreland | | Erlinda | |
|---|---|---|---|---|---|---|---|---|---|---|
| | Men | Women | Men | Women | Men | Women | Men | Women | Men | Women |
| Number of mutual acquaintances with partner when first met:[a] | | | | | | | | | | |
| None | 32.9 | 39.9 | 52.8 | 32.2 | 27.8 | 35.1 | 32.6 | 34.5 | 40.7 | 38.9 |
| 1 | 18.1 | 8.9 | 11.3 | 20.3 | 18.5 | 20.8 | 22.1 | 19.5 | 11.1 | 5.6 |
| 2–4 | 22.6 | 20.9 | 13.2 | 15.3 | 20.4 | 13.0 | 22.1 | 24.8 | 22.2 | 22.2 |
| 5 or more | 26.5 | 30.4 | 22.6 | 32.2 | 33.3 | 31.2 | 23.3 | 21.2 | 25.9 | 33.3 |
| N | 155 | 158 | 53 | 59 | 54 | 77 | 86 | 113 | 27 | 36 |
| Length of time lived in neighborhood:[b] | | | | | | | | | | |
| Less than 1 year | 20.3 | 18.5 | 21.4 | 15.5 | 11.1 | 12.6 | 42.1 | 43.7 | 26.7 | 21.9 |
| 1–4 years | 31.8 | 31.8 | 27.1 | 29.9 | 21.0 | 17.8 | 41.1 | 40.9 | 28.9 | 38.4 |
| 5–9 years | 15.6 | 16.8 | 10.0 | 18.6 | 21.0 | 13.3 | 7.4 | 5.6 | 15.6 | 19.2 |
| 10 years or more | 32.3 | 32.9 | 41.4 | 36.1 | 46.9 | 56.3 | 9.5 | 9.9 | 28.9 | 20.6 |
| At least half of relatives live in Chicago[b] | 62.5 | 64.3 | 52.9 | 51.6 | 84.0 | 76.3 | 35.8 | 28.9 | 53.3 | 54.2 |
| At least half of friends live in Chicago[b] | 79.7 | 78.7 | 78.6 | 69.1 | 84.0 | 85.2 | 70.5 | 71.1 | 80.0 | 71.2 |
| Knows at least half of neighbors[b] | 40.1 | 38.8 | 58.6 | 48.5 | 59.3 | 60.7 | 8.4 | 7.0 | 33.3 | 17.8 |
| N | 192 | 286 | 70 | 97 | 81 | 135 | 95 | 142 | 45 | 73 |

[a]Percentages based only on those who self-identified as heterosexual and met their partner in the last five years.
[b]Percentages based only on those who self-identified as heterosexual and are currently single (not currently married).

Table 3.4 Percentage Distributions of Sex-Market Cultural and Institutional Characteristics: Chicago Adults, Aged 18–59, CHSLS, 1995–97

| | Cook County Cross Section | | Westside | | Southtown | | Shoreland | | Erlinda | |
|---|---|---|---|---|---|---|---|---|---|---|
| | Men | Women | Men | Women | Men | Women | Men | Women | Men | Women |
| Cultural characteristics: | | | | | | | | | | |
| Religious affiliation:[a] | | | | | | | | | | |
| None | 11.5 | 6.6 | 8.6 | 5.2 | 11.1 | 6.7 | 24.2 | 26.1 | 6.7 | 8.2 |
| Mainline Protestant | 13.0 | 10.5 | 2.9 | 4.1 | 3.7 | 8.2 | 14.7 | 15.5 | 6.7 | 1.4 |
| Fundamentalist Protestant | 28.1 | 42.0 | 10.0 | 5.2 | 74.1 | 77.8 | 14.7 | 9.9 | 11.1 | 19.2 |
| Roman Catholic/Orthodox | 39.1 | 36.4 | 74.3 | 80.4 | 8.6 | 6.7 | 30.5 | 33.8 | 75.6 | 67.1 |
| Other religion | 8.3 | 4.6 | 4.3 | 5.2 | 2.5 | .7 | 15.8 | 14.8 | .0 | 4.1 |
| Church attendance:[a] | | | | | | | | | | |
| Not at all | 20.8 | 13.3 | 10.0 | 10.3 | 17.3 | 6.7 | 23.2 | 19.7 | 17.8 | 12.3 |
| Several times per year | 38.5 | 37.4 | 40.0 | 30.9 | 39.5 | 34.1 | 53.7 | 58.5 | 40.0 | 32.9 |
| About once a month | 20.3 | 22.0 | 34.3 | 24.7 | 23.5 | 21.5 | 15.8 | 14.8 | 17.8 | 31.5 |
| Every week or more | 20.3 | 27.3 | 15.7 | 34.0 | 19.8 | 37.8 | 7.4 | 7.0 | 24.4 | 23.3 |
| Attitudes:[a] | | | | | | | | | | |
| Premarital sex is wrong | 19.8 | 35.1 | 42.9 | 45.4 | 23.5 | 39.3 | 4.2 | 4.2 | 37.8 | 50.7 |
| Extramarital sex is wrong | 84.4 | 88.0 | 81.4 | 91.8 | 76.5 | 87.4 | 88.4 | 88.7 | 91.1 | 95.9 |
| Same-sex sex is wrong | 66.2 | 61.4 | 80.0 | 73.7 | 84.0 | 77.0 | 35.8 | 18.6 | 79.6 | 76.1 |

continued

Table 3.4 continued

| | Cook County Cross Section | | Westside | | Southtown | | Shoreland | | Erlinda | |
|---|---|---|---|---|---|---|---|---|---|---|
| | Men | Women | Men | Women | Men | Women | Men | Women | Men | Women |
| Interracial marriage is wrong | 10.4 | 6.0 | 11.4 | 14.4 | 9.9 | 8.2 | 3.2 | 1.4 | 4.4 | 5.6 |
| Traditional gender ideology | 31.6 | 35.9 | 64.3 | 56.7 | 38.3 | 40.3 | 14.7 | 9.2 | 48.9 | 48.6 |
| Best sex is without emotional ties | 20.7 | 16.1 | 23.5 | 17.7 | 21.0 | 19.3 | 7.4 | 3.6 | 31.1 | 23.6 |
| Would not have sex unless in love | 35.6 | 66.1 | 53.6 | 74.2 | 28.8 | 60.7 | 30.5 | 47.5 | 51.1 | 80.8 |
| Sex is very important part of life | 65.6 | 53.9 | 72.9 | 67.0 | 76.5 | 45.2 | 78.7 | 74.7 | 68.9 | 54.8 |
| Religious beliefs guide sexual behavior | 36.3 | 46.5 | 47.1 | 53.6 | 38.3 | 51.9 | 20.0 | 26.8 | 22.2 | 53.4 |
| N | 190 | 286 | 70 | 97 | 81 | 135 | 94 | 142 | 45 | 73 |
| Institutional characteristics: | | | | | | | | | | |
| Type of place goes for health care:[a] | | | | | | | | | | |
| No place in particular | 47.9 | 23.8 | 60.0 | 21.7 | 51.9 | 17.8 | 53.7 | 21.8 | 53.3 | 24.7 |
| Doctor's office | 36.5 | 49.3 | 15.7 | 38.1 | 27.2 | 54.8 | 39.0 | 64.1 | 35.6 | 54.8 |
| Hospital outpatient clinic | 8.9 | 16.1 | 14.3 | 18.6 | 11.1 | 11.9 | 2.1 | 6.3 | 8.9 | 16.4 |
| Emergency room | .5 | .7 | 1.4 | 1.0 | 1.2 | 3.7 | 1.1 | .0 | .0 | .0 |
| Community/Public health clinic | 4.7 | 7.3 | 5.7 | 20.6 | 7.4 | 11.9 | 2.1 | 6.3 | 2.2 | 4.1 |
| Other | 1.6 | 2.8 | 2.9 | .0 | 1.2 | .0 | 2.1 | 1.4 | .0 | .0 |
| N | 192 | 286 | 70 | 97 | 81 | 135 | 95 | 142 | 45 | 73 |

[a]Percentages based on only those who self-identified as heterosexual and are currently single (not currently married).

## Shoreland

The heterosexual sex market in Shoreland exists side by side with the sex markets of the most visible gay and lesbian communities in Chicago. (For a detailed discussion of the gay sex market in Shoreland, see Ellingson and Schroeder [chapter 4 in this volume].) Despite the physical propinquity of these markets, there is, however, very little overlap between them (Schroeder & Mahay, 2000).

SPACE. Because many Shoreland residents are recent college graduates, it is not surprising that about one-third report meeting their most recent partner at school. In terms of the current sex market, however, singles in Shoreland are quite mobile. Of the four neighborhoods, Shoreland has the highest percentage of residents having access to a car and going outside their neighborhood in order to meet potential partners. At the same time, there are numerous bars, restaurants, and clubs within the neighborhood in which individuals can meet partners. These spaces are set aside more or less explicitly for this purpose and signal the types of sex partners, sexual activities, and sexual relationships that one can expect to find inside. They are more or less direct sexual-marketplace institutions and are organized so as efficiently to coordinate search and transactions.

As mentioned above, the heterosexual sex market shares the neighborhood with an active gay sex market. However, there is little overlap in the bars that each group patronizes. In general, bars are known as either gay or straight, which, indeed, allows for more efficient partnering. Any outsider who ventures into a bar in this neighborhood will become immediately aware of which type of bar it is and, thus, the chances of finding his or her preferred partner type there.

SOCIAL NETWORKS. Shoreland residents are young and living lives in transition, disconnected from family and friends. Most singles are recent arrivals, with about 40 percent having moved to Shoreland within the last year, and over 80 percent having lived there for less than five years. Not surprisingly, fewer than 10 percent said that they knew at least half their neighbors. And only about one-third have at least half their relatives living in the Chicago area. Singles in Shoreland were the least likely to be living with a relative or to say that either of their parents knew their most recent sex partner. About one-third of the singles also said that they and their most recent sex partner had no mutual friends on first meeting.

Thus, there is little surveillance by friends and family of singles' sexual-partnering activities and a limited number of stakeholders in their relationships. In addition, Shoreland residents know little about their sex partners before beginning relationships because, having no mutual friends, they have no opportunity to obtain inside information.

CULTURE. Shoreland is a highly secular community. Fully a quarter of the residents profess no religious affiliation, 30 percent are Catholic, 30 percent are Protestant, and the remaining 15 percent are split between Judaism and other religions. Even among those professing a religious affiliation, church attendance is low, and many who do go to church choose congregations or denominations that have liberal viewpoints regarding sexuality (e.g., allowing priests or ministers to perform same-sex commitment ceremonies).[3] The vast majority of both men and women, however, go to church only several times a year or even less frequently. Not surprisingly, then, the residents of Shoreland are also the least likely of any of the residents of the four neighborhoods to say that their religious beliefs shape and guide their sexual behavior.

Also in keeping with their secular orientation and high level of education, singles in Shoreland are quite liberal and nontraditional in their other sexual and gender-role attitudes. Only 4 percent believe that premarital sex is wrong, a rate much lower than those found in the other three neighborhoods. Singles are also much less likely to say that same-sex sex or interracial marriage is wrong or that the husband should work and the wife should stay home and take care of the family (this is what is referred to in table 3.4 as *traditional gender ideology*). However, while singles in Shoreland are less likely than singles in the other neighborhoods to say that they would not have sex unless in love, they are also much less likely to say that sex is *best* without emotional ties.

INSTITUTIONS. Most Shoreland residents are highly embedded in secular, private institutions. The residents, typically college graduates and professionals or technical specialists, are very active in school and work institutions; they have spent more time in school, and they work long hours at their jobs. This explains why so many more Shorelanders (45 percent) than residents of other neighborhoods have met their partner in school or at work.

When seeking health care, most Shorelanders use private doctors rather than public-health services and, thus, have private access to contraception, abortion, and STD (sexually transmitted disease) care. Most of the public-health and social-service organizations are oriented toward the large gay population in the neighborhood.

---

3. For a detailed exploration of neighborhood differences in churches' responses to the problem of sexuality, see Ellingson, Van Haitsma, Laumann, and Tebbe (chapter 11 in this volume).

In sum, the heterosexual sex market in Shoreland can be characterized as explicit, organized in private or semiprivate secular institutions, and disembedded from social networks, particularly family ties. Its cultural context is liberal and secular, with nontraditional gender and sexual attitudes that are permissive regarding the pursuit of sexual pleasure for its own sake.

## Westside

In many ways, the heterosexual sex market in Westside is the opposite of that of Shoreland, having a very religious cultural context and strong family networks, and using more public, but also more geographically circumscribed, space.

SPACE. In fact, the sex market in Westside is the most geographically circumscribed of the sex markets in the four neighborhoods in this study. Singles in Westside live the shortest mean distance from their sex partners, compared to singles in the other neighborhoods. They are the least likely to have access to a car: just over half the single men and 30 percent of the single women in Westside have access to a car. Most activities are conducted within the neighborhood: Westside singles are the least likely to work outside the neighborhood and tend to stay in the neighborhood when visiting friends' homes. They are also much less likely than singles in Shoreland or Southtown to go outside their neighborhood in order to meet potential partners or go to bars.

Thus, not surprisingly, singles in Westside are much more likely than singles in other neighborhoods to have met their most recent partner at a family member's home: more than 16 percent of singles in Westside, compared to just 1 percent of singles in Shoreland, met their most recent partner at a family member's home. However, they are also much more likely than Shoreland singles to have met their most recent partner in a public place: 20 percent of the men and 16 percent of the women in a park or on the street and 19 percent of men and 23 percent of women at a bar, dance club, or nightclub.

Key informants from the neighborhood explained that the lack of private space within the family home—the result of large families and small houses as well as cultural norms about protecting and watching over female sexuality—leads young, single residents to make such public spaces as schools, street corners, and parks primary venues for conducting partner searches. There are two public parks that young people in the community use for recreation, although these two parks are in the territories of two rival gangs and, thus, are frequented by two different groups of people.

Young people also sometimes go to dances sponsored by their church or youth group. There is as well a distinct group of young people who frequent the neighborhood's cafés. This group is interested in the arts, and many of its members are college educated. The cafés are places to talk and play chess; art openings, poetry readings, and musical performances are also held there. There are also many taverns where men go in the evenings.

Thus, while family obviously plays a large role in Westside's heterosexual sex market, its oversight of the process also has the unintended consequence of forcing much sexual-partnering activity beyond its purview. Key informants also reported that people use space differently depending on the type of partner they would like to meet. That is, many people will search for *dating* partners inside the neighborhood (at church functions or other community activities) and for *sex* partners outside the neighborhood (at bars or clubs). Many men even return to Mexico when searching for a wife. This is because they are looking for a woman untainted by North American culture, one who will dedicate herself solely to being a good wife and mother.

SOCIAL NETWORKS. As indicated above, singles in Westside are strongly embedded in family and neighborhood social networks. The majority of the singles in this neighborhood have lived there for five years or more, know at least half their neighbors, and have at least half their friends and family in Chicago. Cultural and linguistic unity is preserved by the ties formed between families and neighbors, ties on which Westside residents pride themselves. Extended families often live together, and people come all the way from Mexico to live with their families.

Families not only live together (usually in apartments or multifamily houses) but also spend their leisure time together. Social activities tend to be family or neighborhood, rather than individual or couple, oriented: church suppers and neighborhood festivals. Family groups are often seen walking down the street together or playing in the park.

CULTURE. In keeping with their Mexican origin, the vast majority of Westsiders are Catholic—over 80 percent (see table 2.1 above). The remainder are mostly Protestant, with a few having other religious affiliations and a few having no religious affiliation. Westside has an unusually high proportion of people who have been born again. Westside singles attend church more frequently than do singles in the other three neighborhoods.

Thus, not surprisingly, singles in Westside have traditional gender-role expectations and sexual attitudes. About 64 percent of single men and 57 percent of single women agree that it is best if the husband works outside the home and the wife stays home and takes care of the family. Singles in Westside are also more likely than singles in Shoreland and Southtown to report that their religious beliefs shape and guide their sexual behavior (about half), that premarital sex is wrong (over 40 percent), and that they would not have sex unless in love (over half of single men and three-quarters of single women). Key informants reported that families do not feel free to talk with their children about sex and related issues. Sexuality is a taboo subject for all family members, but especially for young women, who put on makeup and change their clothes when they get to school. Second- and third-generation residents tend to be more open about sexuality than are immigrants.

Few residents find homosexuality to be culturally or socially acceptable. Although some men will have sex with other men they meet in bars, they do not consider themselves to be gay. This phenomenon has been found in other studies of Hispanic cultures (see, e.g., Carrier, 1995; Lancaster, 1988; Magana & Carrier, 1991) and is discussed in greater depth in Ellingson and Schroeder (chapter 4 in this volume). The official statistics from the city indicate that Westside has a low AIDS rate, but one community leader said that the actual infection rates are probably higher than the data indicate; AIDS is a topic that is not openly discussed.

INSTITUTIONS. Westside has many community organizations vying to control various issues in the neighborhood. The large number of active groups attests to the awareness and commitment of Westside residents. Many of these groups have been active for more than twenty years. However, we were told by many respondents that, when Westside residents have personal problems, they are more likely to go to the church for help than to a secular organization. Indeed, the local church is one institution that is strong in Westside. The social life of Westsiders is centered around the church, and local churches sponsor summer fairs and weekend dances. Women are somewhat more involved in the day-to-day activities of the church than are men, but everyone in the neighborhood comes out for the yearly rituals, such as the Stations of the Cross on Good Friday. As discussed by Ellingson, Van Haitsma, Laumann, and Tebbe (chapter 11 in this volume), when it comes to sex, the churches in Westside tend to be more traditional and conservative than are the churches in Shoreland. Nevertheless, despite the strong influence of the church, many Westside women will go to neighborhood social-service organizations for personal counseling and legal advice (in the case of domestic violence), a fact that complicates the picture of sex roles and sexual interaction in Westside.

There are several community outreach groups oriented toward preventing AIDS, but they are restricted in what they can say and do. One such organization said that it receives regular requests to speak at schools but that restrictions are often placed on presentations. For example, one high school will not allow the organization's representatives to bring along pamphlets that have the word *sex* on the cover. Sometimes condoms cannot be discussed unless the students mention them first. One organization that handed out condoms at a neighborhood festival received some negative reactions from older women and found that the police officers on duty at the festival were similarly unsupportive. Still, many second- and third-generation residents picked up condoms for their teenage children. While people appear to be becoming more aware of AIDS, religious and cultural considerations make it more difficult for Westsiders to address the threat of AIDS than it is for residents of other communities.

In sum, the heterosexual sex market in Westside is highly organized by the family, the church, and neighborhood social networks, a situation that often has the unintended consequence of pushing sex-market activity into public spaces and, thus, beyond these institutions' control. Restrictive social mores regarding homosexuality also appear to have the unintended consequence of a greater-than-usual overlap between the heterosexual and the homosexual sex markets.

## Erlinda

Like Westside, Erlinda is an area characterized by a Hispanic concentration, and the organization of its heterosexual sex market mirrors that of Westside's in many respects. However, because of its greater ethnic diversity, including a large number of Puerto Ricans, there is less cohesion; social networks do not play as strong a role in sexual partnering in Erlinda as they do in Westside, and cultural norms regarding sexual behavior differ among ethnic groups. Furthermore, the more traditional cultural norms among Mexicans and the less traditional cultural norms among Puerto Ricans create a sexual divide between these two ethnic groups despite their physical propinquity.

SPACE. Singles in Erlinda have greater geographic mobility than do those in Westside: they live farther from their sex partners (about twice as far on average), and more have access to a car. However, few say that they go outside the neighborhood in order to meet potential partners, and the percentage who say that they do is similar to that in Westside. The primary places for socializing in the community are the churches, the city park, and a few neighborhood bars. As in Westside, family members' homes are relatively common places in which to meet partners, but more people in Erlinda met their most recent partner at a friend's home or in a public place. There is also one park in this neighborhood that is known as a popular pickup spot where non-gay-identified men will offer drive-up sex to drug dealers from outside the community in exchange for drugs.

SOCIAL NETWORKS. Puerto Rican families in Erlinda tend to be more fragmented than are Mexican families in Westside, where it is not unusual for migrants from the same town in Mexico to settle next to one another on reaching Chicago. The upshot of this "breakdown" is that there is less social control exerted by the local community on Puerto Rican couples and less likelihood that they will get married according to long-standing customs. There is also an attitude among Puerto Ricans that they should mind their own business and not meddle in the affairs of their neighbors. This contributes to greater diversity and less conformity in the rituals of marriage and family among Puerto Ricans. Nevertheless, there is a strong emphasis on family among both Puerto Ricans and Mexicans living in this neighborhood that is maintained though a system of *copadre* and *comadre* or godparent relationships. These ritual relationships are used to establish networks of financial and social obligations that endure for life. It is not uncommon for children to be closer to their *copadre* or *comadre* than to their own parents.

Singles in Erlinda have lived there for a somewhat shorter period of time than singles in Westside have lived there and were, therefore, much less likely than singles in Westside to know at least half their neighbors. However, they were just as likely to have at least half their friends and relatives living in Chicago, and over half those in Erlinda had at least two mutual acquaintances in common with their most recent partner when they first met. But a fairly high percentage (about 40 percent) also said that they had no mutual acquaintances.

CULTURE. Like Westside, Erlinda is heavily Catholic and characterized by high rates of church attendance. However, in Erlinda there can be found more fundamentalist/evangelical Protestants—Baptists and more conservative fundamental and Pentecostal sects—particularly among women. This is consistent with trends in Puerto Rico, where many have become disaffected with the Catholic Church and evangelical Protestants have made many converts.

As in Westside, singles in Erlinda are quite traditional in their sexual attitudes, although there are notable differences between the Mexican Americans and the Puerto Ricans living here. For example, there is a tradition of marrying early in both Westside and Erlinda, although Mexicans Americans are likely to marry earlier than Puerto Ricans, especially if they are first- or second-generation immigrants. Sixteen is considered a fine age for a Mexican girl to marry. For Puerto Rican girls, the preferred age of marriage is the late teens or early twenties.

One reason for early marriage in both the Puerto Rican and the Mexican American communities is the taboo attached to out-of-wedlock pregnancy. In the Mexican American community, parents of sexually active girls are likely to push them to marry in order to prevent the social stigma of an illegitimate birth. Puerto Rican parents are more likely to emphasize birth control. Another reason for early marriage in the Mexican American community is financial security—families want to find the "right" partners for their daughters. Puerto Rican families, by contrast, approach the issue of financial security by encouraging their daughters to get an education so that they will be self-reliant and, therefore, encouraging them to delay marriage and child-birth. Girls themselves, however—both Puerto Rican and Mexican—may prefer to marry early since childbirth is one of the few means to status and prestige open to them.

Among singles in the neighborhood as a whole, over 50 percent of women and about 38 percent of men say that premarital sex is wrong, and over 90 percent of both men and women say that extramarital sex is wrong. However, the traditional gender ideology in this community is characterized by a sexual double standard: married men are allowed to have extramarital relationships, but married women must remain faithful to their husbands. The double standard is verbalized in a tag line popular among married men: "I'm not married; my wife is." It is also evinced by the fact that few Mexican men wear wedding rings but that women must wear them at all times. For our purposes, however, what it means is that marriage takes women, but not men, out of the sex market.[4]

Cultural norms also dictate appropriate sex and marriage partners. Dating between Puerto Ricans and Mexicans is typically frowned on, if not explicitly forbidden. In particular, if a Puerto Rican girl has a child from a previous relationship or marriage, she is unlikely to be accepted by Mexican parents as an eligible partner for their son. The cultural traditions among Mexicans and Puerto Ricans also mean that some women are kept out of the sex market altogether and are not expected to marry at all. These are usually the youngest—and, occasionally, the middle—daughters, who are expected to serve as caretakers for their parents.

About three-quarters of both men and women say that same-sex sex is wrong. However, gays and lesbians seem to be more or less accepted in the community as long as they do not flaunt their sexual orientation. The pressure to hide one's homosexuality is, of course, particularly strong among more traditional families. Thus, men who might in other circumstances be openly gay tend to marry and have children while seeing other men on the side. Puerto Rican families tend to be more open about and accepting of homosexual sexual identities than are Mexican families, but both are hostile to efforts to gain political legitimacy for gay community organizations. A further discussion of issues surrounding gay identity in this neighborhood can be found in Ellingson and Schroeder (chapter 4 in this volume).

Informants working in local social-service and health-care organizations have also identified several aspects of the Puerto Rican culture that have

---

4. This sexual double standard has been documented by other ethnographies of Hispanic neighborhoods as well (see, e.g., Horowitz, 1983; Marín, 1996).

led to Puerto Rican women becoming the fastest-growing group of Latinos affected by HIV. First, some Puerto Ricans believe that sexual relations possess a mystical quality and that asking a man to wear a condom breaks the magic of the moment. Second, Puerto Rican women tend to suffer from low self-esteem, which renders them either unwilling to broach the issue of prophylactic use with their sex partners or afraid of changing established sex practices or, worse, of being accused of infidelity. Third, the sexual double standard, which allows men to have extramarital sexual relations with opposite-sex partners, and the cultural pressure to hide a homosexual sexual orientation, which results in many married men conducting extramarital sexual relations with same-sex partners, both put women in this neighborhood at greater risk for HIV. A detailed discussion of the cultural explanations given by health-care and social-service workers can be found in Ellingson, Mahay, Paik, and Laumann (chapter 12 in this volume).

INSTITUTIONS. Erlinda has a large number of social-service organizations, many of which are oriented toward teens. Most of these organizations belong to a consortium that attempts to coordinate family and individual services. Some social-service organizations are operated by local churches. There is one major treatment center in this neighborhood for STDs. Latino teens typically go to a public STD clinic for treatment rather than to a physician in private practice because the clinic is more confidential, is less expensive, and does not require an appointment. In many cases, however, they will go to an STD clinic outside the neighborhood in order to preserve their privacy. Most of the teens who come to the clinic are referred by their friends and by youth organizations.

To summarize, the organization of Erlinda's sex market is similar to that of Westside's, but the cultural differences between Puerto Ricans and Mexican Americans create a somewhat less cohesive market. For one thing, sexual partnering between these two groups is discouraged. In addition, Puerto Ricans have a somewhat different approach to sexual partnering, marrying later, being more open to the use of contraceptives, and being slightly more accepting of gays and lesbians. This makes it easier for Puerto Ricans to adopt a gay identity than it is for Mexicans. Other cultural aspects of Puerto Rican culture, however, make it harder for women to ask their partners to use contraceptives, leading to the growing rate of HIV infection.

## Southtown

The Southtown heterosexual sex market is very different from any of those discussed above. Southtown singles go largely outside their own neighborhood to meet partners and socialize, and few outsiders come into the neighborhood. While social networks are quite cohesive in Southtown, there is little stigma attached to premarital sex, and there is a high level of concurrency in sexual partnering, possibly due to the low rates of marriage and the unbalanced sex ratio (see Youm, 2000).

SPACE. Singles in Southtown have a high degree of geographic mobility. They are more likely than not to have access to a car (58 percent do) and are, therefore, more likely than those in other neighborhoods to go to parties, dances, and bars outside their neighborhood. Not surprisingly, then, the highest mean distance from sex partners among all four neighborhoods is found in the Southtown data. Interestingly, however, while 39 percent of single men in Southtown said that they go outside the neighborhood in order to meet potential partners, only 17 percent of single women in Southtown do so. (The high degree of geographic mobility among Southtowners has implications for their sexual-networking patterns and risk for STDs and is further analyzed in Youm and Laumann [chapter 9 in this volume].)

Singles in Southtown were more likely to have met their most recent sex partner in a public place, such as in a park, at the beach, or on the street (about 25 percent), than anywhere else. The next most common meeting places are bars, dance clubs, and night clubs (for men), school, work (for men), and friends' homes.

SOCIAL NETWORKS. Singles in Southtown are longtime residents—about half have lived there for ten years or more, a greater percentage than in any of the other neighborhoods. Not surprisingly, these singles are also the most likely to know at least half their neighbors: about 60 percent said that they knew at least half the people in their building or on their street. They are also the most likely to report that at least half their friends and relatives live in Chicago, that at least one of their parents knew their most recent sex partner, and that they lived with a relative (other than children). Thus, Southtowners are highly embedded in local family and neighborhood social networks.

CULTURE. As is true of most African American communities, Southtown is overwhelmingly Protestant, with over 80 percent of the population claiming affiliation with one or another Protestant denomination. The vast majority of the residents are Baptist or affiliated with another more conservative evangelical or fundamentalist group. The remainder are Catholic, profess some other religious affiliation, or have no religious affiliation. Southtown residents are more likely than residents of the other neighborhoods to attend church more than once per week and to say that they have been born again, a pattern of worship consistent with that associated with more conservative Protestant churches.

Given the importance of religion for many in this neighborhood, it is not surprising that singles are fairly traditional in their beliefs about gender roles, although not as traditional as singles in Westside or Erlinda; about 40 percent agreed that men should work outside the home and women should stay at home and take care of the family. They are also quite likely to say that their religious beliefs shape and guide their sexual behavior.

Our key informants confirmed that the Judeo-Christian tradition provides a strong moral basis for the community and that it is on this tradition that the policing of sexuality is based. The desired family arrangement appears to be the male-headed nuclear family. However, across the board there was an understanding that women will work, may at times change partners, and enjoy sex. In addition, key informants reported that cohabitation, divorce, and premarital sex are not stigmatized, although about a quarter of single men and a third of single women still said that they thought that premarital sex was wrong. There is also a high level of concurrency in sexual partnering. Almost two-fifths of the men—but only 13 percent of the women, a gender difference likely due to the unbalanced sex ratio and low marriage rates in the community—were currently maintaining relationships with two sex partners. The relation between family formation and the high rate of concurrency among African Americans is analyzed by Youm and Paik (chapter 6 in this volume), the relation between STDs and concurrency by Youm and Laumann (chapter 9 in this volume).

Community informants attributed the high HIV/AIDS rates among teens in this community to one (or both) of two typical attitudes. The first is that "it can't happen to me." Young people in general tend not to believe that they are at risk of HIV infection and, thus, do not think about the consequences of their actions. The second is that one should "live for today." Young people in Southtown in particular tend to see no future for themselves and, thus, again do not think about the consequences of their actions. Such pessimistic thinking is often attributed by professionals to the economically and otherwise impoverished environment, a position discussed at greater length by Ellingson, Van Haitsma, Laumann, and Tebbe (chapter 11 in this volume).

INSTITUTIONS. Southtown benefits from the services of a large number of health-care organizations and a socially active church but suffers from a lack of social-service organizations and a police department that is regarded with suspicion by many residents. First, the health-care community is extremely well organized and active in Southtown. It is perhaps the community's best-organized institutional network. This may be due in part to the high rates of STDs and HIV in the community. All three Southtown health clinics enjoy good reputations and good working relationships with one another. They have an effective cooperative arrangement that facilitates referral of cases to appropriate service providers when needed. The level of services directed specifically at HIV/AIDS is, however, unfortunately inadequate to meet demand.

The lack of social services, by contrast, was a constant theme in many of the Southtown informant interviews. This situation was attributed to the fact that the West Side of Chicago is thought by the city administration to be in greater need of such services than is the South Side.

While there might be few publicly supported social-service agencies in Southtown, the church has a very strong presence on the social-service scene in the neighborhood. All the big churches, several with literally thousands of parishioners, have numerous well-funded, in-house programs offering such services as domestic-violence and AIDS ministries. Church-sponsored organizations for single families and young people seem to be especially plentiful. But these church programs typically have few outside linkages to other local-community organizations. And the churches themselves are often criticized for not being more community oriented and for being too politically oriented. Further, the rivalry among them sharply curtails their capacity to cooperate with one another (see McRoberts, 2003). Most problematic, since there is still a strong moral stigma associated with HIV/AIDS in the black community, many churches simply do not address the issue. (For an extended discussion of this matter, see Ellingson, Van Haitsma, Laumann, and Tebbe [chapter 11 in this volume].)

Finally, the police in Southtown are not held in high regard, especially among children and teenagers. Their relationship with the neighborhood's young people is often adversarial, or at least this is how it is perceived. Outside the police, there is no organized legal community, with the result that people must go outside the neighborhood for legal advice or counseling. The local police department and one of the churches have, however, recently embarked on several programs that are focused directly on the needs of young African American men.

To summarize, Southtown is a working-class African American neighborhood in which people have lived for a long time. Singles are highly embedded in neighborhood social networks, and their friends and relatives play a large role in their partnering activities. However, residents have a high degree of geographic mobility and are quite likely to go outside the neighborhood for work and social activities. Concurrency in sexual partnering is common, owing in part to the unbalanced sex ratio. This may well contribute to the high level of STDs and risk for HIV/AIDS in the neighborhood.

## Conclusion

The four sex markets described above illustrate the ways in which culture, social networks, space, institutions, and demographic characteristics interact to shape the way in which sex markets are organized. For example, culture clearly shapes the institutions and spaces that are used for sex-market activities. The traditional cultures in Westside and Erlinda encourage some market activities to take place in church or at church-sponsored activities. The restrictive sexual culture may also have the unintended consequence of pushing the search for sex partners into spaces that are less controlled by institutions and family.

Culture also shapes the role of social networks in sexual partnering. For example, the more traditional culture in Westside and Erlinda accords the family a central role in the sex market. In these communities, the family structures whom one meets, acts as a stakeholder in the relationship, and determines the types of people with whom one can have a relationship. In liberal Shoreland, however, family has little control over whom one meets. While culture influences the role of social networks in the sex market, networks also determine how well cultural norms can be enforced. Cultural norms are more likely to be adhered to when there are people involved in the relationship there to enforce them.

Space also determines the degree of surveillance or control that social networks can exert, the institutions and sexual marketplaces to which one has access, and the demographic composition of the pool of available partners. Individuals restricted to their neighborhoods for whatever reason face limited sex-market choices. However, space can also be used in an active way by individuals who wish to go outside the purview of their social networks and cultural context. For example, in Westside, individuals looking for a sex partner rather than a dating or a marriage partner will go to particular kinds of clubs, sometimes outside their own neighborhood. Some men travel back to Mexico to find wives untainted by North American culture.

The institutions that are important in neighborhoods, however—such as the church in Westside and Southtown and work or school in Shoreland—influence the spaces in which partnering occurs, the cultural norms that guide behavior, the role that social networks play in meeting sex partners, even the type of partner one is likely to meet. Thus, like space and social networks, institutions can be used by individuals to facilitate meeting particular types of partners.

In sum, sexual partnering is structured by the ways in which all four of these aspects of sex markets interact. While individuals may be constrained by these forces, they can also use them in strategic ways to achieve specific partnering goals. However, it must be kept in mind that demographic characteristics such as income, race/ethnicity, religion, age, and education level influence the neighborhoods in which people live, the institutions to which they have access, the people whom they know, and the cultural norms to which they adhere in the first place.

# 4 )

# *Race and the Construction of Same-Sex Sex Markets in Four Chicago Neighborhoods*

Stephen Ellingson
and Kirby Schroeder

As Simon and Gagnon (1998, 25) have written: "A central concern underlying [the] options and the management of a homosexual career is the presence and complexity of a homosexual community, which serves most simply for some persons as a sexual market place, but for others as the locus of friendships, opportunities, recreation, and expansion of the base of social life. Such a community is filled with both formal and informal institutions for meeting others and for following . . . a homosexual lifestyle. Minimally, the community provides a source of social support, for it is one of the few places where the homosexual may get positive validation of his own self-image." And, of course, we find such a "homosexual community" in Chicago, which, like many large urban areas in the United States, has an openly gay, predominantly white neighborhood. The city also has a more spatially diffuse but identifiable and largely white lesbian community. Both communities operate much like the generic community described by Simon and Gagnon—except that, as sex markets,[1] they are organized differently.

The operative word here is, of course, *white*. Gay persons of color are offered few opportunities for finding sex partners or otherwise exploring their sexuality by the largely white gay and lesbian communities. At the same time, they find limited and problematic opportunities in the Mexican American, Puerto Rican, and African American neighborhoods in which they live. Faced with both subtle and overt discriminatory practices, they have, thus, been compelled to create separate social and sexual spaces within the larger same-sex sex markets of the city.

This state of affairs raises the following, obvious questions: How are the gay and lesbian sex markets in Chicago organized generally? In particular, how do race and ethnicity shape the sexual culture and sexual geography of same-sex sex markets in four city neighborhoods? How do the different structures of each market affect the nature and trajectory of same-sex sexual relationships, identities, and outcomes (e.g., disease)?

In this chapter, we examine how race, ethnicity, and geography converge in the construction of sexual identities and same-sex sex markets. We identify two general types of markets: *transactional* and *relational*. In the transactional market, the goal of market activity is efficiently finding partners for short-term sexual encounters, and these encounters, or *transactions,* are facilitated by a number of search mechanisms, such as the physical appearance of potential partners and the social spaces designated for meeting others. In the relational market, the goal of market activity is establishing more enduring sexual relationships, and the participants rely on their networks of friends and acquaintances to help them find partners. In practice, both types of markets operate for men and women seeking same-sex sex partners, although we expect the male same-sex market (MSSM) to be primarily transactional and the female same-sex market (FSSM) to be primarily relational. We also expect that same-sex markets are constrained by three interrelated sets of social and cultural structures: group norms and scripts about sexual identity and behavior; the degree of local institutional legitimacy accorded same-sex relationships; and the nature of social space available for same-sex search activities.

In what follows, we first provide a review of past scholarship on same-sex markets in the United States and then identify features of same-sex markets and explore how culture, institutions, and space influence these markets. We then describe how race helps organize the market in the white gay and lesbian communities and how different sexual cultures and varying levels of in-

---

1. On the terms *sex market* and *sexual marketplace* as they are used in this study, see the section "The Social Organization of Sexual Partnering and Sexual Relationships" in Ellingson, Laumann, Paik, and Mahay (chapter 1 in this volume).

stitutional support have led to different types of same-sex markets in three nonwhite neighborhoods.

## A Brief History of Same-Sex Sex Markets in the United States

### MSSMs

MSSMs in both popular and scholarly works on the subject are understood to be organized primarily in terms of transactions rather than relationships. That is, the goal of male same-sex searches tends to be short-term, often anonymous, sexual exchanges that occur in a variety of sexual marketplaces. Participants in MSSMs do not necessarily avoid establishing relationships or relying on friendship networks to meet potential partners, but a relational orientation tends to be secondary (see Sadownick, 1996, 169; Aveline, 1995, 207).[2] Even the language in which the behaviors and spaces of the MSSMs are described conveys the centrality of their transactional nature—*cruising, tricking, anonymous sex, body worship, sport fucking, glory holes, clone.* Such transactional language is much less common in FSSMs and heterosexual sex markets.

MSSMs are powerfully shaped by history, culture, demography, and geography. In particular, these forces have helped form and bolster the transactional nature of MSSMs. The proportion of men who are potential or actual participants in a MSSM is relatively small, which has meant that market participants must *concentrate* themselves physically in order to locate sex partners efficiently—unlike women, gay men often choose to relocate from rural to urban areas as part of their strategy for locating potential sex partners. This has resulted in urban areas of the United States having substantially higher proportions of gay-identified men than do rural areas.[3] In addition to this, the men in the most urban areas have also been found to have the highest prevalence of same-sex contacts (Binson et al., 1995), a pattern that we would not expect to be as strong for heterosexuals or for lesbian women since these groups are less motivated to relocate in search of sex partners.

2.  Murray (1996, 175–81) notes that, historically, sex markets run on alternating cycles of license and suppression, or what he terms *nesting* and *tricking*. Despite relatively stable majorities of gay men who are coupled and the strong normative turn toward coupling in the post-AIDS era, gay sex markets still tend to operate to facilitate efficient, low-cost sexual transactions rather than the creation of same-sex couples.

3.  If we include those men with some degree of same-sex desire, sexual activity, and/or identity as homosexual, this combined figure is around 10 percent (Laumann, Gagnon, Michael, & Michaels, 1994).

In those cities with sufficiently large populations, informal gay districts often appear to further aid and coordinate this concentration within an urban context, although the manifestations of "gay space" take a variety of forms both inside and outside these neighborhoods: bars and dance clubs, bathhouses, and bookstores are a few examples of spaces in which men may seek male partners with relative anonymity. What is common to many of these spaces is that they are either designed or end up serving to facilitate casual or short-term sexual relationships.[4]

Historically, Western MSSMs have operated on the margins or in urban enclaves. The social space for same-sex transactions has tended to be limited to bohemian or working-class districts of cities, where so-called deviant behavior was either tolerated, less regulated, or hidden. Strong taboos and severe sanctions against same-sex activity have led men to seek out same-sex partners in ways that avoid detection or stigmatization. These practices include cruising, or searching for casual-sex partners in those public spaces where control by the police or vigilante groups is difficult to achieve, and congregating in institutions that cater to homosexuals (see Chauncey, 1994, esp. chap. 7; see also Beemyn, 1997).

Gay culture has also fostered the development of a transactional market. Different components of gay culture—from the social rituals of cruising and the use of clothing and mannerisms to signal availability, to definitions of masculinity (e.g., the clone of the 1970s or the muscular or "cut" body of the 1990s), to a rich literature of fictional and nonfictional works on what it means to be homosexual—sanction and celebrate a transactional orientation toward sexual partnering. This is especially true of male same-sex scripts, especially those cultural scenarios and interpersonal scripts that are a central feature of the culture surrounding same-sex markets.[5]

4. To these geographic contexts may be added other transactional sexual marketplaces: the long-standing marketplace of the personal ad and the much more recent and still largely unexplored marketplace of the Internet. Here, geography plays a diminished but still important role: partners may locate each other from a distance, but they must still meet each other in person in order for sex to take place—the greater the distance between potential partners, the less likely those partners are, we would expect, to have sex. Since people who meet in these ways are unlikely to have overlapping social networks, the structural factors that might encourage a relational interaction are weak, and a transactional exchange becomes much more likely, although there is some evidence among personal ads that the AIDS epidemic has resulted in an increased interest in sexual exclusivity (Davidson, 1991).

5. According to Simon and Gagnon (1987, 364–65): "Sexual scripts can be said to exist at three analytically distinct levels: *cultural scenarios* (paradigmatic assemblies of the social norms that impinge on sexual behavior), *interpersonal scripts* (where social convention and personal desire must meet), and *intrapsychic scripts* (the realm of the

In the United States, pre–World War II scripts provided for a number of homosexual identities (e.g., fairy, trade, queer) and roles (e.g., the straight man who takes the active or masculine sex role, the effeminate self-identified homosexual man who adopts the passive role) while defining male same-sex encounters in terms of their position along a continuum of marginally legitimate to deviant. Many scripts framed same-sex sexual behavior in the context of a casual exchange rather than that of a long-term relationship. For example, a working-class script allowed for same-sex activity in order for the working-class straight man to find sexual release, while a number of scripts for sex in public developed to overcome obstacles to transactions (e.g., lack of privacy or police harassment) (see Chauncey, 1994, 195–201).

In the 1970s, a new cultural scenario developed that celebrated and encouraged sexual experimentation and the separation of sex from intimacy among gay men; this, in turn, reinforced the transactional nature of the market as anonymous sexual encounters and multiple partners became normative (see Murray, 1996, 175; Sadownick, 1996, 77–112). Levine (1992, 83) summarizes the effect of gay liberation on gay sexual scripts: "Gay liberation's redefinition of same-sex love as a manly form of erotic expression provoked masculine identification among clones, which was conveyed through butch presentational strategies, and cruising, tricking, and partying. . . . In a similar vein, the roughness, objectification, anonymity, and phallocentrism associated with cruising and tricking expressed such macho dictates as toughness and recreational sex. . . . The cultural ideal of self-gratification further encouraged these patterns, sanctioning the sexual and recreational hedonism inherent in cruising, tricking, and partying." While relational sex or coupling and safe sex may have become symbolically important in the 1980s and 1990s, scripts that legitimate the transactional market are still prominent, and there is no conclusive evidence that the market has become relational (see Sadownwick, 1996, chaps. 5–7; Murray, 1996, 175–78; cf. Levine, 1992, 79–82).

## FSSMs

Research on lesbian partnering practices suggests that the FSSM is more likely to be organized in terms of relationships than in terms of transactions. The

---

self-process)." In particular: "Interpersonal scripts represent the actor's response to the external world and draw heavily on cultural scenarios, invoking symbolic elements expressive of such scenarios. It is at this level that the actors must work out their strategies for embodying their own sexual wishes and plans in terms of the experiences and anticipated responses of specific others. . . . Interpersonal scripts might be defined as the representation of self and the implied mirrorings of the other or others that facilitate the occurrence of a sexual exchange."

goal of female same-sex searches tends to be long-term, committed partnerships rather than short-term sexual exchanges, and the search process itself
seems to be facilitated more by an individual's social networks than by anonymous market mechanisms. In their review of the literature, Garnets and
Kimmel (1993b, 27) report: "Lesbians are more likely to have sexual experiences in the context of emotional relationships with one woman or a series
of special women" (see also Ponse, 1978; Vetere, 1983; Blumstein & Schwartz,
1983). Although casual, even anonymous sex occurs among women, the
more common pattern is serial monogamy or, more colloquially, "the lesbian
shuffle" (Barnhart, 1975; Kennedy & Davis, 1997, 28–29).[6]

Market space is coded and used differently by women. The FSSM is organized to help women develop social networks that in turn serve as points of
entry into sexual relationships rather than as means to foster sexual exchanges,
as in the MSSM. Several studies of lesbian bar culture from the 1930s through
the 1970s report that these spaces were organized primarily to facilitate socializing and socialization into lesbianism and only secondarily to facilitate
meeting partners. Cruising, or searching for casual sex, was an activity engaged in only by some lesbians and, even then, relatively infrequently. Middle-
class lesbians, both white and African American, tended to reject such practices (see Thorpe, 1997; Gilmartin, 1996; Kennedy & Davis, 1997). More
recent work on lesbian dating in the 1980s and 1990s indicates that the contemporary FSSM operates primarily as a relational market (e.g., Creith, 1996).

Women's athletics, especially softball leagues, has been a second public
space used for socializing, identity formation, and partnering activities. Cahn
(1999, 55) notes: "The athletic setting [i.e., softball] provided a public space
for lesbian sociability without naming it as such. . . . This environment could
facilitate the coming-out process, allowing women who were unsure about
or just beginning to explore their sexual identity to socialize with gay and
straight women without having to make immediate decisions or declara-
tions." Similarly, in her study of the lesbian community in a Northeastern
city, Esterberg (1997, 127) finds that the summer softball league is the place
for lesbians to connect with one another, "a place to see and be seen": "Even
women who don't like softball may come down to the fields to hang out with
friends, eat hot dogs, and enjoy the atmosphere."

---

6. Newton (1993, 536–37) notes that the lesbians on Fire Island whom she
studied understand their sexuality in relational rather than transactional terms and
briefly chronicles the conflict over gay men's use of an area of the public beach for casual, anonymous sex. The area, known as the "Meat Rack," was parodied by the
creation of a fictional women's casual-sex zone on the beach playfully called the
"Doughnut Rack."

More generally, the nature of the space in which partner searches are conducted has helped determine what type of market will be dominant in a given neighborhood. Historically, gay men have been more successful than lesbians in creating visible, distinct neighborhoods by controlling residential and commercial property and, thus, being able to create concentrations of gay residential and business areas as well as networks of social service and voluntary organizations (Adler & Brenner, 1992; D'Emilio, 1989; Knopp, 1995). The simple concentration of gay men in a spatially bounded area, in conjunction with particular cultural scripts (e.g., those that sanction anonymous sexual encounters), encourages the formation of a transactional market. Lesbians have tended to be more residentially diffuse and less likely to possess the economic resources necessary to establish lesbian-oriented businesses (see Wolf, 1979; Lauria & Knopp, 1985).[7] Rothenberg's (1995) study of a lesbian neighborhood in Brooklyn suggests that lesbians use their urban space, not for partner searches, but for a variety of household and socializing activities.

## Historical Lessons

The preceding historical overview suggests that space, culture, and institutions powerfully shape and constrain same-sex sex markets.[8] Sex markets— and sexual marketplaces—are organized by the system of meanings or the sexual culture of particular groups in each market, and this internal culture exists within larger sexual cultures of the broader society. Markets are also shaped, at least indirectly, by the activities of stakeholders from different institutional spheres as well as by stakeholders within the particular sex market.

The internal culture of same-sex markets is composed of alternative sets of scripts for behavior and identity. These scripts specify how to act in the market, offer identities or roles to adopt in given contexts, and provide definitions of appropriate and inappropriate partners and relationships. In gay and lesbian markets, participants select from a variety of identities or roles (e.g., top/bottom, butch/femme), learn where to find potential partners, and become connected to other members through a shared culture (see Murray, 1996, 178–214; Davis & Kennedy, 1989; Klinkenberg & Rose, 1994; Fader-

---

7. Adler and Brenner (1992) argue that the literature on the differences between gay and lesbian urban space is ambiguous. In their study of an unnamed Northwestern city, they found a clear spatial concentration of lesbian residences and businesses (see also Rothenberg, 1995).

8. On the centrality of sexual geography and sexual culture for understanding gay and lesbian sex markets, see Parker and Carballo (1990), Murray (1996, 182–216), Knopp (1995), and Weeks (1996, 54–59).

man, 1992).[9] At the same time, individuals who participate in same-sex markets must attend to external sexual cultures. These include the broad cultural scenario of heterosexual monogamy and particular group sexual cultures such as machismo among Hispanics or the "don't ask, don't tell" position on homosexuality common among African American groups.

Internal and external cultures will be powerful to the extent that participants in same-sex markets are embedded in relationships and institutions that carry or support particular sexual cultures. For gay men and lesbians, peers, the gay/lesbian press, local service providers, and the community itself are important stakeholders, who, as noted above, exert pressure on participants in the market to conform to particular identities, as in the case of the butch/femme dichotomy in the 1950s, and to follow particular behavioral repertoires, such as safe-sex regimes advocated by medical- and social-service providers. Herdt's (1992a) study of a youth counseling center in Chicago highlights the importance of stakeholders. He reports that the center's staff strongly encourages gay and lesbian teens to come out. The process is facilitated by the group counseling sessions and activities in which peers and adults act as role models, reinforce positive self-identities as homosexual men and women, and teach newcomers how to be gay. Given the strong code of solidarity and the intense inductive socialization sessions, it would be difficult for a participant at the center not to adopt one of the accepted identities (e.g., queer, dyke) or lifestyles.

The power and salience of internal stakeholders in the organization of same-sex markets may be tempered by the activities of external stakeholders—family, straight friends, work, religion (see Laumann & Gagnon, 1994, 194, 198–99). The literature on same-sex markets suggests that external stakeholders will be more salient and powerful among white working-class, Hispanic, and African American populations and more attenuated among white, middle-class groups. We expect to find this pattern replicated in our interview data with various institutional actors or stakeholders in Chicago.

We expect space, culture, and institutional forces to mutually constitute and influence same-sex sex markets in an additive manner. For example, a neighborhood sexual culture that condemns homosexual identity and behavior is likely to be reinforced by institutional support from religious or-

9. This ideal-typical construction of same-sex culture emphasizes choice and intentionality, but, in practice, choices may be highly constrained by group norms or social opportunities. For example, in pre-Stonewall America, two roles were available to lesbians: butch and femme. However, these roles were enacted mostly in private or semiprivate settings (homes or bars catering to lesbians), the only places in which most lesbians could be open about their sexuality (see Gilmartin, 1996; Davis & Kennedy, 1989).

ganizations, families, and social-service providers. In turn, this lack of cultural and institutional support for same-sex sexuality will discourage the creation of social space that serves a lesbian and gay population. Under such conditions, we expect that the same-sex market in this type of neighborhood will be forced underground or created in private spaces.[10]

The historical record also indicates that race and ethnicity structure same-sex markets in significant ways. First, racial and ethnic groups vary in terms of how they construct and sanction homosexuality, that is, in terms of creating group-specific opportunities and obstacles related to homosexual identity, behavior, and relationships. As noted above, among Latino groups in the United States (and elsewhere), simply engaging in same-sex sexual activity does not necessarily mean that a man has adopted a gay identity. Object choice is less important for personal identity than is following sharply defined sex roles. Men who take the active, masculine role and penetrate other men in anal intercourse are not considered homosexuals, and their masculinity is neither compromised nor stigmatized by such behavior, especially if they also have sex with women. However, men who are penetrated are considered to have assumed the passive, feminine role and, thus, to be homosexual (see Alonso & Koreck, 1993; Magana & Carrier, 1991; Carrier, 1989; Lancaster, 1988; Diaz, 1998, 63–88). In this context, it is difficult to create a clearly defined gay community even though the market of men looking for same-sex sexual encounters may be very large. These encounters may become highly ritualized, as in the case of men going to bars seeking a transvestite partner or finding partners among male friendship cliques that develop among new immigrant populations (see Parker & Carballo, 1990, 507).

Latina lesbians face a more restrictive environment. Generally, Latino groups in the United States strongly reject lesbianism, for a number of reasons. Lesbianism violates gender-role expectations and norms that emphasize passivity, deference to men, and the centrality of childbearing. It therefore threatens the family—the primary economic and social institution for Latino groups. Also, being openly homosexual—and especially being openly les-

10. Murray (1996, 72–77, 190–91) suggests that institutional elaboration or the development of a relatively complete set of basic social services (i.e., bookstores, leisure-oriented associations such as musical groups or athletic leagues, residential housing, medical- and social-service providers) encourages the concentration of gay and lesbian populations in urban areas and, thus, helps create more enduring sex markets. The process of institutional elaboration is most developed in urban white middle-class gay-male communities, while white lesbian urban populations tend to be more diffuse, with a less elaborated institutional infrastructure. The markets in ethnic and racial neighborhoods are often even more attenuated (Binnie, 1995; Rothenberg, 1995; Adler & Brenner, 1992; Kreiger, 1982).

bian—is often interpreted as a betrayal, not only of one's family, but also of the broader ethnic community (see Almaguer, 1991, 90–95; Espin, 1987; Garnets & Kimmel, 1993a, 332–36; Diaz, 1998, 89–112). Given these strictures, Latina lesbians have few, if any, public spaces, social services, or social networks available to them in their own communities. They commonly must seek them out in the white lesbian community or cope with the lack of spaces, services, and resources within their own ethnic communities (see Espin, 1987).

Second, race/ethnicity serves as an alternative—often the primordial—identity for persons of color who engage in homosexual behavior. In a brief review of research on gay and lesbian African Americans, Murray (1996, 239) concludes: "Race generally is a more important basis of self-identification than sexual orientation for African American gay men." Several African American scholars document the role conflict and tensions involved in being black and gay. Lorde (1984) notes that lesbianism is generally considered incompatible with gender-role expectations in the black community, and Icard (1986) finds that black gay men and lesbians struggle to find acceptance both in the black community and among white gays and lesbians (see also Peterson, 1992, 150–55; Scott, 1994). In brief, one can hide being gay, but one cannot hide being African American, and, in a community that reports strong negative attitudes toward homosexuality, keeping one's homosexuality hidden may be the preferred option.

Some African Americans believe that homosexuality is a white cultural phenomenon and that the gay community is white. "Consequently," according to Herek and Capitanio (1995, 97), "some heterosexual blacks' attitudes may be premised on the assumption that gay people are different from themselves not only in sexual orientation but also in race, ethnic identification and the values associated with being African American" (see also Icard, 1986; Loiacano, 1989). Similarly, according to Espin (1987, 40), some Hispanics believe that lesbianism is a "sickness" passed along by Anglos and Anglo culture. Strong pressures to maintain their racial or ethnic identity may make it difficult for gay persons of color to establish a separate gay/lesbian community within their own communities. For example, according to Cohen (1996), black gay men and lesbians who are deemed to be outside the boundaries of "acceptable blackness"—that is, those individuals who can neither conform to heterosexual standards nor hide their homosexuality—are often forced to leave the community altogether. In sum, gay persons of color lack what Stokes, Vanable, and McKirnan (1996, 374) call the "social support and institutional resources that gay communities can provide," a situation that reinforces negative attitudes about homosexuality among the larger heterosexual communities in which these gays and lesbians find themselves and helps keep same-sex sexual behavior, relationships, and organizations private.

Third, there is a perception among gay persons of color, usually based on individual experiences of discrimination and exclusion, that the gay community is white and racist. This tends to keep gay and lesbian persons of color from fully participating in the life of the broader lesbian and gay communities (see Stokes, Vanable, & McKirnan, 1996, 374; Herek & Capitanio, 1995, 97; Weston, 1995, 272–73). Icard (1986, 89–90) claims that black gays are often viewed as inferior members of the larger gay community and subject to a variety of racist practices in public settings (e.g., triple carding,[11] higher cover charges, and slower service at bars) (see also Peterson, 1992, 152–53; Weston, 1995, 272–73; Loiacano, 1989, 23). Similarly, Diaz (1998, 124–25) reports that most of the acculturated Latino gay men whom he interviewed experienced "blatant racism" and the feeling of being either objectified as exotic or simply invisible in gay bars and clubs (see also Garnets & Kimmel, 1993a, 335–36).

## Chicago's MSSMs

### *The MSSM in Shoreland*

Shoreland represents the gay center of the city of Chicago, and, while the city's MSSM is by no means limited to the borders of the neighborhood, Shoreland is the most explicit, the most public, and probably the largest physical space within the city where male same-sex activity is commonplace and accepted. Of the four sample areas of the Chicago Health and Social Life Survey (CHSLS), the Shoreland sample contains the largest number of cases of gay-identified, sexually active men. Both the survey questionnaire and the open-ended interviews provide important insights into the sex-market operations of this section of the city and illustrate the roles of sexual-marketplace coordination, network embeddedness, and sexually transmitted infections (STIs) in the Shoreland MSSM.

Strictly speaking, membership in a same-sex sex market is determined by sexual behavior: those who participate are members. However, two other important aspects of same-sex sexuality—identity and desire—also play important roles. The combination of identity, desire, and behavioral characteristics creates a three-dimensional spectrum of possible sexual types of individual. This spectrum can, however—with only some oversimplification—be reduced to eight basic classes of individuals who either possess or lack the same-

---

11. The reference here is to the practice of requiring multiple forms of identification to enter bars and clubs.

sex attribute in each category. The scheme presented here is intended, not to be a definitive description of same-sex sexuality, but, rather, to provide a convenient framework for understanding the results of the CHSLS investigation of the Shoreland same-sex sex market.

Of the Shoreland male sample (weighted cases), 67.2 percent portrayed themselves as exclusively heterosexual, expressing no amount of same-sex desire, identity, or behavior. The remaining cases are broken down in figure 4.1. Figure 4.1 includes all individuals in the Shoreland sample who expressed *any amount* of same-sex identity, desire, or behavior in adulthood. In this fig-

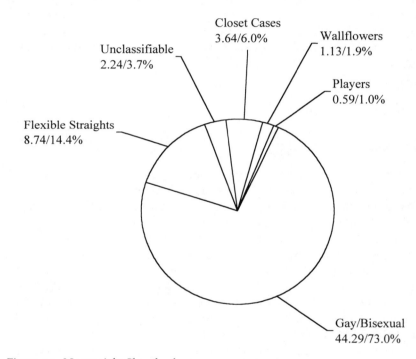

Figure 4.1. Nonstraight Shoreland men.

*Note:* Cases weighted by SAMPWGT. *Players* = straight-identified men who express no attraction to members of the same sex yet have had more than five same-sex partners in adulthood. *Closet cases* = straight-identified men who are strongly attracted to men but who have had no adult same-sex partners. *Flexible straights* = men who identify as heterosexual yet have either had a single same-sex experience in adulthood or expressed a mild attraction to members of the same sex. *Wallflowers* = gay-identified men who are attracted to men but who have had no adult same-sex partners. *Gay/bisexual* = men have a gay or bisexual identity, are attracted to other men, and have had at least five adult same-sex partners. *Unclassifiable* = those men who refused to answer one or more questions about their sexual identity, desire, or behavior and, therefore, could not be placed in any particular category.

ure, *players* are straight-identified men who express no attraction to members of the same sex yet have had more than five same-sex partners in adulthood;[12] *closet cases* are straight-identified men who are strongly attracted to men but who have had no adult same-sex partners; the category *flexible straights* constitutes a gray area and includes men who identify as heterosexual yet have either had a single same-sex experience in adulthood or expressed a mild attraction to members of the same sex; *wallflowers* are gay-identified men who are attracted to men but who have had no adult same-sex partners; *gay/bisexual* men have a gay or bisexual identity, are attracted to other men, and have had at least five adult same-sex partners; the category *unclassifiable* refers to those men who refused to answer one or more questions about their sexual identity, desire, or behavior and, therefore, could not be placed in any particular category.[13]

## Shoreland Market Arrangements

The MSSM in Shoreland is organized very differently from Chicago's heterosexual sex market and from the FSSM. Some of the patterns are ones predicted by popular culture; others are unexpected. The MSSM is fundamentally a transactional market, as evinced by the institutionalized sexual culture of the neighborhood and by the sex practices of individuals who participate in this market.

---

12. The Shoreland sample includes a gap between one and five same-sex partners, no individuals reporting two, three, or four same-sex partners.

13. As presented here, this classification scheme contains three theoretical gaps: (1) sexually active gay-identified men who paradoxically claim no amount of same-sex desire; (2) gay-identified men who deny any same-sex desire as well as any adult same-sex behavior; and (3) gay-identified men who express at least some same-sex desire but who report only between one and five same-sex partners in adulthood. We exclude the first two categories as nonsensical under the intuitive assumption that the adoption of a gay identity must derive from some sense of same-sex desire (therefore, such cases would result only from inaccuracies, such as a respondent's deliberate misrepresentation or a coding error). We propose the response rate of more than five same-sex partners (rather than at least one) as a qualifier for assignment to the category *gay/bisexual* in order to make such classification both substantive and unequivocal in terms of marketplace participation, especially given the tendency for sexually active gay men in the sample to report large numbers of partners relative to their straight counterparts; while the present scheme would place those gay men with between one and five partners in the category *unclassifiable,* a more refined definition based on a larger sample might have permitted the assignment of such individuals to an additional category, perhaps *homebodies,* or else their prudent collapse into the general category *gay/bisexual men.*

INSTITUTIONALIZED SEXUAL CULTURE. Like other gay ghettos, Shoreland has an institutionalized gay culture that encourages the creation and maintenance of a transactional sex market. Informants from several institutional spheres noted the common expectation among white gay men of having multiple casual sex partners. Ads for gay bars and clubs convey the message that being gay is about having sexual encounters, not relationships, with a particular male ideal (i.e., the cut or athletic clean-cut stud). The majority of personal ads in city papers under the heading *men seeking men* identify casual sex rather than long-term relationships as their goal.

Neighborhood bars, dance clubs, and the two bathhouses help individuals fulfill the expectation of transactional sexuality. Although several informants noted that gyms and churches increasingly serve as spaces in which to meet potential partners, bars and dance clubs continue to remain important places for men to meet male partners. Tables 4.1 and 4.2 show where men in Shoreland met their two most recent sex partners, by that partner's gender (note that the distinction by gender is a proxy for membership in the MSSM)—the role of bars as market coordinators is obviously strong in the MSSM. In both tables, men met at least half of all *male* partners in bars or dance clubs—three times the proportion of *female* partners met in this con-

Table 4.1 Places Where Shoreland Men Met Most
Recent Sex Partner, by Partner's Gender (N)

|  | Male | Female |
|---|---|---|
| Work | 4 | 27 |
|  | (8.7) | (19.6) |
| School | 0 | 32 |
|  | (0.0) | (23.2) |
| Church | 0 | 1 |
|  | (0.0) | (0.7) |
| Bar/dance club | 23 | 23 |
|  | (50.0) | (16.7) |
| Friend or family member's home | 6 | 15 |
|  | (13.0) | (10.8) |
| Public place | 6 | 9 |
|  | (13.0) | (6.5) |
| Other | 7 | 31 |
|  | (15.2) | (22.5)[a] |
| Total[b] | 46 | 138 |
|  | (100.0) | (100.0) |

*Note:* Percentages are given in parentheses.

[a]This high percentage is made up largely of meetings at private events and parties not collapsible into other categories.

[b]One person refused to indicate most recent partner's gender.

Table 4.2 Places Where Shoreland Men Met Second
Most Recent Sex Partner, by Partner's Gender (N)

|  | Male | Female |
| --- | --- | --- |
| Work | 2 | 27 |
|  | (4.5) | (20.9) |
| School | 0 | 27 |
|  | (0.0) | (20.9) |
| Church | 0 | 1 |
|  | (0.0) | (0.8) |
| Bar/dance club | 25 | 21 |
|  | (56.8) | (16.3) |
| Friend or family member's home | 6 | 32 |
|  | (13.0) | (24.8) |
| Public place | 7 | 9 |
|  | (15.9) | (7.0) |
| Other | 8 | 12 |
|  | (18.2) | (9.3) |
| Total[a] | 44 | 129 |
|  | (100.0) | (100.0)[b] |

*Note:* Percentages are given in parentheses.
[a]Nine respondents did not have a second sex partner.
[b]Two female partners were legitimately skipped in the survey; one person refused to indicate where met most recent female partner.

text and over twice the proportion of women met in any other specified context. Bars and dance clubs have primacy when it comes to the physical space organizing the MSSM.

There are other important ways—besides space where sex partners are located—in which participants in the MSSM differ from nonparticipants. Three important differences are the number of sex partners in adulthood, the degree to which partners are embedded in respondents' social networks, and the rate of STIs among members of Shoreland's MSSM. Taken together, these differences suggest that the Shoreland MSSM is a more fundamentally transactional market than is the Shoreland heterosexual sex market.

*Number of adult sex partners.* Table 4.3 presents a cross-tabulation of number of sex partners of Shoreland men by participation in the MSSM (i.e., those with five or more adult same-sex partners vs. those with fewer) among those with at least one adult sex partner. This table shows that *well over half* (61.3 percent) of the MSSM participants reported more than thirty adult sex partners, compared with just over 20 percent of their nonparticipant equivalents; a very large proportion (42.9 percent) of MSSM participants had more than sixty partners, compared with a very small fraction (3.8 percent) of the nonparticipants. Such a discrepancy shows a *much* greater frequency of short-

Table 4.3 Number of Sex Partners of Shoreland Men
in Adulthood, by Participation in the MSSM (N)

|  | Non–MSSM[a] | MSSM[b] |
|---|---|---|
| 1–5 | 37 | 1 |
|  | (34.9) | (2.0) |
| 6–15 | 24 | 5 |
|  | (22.6) | (10.2) |
| 16–30 | 23 | 13 |
|  | (21.7) | (26.5) |
| 31–60 | 18 | 9 |
|  | (17.0) | (18.4) |
| > 60 | 4 | 21 |
|  | (3.8) | (42.9) |
| Total | 106 | 49 |
|  | (100) | (100) |

*Note:* Percentages are given in parentheses.
[a]Sexually active straights, flexible straights, and closet cases.
[b]Gay/bisexual men and players.

term relationships among participants in the MSSM, a strong indication of the transactional nature of this market.

*Network embeddedness of partners.* All CHSLS respondents were asked (with regard to their two most recent sex partners), "About how many people you knew at the time you and [partner] met, knew [partner] before you did?" This question allows us to examine the degree of network embeddedness of those sex partners. Tables 4.4 and 4.5 show the Shoreland men's responses to this question, divided by the gender of the partner in question,[14] for those with at least one adult sexual experience. We can conclude from these tables that male partners (by definition located within the MSSM) are much less likely to be embedded within an existing social network than are female partners. For both the most recent and the second most recent sex partners, male partners were consistently twice as likely to be *completely* outside the respondent's social network than were female partners (59.1 percent vs. 30.3 percent for the most recent partner, 52.5 percent vs. 22.6 percent for the second most recent). This, again, demonstrates the transactional nature of the MSSM.

One final behavioral indicator of the transactional nature of Shoreland's MSSM is the rate of disease transmission. Disease transmission is driven, in part, by the number of partners an individual has; higher rates of disease signal greater numbers of partners (see Laumann, Gagnon, Michael, & Michaels,

14. As in tables 3.1 and 3.2 above, gender of most recent partner is used as a proxy for MSSM membership.

Table 4.4 Number of People Respondent Knows Who Knew Most
Recent Sex Partner before Respondent Did, by Partner's Gender (N)

|  | Male | Female |
|---|---|---|
| None | 26 (59.1) | 33 (30.3) |
| 1 | 5 (11.4) | 18 (16.5) |
| 2–4 | 10 (22.7) | 26 (23.9) |
| 5 or more | 3 (6.8) | 32 (29.4) |
| Total | 44 (100) | 109 (100) |

*Note:* Percentages are given in parentheses.

Table 4.5 Number of People Respondent Knows Who Knew Second Most
Recent Sex Partner before Respondent Did, by Partner's Gender (N)

|  | Male | Female |
|---|---|---|
| None | 23 (52.5) | 24 (22.6) |
| 1 | 9 (20.9) | 18 (17.0) |
| 2–4 | 2 (4.7) | 33 (31.1) |
| 5 or more | 9 (20.9) | 31 (29.2) |
| Total | 43 (100) | 106 (100) |

*Note:* Percentages are given in parentheses.

1994, 385). It is also driven by the nature of the sex market in question; since MSSMs tend to be relatively closed, located in urban areas where searches are easier (because of the higher density of potential partners), and highly organized through organizations such as bars, participation in them often results in higher rates of STIs. The rate of having any STI (i.e., gonorrhea, syphilis, herpes, genital warts, hepatitis B, nongonococcal urethritis, HIV) in the non–MSSM-participating male population of Shoreland is approximately 14.8 percent. By contrast, the rate among MSSM participants is a much higher 55.1 percent, a difference that is significant at the .001 level and suggests that STIs have an important effect on Shoreland's MSSM.

The organization of Shoreland's MSSM also differs from that of other sex markets in the city in terms of the role of stakeholders. Stakeholders play a limited role in defining legitimate partners, sanctioning behaviors, and assisting individuals in locating partners. In Shoreland, the influence of two key stakeholders, the church and the family, appears to be weak: church attendance is low, and family members live far away.

Most Shoreland residents do not live near their families. Almost 70 percent of the Shoreland respondents indicated that either less than half or none of their relatives lived in the Chicago area, compared with 50.8 percent of respondents in Westside, 42.4 percent in Erlinda, and 23.4 percent in Southtown.[15] Moreover, when compared with residents of other neighborhoods, Shoreland residents were more likely to indicate that their social networks consisted of non–family members—between 79.7 and 83.7 percent of the first three listed members of Shoreland residents' social networks were non–family members, whereas the equivalent figure is never above 65 percent in any other neighborhood.[16] Such a result corroborates findings from interviews: in its different aspects, Shoreland is a refuge for homeless teenagers as well as a new home for both urban gay men who have relocated to facilitate finding sex partners and upwardly mobile young heterosexual singles. The absence of the family as a stakeholder in the location of sex partners in this neighborhood allows gay men to claim a sexual identity (both homosexual and transactional) that might conflict with their identities as members of their families.

Similarly, religious organizations are not influential stakeholders in the MSSM. Shoreland residents are the least religious of the residents of the four ethnic neighborhoods in the CHSLS study. Fewer that 25 percent of respondents indicated that they attend religious services more often than several times a year; one in five indicated never attending religious services. As a result, very few respondents reported finding sex partners (of either sex) through religious activities (see tables 4.1 and 4.2 above). Many churches in the neighborhood, from mainline Protestant to Roman Catholic to Reform Jewish, are supporters of gay and lesbian identities and relationships. Most are welcoming of gays and lesbians; some engage in advocacy for gay rights; some perform same-sex commitment ceremonies.

As suggested above, peers are the most important stakeholder in Shoreland. Over 75 percent of the participants in the Shoreland MSSM claimed that most or all the people they know are gay, lesbian, or bisexual, whereas only 2.9 percent of the nonparticipants made this claim. In short, the social circles of gay men consist of other gay men. Although this result is hardly surprising, its implications are large: anyone entering a social network where

---

15. This difference between Shoreland and each of the other neighborhoods is significant beyond the .001 level.

16. A difference that is consistently significant beyond the .001 level.

having a large number of partners is the social norm might be encouraged by members of that network to imitate this pattern and to pursue transactional sex partners rather than more relational ones.

The following combination of market factors, then, results in a relatively transactional MSSM:

- the presence of centralized, convenient, popular public meeting places geared toward transactional relations;
- the relative unembeddedness of social relations between sex partners;
- the absence of stakeholders who traditionally limit transactional relations and the presence of stakeholders who encourage them; and
- the absence of cultural forces that encourage monogamy and the presence of cultural forces that encourage large numbers of sex partners.

PRIVATE AND PUBLIC ETHNIC SEXUAL MARKETPLACES. In the daily and weekly round of the gay sex market of Shoreland, the dominance of the white population—the sheer fact of the neighborhood's whiteness—works covertly to exclude ethnic minorities. This exclusion is institutionalized when bars or clubs make it complicated or awkward for minorities to enter. Several informants noted that triple carding was still used by a few Shoreland bars, and some used a dress code to deny admission to nonwhite would-be patrons. Those minorities who gain admission may face other forms of discrimination or exclusion—being eroticized, objectified, or treated as hustlers or gay-bashers. In brief, Shoreland's whiteness ensures that minorities who enter this neighborhood's sexual marketplaces are unlikely to find many other market participants of their own ethnicity, and this simple fact becomes a self-fulfilling prophecy.

However, while whites remain the dominant racial/ethnic group at all gay sexual marketplaces in Shoreland, the three major barriers to minority sex-market participation—the overt and covert discrimination problems and the coordination problem—are lifted at larger-scale public events: Overt discrimination is eliminated because identification requirements and dress codes are impossible to enforce at such events. Covert discrimination in the form of overbearing whiteness is eliminated since large public events attract a certain critical mass of ethnic minorities. And, because the barrier of whiteness has been eliminated, the coordination problem is also eliminated: substantial numbers of ethnic minorities will choose to attend such events because they know that they will find substantial numbers of ethnic minorities there.

Thus, it is in the regular, small-scale, private sexual marketplaces that African Americans and Hispanics find themselves at a loss in the city of Chicago. Although gay men in most ethnic neighborhoods have one or two gay-friendly places to go, none have as many options as the gay men in Shoreland. The gay men of the African American neighborhood of Southtown are a case in point. There are available to them across the entire South Side only three gay bars and two dance clubs. (There used to be more, but, in the early 1990s, several downtown gay bars that catered to African American men closed.) There are several cruising zones scattered across the city that are frequented by African American men, but only one of these is in Southtown itself. Therefore, house parties—advertised by word of mouth—and private social networks serve as important avenues by which African American men find male partners.

The African American same-sex market is primarily a transactional market, especially among bisexual or straight-identified men. However, one informant claimed: "There is definitely a trend toward long-lasting and committed relationships in the gay-male community." While the private market may be organized to facilitate such relationships, the public market is set up to facilitate more short-term sexual exchanges. For example, the primary place in which to find partners is a large public park on the South Side of the city. Here, straights, bisexuals, and gays look for same-sex sexual encounters, often trading sex for drugs, with little expectation—especially among the married men who frequent this space—that the encounter will develop into a long-term relationship. It should be noted, however, that, while bisexual practice occurs, often driven by the drug trade (i.e., substance abusers who self-identify as straight are willing to engage in homosexual acts for drugs), public, bisexual identities are uncommon. According to two informants, there is no cultural sanctioning of bisexuality in the African American neighborhood as there is in Latino communities.

The African American same-sex market has been significantly shaped by the sexual culture of the African American community and by the lack of institutional support for homosexuality. Health-care workers and informants from the social-service sector reported that, while the black community is highly homophobic, it does tolerate homosexuality as long as individuals do not present themselves publicly as being gay. The black church—a significant force in the definition of legitimate and illegitimate sexual identities and behaviors in the black community—is the strongest proponent of this "don't ask, don't tell" position. One health educator claimed that the church has, in fact, effectively silenced discussion of homosexuality and AIDS in Southtown. This claim was supported by interviews with neighborhood clergy, who either denied the existence of homosexuality and AIDS in the South Side black community, affirmed the church's inadequate response to the problem of AIDS, or repeated its moral teachings against homosexuality. The church's stance against homosexuality, together with the broader community's negative attitudes toward homosexuality, has, thus, forced Southtown's MSSM largely underground.

Similarly, the stigma attached to homosexuality limits the public face of the same-sex market in the two Latino neighborhoods, Westside and Erlinda. Sharply defined sex roles and the culture of machismo limit the demand for an openly gay community. Carlos Munez, a gay activist in Erlinda, notes: "Latin American culture has very strongly defined sex roles; being homosexual is very taboo. Some men won't have sex with other men unless they are dressed like drag queens. This type of behavior in which a man acts in the active role is considered masculine and not associated with homosexuality." He continued: "The typical Latino identifies homosexuality with the Hollywood stereotype of the poodle-carrying man and not with his own hypermasculine behavior" (see also Magana & Carrier, 1991, 434–35).[17]

Community norms that are antithetical to homosexuality are rigorously enforced: the few openly gay men in the neighborhood are routinely harassed, as are the men frequenting those neighborhood bars known to facilitate same-sex exchanges. Such targeting is facilitated by the high degree of embeddedness of individuals in networks of family and friends (48.1 percent of the men in Westside and 58.6 percent of the men in Erlinda report that at least half their family lives in the city, compared to just under 30 percent of the men in Shoreland), which means that sexual proclivities tend to be generally known. Informants suggested that families in both Westside (predominantly Mexican) and Erlinda (largely Puerto Rican) are likely to reject a family member who is openly gay (although outright rejection is more likely among Mexican families). The high value placed on marriage and family and the financial demands placed on male breadwinners to provide for the extended family further hinder the adoption of a gay identity in the Latino community.

The result of this pressure to conform and lack of public space has been a MSSM that is small and mostly hidden. It is also primarily transactional. Few participants are involved in or looking for long-term relationships (those gay-identified Latino men who are tend to live in Shoreland), and many are, in fact, straight.

What public markets there are in these neighborhoods tend to be based in parks and bars and to cater to straight men seeking the occasional male partner. In Erlinda, the common pattern is Puerto Rican men trading sex for drugs, or for money for drugs, in parks. In Westside, the common pattern is married Mexican men seeking casual sex with men in bars, the object being sexual release and a demonstration of masculinity. Such bars tend to be frequented mostly by recent immigrants and working-class men since in them gay-identified men are pressured to adopt the effeminate role—the *maricón,* the *joto,* the *pasivo.* More acculturated gay-identified Latinos—whose sex-

---

17. Men from Westside, the Mexican neighborhood, are more likely to be straight but have sex with other men, while men from Erlinda, the Puerto Rican neighborhood, are more likely to be gay.

ual preferences more closely resemble those of gay white men[18]—find them less hospitable.

There is, unfortunately, no publicly defined community for gay men of color within the city of Chicago. Therefore, many Latino men go to Shoreland in search of partners—probably because, as some informants suggested, it is a safe, anonymous environment.[19] At the same time, according to Diego Juarez, a public-health educator, gay white men from Shoreland cruise the parks in Latino or African American neighborhoods to pick up non-gay-identified men. The pattern of transcommunity cruising is, however, mostly a Latino and, to a lesser extent, African American phenomenon. Whites are more likely to find potential Latino or African American partners in their own neighborhood—men who have been integrated into the gay white community or who hang out in the lakeside parks—and, thus, not to stray beyond its boundaries.

Since the mid-1990s, gay men from the three ethnic neighborhoods have been working to create a visible gay presence within the broader Latino and African American communities in the city. For example, one organization based in Erlinda provides counseling, education, and support for gay men, uses the Latino press to highlight issues facing gay Latinos, marches in parades, and organizes fund-raisers, all in order to get the word out that a gay community exists within the larger Latino community of Chicago. A prominent goal of the organization is to change culturally received ideas about homosexuality in the broader Latino community. This would help create a space like Shoreland for Latino gay men who wish to stay in the community and reduce the conflict that many feel between their sexual and their ethnic identities. In Southtown, small numbers of gay men have formed relatively short-lived support groups meant to address such problems as HIV/AIDS, coming out in the neighborhood, and finding gay-friendly social activities. Gay African American men have also participated in larger coalitions with African American lesbians to promote visibility for the lesbian and gay community on the South Side and to mobilize support for HIV/AIDS education.

18. Munez, e.g., remarked that, because it is so well organized, the white gay community dominates Chicago and that it is, therefore, hard for a Latino to adopt a gay identity without adopting a gay white identity. For a more extended discussion of the relation between acculturation and sexuality among Latinos, see Diaz (1998, 129–36).

19. Although gay white Shoreland is "not happening" for many Latinos, some have been able to carve out their own social space: taking over one or two bars in the neighborhood or at least pressuring owners to set aside one night (e.g., "salsa night") for ethnic groups; using the neighborhood's major park as a cruising zone; and creating their own celebrations of gay Latino identity as part of the larger neighborhood celebrations.

In sum, any attempt to create a visible gay presence in these neighborhoods requires both altering the structure of existing same-sex markets and creating a gay-friendly space within a hostile sexual culture. The struggle is, therefore, ongoing because it faces continued resistance or indifference within these neighborhoods.

## Chicago's FSSMs

Chicago's FSSMs differ significantly from its MSSMs in several ways. Most prominent is that they are organized in relational rather than transactional terms. While some informants discussed cruising and the search for casual partners among lesbians under thirty, this type of behavior was framed as the exception rather than the rule. Space is defined and used primarily to help women build relationships and communities, sometimes across racial and ethnic groups, and only secondarily to meet partners for casual sex. Unlike the MSSMs, the FSSMs are not centered geographically in a white, middle-class neighborhood; rather, they are scattered across several ethnically and economically diverse North Side neighborhoods and a few, largely African American South Side neighborhoods. They also lack the same institutional infrastructure (e.g., bars and cafés, bookstores, and social and health-care services) that is available in Shoreland. This is especially true in African American and Latino neighborhoods, where, consequently, the markets tend to operate in private rather than public space.

There are, however, similarities. Like the MSSMs, the FSSMs are largely segregated by race, and women of color often experience discrimination when they enter white neighborhoods. And, like minority men, minority women face strong, if not stronger, pressures from stakeholders to conform to heterosexual notions of identity and behavior.

### The White FSSM

Although Shoreland is home to several businesses and service organizations that serve lesbian and/or bisexual female clients, it is not the geographic center of the white FSSM.[20] This market is scattered throughout the city: lesbian residential pockets can be found in most of the North Side lakeside neighborhoods, in a few South Side neighborhoods, and in one or two suburbs. One recurrent complaint voiced by our informants was the lack of space in Shore-

20. Informants claimed that this market is primarily lesbian with a small bisexual clique. No one identified the phenomenon of white heterosexual women seeking female partners.

land and other North Side neighborhoods dedicated to market and nonmarket concerns of women seeking female partners. Several lesbian bars in Shoreland had been taken over by gay men prior to the fielding of the CHSLS, and many public spaces in the neighborhood are considered too male and hostile to women.[21] According to our informants, many lesbians are looking for a safe place to meet other women and, even more basically, simply a place to belong. Thus, in several neighborhoods, women have created a number of public and private spaces in which to find potential partners and friends: bookstores, coffeehouses, service organizations, house parties, and barbecues.

These marketplaces are defined as spaces in which women can build community and develop relationships. Several informants noted that many women on the city's North Side meet partners through participating in support groups, volunteering at women's-issues organizations (e.g., the Lesbian Community Cancer Project), and playing in one of the city or suburban softball leagues. Partnering is depicted as a fortuitous outcome of the more important work of building community rather than as the goal of participation. Private parties and political organizing at private residences are also common means of meeting potential partners.

The institutional support for the FSSM on the North Side is reinforced by the sexual culture. Women's sexuality, especially that of lesbians, is seen as being antithetical to the promiscuity that characterizes gay-male sexuality. Barbara Boyer, a therapist at a Shoreland clinic, noted that most lesbians, especially over the age of thirty, are seeking relationships and that even those younger women who take a more casual approach to sex are not seeking anonymous, one-time meetings but, rather, are engaged in a process of narrowing the pool of potential long-term partners and remain monogamous as long as a relationship endures. The centrality of relationships is also evident in the humor about lesbian sexuality. Nearly every informant told the same old joke: after one date lesbians rent a U-Haul and move in together. Ultimately, the values—loyalty, honesty, monogamy—prized by the North Side lesbian community, young and old alike, reinforce relational rather than transactional sexual relationships.

This codification of relational values suggests that the lesbian community on the North Side is, perhaps, the most powerful stakeholder shaping the FSSM. The power of the community is evident in the ability of different lesbian groups to stigmatize bisexuality and keep bisexual women from exercising any power in lesbian organizing and politics. According to Marie

21. The lack of public space in Shoreland is also caused by gay men's control of property in the neighborhood as well as by women's more limited financial resources. On the relation between financial resources and urban space among lesbians, see Adler and Brenner (1992) and Rothenberg (1995).

Anderson, a lesbian police officer, bisexuals are viewed with suspicion in the community as being more promiscuous and likely to carry "social diseases." They threaten to undercut the identity of lesbians and the communal ideals of sexual behavior. Few other stakeholders seem to exercise much power in the North Side FSSM.

Discussion of families was conspicuously absent from many of the interviews. Anderson claimed that the lesbian community is filled with individuals who have moved to Chicago from other Midwest cities and for whom the family that matters is the family by choice, not the family by birth (even as she lives near her own family). Nearly 50 percent of the women who live in Shoreland report that they have no family living in Chicago. Barbara Boyer echoes Anderson's claim, noting that, among her clients, families seem to be more important to lesbians of color than to white lesbians.

Boyer also argued that organized religion had largely been abandoned by North Side lesbians, replaced by some form of individualistic spirituality or the lesbian community itself. An excerpt from an interviewer's field notes, for example, reports: "I asked how these clients generally resolve these conflicts [i.e., conflicts between religious beliefs and one's sexual orientation]. Barbara said that generally they dump religion. Many seek groups like Dignity, which serves gay Catholics, but these groups tend to be dominated by men. Women, she said, are more likely to try other faiths, especially from the East, or 'women's communities' provide a substitute for the sense of community provided by a church."[22]

In short, the community, rather than more traditional stakeholders, such as religion and family, is a more powerful force shaping the FSSM on Chicago's North Side. Community and culture together legitimize a relational orientation among participants in the FSSM and channel behavior toward relational outcomes (albeit, often in the form of serial monogamy).

## The Same-Sex Market for Women of Color

Informants identified and described several groups of participants in the same-sex market for women of color. These different market groups include an under-thirty politically active and openly lesbian clique; an over-thirty crowd, many of whom have moved to the North Side while retaining family ties in their home neighborhoods; a large closeted and isolated group that is not aware of the events, house parties, and public spaces available to lesbians; and

---

22. The CHSLS data provide additional evidence of religion's minimal power as a stakeholder. Twenty-six percent of the Shoreland sample (both men and women) report having no religious affiliation, and just over 85 percent of the women in the sample report attending religious service no more than a few times per year.

a group of bisexual women in the projects who may not openly identify themselves as homosexual but who have a woman as their primary partner even at the same time as they have sex with men to maintain social legitimacy or acquire financial resources for child care or drugs. As is to be expected, both similarities and differences between the various FSSMs emerged.

The same-sex market for women of color, like that for white women, tends to be relational. While women under thirty may engage in casual sex or cruising, our informants claimed that this behavior was not common. A Latina activist, for example, argued that casual sex was simply not an option for Latina lesbians: "There is not the same freedom to have casual sex. If you are in a relationship with another lesbian, you talk about forever/expectation of monogamy. Latinos and gays in general will look for someone to have for the weekend, regardless of whether they are gay, bi, or straight. Lesbians, on the other hand, view this type of behavior in a woman as totally unacceptable."

Similarly, none of our African American informants identified casual sex as a common practice, although an organizer of house parties claimed that, when it occurs, it tends to be among the under-thirty crowd attending her parties. In the African American market, as in the white North Side market, the goal of cruising seems to be finding a long-term partner rather than a casual sexual encounter. Connie Blake, the party organizer, identified serial monogamy as the common outcome of cruising, with many of the resultant relationships lasting between six and twelve months.

It should be noted, however, that, while long-term relationships were important in both the Latina and the African American markets, friendship networks tended to be more central in the African American. Another difference between the two markets is that, while bisexuality is more common in them than in the white market, it was more likely to be by choice in the Latina market and by necessity in the African American market. Nevertheless, informants across the African American, Puerto Rican, and Mexican neighborhoods generally considered bisexuality not to be a legitimate option.

Women of color face a restrictive environment in terms of little public space allocated to and limited institutional support for participation in a same-sex market. Informants from the African American and the two Latino neighborhoods reported that, in them, lesbians, like gay men, are nearly invisible and that there is little sense of community among them. In Southtown, the market is largely privatized. Socializing and partner search take place primarily at private house parties, and, while a few of these parties may draw several hundred people, most are small and involve friendship networks. Judy Boles, a lesbian writer, noted that many women are unaware both of these parties and of the few public spaces—two dance clubs and a few bars that tolerate homosexual customers—frequented by the small openly lesbian community on the South Side.

One strategy to expand the public space open to African American lesbians has been to co-opt one of the Shoreland lesbian bars. Another has been to organize politically and socially on the South Side. In 1995, there were six organizations established to serve as support groups for African American lesbians and/or politically mobilize South Side gays and lesbians. In recent years, lesbians (and some gay men) formed an association (Active Proud Black Lesbians and Gays) that became the first openly homosexual group to march in the annual Bud Billiken Parade on the South Side, organized a PFLAG (Parents and Friends of Lesbians and Gays) chapter on the South Side, and began work to bring health clinics and youth centers to the neighborhood. Like the spaces sponsored by North Side groups, these South Side spaces operate less as sites in which to meet partners and more as sites in which to develop relationships and a larger lesbian (and gay) community among African Americans.

Latina lesbians face a more pronounced lack of public and private space in Westside and in Erlinda. Few informants in these neighborhoods acknowledged the existence of Latina lesbians. Like openly gay Latinos, openly lesbian Latinas find it difficult to reside in the neighborhood. One Puerto Rican informant claimed that most lesbians lead double lives, acting straight at work and in the neighborhood and adopting their homosexual personas outside the neighborhood. No bars or dance clubs in these neighborhoods are open to Latina lesbians, many of whom frequent the two clubs in Shoreland that offer salsa nights as a way of attracting Latina customers. Private house parties, when they exist, are one of the few means that Latina lesbians have of meeting potential partners and developing a community. Also, several neighborhood activists have established support and social groups, both of which have struggled to attract participants and stay together.

Women of color face a restricted market owing to the exclusionary practices of the North Side white gay and lesbian community and to the homophobic pressures of several stakeholders in their neighborhoods. Like gay men of color, African American and Latina lesbians experience discrimination when they go to bars and community events in Shoreland. In terms of local politics, the concerns of lesbian women of color are routinely ignored by white-run lesbian community organizations. One African American activist noted that the white North Side community was supportive of the effort of the group Active Proud Black Lesbians and Gays to be allowed to march in the Bud Billiken Parade but that such support is exceptional. She stated: "The North Side is not a haven for blacks. They are much more likely to be called a 'nigger' there than in any other part of the city. White North Siders don't deal with racial issues. I sometimes get calls from them on issues concerning race, but I'm not invited to sit on their boards; they don't want to give me that kind of power." Other informants reported common experiences of triple carding at Shoreland bars unless individuals are light skinned and, thus, can pass as white. Latinas with limited English-language skills are targeted for ex-clusion as well. In addition to discrimination based on race, many women experience discrimination based on gender as well—indeed, they face out-right hostility in many Shoreland gay bars, to which they often have to resort owing to the currently limited number of lesbian bars in operation.

The commonplace exclusion from an important stakeholder—the broader Chicago lesbian and gay community—creates identity problems for women of color and forces them into racially separate and smaller FSSMs. The racism of the North Side community makes it difficult for Latinas and African Amer-ican women to identify first as lesbians. Instead, many claim a stronger iden-tification with their ethnic/racial community. But, given community norms and institutional pressures strongly favoring heterosexuality over homosexu-ality, such an identification just makes it that much more difficult to be open about one's sexual orientation and partner preferences. Efforts to establish lesbian organizations—a specifically Erlinda group that met in Shoreland be-cause it could not meet safely in Erlinda and other, pan-Latina groups—have floundered owing to a lack of participation. And South Side African Amer-ican informants suggested that they, too, struggle to establish and maintain gay and lesbian organizations, in part because many in the community do not wish to be openly identified as a homosexual.

In all three neighborhoods—Erlinda, Westside, and Southtown—the FSSMs are constrained by the strong antihomosexual attitudes held by the ethnic or racial community itself. Taboos against female homosexuality are especially strong in Westside and Erlinda. The central concern there is to pre-serve the family as this institution provides the social foundation for these two immigrant neighborhoods. Almaguer (1991) notes that family is so critical for Latinos because it is the means to resist racism and the effects of economic inequality in the United States. However, according to Almaguer, the Latino family structure "exaggerates unequal gender roles and suppresses sexual non-conformity. Therefore any deviation from the sacred link binding husband, wife, and child not only threatens the very existence of *la familia,* but also po-tentially undermines the mainstay of resistance to Anglo racism and class ex-ploitation" (90). He also notes that these familial norms are relaxed for men—thus permitting homosexual activity—but not for women. Lesbianism among Latinas is not a culturally acknowledged possibility, especially for new immigrants and members of older generations (see Alonso & Koreck, 1993).

Interviews with residents of Erlinda and Westside confirm the findings of earlier research. These informants indicate that many women fear being os-tracized if they come out (a few informants noted that a Mexican family is more likely to reject a homosexual daughter than is a Puerto Rican family), and daughters seem concerned with injuring their relationships with their mothers and grandmothers (see Espin, 1987). Like their male counterparts,

Latinas are more tightly embedded in family networks than are white women; over 50 percent of the respondents in the two Latino neighborhoods reported that at least half their family lives in Chicago.

Moreover, the deep-seated culture of silence surrounding sexuality makes any discussion of sexual identity and behavior problematic for Latina lesbians. Several Erlinda and Westside health-care workers noted that families rarely talk about sexuality, especially women's sexuality. More recent immigrants lack even a vocabulary with which to talk about their bodies, their sexual desires, or their sexual identity. Not only is discussion about alternative sexualities prohibited, but it may be impossible within some Latina populations. Finally, norms and scripts about gender roles place women in such a position that their only legitimate relation to men is as a subordinate—usually the submissive wife/mother or aunt. This leaves lesbians little cognitive or social space in which to express alternative identities and roles. In short, stakeholders' antihomosexual views and the lack of institutional support for FSSMs in Erlinda and Westside compel many Latinas to remain closeted or to adopt a seemingly straight persona (e.g., a femme). Without cultural and institutional support, the FSSM for Latinas exists largely in white neighborhoods or in private venues.

The FSSM in Southtown, the African American neighborhood, is also relegated largely to private space—again owing to community norms. Nevertheless, many young gays and lesbians are choosing to stay in the neighborhood, although how open they are about their sexual preferences is unclear. For example, several informants from the fields of health care and social service discussed only male homosexuality and, when pressed, claimed that they had not encountered lesbians in their professional work. The interviews generally support earlier work documenting strong antihomosexual attitudes in the black community (e.g., Cohen, 1996; Icard, 1986). Several informants noted that women who are openly butch are often harassed on the street (femmes more easily pass as straight). Some older lesbians believe that they cannot be open and live safely on the South Side and have, therefore, moved to more homosexual-friendly North Side neighborhoods.

African American families voice strong disapproval of daughters who are involved sexually with other women. Such a taboo does not appear to be as strong as it is among Latino families, however, the common approach among African American families being to adopt a "don't ask, don't tell" policy. Most churches in the neighborhood follow this strategy. One Presbyterian minister claimed that, while homosexuality may be publicly denounced as immoral, especially in conservative churches, it is nevertheless generally tolerated. The interviewer's field notes captured this minister's final assessment of homosexuality in the African American community: "He said, 'These are the kinds of people [i.e., gays and lesbians] you should stay away from,' his mother used to tell him. But she never talked badly of them, and they were always accepted members of the church community. They were just seen as different and were equally involved in the church as he was. Churches would cater to such differences, but you still would never hear anyone talking about them. It was simply understood that there were certain churches where you could go if you were of that persuasion." Although this quiet tolerance of homosexuality by a key stakeholder in Shoreland may provide "church queens and dykes" a modicum of institutional support, it does not legitimate alternative sexual identities and relationships in the larger African American community and, thus, helps to keep lesbians hidden.

Perhaps the strongest community constraint on the black FSSM is the conflict between racial and sexual identities. In a community that prefers to keep public discussions and displays of homosexuality muted and in which racial solidarity is highly valued, being openly homosexual, and especially being openly lesbian, is problematic. Several informants discussed the tension between older lesbians, who tend to identify first as gay and second as black, and younger cohorts, who place race first and sexual orientation second. This tension is played out in both the political and the social arenas, as indicated by the difficulties faced by those mostly younger women attempting to organize and sustain lesbian political interest groups as well as by those attempting to create lesbian public spaces. The older generations are likely to dismiss these efforts as relatively unimportant.

In sum, the ideological and social pressures to keep homosexuality hidden, the lack of institutional support for lesbianism, and the concomitant dearth of public space and social or political events for lesbians have led to the creation of a largely private black FSSM.

## Conclusion

This chapter has demonstrated how same-sex markets operate in four Chicago neighborhoods. We have argued that MSSMs are organized to facilitate transactions and that FSSMs are organized to facilitate relationships. The particular shapes that the various markets take depend on group-specific sexual cultures, the role of institutional stakeholders, the salience of racial or ethnic identity, and the availability of space for same-sex market activities.

MSSMs are constructed as transactional for several reasons. First, the white gay sexual culture allows for and even celebrates casual, episodic sexual encounters, as in the case of Shoreland. A more restrictive sexual culture, as exemplified in the Latino neighborhoods, legitimizes same-sex activity for straights—as long as they adopt the active role in the encounter—and stigmatizes homosexual behavior. A homophobic sexual culture in the African

American neighborhood makes long-term, openly gay relationships difficult to sustain, and, thus, short-term sexual exchanges become the most viable avenue for same-sex sexual expression. Conversely, the sexual cultures of the three FSSMs hold up monogamous, committed relationships as the ideal, which is reinforced by the way in which market space is defined and organized as space to build relationships and community rather than as space to find casual sex partners.

As suggested above, the meanings that shape and direct same-sex markets are reinforced and made operative by the availability and organization of social space in which to seek out potential partners and the role of institutional stakeholders in sanctioning same-sex activities. For example, the strong taboo against lesbianism, coupled with strong norms favoring traditional gender roles, creates difficulties for Latina lesbians attempting to carve out public space for themselves. This lack of public space creates an additional network problem: knowing who is in the market is problematic because there are few places in which to find potential partners. As a result, Latina lesbians have been forced into Shoreland in order to make contact with one another and with the larger lesbian community.

Finally, the analysis has shown how same-sex markets are differentiated by (relatively impermeable) racial and ethnic boundaries. Both crossing the boundaries and staying within them exact costs on market participants. On the one hand, because racial/ethnic identity is often set in opposition to sexual identity among African Americans and Latinos, staying within the boundaries means staying closeted. (Younger Latino and African American gays and lesbians, however, are resisting the pressure to stay closeted and, instead, working to create space and social approval for same-sex market activities in their neighborhoods.) On the other hand, crossing the boundaries means subordinating a racial/ethnic identity to a gay or lesbian identity that, more often than not, is pegged to white experience and expectations. It also means facing possible hostility in white gay and lesbian spaces or creating alternative space in the host market, as gays and lesbians of color do during the annual pride parade in Shoreland.

In short, the cost of adopting a gay or lesbian identity and pursuing same-sex partners is determined by three interrelated social forces: group-specific sexual cultures; the space set aside for meeting potential partners; and the degree of embeddedness in social institutions (e.g., family, religion, neighborhood, homosexual community) that are locally powerful in sanctioning or suppressing same-sex market activities.

# Part Three )

*Sexual and Social Consequences
of Sexual Marketplaces*

# 5 )

# *Meeting and Mating over the Life Course*

Jenna Mahay and
Edward O. Laumann

Americans today find themselves in the sex market for longer periods of time, and at older ages, than at any other time in the past hundred years.[1] Both men and women are marrying later, about half those who do marry will divorce, and rates of remarriage are declining (Bumpass, Sweet, & Martin, 1990; Cherlin, 1992; DaVanzo & Rahman, 1993; Fitch & Ruggles, 2000; Ra-

A version of this chapter was presented as "Meeting and Mating over the Life Course: A New Approach to Understanding Union Formation" at the annual meeting of the American Sociological Association, Chicago, 20 August 2001.

1. On the terms *sex market* and *sexual marketplace* as they are used in this study, see the section "The Social Organization of Sexual Partnering and Sexual Relationships" in Ellingson, Laumann, Paik, and Mahay (chapter 1 in this volume).

ley, 2000). Thus, the majority of people today will find themselves in the sex market at successively later stages of the life course, and the conditions under which they must form relationships will be very different at different stages of the life course. For example, people in their forties are likely to find themselves in a different market position than they were in when they were in their twenties, and they may have altogether different attitudes toward forming sexual unions.

At the same time, there is little social support, and few institutionalized guidelines, for forming intimate unions in later life, which is not considered the normative time to be searching for a partner (Rodgers & Conrad, 1986). Yet there is a lot at stake here since the ability to form warm, committed, ongoing relationships affects emotional, physical, and financial well-being—in short, the quality of life (Horwitz, White, & Howell-White, 1996; House, Landis, & Umberson, 1988; Marks & Lambert, 1998; Ross, 1995; Waite, 1995; Waite & Gallagher, 2000). In fact, evidence suggests that forming such relationships may be particularly important for well-being in later life (Waite & Hughes, 1999).

Thus, the questions that we address in this chapter are the following: How does age affect the process of union formation? And does it affect men and women differently? The way in which a sexual partnership is formed and maintained is a critical issue because the process has consequences for whether the partnership leads to the kind of committed, enduring relationships that have such a positive effect on the quality of life.

## Background

### *Changes in the Timing and Process of Relationship Formation*

The presence of Americans in the sex market at increasingly older ages is due to the confluence of three major demographic trends.

First, both men and women are marrying later now than at any other time in the past hundred years (Cherlin, 1992; DaVanzo & Rahman, 1993; Fitch & Ruggles, 2000; Raley, 2000). Between 1960 and 1999, the median age at first marriage increased by almost five years (to 24.5) for white women and by over four years (to 26.6) for white men. For African Americans, the delay in first marriage has been even more striking, with the median age climbing to 27.3 for women and 28.6 for men (Fitch & Ruggles, 2000). Thus, now fully 25 percent of people aged thirty to thirty-four have not yet married (U.S. Bureau of the Census, 1998). Rising rates of cohabitation do not account for all the increase in the age at marriage, and, because cohabitation is a less stable form of union than marriage, a high percentage of cohabitations dissolve within the first few years, leaving these individuals single again at older ages (Bumpass, Sweet, & Cherlin, 1991).

Second, the divorce rate is climbing. It is by now well-known that about half of all marriages end in divorce (see Cherlin, 1992; McLanahan & Casper, 1995), placing unprecedented numbers of people back in the sex market at later stages of the life course. While the annual rate of death for married persons has declined at the same time that the annual rate of divorce has been rising, the rising divorce rate since 1970 has pushed the total dissolution rate well above its historical high (Cherlin, 1992).

Third, the rate of remarriage is declining, and men and women are increasingly cohabiting rather than remarrying after divorce (Bumpass, Sweet, & Martin, 1990; Wilson & Clarke, 1992), that is, entering a form of union that is, again, less stable than marriage. In addition, even when people do remarry, the rate of divorce for remarriages is substantially higher than the rate of divorce for first marriages, and, thus, 16 percent of the 1970 birth cohort is projected to experience two divorces over the life course (Cherlin, 1992).

The end result of these three demographic trends is that more people are in the sex market for longer periods of time and at older ages than ever before in the past hundred years.

While this fact has been well established, there has been relatively little research conducted on how age affects the process of relationship formation, for example, on how people meet their partners and develop intimate relationships. The National Health and Social Life Survey (NHSLS) did examine such aspects of intimate unions as where respondents met their partners, how they were introduced to their partners, and how quickly the relationship developed (see Laumann, Gagnon, Michael, & Michaels, 1994, 225–68). However, it did not analyze age differences in these aspects of the relationship-formation process. Other, more social-psychological studies of the development of relationships once people have met their partners have also not typically examined how the process changes with age (see Benson, Larson, Wilson, & Demo, 1993; Eggert & Parks, 1987; Houts, Robins, & Huston, 1996; Johnson & Milardo, 1984; Leslie, Huston, & Johnson, 1986; Lloyd, Cate, & Henton, 1984; Sacher & Fine, 1996; Sprecher & Felmlee, 1992; Surra & Gray, 2000), often relying on samples of college students. Those studies that have examined age differences in the partnering process tend to examine only one aspect of the process, such as where people met or the length of courtship before marriage (Kalmijn & Flap, 2001; O'Flaherty & Eells, 1988; Peters, 1976; Whyte, 1990), and have used unrepresentative samples (for an exception, see Kalmijn and Flap [2001]). These studies also analyze only marriages or compare only first marriages and second marriages and, thus, in a critical sense select on the dependent variable; they do not analyze the effect of age on the process of forming intimate relationships.

## Critical Processes of Relationship Formation

We propose that there are three aspects of the partnering process—discussed in Ellingson, Laumann, Paik, and Mahay (chapter 1 in this volume), which outlined our theory of the sex market—that are particularly important for determining whom one meets and the outcome of the ensuing relationship: institutional embeddedness; social-network embeddedness; and relational embeddedness. We discuss each in turn.

1. *Institutional embeddedness.* Some settings are more "efficient" than others for those searching for a partner (see England & Farkas, 1986; Kalmijn, 1991a, 1994; Kalmijn & Flap, 2001; Oppenheimer, 1988; Scott, 1965). In other words, there is a higher likelihood of finding a good match with each unit cost of investment in a setting (Oppenheimer, 1988). Institutionally embedded settings, such as school, work, or church, tend to be socially preselective, with the result that individuals' preferences for similar mates are combined with interaction opportunities that make it more likely that they will meet potential partners with similar characteristics, such as age, race, level of education, or religion (Kalmijn, 1998; Kalmijn & Flap, 2001; Laumann, Gagnon, Michael, & Michaels, 1994, 225–68). An individual is likely, therefore, to have a good deal more in common with those partners met in an institutionally embedded setting than with those met in more public, less institutionally embedded settings, such as a beach, park, bar, or mall, which are less socially preselective. Indeed, Laumann, Gagnon, Michael, and Michaels (1994, 233–68) found that partners who met in a bar were less likely to be similar with respect to age, education, and religion than were those who met in more institutionally embedded, socially preselective settings, such as at school or work. Partners who share social characteristics are more likely to have the shared cultural resources and worldviews that have been found to facilitate personal attraction (Byrne, 1971) and the development of intimacy that leads to marriage (DiMaggio & Mohr, 1985). Thus, the institutional embeddedness of the setting in which one meets one's partner typically affects the type of person one meets, how much one is likely to have in common with that person, and, ultimately, the outcome of the relationship. We refer to whether one meets one's partner in an institutionally embedded setting as *institutional embeddedness.*

2. *Social-network embeddedness.* Social networks play multiple roles in the partnering process. First, owing to the high level of social homogeneity found in social networks (see Fischer, 1982; Laumann, 1966, 1973; Marsden, 1988), individuals are more likely to share important characteristics with a partner met through a mutual friend or a family member than with someone outside their social network. Second, partners who from the beginning of their relationship have mutual acquaintances have more sources of information about each other and, thus, are more likely to know whether they can trust each

other or whether they share common values (Youm, 2001; see also Ellingson, chapter 10 in this volume); relationship formation depends, not only on the supply of available mates, but also on the availability and reliability of information about both the searcher and potential partners (Oppenheimer, 1988). Finally, the presence of mutual friends in a romantic relationship has been shown to support the relationship and increase relational stability—if these "stakeholders" approve of the match (see Youm & Paik, chapter 6 in this volume; Sprecher & Felmlee, 1992; Laumann, Gagnon, Michael, & Michaels, 1994). We refer to whether partners meet through social networks as *social-network embeddedness*.

3. *Relational embeddedness.* Finally, the relational context in which an individual begins a sexual partnership affects the durability of the relationship and the likelihood that it will lead to marriage. An individual who has known a partner for a longer period of time before initiating a sexual relationship has a greater investment and greater satisfaction in the relationship, knows more about that partner in terms of trustworthiness, values, and common interests, and is, ultimately, more likely to marry that partner (Laumann, Gagnon, Michael, & Michaels, 1994; Lloyd, Cate, & Henton, 1984). In addition, more committed partnerships have a higher probability of enduring and providing higher levels of satisfaction than do sexual relationships in which the partners are uncommitted (Rusbult, Johnson, & Morrow, 1986; Waite & Joyner, 2001). We refer to whether the sexual relationship begins within the context of a long-term, committed relationship as *relational embeddedness*.

## Theories of the Effect of Age on the Partnering Process

While little empirical research has addressed how these aspects of the partnering process vary with age, the theory of the sex market outlined in Ellingson, Laumann, Paik, and Mahay (chapter 1, in this volume) includes two elements—*market position* and *sexual culture*—that suggest conflicting hypotheses.

THE INFLUENCE OF MARKET POSITION. One of the basic assumptions underlying the theory of the sex market is that the partnering process is governed by the rational choices that individuals make in order to optimize their utility, choices based on the costs and benefits of the potential match (see Becker, 1981; Becker, Landes, & Michael, 1977; England & Farkas, 1986). Individuals' ability to realize their preferences in a partner depends on the demand for, and the availability of, the desired characteristics as well as on the relative desirability of their own characteristics (see England & Farkas, 1986; Oppenheimer, 1988; Becker, 1981; Laumann, Gagnon, Michael, & Michaels, 1994).

On the basis of this assumption, we would expect that, with age, the partnering process will become less embedded in institutionally organized settings, social networks, and long-term committed relationships and that the negative effect of age will be greater for women than for men, for a number of reasons.

For one thing, in terms of "search costs" and the structure of opportunities in the market, both older men and older women are less likely to be embedded in the more "efficient" market institutions, such as schools, than are their younger counterparts (see Kalmijn, 1991a, 1994; Oppenheimer, 1988). While older singles are embedded in other institutionally organized settings, such as the workplace or church, these other settings are somewhat problematic as sexual marketplaces: workplaces often have proscriptions against romantic relationships (Kalmijn & Flap, 2001), and singles are less likely to attend church on a regular basis than are those who are married (Hertel, 1995; Stolzenberg, Blair-Loy, & Waite, 1995). Thus, we would expect older individuals to have to go outside these more institutionally organized settings to meet their partners and search in more public places, such as in bars or through personal ads (England & Farkas, 1986; Ahuvia & Adelman, 1992).

For another, as their friends get married, older individuals' social networks tend to include fewer singles than do the social networks of those who are younger, and there may also be some uneasiness among married acquaintances about having a friend who is in the market (Bumpass, Sweet, & Martin, 1990). Thus, we would expect that, compared to their younger counterparts, older singles will be more likely to have to go outside their existing social networks in order to meet partners and, thus, that they will meet their partners in ways that will be less embedded in their social networks.

While these two aspects of the structural opportunities in the sex market change with age similarly for both men and women, there are also several ways in which men's and women's position in the sex market changes differently as they age.

First, strictly in terms of numbers, with age the sex ratio becomes less favorable for women and more favorable for men. Excess male mortality and higher remarriage rates among men than among women, combined with the fact that men tend to marry younger women, contribute to the relative deficit of available men at older ages (South & Lloyd, 1992; Oppenheimer, 1988; South, 1991; Laumann, Gagnon, Michael, & Michaels, 1994, 251–54). The shortage of available men has been found to be even more acute among African Americans (see Lichter, LeClere, & McLaughlin, 1991; Lichter, McLaughlin, Kephart, & Landry, 1992; Mare & Winship, 1991; South & Lloyd, 1992; Youm, 2000).

Second, women, but not men, are considered less sexually desirable as they age. Our cultural standards still define women's beauty partly in terms of youthful looks, while men's attractiveness is largely defined in terms of power and socioeconomic status, which usually increase with age (Blumstein & Schwartz, 1983; England & Farkas, 1986).

Third, older single women are more likely to have children than are older single men, either because they have custody of children from a previous marriage or because they have had children out of wedlock (Bumpass, Sweet, & Martin, 1990). Children represent a "cost" to a prospective partner from the market-position perspective, making women with children less desirable as partners (Becker, Landes, & Michael, 1977; Bumpass, Sweet, & Martin, 1990; Koo, Suchindran, & Griffith, 1984; Smock, 1990; Sweeney, 1997).

These three factors—the sex ratio, cultural definitions of attractiveness, and the presence of children—put older women in a relatively weaker sex-market position compared to older men. Thus, we would expect older single women to be even more likely than older single men are to have to search farther afield for partners and, therefore, to have their partnering process be less embedded in institutionally organized settings or within their social networks. In fact, owing to the compounding of these factors, we may even expect a curvilinearly negative effect for women; that is, we may expect the effect of age to become progressively more negative for women at older ages. On the other hand, we would expect an overall positive curvilinear effect for men, the likelihood of finding a partner in an institutionally embedded setting decreasing somewhat with age as men leave efficient sex-market settings such as school but then actually increasing at older ages given men's advantage in terms of the sex ratio and cultural definitions of attractiveness.

In addition, we would also expect less relational embeddedness in the partnering process for older women and men compared to their younger counterparts. Since older women are in a weaker market position, they have fewer alternatives in terms of partners and, thus, less bargaining power when it comes to shaping the development of the relationship (see England & Kilbourne, 1990). We would, therefore, expect that they would have to comply with men's sexual attitudes, which studies have shown to be less traditional than women's (see Blumstein & Schwartz, 1983; Laumann, Gagnon, Michael, & Michaels, 1994; Mahay, Laumann, & Michaels, 2001). And, because older women must conform to men's sexual attitudes and older men are better able to shape the development of the relationship according to their less traditional attitudes, we would expect both older women and older men to be less likely than their younger counterparts to have sex within a long-term, committed relationship.

Finally, to the degree that African American women face an even more acute shortage of available men than do white women, we would expect African American women's partnering process to be less embedded than white women's. This perspective also predicts that the negative effect of age on women's market position may be offset by greater socioeconomic resources, which have been shown to be increasingly important and attractive to men and may also increase women's number of contacts with potential partners (Kalmijn, 1994; Mare, 1991; Oppenheimer & Lew, 1995; Schoen & Wooldredge,

1989; South, 1991; Waite & Spitze, 1981). Therefore, we would expect an interaction effect between socioeconomic status and age, where the negative effect of age would be reduced for women of higher socioeconomic status.

THE INFLUENCE OF SEXUAL CULTURE.  On the other hand, the theory of the sex market also acknowledges the effect of culture on sexual partnering; the formation of sexual unions is influenced by cultural norms and symbolic displays of masculinity and femininity (see Butler, 1990; Fenstermaker, West, & Zimmerman, 1991; Simon & Gagnon, 1987; Goffman, 1977; West & Zimmerman, 1987). These cultural constraints are likely to have an opposite effect on the partnering process for older singles, suggesting that the partnering process will actually be more embedded for both older single men and women than for their younger counterparts.

Perhaps the most dramatic societal shift in cultural attitudes and norms regarding sexual partnering occurred during the Sexual Revolution of the late 1960s. Indeed, numerous studies have shown more liberalized sexual attitudes and practices among people who came of age during and after the 1960s (see Baumann & Wilson, 1976; Bell & Chaskes, 1970; Bell & Coughey, 1980; King, Balswick, & Robinson, 1977; Laumann, Gagnon, Michael, & Michaels, 1994; Reiss, 1986; Robinson & Jedlicka, 1982; Robinson, Ziss, Ganza, & Katz, 1991; Scanzoni, Teachman, & Thompson, 1989; Seidman, 1989; Joyner & Laumann, 2001). Given the influence of the Sexual Revolution, we would expect older individuals who came of age before the 1960s to have more traditional or conventional partnering processes than do younger people. More traditional partnering processes tend to be more embedded, such as meeting partners in everyday, institutionally organized, socially preselective settings (school, work, or church) rather than searching farther afield (in bars or through personal ads). Meeting partners through social networks, rather than through self-introduction, is also more traditional. And, in terms of relational embeddedness, it is more traditional to have sex within the context of a long-term, committed relationship. Thus, we would expect the relationship-formation processes of those who came of age before the 1960s to be more embedded in institutionally organized settings, social networks, and long-term, committed relationships.

While we would expect this cohort difference to hold generally for both men and women, we expect to find a larger difference for women since research has found that the effect of the Sexual Revolution on women's attitudes and behavior was more dramatic than it was on men's and that the 1960s marked a decline in the sexual double standard (Robinson, Ziss, Ganza, & Katz, 1991; Sprecher, McKinney, & Orbuch, 1987).

Several other factors that are associated with age are also likely to influence the partnering process through cultural mechanisms rather than through the calculation of costs and benefits. For example, religious participation has been found to increase with age, even after taking into account marriage (Hout & Greeley, 1987; Stolzenberg, Blair-Loy, & Waite, 1995). Women tend to have higher religious participation than do men (de Vaus & McAllister, 1987), and women's religious participation actually increases with divorce and parenthood, which are also positively associated with age (Stolzenberg, Blair-Loy, & Waite, 1995). To the extent that most religions promote traditional lifestyles, particularly when it comes to sexual behavior (Bearman & Bruckner, 2001; Laumann, Gagnon, Michael, & Michaels, 1994), we would, thus, expect older individuals to have more embedded partnering processes.

Older men and women are also less likely to have experienced parental divorce while they were growing up since the dramatic increase in divorce did not begin until the 1970s. Numerous studies have shown that individuals who experienced parental divorce have less traditional sexual attitudes and behavior (Axinn & Thornton, 1996; Booth, Brinkerhoff, & White, 1984; Thornton & Camburn, 1987). For this reason, we would also expect older men and women to have more traditional, embedded partnering processes.

Finally, older singles are more likely to have children, and parenthood has also been shown to be associated with more traditional sexual attitudes (Morgan & Waite, 1987; Trent & South, 1992). Parents may also be more conservative in their partnering processes because they want to set a good example for their children. Thus, we would expect older singles to have more embedded partnering processes. Since single women are more likely to have custody of their children than are single men, we would expect this effect to be larger for women.

Overall, then, owing to cultural influences, such as the Sexual Revolution and age differences in religious participation, the experience of parental divorce, and parenthood, we would expect both older single men and older single women to have more traditional sexual attitudes than do younger singles. Thus, we would expect the partnering processes of those forming sexual unions at older ages to be more embedded in their everyday institutions and social networks and within the context of long-term, committed relationships. We would expect a particularly sharp difference between those who came of age before and those who came of age during or after the 1960s, especially for women.

## Data and Methods

The Chicago Health and Social Life Survey (CHSLS), described in Van Haitsma, Paik, and Laumann (chapter 2 in this volume), is ideal for our purposes here in that it included detailed questions about the three aspects of the intimate-union-formation process described above and asked these questions of people forming unions over a wide age range. In addition, while the NHSLS (Laumann, Gagnon, Michael, & Michaels, 1994) included similar questions, the CHSLS has the advantage of representing a local sex market. As recent studies have recognized (see Lichter, LeClere, & McLaughlin, 1991; Lichter, McLaughlin, Kephart, & Landry, 1992), sex and marriage markets are not national in scope, as has been implicitly assumed in previous research. Intimate-union formation is fundamentally a local process; two people must live within reasonable geographic proximity in order to initiate and develop an intimate relationship.[2] Thus, sexual partnering typically occurs within a geographically bounded area, with the demographic realities, institutions, social-network patterns, and cultural orientations that define partnering opportunities and norms. Since we will be testing the effects of the sex market and cultural norms, it is critical that the data reflect an actual local sex market and cultural milieu.

For our analysis of partnering processes, we use data only for the most recent partnership and include only people who met their most recent partner within the last five years, whose most recent partnership was heterosexual, and who are between twenty and fifty-nine years of age.[3] Thus, the final sample used for our analysis of partnering processes consists of 338 men and 402 women aged twenty to fifty-nine who met their most recent opposite-sex partner within the last five years.

2. While it is possible for two people to *meet* without being in geographic proximity, such as via the telephone or the Internet, they must be in geographic proximity to have a sexual relationship.

3. Since some people may have met their most recent partner twenty years ago or more, in order to reduce period effects we analyze only partnerships that began in the last five years. In addition, restricting our analysis to relationships that began in the last five years reduces the selection bias toward those relationships that ended in marriage, which, because they are likely to last longer than other sexual relationships, would be overrepresented among all partnerships in a cross-sectional sample such as this. Since same-sex partnerships have been found to have different partnering processes than do heterosexual partnerships (see Ellingson & Schroeder, chapter 4 in this volume), and since we do not have sufficient numbers of same-gender partnerships to fully examine the effect of age on both types of partnerships separately, we also restrict our analyses to those whose most recent partnership was heterosexual. Finally, because respondents were asked only about the highest degree already completed and whether they were currently in school, we restricted our analysis to individuals twenty to fifty-nine years of age so that we can distinguish between those who went to college but did not go directly after high school and those who probably did not plan to go to college at all.

## Addressing Sample Selection Bias

In our analysis of age differences in the partnering process, it is possible that a sample selection bias exists, in which those with more traditional sexual attitudes may marry relatively early and remain married throughout the life course (and are, therefore, selected out of our sample of older singles), whereas those with less traditional attitudes or those who are not looking for a marriage partner either marry later or do not marry at all (and are, therefore, overrepresented in our sample of older singles). While there are a variety of techniques for correcting sample selection bias (e.g., Heckman, 1976, 1979; Winship & Mare, 1992), recent work has shown that these often do more harm than good (Stolzenberg & Relles, 1990, 1997). For this analysis, perhaps the most intuitive way to test for selection bias is to examine age differences in the sexual attitudes of those who are currently single. If there is a sample selection bias, we should find that those who are single at older ages have less traditional sexual attitudes. Thus, we conduct a separate analysis of the sexual attitudes of those who are currently single (defined as not currently cohabiting or married and also restricted to those who self-identified as heterosexual). Because this is a cross-sectional sample, we cannot include attitudes as independent variables in our analysis of the partnering process since the CHSLS measured attitudes only at the time of the survey, not when respondents met their most recent partner. The final number of cases for our analysis of sexual attitudes is 360 men and 549 women aged twenty to fifty-nine.

## Sexual Attitudes

The CHSLS asked four questions regarding sexual attitudes that are relevant to the partnering process. First, respondents were asked to agree or disagree with the following statements: "I would not have sex with someone unless I was in love with them"; "My religious beliefs shape and guide my sexual behavior"; and "It is much better for everyone if the man earns the main living and the woman takes care of the home and family" (referred to as *traditional gender ideology*). Response categories ranged from 1 to 4, with 1 labeled *strongly agree,* 2 *agree,* 3 *disagree,* and 4 *strongly disagree.* Respondents were also asked to indicate their approval of "a man and a woman having sexual relations before marriage." Response categories ranged from 1 to 4, with 1 labeled *always wrong,* 2 *almost always wrong,* 3 *wrong only sometimes,* and 4 *not wrong at all.*[4]

4. The direction of all attitude scores is reversed in the analyses, higher scores indicating more traditional sexual attitudes.

## Partnering Processes

INSTITUTIONAL EMBEDDEDNESS. Respondents were asked, "Where did you meet [Partner]?" For the purposes of this analysis, the response categories were recoded into a dichotomous variable: 0 = met partner in a more public, less institutionally embedded setting (e.g., park, beach, mall, street, personal ads, vacation/trip, restaurant, bar, bowling alley, theater, concert, gallery, or museum); 1 = met partner in a more institutionally embedded, socially preselective setting (e.g., school, work, church, family member's home, friend's home, private party, wedding, gym, or voluntary activity).

SOCIAL-NETWORK EMBEDDEDNESS. Respondents were asked, "How many people you knew at the time you and [Partner] met knew [Partner] before you did?" This indicates whether the respondent had any mutual acquaintances when they first met or whether the partner came from within the respondent's social network. For this analysis, the response categories were recoded as either 0 (= had no mutual acquaintances when first met partner) or 1 (= had any mutual acquaintance when first met).

RELATIONAL EMBEDDEDNESS. The CHSLS includes two measures of relational embeddedness. Respondents were asked about the type of relationship that they had with their partner at the time of sexual involvement: "How would you characterize your relationship with [Partner] at the time when you first had sex?" Responses were recoded as 0 (= not in a committed relationship at the time of first sex with that partner) or 1 (= in a committed relationship at the time of first sex with that partner).[5] And respondents were also asked how long they knew their partner before engaging in sex: "Think about the time you first became romantically involved with or began dating or seeing [Partner]. About how long was it between that time and the time you first had sex?" Responses were recoded as 0 (= one month or less) and 1 (= more than one month).

---

5. The original response categories were as follows: 1 = "you paid partner for sex"; 2 = "your partner paid you for sex"; 3 = "your partner was someone you just met"; 4 = "your partner was an acquaintance"; 5 = "your partner was a friend but you had not gone out on a date with him or her"; 6 = "you were seeing or going out with your partner, but not seriously"; 7 = "you were in a serious relationship with your partner but not engaged"; 8 = "you were engaged to your partner"; 9 = "you were married to your partner"; or 10 = "some other relationship (specify)." Those who answered 1–6 were recoded as 0 (= not in a committed relationship at the time of first sex with that partner). Those who answered 7–9 were recoded as 1 (= in a committed relationship at the time of first sex with that partner).

## Independent Variables

AGE. The main independent variable of interest in our analysis of sexual attitudes is AGE, measured in years.[6] In the analysis of partnering processes, we use AGE MET, which is the age at which the respondent met his or her most recent partner (in years). Again, note that we have restricted our sample to include only those who met their most recent partner within the last five years. We use AGE MET$^2$ as a measure of the curvilinear effect of age that was predicted for both men and women by the market-position perspective. Finally, in our analysis of both sexual attitudes and partnering processes, we include SEXREV, a dummy variable reflecting the cohort effect that we would expect under the cultural perspective. This variable is coded as 0 if the respondent came of age (turned fourteen) during or after the Sexual Revolution (1967) and as 1 if the respondent came of age before (see Joyner & Laumann, 2001).

DEMOGRAPHIC VARIABLES. For the analysis of both sexual attitudes and partnering processes, we include dummy variables for race/ethnicity, education level, and socioeconomic background as important demographic variables that may also influence both market position and cultural scripts. Dummy variables for race/ethnicity include NONHISPANIC BLACK and HISPANIC, with NONHISPANIC WHITE as the reference category. Unfortunately, we could not include members of other racial and ethnic groups or further refine the HISPANIC category because there were too few cases. For education level, dummy variables include HIGH SCHOOL DEGREE and SOME COLLEGE OR MORE, with LESS THAN HIGH SCHOOL DEGREE as the reference category.[7] Finally, as a measure of socioeconomic

6. Curvilinear effects of age, measured as AGE$^2$, were tested but were not significant and, therefore, not included in the models predicting sexual attitudes.

7. The CHSLS asked respondents only about the highest degree that they had completed and whether they were currently in school. Thus, those with junior college and associate's degrees and those with bachelor's and graduate degrees as well as those who already have a high school degree and reported being currently in school are all included in the SOME COLLEGE OR MORE category. This may, therefore, be a conservative measure since it does not capture those who may have had some college but are not currently enrolled in school. In addition, this is a measure of current education level rather than of the education level at the time the respondent met his or her most recent partner (which may have been up to five years ago). However, this is more of a problem for those at younger ages since education is typically completed fairly early in the life course. In addition, plans for going to college are typically made several years before one actually attends, and, thus, we felt that current education level was still an important and appropriate measure of socioeconomic status and structural opportunities for meeting partners.

background, we include the dummy variable SES BACKGROUND: PAR-
ENTS' COLLEGE, coded as 0 if neither parent had a college degree and as
1 if either parent had a college degree.

OTHER SEX-MARKET AND CULTURAL INDICATORS. For the analy-
ses of both sexual attitudes and partnering processes, we also include several
other measures of market position and cultural influences that may be associated with age in our models. Because it may affect both market position and
own attitudes toward relationship formation, the dummy variable PREVI-
OUSLY MARRIED was included (in the analysis of partnering processes,
this variable indicates whether respondents were married *at the time they met
their most recent partner*), coded as 0 for never married and as 1 for previously
married. We also included the dummy variable CHILDREN (in the analysis
of partnering processes, this variable indicates whether the respondent had
any children at the time he or she met his or her most recent partner), coded
as 0 for no children and as 1 for any children.[8]

A measure of family background, INTACT, is a dummy variable scored as
0 for respondents who did not live with both parents at age fourteen and as
1 for those who did live with both parents at age fourteen. And RELIGIOUS
AFFILIATION was coded as five dummy variables—MAINLINE PROT-
ESTANT, FUNDAMENTALIST PROTESTANT, ROMAN CATHOLIC/
ORTHODOX, and OTHER, with NO RELIGIOUS AFFILIATION as
the reference category. Because Protestant churches constitute a diverse array of denominations that can have quite different orientations, we follow
Laumann, Gagnon, Michael, and Michaels (1994) in coding Protestants into
two groups. Methodists, Lutherans, Presbyterians, Episcopalians, and members of the United Church of Christ were coded as MAINLINE PROTES-
TANTS. Baptists, Pentecostals, and members of the Churches of Christ and
the Assemblies of God were coded as FUNDAMENTALIST PROTES-
TANT. This latter group is more likely to have an evangelical or fundamentalist worldview and tends to be more conservative (for more on this variable,
see Laumann, Gagnon, Michael, & Michaels [1994, 146–47]).[9]

8. Unfortunately, we did not have information on whether the children were living in the home. Thus, this is a conservative measure since it includes those who had
a child who was not living in the home, while we would expect the greatest effect to
be for those who had a child living in the home.

9. We use respondent's current religion rather than the religion in which respondent was raised because we believe that current religion is more likely to affect behavior—particularly at older ages. We did not use frequency of church attendance
because church attendance is something that is, we believe, more likely to change after meeting a partner than is religious affiliation and we did not have this information
for the time at which the respondent met his or her partner.

Finally, in the analysis of partnering processes we also include two other measures of market position. We include the dummy variable LARGE SO-CIAL NETWORK, which is based on the question, "Some people see themselves as having a great many friends. Others see themselves as having fewer. Think about the people you consider to be your friends, both your closest friends and the people with whom you are pretty good friends. About how many friends would you say that you have?" Those who had fewer than ten friends were coded as 0, those with ten or more friends as 1. In addition to measuring the size of one's social network, this variable may also measure basic outgoingness or social competency.

We also include the dummy variable ATTRACTIVENESS, which is based on responses to the question, "[On a scale of 1 to 7, where 1 is very unattractive and 7 is very attractive], how would you rate yourself in terms of attractiveness compared to other [men/women] in your age group?" (If the partner in question was not current, interviewers added the phrase "during the time you were involved with [Partner]?") Those who responded that they were less than average or average (1–4) were coded as 0, those who responded that they were more attractive than average (5–7) as 1. While this measure may not be completely objective, it nevertheless measures a respondent's level of confidence about his or her attractiveness to others and is likely to reflect the response of others to that person's attractiveness.

## Analytic Strategy

First, we use OLS regression for our analysis of age differences in sexual attitudes among singles in order to test whether there is a selection effect. In the first model, we examine the effect of age after controlling only for pooling effects. In the second model, we include controls for race/ethnicity, education level, parent's education level, coming of age before the Sexual Revolution, previously married, ever had any children, religious affiliation, and whether the respondent lived with both parents at age fourteen.

We then use logistic regression to test our hypotheses regarding the effect of the age at which one meets one's partner on the four measures of the partnering process described above. We first estimate models including the continuous variable for age at which the respondent met his or her partner (AGE MET) and the cohort variable for coming of age before the Sexual Revolution (SEXREV), along with the basic demographic variables. By including both the continuous variable for the effect of age met and the cohort variable for those who came of age before versus after the Sexual Revolution, we hope to gain some insight into the relative effects of market position and sexual culture. For the continuous age–met variable, we examined both linear and curvilinear effects. Where curvilinear effects were not found, we include only the linear effects of AGE MET in the model. In the second model, we included other measures of market position, such as divorced, presence of children, social network, and attractiveness, in order to examine the extent to which they mediate the effect of age or cohort. Finally, we also tested for interaction effects between AGE MET and the education-level variables and between AGE MET and the race/ethnicity variables.

For the analysis of both sexual attitudes and partnering processes, all the models were run for men and women separately because much of the theoretical framework involves within-gender comparisons and different effects of many of the independent variables on women and men. For all analyses, we pooled the five samples included in the data set and controlled for pooling effects by including all significant main effects of sample and significant interaction effects between sample and each of the other independent variables in the model.

## Results

### Sexual Attitudes of Singles

Table 5.1 presents the means and standard deviations of each of the sexual-attitude variables. Consistent with previous studies discussed above, this table reveals that, on average, women have more traditional sexual attitudes than do men, with the exception that, on average, men have more traditional *gender* ideologies than do women (see, e.g., Thornton, 1989). The differences between men and women are all significant at the $p < .05$ level. For women, the average response to the statement, "I would not have sex with someone unless I was in love with them," was closest to "agree," while the average response for men was closer to "disagree." The average response to the statement, "My religious beliefs shape and guide my sexual behavior," was halfway between "disagree" and "agree" for women and closer to "disagree" for men. On average, both men and women said that they thought that premarital sex was "wrong only sometimes," but men's average response fell somewhat closer to "not wrong at all" than did women's. Finally, the average response to the statement, "It is much better for everyone if the man earns the main living and the woman takes care of the home and family," was closest to "disagree," although men's average was slightly closer to "agree" than was women's.

Table 5.2 presents the results from the OLS regression of sexual attitudes for single men and women separately. Model 1 presents the regression of the sexual-attitude variables on age alone, controlling only for pooling effects, while model 2 presents the effect of age after controlling for race/ethnicity, education level, parents' education, coming of age before the Sexual Revo-

Table 5.1 Means and Standard Deviations of Sexual Attitudes, by
Gender: Single<sup>a</sup> Chicago Adults, Aged 20–59, CHSLS, 1995–97

| Variable | Women | Men | P-Value of Difference between Men and Women |
|---|---|---|---|
| | Means (SD) | | |
| Would not have sex unless in love (strongly disagree = 1; strongly agree = 4): | | | |
| Mean | 2.862 | 2.425 | .001 |
| Standard deviation | (.038) | (.044) | |
| N | 537 | 351 | |
| Religious beliefs shape sexual behavior (strongly disagree = 1; strongly agree = 4): | | | |
| Mean | 2.500 | 2.288 | .001 |
| Standard deviation | (.038) | (.044) | |
| N | 536 | 351 | |
| Premarital sex is wrong (not wrong at all = 1; always wrong = 4): | | | |
| Mean | 1.996 | 1.776 | .01 |
| Standard deviation | (.053) | (.059) | |
| N | 537 | 353 | |
| Traditional gender ideology (strongly disagree = 1; strongly agree = 4): | | | |
| Mean | 2.125 | 2.284 | .05 |
| Standard deviation | (.043) | (.049) | |
| N | 535 | 352 | |

<sup>a</sup>Attitude analyses are restricted to those who are currently single (not cohabiting or dating) and those who self-identified as heterosexual.

lution, divorced, children, religious affiliation, intact family background, and pooling effects.[10]

Recall that, under the selection effect, we would expect older singles to have less traditional sexual attitudes and gender-role ideologies than their younger counterparts. Results show that, for women, age actually has a *positive* effect on traditional sexual attitudes; older single women are significantly more likely to say that they would not have sex unless in love, that religious beliefs shape their sexual behavior, and that premarital sex is wrong and to have a traditional gender ideology, compared to their younger counterparts. While the effect of age on some of women's sexual attitudes is reduced after controlling for other factors in model 2, in no case is the effect of age negative. For men, there are no significant effects of age except that older single

10. Curvilinear effects of age were tested but were not significant.

Table 5.2 Unstandardized Coefficients from the OLS Regression of Sexual Attitudes on Selected Independent Variables: Single Chicago Adults, Aged 20–59, CHSLS, 1995–97

| | Would Not Have Sex unless in Love | | Religious Beliefs Shape Sexual Behavior | | Premarital Sex Is Wrong | | Traditional Gender Ideology | |
|---|---|---|---|---|---|---|---|---|
| | Model 1 | Model 2 | Model 1 | Model 2 | Model 1 | Model 2 | Model 1 | Model 2 |
| **Women:** | | | | | | | | |
| Age | .012** | .014* | .014*** | .012† | .021*** | .008 | .022*** | .024*** |
| | (.003) | (.006) | (.003) | (.007) | (.005) | (.009) | (.004) | (.007) |
| Constant | 2.392 | 2.161 | 2.073 | 1.255 | 1.378 | 1.539 | 1.403 | 1.157 |
| N | 537 | 537 | 536 | 536 | 537 | 537 | 535 | 535 |
| **Men:** | | | | | | | | |
| Age | −.005 | −.002 | .001 | .007 | −.003 | −.003 | .018*** | .016* |
| | (.004) | (.007) | (.004) | (.007) | (.006) | (.010) | (.004) | (.008) |
| Constant | 2.606 | 2.173 | 2.277 | 1.414 | 1.855 | 1.701 | 1.635 | 1.613 |
| N | 351 | 351 | 351 | 351 | 353 | 353 | 352 | 352 |

*Note:* Numbers in parentheses are standard errors. Model 1 controls only for sample and any interaction effects with sample and age. Model 2 adds controls for race/ethnicity, education level, parents' education, coming of age before the Sexual Revolution, divorced, children, religious affiliation, parents divorced, and any other significant interaction effects between sample and the other independent variables. Analyses include only those who are currently single (not currently cohabiting or married) and those who self-identified as heterosexual.

*$p < .05$ (two–tailed test).

**$p < .01$ (two–tailed test).

***$p < .001$ (two–tailed test).

†$p < .10$ (two–tailed test).

men are more likely to have a traditional gender ideology than are younger single men. Thus, older singles do not have less traditional sexual attitudes or gender-role ideologies than younger singles, as we would have expected if there was a selection effect. In fact, as predicted by the cultural perspective, even among singles, older women in fact have *more* traditional sexual attitudes than their younger counterparts, and the effect of age is not significant for men.

In terms of gender differences, it is interesting to note that, at the youngest ages, men's and women's sexual attitudes are very similar. For example, calculations from model 1[11] show that the estimated average responses to the statement, "I would not have sex unless in love," for single men and women at age twenty are very close, at 2.5 for men and 2.6 for women (halfway between "agree" and "disagree"). However, the sexual attitudes of men and

11. $Y = \alpha + \beta_{AGE} \times AGE$, calculations not shown.

women diverge at older ages; older single women have significantly more traditional sexual attitudes than their younger counterparts, while older men do not. Next, we examine age differences in the actual partnering process.

## The Process of Partnering

First, in our sample of people who met their most recent partner in the last five years, about 60 percent of both men and women met their partner in an institutionally embedded, socially preselective setting, such as work, school, church, or a family member's or friend's home. And about 63 percent met their partner through their social network or had mutual acquaintances with their partner when they first met. These figures are consistent with the results from the national study, the NHSLS, conducted in 1992 (see Laumann, Gagnon, Michael, & Michaels, 1994). For means and standard deviations of all the variables used in this analysis, see appendix table 5A.1.

In terms of relational embeddedness, just over half of women were in a committed relationship with their partner when they first had sex with him, while the equivalent percentage is somewhat lower for men. In addition, about one-third of women had dated their partner for more than a month before sex, while the equivalent percentage is only about one-quarter for men. These gender differences have been found in many other surveys and could be due to several factors, including reporting bias and differences in perceptions and definitions of dating relationships (Laumann, Gagnon, Michael, & Michaels, 1994). Because all our models are run for men and women separately, gender differences in the level of reporting for these variables should not affect our analyses of age differences.

## Institutional Embeddedness

The logistic regression analyses (for coefficients, see appendix table 5A.2) reveal very different age patterns in the level of institutional embeddedness for men and women. While there is a curvilinear effect of AGE MET on the likelihood of meeting in an institutionally embedded setting for both women and men, it is negative for women and positive for men. The comparison of the effect of AGE MET for men and women can perhaps best be seen in figure 5.1, which depicts the relation between the age at which one met one's most recent partner (within the last five years) and the probability of meeting that partner in an institutionally embedded setting.[12]

For women, the probability of meeting one's partner in an institutionally

---

12.  These estimated probabilities are derived from model 1 ($p = e^y/[1 + e^y]$), holding all other variables except AGE constant at their respective means.

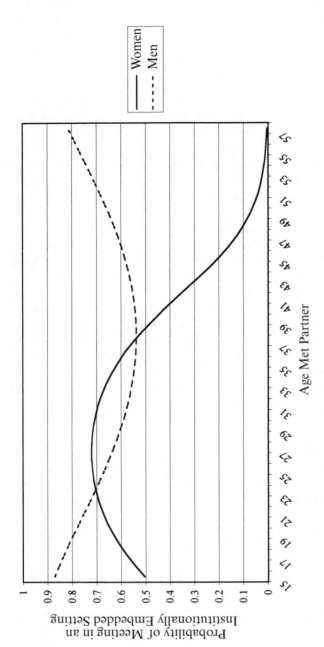

Figure 5.1. Probability of meeting in an institutionally embedded setting by gender and age met partner, Chicago adults, aged twenty to fifty-nine, CHSLS (1995–97).

*Note:* The lines for those who came of age before and during or after the Sexual Revolution overlap between the ages of thirty-eight and forty-two because this is a measure of age, while the x-axis is age met most recent partner, and our analysis is restricted to those who met their partner in the last five years. Thus, those who were forty-three at the time of the survey would be categorized as coming of age before the Sexual Revolution, although they could have met their partner when they were as young as thirty-eight and still be included in our sample.

embedded setting increases from about .50 at the youngest ages up to .72 at age twenty-seven, after which it declines fairly rapidly. For men, the probability of meeting in an institutionally embedded setting declines from .87 at the youngest ages to .54 at age thirty-seven, after which it actually increases. The patterns follow those predicted by the market-position perspective, in which women's market position becomes weaker as they age while men's becomes stronger. Thus, older women must look farther afield in their search for a partner as they age, while men are more likely to find available partners in their everyday institutional settings as they age. There is no significant effect of coming of age before the Sexual Revolution, as would have been predicted by the cultural hypothesis. Thus, despite their more traditional attitudes, older women are more likely than are their younger counterparts to meet their partners in less socially preselective, institutionally embedded settings, such as parks, bars, nightclubs, or restaurants. In these venues they are less likely to meet partners with whom they have a great deal in common or even with whom they share similar social characteristics, such as age, race, education, and religion, which have been found to be so important for developing intimacy and, ultimately, predictive of marriage.

After controlling for the other variables (in model 2), we found that African American men were more likely to meet their partner in an institutionally embedded setting than were white men, something that we would expect given the relatively more advantaged market position of African American men (a position that is due to the sex ratio), particularly after controlling for socioeconomic status. In model 2, we also found that women from more advantaged socioeconomic backgrounds are more likely to meet their partner in an institutionally embedded setting, perhaps because of their better market position as well as greater access to private, more socially preselective settings, such as private clubs, or work environments that are more conducive to finding a similar mate and developing a relationship.

In addition, for women, having a child significantly increases the likelihood of meeting a partner in an institutionally embedded setting rather than a more public one. This finding contradicts the market-position perspective that children represent a "cost" to a prospective spouse and that women with children must search farther afield than women without children. However, it makes sense from the cultural perspective when we consider the culturally defined rules for the appropriate places for mothers to go with their children and the fact that going to places where there are likely to be many other singles, such as a bar, becomes much more difficult when one must first find a baby-sitter. As predicted, the effect of having a child is not significant for men, most likely because it is usually the mother who actually has custody of the child.

There was another cultural influence on where people meet their partners: religious affiliation. Fundamentalist Protestants in particular are more likely than are those with no religious affiliation to meet their partner in an institutionally embedded setting. This may be due either to fundamentalist Protestants' more conservative sexual attitudes or to the fact that more of their social activities are church related and, thus, take place in an institutionally organized setting. In addition, some social institutions, such as churches, are beginning to provide opportunities for older singles to meet similar others in a safe environment, such as church-sponsored singles' clubs.

Controlling for these other factors, however, does not eliminate the curvilinear effects of AGE MET for either men or women. Thus, the age pattern follows that predicted by the market-position perspective. We found no significant interaction effects between either the linear or the curvilinear effects of AGE MET and the education-level or race/ethnicity variables.

## *Social-Network Embeddedness*

How does age affect the social-network embeddedness of sexual partnering? We find that the likelihood of social-network embeddedness in the partnering process declines significantly with age for women but that it is significant for men only after controlling for the market-position and cultural variables (for logistic regression coefficients, see appendix table 5A.3). Although the effect of age is not curvilinear, as we might have expected, the results are consistent with the market-position perspective. In general, older singles must search for partners outside their existing social networks, probably both because their networks are likely to contain fewer other singles than they did when they were younger and because they are now more likely to meet their partners in public settings, where they are less likely to know people in common. As expected, however, this effect of age is somewhat mitigated for men, who experience a more favorable sex ratio at older ages.

However, the results show that, for women, there are also opposing cultural influences, in that women who came of age before the Sexual Revolution are significantly more likely to have mutual acquaintances when they first met their partner. In fact, women who came of age before the Sexual Revolution are 2.7 (= exp[1.007]; see table 5A.3) times more likely to have met their partner through social networks than are women who came of age during or after, after controlling for the other variables in the model. Also consistent with the cultural perspective, the effect of coming of age before the Sexual Revolution is not significant for men.[13]

---

13. Because we hypothesized that coming of age before the Sexual Revolution would have a positive effect on social-network embeddedness, a one-tailed test is most appropriate for determining significance. Using the one-tailed test, the effect is significant at the .05 level for women but not significant for men.

The effects of AGE MET and SEXREV on the probability of social-network embeddedness is graphically represented in figure 5.2.[14] The effect of coming of age before the Sexual Revolution is included in the graph only for women since it is not statistically significant for men.[15] This graph shows that the probability of having mutual acquaintances with one's partner is similar for men and women, at about .80 for women and .71 for men, at the youngest ages. However, while for women the probability of social-network embeddedness declines significantly with age, to .42 for women who met their partner at age forty, for men the probability does not decline significantly and is .57 at age forty.

As mentioned above, however, women who came of age before the Sexual Revolution have a significantly higher probability of meeting their partners through social networks than do women who came of age during or after. Those who came of age before were forty-three years of age or older at the time of the survey. Because those included in this analysis may have met their most recent partner up to five years ago, those who came of age before the Sexual Revolution could have been as young as thirty-eight when they met their most recent partner. For women who came of age before and met their partner at age forty, the probability of social-network embeddedness jumps to about .66, although it still declines with age, indicating the continuing conflict that older women face between their weaker market position and their more traditional sexual attitudes.

In model 2, we also find for women positive effects of another cultural influence: religious affiliation. Specifically, fundamentalist Protestant women, and, to a lesser extent, Catholic women, are more likely to have their partnering processes embedded in their social networks than are those with no religious affiliation. This is what we would expect from the cultural perspective; adherents of more traditional faiths form unions in more traditional ways. Religious affiliation may also have this effect because it provides a more extensive network of acquaintances through which to safely meet partners, especially partners who have the same religious affiliation and who are likely

14. Probabilities are calculated from model 1 of table 5A.3, holding all other variables constant at their respective means.

15. The lines for those who came of age before vs. during or after the Sexual Revolution overlap between the ages of thirty-eight and forty-two because this is a measure of age, while the *x*-axis is the age at which respondents met their most recent partner, and our analysis is restricted to those who met their partner in the last five years. Thus, those who were forty-three years of age at the time of the survey would be categorized as coming of age before the Sexual Revolution, although they could have met their partner when they were as young as thirty-eight and still be included in our sample.

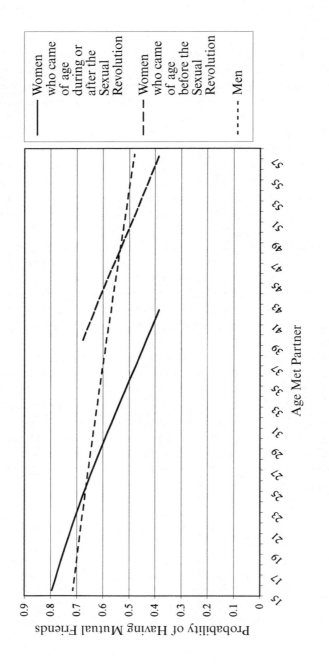

Figure 5.2. Probability of having mutual acquaintances when met partner by gender, age met partner, and cohort, Chicago adults, aged twenty to fifty-nine, CHSLS (1995–97).

*Note:* See figure 5.1.

to share a common worldview. However, we found for men no significant effect of religious affiliation, which is likely due to the fact that women are more involved in church than are men (de Vaus & McAllister, 1987) and are also more likely to say that their religious beliefs influence their sexual behavior (see table 5.1).

Overall, however, while coming of age before the Sexual Revolution and religious affiliation appear to have some protective effect, women's partnering processes are still less embedded in their social networks as they age, which means that they are less likely to share important social characteristics and interests with their partner and also that they are likely to have less information about their partner, fewer stakeholders to support the relationship, and fewer sources of social control over their partner. As discussed above, research has shown that these factors make the relationship less stable, more tenuous, and, ultimately, less likely to lead to marriage. We found no significant interaction effects between AGE MET and the variables for education level or race/ethnicity.

## Relational Embeddedness

Finally, how does age affect relational embeddedness in the partnering process? Results reveal a similar pattern of age to that which we found for social-network embeddedness (see appendix tables 5A.4 and 5A.5).

The likelihood of dating more than one month before sex with a partner declines significantly with age met for women but not for men. While this pattern of relational embeddedness is consistent with the market-position perspective, in which women have less bargaining power in the relationship as they age owing to their declining market position, cultural influences also have a significant, and opposite, effect. Women who came of age before the Sexual Revolution are 6.3 (= exp[1.833]; see model 1 of table 5A.4) times more likely to date for more than one month before sexual involvement with their partner than are women who came of age during or after. For men, the effect of coming of age before the Sexual Revolution is positive, but not significant. This is also consistent with the cultural perspective, which predicted a stronger effect of the Sexual Revolution on women than on men.

These effects are graphically depicted in figure 5.3. Note that women have an overall higher probability of having dated for more than one month before sex. For women at the youngest ages, the probability of dating for more than one month before sex is .76, compared to .52 for men at the youngest ages. However, for women, the probability of dating for one month or more declines rapidly and significantly with age, to only .44 at age forty. For men, the decline in probability is not steep or significant and, therefore, only somewhat lower than for women at age forty. Thus, women engage in riskier

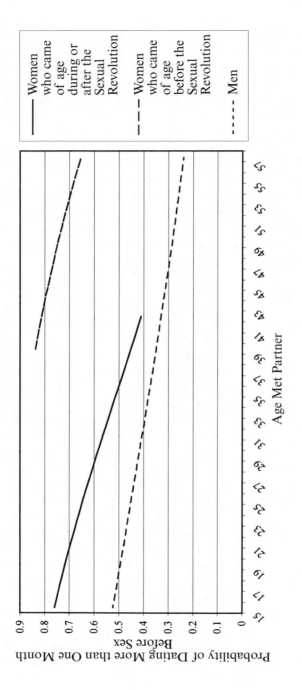

Figure 5.3. Probability of dating more than one month before sex with partner by gender, age met partner, and cohort, Chicago adults, aged twenty to fifty-nine, CHSLS (1995–1997).

*Note:* See figure 5.1.

partnering behavior as they age; they have less information about their partner owing to the short interval of dating before sexual involvement, and this is compounded by the fact that they are less likely to have met their partner in a socially preselective, institutionally embedded setting or to have mutual acquaintances who could provide outside sources of information about, and social control over, their partner. This could lead to greater risk of exposure to sexually transmitted infection (STI) or violence. However, again, coming of age before the Sexual Revolution appears to have a protective effect for women, increasing their probability of dating more than a month before sex to .83 at age forty, although it still declines with age.

Another aspect of relational embeddedness is the level of commitment at the time of sex. Again, consistent with the market-position hypothesis, the likelihood of being in a committed relationship at the time of sexual involvement with one's partner declines with age for women (see table 5A.5). For men, the effect of age met is actually curvilinearly positive on the likelihood of being in a committed relationship at the time of first sex with partner. However, as with the length of time dating, women who came of age before the Sexual Revolution are much more likely to have sex within the context of a committed relationship. These women are 4.5 (= exp[1.502]; see table 5A.5, model 1) times more likely to be in a committed relationship at the time of first sex with their partner than are women who came of age during or after the Sexual Revolution.

Figure 5.4 shows that the probability of being in a committed relationship at the time of sexual involvement with one's partner is very similar for men and women at the youngest ages, at about .59. For women, the probability declines steeply with age, to about .20 at age forty.

However, coming of age before the Sexual Revolution increases women's probability of being in a committed relationship at the time of sex to .55 at age forty, although, again, the probability still declines with age. Thus, the realities of the sex market and the cultural scripts of those who came of age before the Sexual Revolution are at odds with one another, pulling single women in their forties and fifties in opposite directions when it comes to developing sexual relationships. For men, figure 5.4 shows that the probability of being in a committed relationship decreases until age thirty-five, when it reaches a low of .16. However, after that age, the probability increases rapidly.

## Discussion

By analyzing differences in the process of relationship formation over a wide age range, we have shown that how people meet partners and develop intimate unions varies systematically with age and in different ways for men and

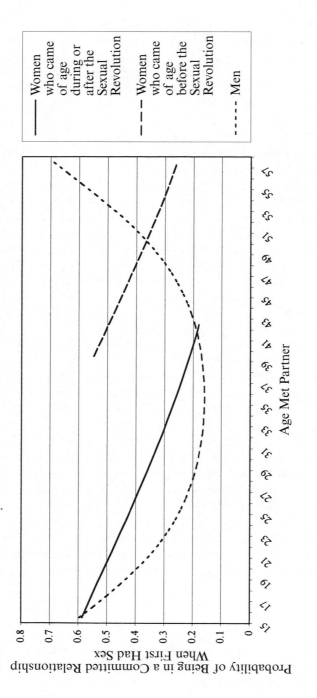

Figure 5.4. Probability of being in a committed relationship when first had sex with partner by gender, age met partner, and cohort, Chicago adults, aged twenty to fifty-nine, CHSLS (1995–1997).

*Note:* See figure 5.1.

women. In fact, we found that, among women, the partnering processes that are more prevalent at older ages are likely to reduce the probability that the relationship will lead to marriage, whereas older men's partnering processes are more likely to lead to marriage.

Specifically, consistent with the market-position perspective, women forming relationships at older ages are less likely than are their younger counterparts to meet their partner in a socially preselective, institutionally embedded setting and are, thus, less likely to share the same religion, education level, age, or cultural worldview with that person, characteristics known to be important in selecting a marriage partner. For men, however, the likelihood of meeting a partner in their everyday, institutionally embedded settings actually increases with age after the late thirties, reflecting their greater advantage in the sex market.

Again consistent with the market-position perspective, women forming relationships at older ages are also less likely than are their younger counterparts to have mutual acquaintances with their partner when they first meet. In other words, they are less likely to meet partners from within their social networks. Thus, they have fewer outside sources of information about their partner, making it less likely that they will share important social characteristics and cultural worldviews and more likely that they will have fewer stakeholders who can help support and maintain the relationship. There is no significant effect of age on the social-network embeddedness of the partnering process for men, however, except after controlling for other sex-market and cultural variables.

Finally, women's partnering processes are also less likely to be embedded in long-term, committed relationships with age. Not only does this reduce the likelihood that older women's relationships will lead to marriage, but it may also increase their exposure to STIs or physical violence. The shorter duration of dating before sexual involvement means that older women will have less information about their partner, which is compounded by the fact that the relationship is also less likely to be embedded in institutions or social networks that could provide outside sources of information and social control that would reduce these risks. Older men, however, are not significantly less likely to have dated for a month or more before sexual involvement with their partner, and the likelihood of being in a committed relationship at the time of sexual involvement actually increases for them after age thirty-five.

Consistent with the cultural perspective, however, women who came of age before the Sexual Revolution are significantly more likely to have met their partner within their social network and to have sex within the context of a more long-term, committed relationship. Thus, older women are pulled between the competing pressures of their weaker position in the sex market and their more traditional sexual attitudes. This occurs at a time when there is little social or institutional support for dating at older ages, providing fewer culturally sanctioned guidelines for how to act (see Rodgers & Conrad, 1986). Our results also suggest that there is greater potential for conflict between men and women in the partnering process at older ages since the gender differences in singles' sexual attitudes increase with age.

Ultimately, this analysis highlights the importance of integrating the market-position and the cultural perspectives on relationship formation, a move that clearly helps us more fully understand the experiences of women and men forming relationships at older ages as well as why the likelihood of marriage declines with age, particularly for women. In addition, we show that, as growing numbers of people enter the sex market at older ages, either because of the later age at first marriage or because of the high level of divorce, the way in which the partnering process varies with age is important for understanding future trends in marriage and remarriage and, thus, the aspects of the quality of life associated with marriage. For example, both married men and married women are happier, have lower levels of mortality, enjoy more active and satisfying sex lives, and have greater wealth than do their single counterparts (Laumann, Gagnon, Michael, & Michaels, 1994; Marks & Lambert, 1998; Mastekaasa, 1994; Mirowsky & Ross, 1989; Waite, 1995; Waite & Gallagher, 2000). In addition, among those in late middle age, married couples have higher levels of physical, mental, and emotional functioning compared to singles (Waite & Hughes, 1999). Children of married couples also tend to be better off financially, have more supervision, and have higher school achievement, social capital, and levels of health (Angel & Worobey, 1988; McLanahan & Sandefur, 1994; Waite & Gallagher, 2000). Thus, the ability to form committed, enduring relationships at older ages has a number of important consequences for both individuals and society as a whole. Growing numbers of singles at older ages may increase the costs of public health-care services and financial assistance.

On the other hand, forming new partnerships may not be as beneficial for older women, given the lower quality of their pool of potential partners. In addition, marrying at older ages may be associated with a loss of feelings of independence for women and is likely to create the added stress of integrating families from previous marriages (Cherlin, 1978; Rodgers & Conrad, 1986).

While the analysis is limited by the cross-sectional nature of the data and the small sample size, it clearly reveals the importance of studying the partnering processes across the full life course and indicates a need for further collection of data on the partnering process at older ages. The proportion of people who are single at older ages is already large, and recent studies have indicated that the age at first marriage continues to rise. Thus, it is important that our research reflect these changes and seek to better understand how this affects the processes and outcomes of relationship formation.

# Appendix

Table 5A.1 Means and Standard Deviations for Variables in the Analysis of Union-Formation Processes, by Gender: Chicago Adults, Aged 20–59, CHSLS, 1995–97

| Variable | Description | Mean (SD) Women | Men |
|---|---|---|---|
| **Dependent variables:** | | | |
| Institutional embeddedness | Met in a private, socially pre-selective setting[a] = 1, met in a public, less socially pre-selective setting[a] = 0 | .608 (.489) | .618 (.487) |
| Social-network embeddedness | Had any mutual acquaintances with partner when met = 1, had no mutual acquaintances with partner when met = 0 | .629 (.484) | .624 (.485) |
| **Relationship embeddedness:** | | | |
| Commitment before first sex with partner | In a committed relationship when had sex with partner = 1, not in a committed relationship when had sex with partner = 0 | .558 (.497) | .421 (.494) |
| Time dating before first sex | Dating more than 1 month when had sex with partner = 1, dating 1 month or less when had sex with partner = 0 | .355 (.479) | .243 (.430) |
| **Independent variables:** | | | |
| AGE MET | Age at which respondent met most recent partner (years)[c] | 27.9 (7.6) | 29.2 (9.1) |
| SEXREV | Turned 14 before 1967 = 1, turned 14 in 1967 or later = 0 | .067 (.251) | .101 (.301) |
| NONHISPANIC BLACK | Non-Hispanic black | .271 (.445) | .269 (.444) |
| HISPANIC | Hispanic | .284 (.451) | .305 (.461) |
| HIGH SCHOOL DEGREE | Had a high school degree | .226 (.419) | .299 (.458) |
| SOME COLLEGE OR MORE | Had some college or vocational school after high school | .587 (.493) | .518 (.500) |
| SES BACKGROUND: PARENTS' COLLEGE | Either parent has college degree = 1, neither parent has college degree = 0 | .326 (.469) | .287 (.453) |
| PREVIOUSLY MARRIED | Previously married when met partner = 1, never married when met partner = 0 | .251 (.434) | .213 (.410) |
| CHILDREN | Had at least one child when met partner = 1, had no children when met partner = 0 | .326 (.469) | .266 (.443) |
| LARGE SOCIAL NETWORK | Has 10 friends or more = 1, has less than 10 friends = 0 | .351 (.478) | .459 (.499) |
| ATTRACTIVENESS | Rates self as more attractive than average = 1, rates self as average or less attractive = 0 | .704 (.457) | .609 (.489) |
| MAINLINE PROTESTANT | Episcopalian, Methodist, Lutheran, Presbyterian | .124 (.330) | .101 (.301) |

*continued*

| Variable | Description | Mean (SD) Women | Men |
|---|---|---|---|
| FUNDAMENTALIST PROTESTANT | Baptist, Pentecostal, Apostolic, Church of Christ | .249 (.433) | .263 (.441) |
| ROMAN CATHOLIC/ ORTHODOX | Roman Catholic or Orthodox | .430 (.496) | .426 (.495) |
| OTHER | Other religions | .055 (.228) | .071 (.257) |
| INTACT | Lived with both biological parents at age 14 = 1, did not live with both biological parents at age 14 = 0 | .629 (.484) | .678 (.468) |

[a]Work, school, church, gym, family member's home, friend's home, private party, wedding, voluntary activity.
[b]Park, beach, mall, street, personal ads, vacation/trip, restaurant, bar, bowling alley, theater, concert, gallery, museum.
[c]All analyses are restricted to those who met their partner in the last five years.

Table 5A.2 Coefficients from the Logistic Regression of Having Met Partner in an Institutionally Embedded Setting[a] on Selected Independent Variables: Chicago Adults, Aged 20–59, CHSLS, 1995–97

| Independent Variables | Women Model 1 | Model 2 | Men Model 1 | Model 2 |
|---|---|---|---|---|
| Age effects: | | | | |
| AGE MET (years) | .371* (.147) | .304$^\dagger$ (.155) | −.261* (.111) | −.320** (.119) |
| AGE MET$^2$ (years$^2$) | −.007** (.003) | −.006* (.003) | .003$^\dagger$ (.002) | .004* (.002) |
| SEXREV | .934 (.737) | 1.079 (.766) | .151 (.779) | −.150 (.850) |
| Demographic variables: | | | | |
| NONHISPANIC BLACK | .062 (.403) | −.267 (.461) | .484 (.421) | 1.108* (.551) |
| HISPANIC | .366 (.349) | .183 (.386) | −.398 (.351) | −.276 (.387) |
| HIGH SCHOOL DEGREE | .374 (.357) | .389 (.370) | −.132 (.368) | −.083 (.390) |
| SOME COLLEGE OR MORE | .304 (.337) | .447 (.360) | .122 (.383) | .081 (.404) |
| SES BACKGROUND: PARENTS' COLLEGE | .550$^\dagger$ (.325) | .719* (.343) | .206 (.319) | .115 (.337) |

Table 5A.2 *continued*

| Independent Variables | Women Model 1 | Women Model 2 | Men Model 1 | Men Model 2 |
|---|---|---|---|---|
| Other marriage-market and cultural indicators: | | | | |
| PREVIOUSLY MARRIED | | −.106 | | .738[†] |
| | | (.355) | | (.397) |
| CHILDREN | | .813[*] | | −.366 |
| | | (.348) | | (.377) |
| LARGE SOCIAL NETWORK | | −.077 | | .055 |
| | | (.298) | | (.264) |
| ATTRACTIVENESS | | .014 | | −.146 |
| | | (.256) | | (.277) |
| Religion: | | | | |
| MAINLINE PROTESTANT | | .467 | | −.222 |
| | | (.453) | | (.543) |
| FUNDAMENTALIST PROTESTANT | | .933[*] | | −.987[*] |
| | | (.454) | | (.497) |
| ROMAN CATHOLIC/ORTHODOX | | .392 | | −.493 |
| | | (.372) | | (.422) |
| OTHER | | .676 | | .808 |
| | | (.608) | | (.686) |
| INTACT | | −.076 | | .076 |
| | | (.256) | | (.293) |
| Constant | −4.610[*] | −4.063[†] | 4.924[**] | 6.283[**] |
| | (2.051) | (2.237) | (1.730) | (1.937) |
| Chi-square | 32.45[**] | 49.10[**] | 22.47[*] | 41.16[**] |
| Degrees of freedom | 13 | 23 | 11 | 22 |
| N | 375 | 375 | 322 | 322 |

*Note:* Numbers in parentheses are standard errors. Analysis is restricted to those who met their partner in the last five years.

[a]Met in an institutionally organized setting (e.g., family member's home, friend's home, private party, wedding, work, school, gym, voluntary activity) vs. meeting in a more public, less institutionally organized setting (e.g., beach, mall, street, personal ads, vacation/trip, restaurant, bar, bowling alley, theater, concert, gallery, museum).

*$p < .05$ (two-tailed test).

**$p < .01$ (two-tailed test).

***$p < .001$ (two-tailed test).

†$p < .10$ (two-tailed test).

Table 5A.3 Coefficients from the Logistic Regression of Having Mutual Acquaintances When Met Partner on Selected Independent Variables: Chicago Adults, Aged 20–59, CHSLS, 1995–97

| Independent Variables | Women | | Men | |
|---|---|---|---|---|
| | Model 1 | Model 2 | Model 1 | Model 2 |
| Age effects: | | | | |
| AGE MET (years) | −.068*** | −.068** | −.024 | −.047* |
| | (.018) | (.022) | (.020) | (.023) |
| AGE MET² (years²)[a] | . . . | . . . | . . . | . . . |
| SEXREV | 1.007† | 1.058† | .070 | .477 |
| | (.526) | (.544) | (.577) | (.597) |
| Demographic variables: | | | | |
| Race/ethnicity: | | | | |
| NONHISPANIC BLACK | −.128 | −.466 | .378 | .899† |
| | (.281) | (.368) | (.337) | (.469) |
| HISPANIC | −.281 | −.523 | −.458 | −.190 |
| | (.307) | (.354) | (.348) | (.397) |
| Education: | | | | |
| HIGH SCHOOL DEGREE | −.194 | −.204 | .080 | .183 |
| | (.344) | (.349) | (.352) | (.375) |
| SOME COLLEGE OR MORE | .006 | .083 | .032 | −.066 |
| | (.320) | (.336) | (.374) | (.394) |
| SES BACKGROUND: PARENTS' COLLEGE | .173 | .190 | .428 | .568† |
| | (.275) | (.281) | (.327) | (.343) |
| Other marriage-market and cultural indicators: | | | | |
| PREVIOUSLY MARRIED | | .013 | | −.440 |
| | | (.320) | | (.385) |
| CHILDREN | | .058 | | .584 |
| | | (.300) | | (.385) |
| LARGE SOCIAL NETWORK | | .251 | | .192 |
| | | (.244) | | (.262) |
| ATTRACTIVENESS | | .210 | | .278 |
| | | (.241) | | (.284) |
| Religion: | | | | |
| MAINLINE PROTESTANT | | .086 | | −.309 |
| | | (.416) | | (.532) |
| FUNDAMENTALIST PROTESTANT | | .830* | | −.758 |
| | | (.402) | | (.488) |
| ROMAN CATHOLIC/ORTHODOX | | .661† | | −.165 |
| | | (.346) | | (.412) |
| OTHER | | −.142 | | .084 |
| | | (.529) | | (.588) |
| INTACT | | −.168 | | .569† |
| | | (.243) | | (.305) |

| Independent Variables | Women | | Men | |
|---|---|---|---|---|
| | Model 1 | Model 2 | Model 1 | Model 2 |
| Constant | 2.469*** | 1.944* | 1.141 | 1.283 |
| | (.613) | (.752) | (.702) | (.847) |
| Chi-square | 18.79** | 28.43* | 24.42** | 42.33** |
| Degrees of freedom | 7 | 16 | 9 | 20 |
| N | 399 | 399 | 335 | 335 |

*Note:* Numbers in parentheses are standard errors. Analysis is restricted to those who met their partner in the last five years.

ªThe curvilinear effect of AGE MET was not significant and, therefore, not included in the model.

*p < .05 (two-tailed test).

**p < .01 (two-tailed test).

***p < .001 (two-tailed test).

†p < .10 (two-tailed test).

Table 5A.4 Coefficients from the Logistic Regression of Dating More than One Month When Had Sex with Partner on Selected Independent Variables: Chicago Adults, Aged 20–59, CHSLS, 1995–97

| Independent Variables | Women | | Men | |
|---|---|---|---|---|
| | Model 1 | Model 2 | Model 1 | Model 2 |
| Age effects: | | | | |
| AGE MET (years) | −.056** | −.075** | −.030 | −.022 |
| | (.018) | (.023) | (.018) | (.022) |
| AGE MET² (years²) | . . . | . . . | . . . | . . . |
| SEXREV | 1.833** | 2.087** | .334 | .071 |
| | (.585) | (.616) | (.555) | (.588) |
| | | | | |
| Demographic variables: | | | | |
| Race/ethnicity: | | | | |
| NONHISPANIC BLACK | −.046 | .282 | .144 | .283 |
| | (.307) | (.383) | (.311) | (.489) |
| HISPANIC | .566† | .754* | .726* | .855* |
| | (.340) | (.378) | (.337) | (.365) |
| Education: | | | | |
| HIGH SCHOOL DEGREE | .171 | .127 | .336 | .406 |
| | (.357) | (.366) | (.353) | (.369) |
| SOME COLLEGE OR MORE | .455 | .371 | .754* | .710† |
| | (.337) | (.358) | (.371) | (.385) |
| SES BACKGROUND: PARENTS' COLLEGE | −.114 | −.047 | −.167 | −.153 |
| | (.275) | (.282) | (.299) | (.312) |

*continued*

| Independent Variables | Women | | Men | |
|---|---|---|---|---|
| | Model 1 | Model 2 | Model 1 | Model 2 |
| Other marriage-market and cultural indicators: | | | | |
|   PREVIOUSLY MARRIED | | .758* | | .200 |
| | | (.334) | | (.397) |
|   CHILDREN | | −.548† | | −.841* |
| | | (.314) | | (.373) |
|   LARGE SOCIAL NETWORK | | −.364 | | .065 |
| | | (.297) | | (.247) |
|   ATTRACTIVENESS | | −.244 | | .044 |
| | | (.248) | | (.249) |
| Religion: | | | | |
|   MAINLINE PROTESTANT | | .780† | | .748 |
| | | (.433) | | (.505) |
|   FUNDAMENTALIST PROTESTANT | | .318 | | .658 |
| | | (.410) | | (.475) |
|   ROMAN CATHOLIC/ORTHODOX | | .434 | | .726† |
| | | (.356) | | (.399) |
|   OTHER | | .214 | | .946† |
| | | (.572) | | (.548) |
|   INTACT | | .026 | | −.408 |
| | | (.247) | | (.272) |
| Constant | 1.577* | 1.836 | −.195 | −.699 |
| | (.628) | (.782) | (.648) | (.807) |
| Chi-square | 43.87*** | 60.11*** | 11.90* | 29.35* |
| Degrees of freedom | 8 | 18 | 7 | 18 |
| N | 396 | 396 | 335 | 335 |

*Note:* Numbers in parentheses are standard errors. Analysis is restricted to those who met their partner in the last five years.

*$p < .05$ (two-tailed test).

**$p < .01$ (two-tailed test).

***$p < .001$ (two-tailed test).

†$p < .10$ (two-tailed test).

Table 5A.5 Coefficients from the Logistic Regression of Being in a Committed Relationship When Had Sex with Partner on Selected Independent Variables: Chicago Adults, Aged 20–59, CHSLS, 1995–97

| | Women | | Men | |
|---|---|---|---|---|
| Independent Variables | Model 1 | Model 2 | Model 1 | Model 2 |
| Age effects: | | | | |
| AGE MET (years) | −.069*** | −.053* | −.359** | −.398** |
| | (.019) | (.024) | (.124) | (.132) |
| AGE MET$^2$ (years$^2$) | . . . | . . . | .005* | .005* |
| | | | (.002) | (.002) |
| SEXREV | 1.502** | 1.301* | −1.080 | −.973 |
| | (.574) | (.601) | (1.183) | (1.199) |
| Demographic variables: | | | | |
| Race/ethnicity: | | | | |
| NONHISPANIC BLACK | −.200 | −.302 | .373 | .838 |
| | (.326) | (.484) | (.452) | (.600) |
| HISPANIC | .751* | .700 | −.180 | −.232 |
| | (.338) | (.426) | (.473) | (.490) |
| Education: | | | | |
| HIGH SCHOOL DEGREE | −.396 | −.573 | −.338 | −.214 |
| | (.362) | (.392) | (.457) | (.469) |
| SOME COLLEGE OR MORE | .073 | −.151 | .503 | .543 |
| | (.332) | (.368) | (.466) | (.479) |
| SES BACKGROUND: PARENTS' COLLEGE | .216 | .224 | −.273 | −.094 |
| | (.294) | (.305) | (.355) | (.372) |
| Other marriage-market and cultural indicators: | | | | |
| PREVIOUSLY MARRIED | | .047 | | 1.120* |
| | | (.381) | | (.483) |
| CHILDREN | | −.468 | | −.520 |
| | | (.346) | | (.471) |
| LARGE SOCIAL NETWORK | | .186 | | .185 |
| | | (.259) | | (.303) |
| ATTRACTIVENESS | | .394 | | .275 |
| | | (.280) | | (.308) |
| Religion: | | | | |
| MAINLINE PROTESTANT | | .497 | | 1.043 |
| | | (.482) | | (.662) |
| FUNDAMENTALIST PROTESTANT | | .825† | | .523 |
| | | (.473) | | (.635) |
| ROMAN CATHOLIC/ORTHODOX | | .586 | | 1.256* |
| | | (.403) | | (.534) |
| OTHER | | .178 | | .684 |
| | | (.643) | | (.757) |
| INTACT | | .486† | | −.1088 |
| | | (.281) | | (.333) |
| Constant | 1.213† | −.265 | 4.338* | 3.747† |
| | (.645) | (.840) | (1.812) | (1.989) |

continued

| Independent Variables | Women | | Men | |
|---|---|---|---|---|
| | Model 1 | Model 2 | Model 1 | Model 2 |
| Chi-square | 41.77*** | 66.86*** | 37.89*** | 52.22*** |
| Degrees of freedom | 8 | 23 | 12 | 21 |
| N | 394 | 394 | 332 | 332 |

*Note:* Numbers in parentheses are standard errors. Analysis is restricted to those who met their partner in the last five years.

*$p < .05$ (two-tailed test).

**$p < .01$ (two-tailed test).

***$p < .001$ (two-tailed test).

†$p < .10$ (two-tailed test).

# 6 )

# The Sex Market and Its Implications for Family Formation

Yoosik Youm and Anthony Paik

How do men and women participate in sex markets?[1] How do they find part-ners, and what kind of sexual relationships do they seek to form? We pursued these questions in many of our interviews with key organization informants across the neighborhoods. Some examples of responses follow:

An earlier version of this chapter was presented as "Network Effects on Family Formation: Why Are African Americans Less Likely to Marry" at the annual meet-ing of the American Sociological Association, Anaheim, Calif., August 2001. We thank session participants for their helpful comments. We also thank Steve Ellingson for his crucial feedback.

1. On the terms *sex market* and *sexual marketplace* as they are used in this study, see the section "The Social Organization of Sexual Partnering and Sexual Relationships" in Ellingson, Laumann, Paik, and Mahay (chapter 1 in this volume).

In explaining how gay men form enduring, committed relationships, one activist noted: "Straight guys go out on a couple of dates and then decide if they are going to pursue a sexual relationship. Gays sleep with people first and then decide if they are going to pursue a relationship. The sex thing usually always plays itself out first in gay-male relationships."

A worker at a health-care clinic in Erlinda described her clients in the following manner: "One [type] is younger and more promiscuous, doesn't like condoms or wear them. These individuals may have had anywhere from six to thirty lovers by their early thirties. The other type is the family man, . . . who will go outside the marriage relationship to have oral sex performed on them without protection. Generally the family men will be on their second or third marriage. Most of them are parents, and roughly 35 percent have steady female lovers on the side. A few have same-gender partners."

An informant knowledgeable about the black lesbian community in Chicago spoke about the prevalence of lesbianism in the projects and the complex sexual partnerships that lesbians hold together: "A lot of women in the projects are lesbians. They might have a house full of kids. It's weird. Hard butch lesbians, they are out, call themselves lesbians, but sleep with men. Others don't identify as lesbians but say they like women. But because of economic pressures and social pressures present in the projects they sleep with men or enter relationships with men for money. Women need money to take care of their kids and sometimes for drugs."

These informants identify a range of strategies that individuals employ to navigate their particular situation in sex markets and to organize their sex lives. Some strategies have a strong relational focus; others are more transactional. Some help individuals maintain multiple partnerships at the same time, while others narrow the possibilities to one relationship.

Mahay and Laumann (chapter 5 in this volume) focused on the search for partners in sex markets. Here, we take up a related, successive issue: the problem of organizing the resulting, sex-market interactions. When a business organization requires critical resources or services for its operations, it makes a decision between producing these goods internally and procuring them on the open market—what Oliver Williamson (1981, 1985) calls the *make or buy* decision. Likewise, men and women pursuing the benefits of sex, which can range from immediate gratification to sharing a life with another person, make decisions about how to organize their sex lives. For many, sex takes place in monogamous, long-term relationships; for others, sex is exchanged with numerous others, sometimes even anonymously. Still others maintain several sexual relationships simultaneously, some overlapping for only brief periods, others overlapping for longer periods of time. The primary aim of this chapter is to investigate the variety and the social consequences of *sexual-matching strategies* employed by men and women in their interactions with sex markets.

This issue—how men and women participate in sex markets—also has theoretical and empirical import. Previous chapters in this volume focused on the embeddedness of sex markets, describing how they are organized by institutional forces such as social networks, institutions, local culture, and space. One feature of sex markets was the tendency to be either transactional or relational. In this chapter, we take the perspective of the individual and focus on individual decisionmaking. Like sex markets, individuals can have either *transactional* or *relational strategies.* However, we also argue that individuals frequently deploy a *hybrid* strategy of maintaining concurrent sexual relations, a topic that has received scant attention in sociological research.[2]

Moreover, the distribution of these different sex-market strategies among everyday Americans has important implications for several outcomes, including out-of-wedlock fertility (Willis, 1999), sexually transmitted infections (STIs) (Morris & Kretzschmar, 1995), and, as we demonstrate below, marriage. We use formal models and statistical analyses to show how different sex-market strategies affect participation in the marriage market. In the following sections, we first provide a perspective on sex-market strategies as well as their relevance for marriage markets. Next, we describe the major patterns of sexual-matching strategies in the Chicago Health and Social Life Survey (CHSLS) samples. We then present a rational-choice model that explains some of the associations among demographic characteristics, sexual-matching strategies, and marriage. Finally, we conclude by investigating how structural embeddedness is a key, intervening mechanism for the effects of the sex market on the marriage market.

## Conceptual Approach

Prior to the latter half of the twentieth century, in the United States an individual's first marriage partner was frequently his or her first sex partner.[3] The decision to marry was, in effect, the decision to have sex with a particular person, so men and women participated only in the marriage markets. Since the 1960s, which marked the advent of effective birth-control technology (Westoff & Ryder, 1977), these two decisions more often than not occur at considerably different points in time and often involve different people. According to the 1992 National Health and Social Life Survey (NHSLS), over 40 percent of the people aged fifty to fifty-nine had their first intercourse ex-

2. The distinction among transactional, relational, and hybrid strategies is based on Baker's (1990) typology of organization-market interfaces.

3. This is more accurate for women than for men since a sizable minority of men had sex with prostitutes prior to marriage.

perience with their spouse; in contrast, this figure is only 5 percent for those aged eighteen to twenty-four (see Laumann, Gagnon, Michael, & Michaels, 1994). Also, only 23 percent of the older age cohort was motivated to have this experience out of sexual curiosity; nearly half the younger cohort had sex as a result of curiosity.[4]

Thus, Americans currently participate in two distinct but related matching markets: the sex and the marriage markets. The comment quoted above from the Erlinda health-care worker illustrates one way in which individuals engage in both markets. These changing sexual and marital patterns point to the two topics with which we deal in this chapter. First, how do Chicagoans organize their intimate relations in sex markets? What are the sexual-matching strategies deployed by our CHSLS respondents? Do they maintain monogamous relationships, engage in a series of short-lived sexual encounters, or juggle several sorts of relationships at once? Second, what effect does an individual's decisions in sex markets have on his or her decisions about marriage? Because individuals can pursue a variety of sexual-matching strategies that do not involve marriage, sexual-matching strategies should affect the likelihood of marriage. Indeed, we suggest that prior studies of family formation may be incomplete (even misleading) since most marriage models do not account for the effect of the sex market.

## The Individual-Market Interface of Sexual Matching

While prior research has traditionally made couples the locus of study for understanding sexual behavior (see, e.g., Blumstein & Schwartz, 1983; Laumann, Gagnon, Michael, & Michaels, 1994; Christopher & Sprecher, 2000), recent work on sexual infidelity highlights the notion that sexual relations are frequently more complex than simple dyads (Forste & Tanfer, 1996; Treas & Giesen, 2000). In terms of ideal types, an individual's relations in sex markets can be *relational, transactional,* or a *hybrid* of these two types. The *relational* type encompasses monogamous couples, the *transactional* type individuals pursuing short-term, serial relationships, and the *hybrid* type individuals pursuing a combination of relational and transactional strategies, resulting in concurrent sexual relationships. The key advantage of this approach over others is that it emphasizes the diversity of strategies for finding partners and organizing sexual relationships.

There are two theoretical grounds for differentiating among relational, transactional, and hybrid sexual-matching strategies. First, relational strategies are not well suited for some of the goals of sex. Briefly, people engage in

---

4. These percentages are estimated among those whose first sex was wanted (as opposed to forced).

sex for a variety of reasons: to pursue sexual pleasure; to feel intimacy; to have children; to establish a "good" reputation among friends, family, or acquaintances (Laumann, Gagnon, Michael, & Michaels, 1994, 8). For most goals, researchers argue that sex is advantageously embedded in long-term, sexually exclusive relationships (Laumann, Gagnon, Michael, & Michaels, 1994; Waite & Joyner, 2001). However, some individuals may prefer transactional or hybrid strategies if the benefits of maintaining short-term or multiple sexual relations increase or if the costs decrease. For example, sexual "libertarians" may prefer to engage in many short-term relationships because having new sex partners tends to heighten sexual excitement.

Second, two major theoretical perspectives currently applied to the study of couples—the transaction-cost (Pollak, 1985; England & Farkas, 1986; Treas, 1993) and network-exchange approaches (Laumann, Gagnon, Michael, & Michaels, 1994)—also include multiple sexual relations in their conceptual schemes, although relatively little work has been devoted to this aspect. While most applications of transaction-cost theory focus on married and cohabiting couples, this perspective calls attention to alternate organizational forms, such as the transactional and the hybrid. Likewise, network-exchange perspectives have long emphasized the importance of alternate sex partners (see, e.g., Blau, 1964). Thus, we argue that the limitation of these perspectives to only dyadic situations is overly restrictive. Below, we apply these two perspectives to the different types of sex-market strategies.

RELATIONAL STRAGEGIES. The network perspective emphasizes how these longer-term relationships are structurally embedded in social relations, such as those between friends, family, acquaintances, and the partners themselves, which all exert control over the behavior of each sex partner through expectations and obligations (Laumann, Gagnon, Michael, & Michaels, 1994). These sexual partnerships tend to be characterized by extensive commitments, are highly intimate, and incorporate expectations of sexual exclusivity.

The transaction-cost perspective, on the other hand, emphasizes how the relational form is well adapted for producing frequent, complex interactions over a long time period, allows for developing relation-specific capital, and provides for ample monitoring opportunities between sex partners (Treas, 1993). Indeed, the transaction-cost perspective treats marriage as the exemplar of "relational contracting" (Pollak, 1985). Because forming sexual relationships is costly in terms of time, money, and energy and is fraught with uncertainty and limited information, relational forms are efficient ways for organizing sexual behavior, lowering transaction costs, and facilitating specialized investments, especially as they relate to sex and the household. The relational form also allows for substantial emotional investments, expressed as intimacy, having and raising children, and even developing better sexual skills.

Empirical research focuses on highlighting differences between two relational forms—cohabitation and marriage (Treas, 1993; Brines & Joyner, 1999; Waite & Joyner, 2001)—but many dating relationships also have relational orientations and are part of the courtship process that eventuates in marriage.

TRANSACTIONAL STRATEGIES. The transactional form, in contrast, facilitates the pursuit of individualized sexual goals and is denoted by sexual relationships of shorter duration. Here, the ideal example is the one-night stand. Because of their short duration, network and transaction-cost perspectives characterize these relationships as having few joint investments and commitments and as being oriented toward brief encounters primarily about sexual exchange (Laumann, Gagnon, Michael, & Michaels, 1994). Transactional forms are more sexual in nature either because there are few other developed expectations and exchanges to organize the relationship or because this strategy is well suited for individuals interested primarily in sexual conquests. In the analyses presented below, we call these *multiple, short-term relationships.*

HYBRID STRATEGIES. Theoretically, there should be hybrid forms between the polar opposites of relational and transactional forms. The focus of most research purportedly dealing with such hybrid forms is probably closer to the relational pole, where an individual in one highly committed partnership maintains a secondary partner (Treas & Giesen, 2000; Christopher & Sprecher, 2000). Extramarital affairs are a good example. Closer to the transactional pole are overlapping relationships, but here the overlap is almost incidental because the beginnings and the endings of many of these relationships are somewhat ambiguous. For example, people involved in dating relationships sometimes have brief periods during which they are seeing more than one partner. Laumann, Gagnon, Michael, and Michaels (1994) found a strong association between the number of partners during a twelve-month interval and the percentage reporting concurrency. We term this *short-term polygamy.* Finally, a third possible alternative is somewhere in the middle, where an individual is not in any highly established relationships but has sexual interactions with multiple partners over a longer time period. Indeed, this third possible hybrid form, a pattern that we term *long-term polygamy,* is likely to have profound implications for well-being, STI transmission, and marriage, yet it has received almost no scholarly attention (but see Anderson, 1999; Bowser, 1994).

Few prior studies have attempted to assess the variety of sex-market strategies of men and women, so little is known about the prevalence of each type of strategy and the concentrations of each within specific population segments. Moreover, little is known about what leads individuals to choose one strategy over another. In the next section, we investigate two causes that lead

individuals, particularly African American men, to form long-term polygamous relationships. These are the changing economic fortunes of African
American men in the postindustrial economy and structural embeddedness.

## The Relevance of Sexual-Matching Strategies for Family Formation

It is our contention that greater attention to sex markets offers a potential explanation for the so-called racial gap in marriage. A long-standing social fact
in demography is that African Americans are much less likely to marry than
are whites (Bumpass, 1990; Ellwood & Crane, 1990). According to one estimate, among women born in the 1950s, 91 percent of whites but only 75 percent of African Americans will eventually marry (Bennett, Bloom, & Craige,
1989). Another estimate projects that only 70 percent of African American
women will ever marry (Rogers & Thornton, 1985). As shown in figure 6.1,
African Americans were increasingly less likely to marry after 1970. Although
this divergence in family formation between racial/ethnic groups generated
considerable debate, a satisfactory explanation is still lacking.

One of the most common explanations for this racial gap in marriage
points to highly imbalanced sex ratios in the African American population.
Guttentag and Secord (1983) argue that a shortage of men has led to higher
rates of singlehood, divorce, out-of-wedlock births, adultery, and transient
relationships. However, African American sex ratios have been declining
since 1920 even though the marital decline has been evident only since the

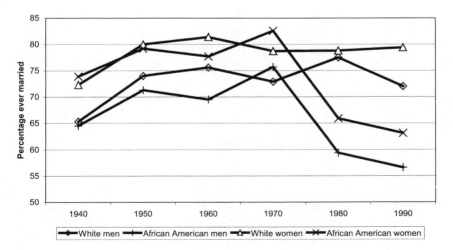

Figure 6.1. Percentage ever married by gender and race.

*Source:* Tucker & Mitchell-Kernan (1995).

1960s (Espenshade, 1985). Indeed, there is only limited empirical support for the sex-ratio hypothesis (South, 1986; South & Messner, 1988; Tucker, 1987).

Some scholars have added economic factors to the sex-ratio explanation. One argument that has drawn some empirical support (Fossett & Kiecolt, 1991; Lichter, LeClere, & McLaughlin, 1991; South & Lloyd, 1992) is the so-called pool-of-marriageable-men explanation, which focuses on the numbers of men who earn enough to support a family. These scholars argue that the feasibility of African American marriage declined as a result of the increasing economic marginality of black men, which made them less attractive to women as potential husbands and less interested in becoming husbands because of their limited ability to fulfill the provider role in marriage (Darity & Myers, 1987; Wilson & Neckerman, 1986; Wilson, 1987). This argument is related to Gary Becker's (1991) notion of household surplus. In general, there is a smaller income differential between African American men and women than between white men and women. Thus, the gain in sharing a household relative to staying single is lower for African Americans than for whites. However, several researchers point out that this argument can explain only a small part of the drastic decline in marriage rates over the last thirty years (Mare & Winship, 1991; Lichter, McLaughlin, Kephart, & Landry, 1992; South & Lloyd, 1992). In addition, other studies show that, not only unemployed African American men, but also employed African American men are less likely to marry than are their white counterparts, a pattern that is discrepant with the pool-of-marriageable-men explanation.

A third approach to the racial gap in marriage rates explores cultural, historical, and attitudinal considerations. One basic argument suggests that African Americans have weak nuclear families because kin networks extending across households were traditionally more important than husband–wife units, a consequence attributed to both the social organization of African societies and slavery (Cherlin, 1992; Gutman, 1976). However, this account does not explain why we observe such sharp discrepancies between racial/ethnic groups only after the 1970s. Also, since 1960 there have been no significant shifts among African Americans in the desire to marry eventually or the desire to remain single or childless (Thornton, 1989; Thornton & Freedman, 1982).

So support for the sex-ratio, economic, and cultural arguments is mixed, and the strength of these effects is far too small to provide a satisfactory, comprehensive account. We argue that previous research has focused only on macro-level factors and has neglected two essential factors in marriage: the character of the sexual-matching strategies at the individual level and the structural embeddedness of couples at the dyadic level. Specifically, we shall relate the opportunities and the constraints in the sex market to those in the marriage market. We argue that the opportunities in the sex market act as constraints in the marriage market, and vice versa; therefore, polygamy in relationships is an alternative to marriage. We demonstrate this point using a dynamic, game-theoretic model of both the sexual and the marriage markets showing that, under some conditions, a small decrease in the relative benefits of marriage can lead to a relatively large decrease in the marriage rates of a population.

Figure 6.2 illustrates how different sexual-matching patterns can produce quite different marriage rates even when the sex ratio is constant. In the strict monogamous condition, depicted in the left panel, the marriage rate is completely determined by the sex ratio. However, the addition of multiple sex partners, as shown in the right panel, produces an even lower marriage rate because most individuals engaged in multiple sexual relations are not married.[5] Therefore, in order to fully explain the marriage rate, we need to account for how individuals make decisions regarding sexual-matching strategies and how those actions aggregate into equilibria in the sex and marriage markets.[6] In addition, we argue that a key factor that guides decisions about sexual-matching strategies and marriage is social embeddedness. Specifically, we incorporate social structure in terms of network embeddedness into our game-theoretic modeling, thus avoiding the assumption of atomized decisionmaking while taking advantage of the power of formal models.

Social embeddedness is relevant because of search costs and uncertainty. Marriage involves highly idiosyncratic decisions in the sense that people engage in limited search even though the costs of choosing unsuitable partners are extremely high. According to the NHSLS, for more than one-third of Americans aged twenty to thirty, the decision to marry is also the same as the decision to engage in first sexual intercourse (Laumann, Gagnon, Michael, & Michaels, 1994). Studies in Europe reveal the same pattern (Michael, Gagnon, Laumann, & Kolata, 1994). This notion is further buttressed by the observation that most partnerships, even casual sexual relationships, are homogeneous in terms of race, geography, education, etc. (Kerckhoff, 1974; Laumann, Gagnon, Michael, & Michaels, 1994). Thus, the decision to marry takes place with little search activity and within homogeneous marriage markets. In other words, it is a socially embedded activity.[7]

Even if two people like each other intensely, they cannot be sure about

5. According to the NHSLS, nearly 11 percent of Americans had at least one concurrent sexual relationship during the twelve months prior to being interviewed (Laumann, Gagnon, Michael, & Michaels, 1994). The prevalence among married individuals, however, was less than 4 percent (Christopher & Sprecher, 2000).

6. To achieve this goal, we integrated Becker's (1991) theory of polygamy into a game-theoretic model.

7. Our approach improves on the neoclassical economic approach, which simply does not provide an adequate model of marriage decisions (Frey & Eichenberger, 1996).

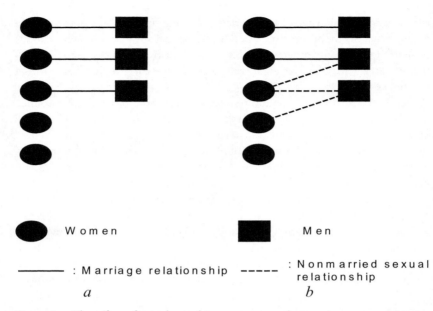

Figure 6.2. The effect of sexual-matching patterns on the marriage rate. *a,* Monogamous. *b,* Polygamous.

*Note:* In both panels, the sex ratio of men to women is 0.6. In panel *a,* the marriage rate is 0.6 for women and 1 for men. In panel *b,* the marriage rate is 0.4 for women and 0.66 for men.

marriage. In general, people have two beliefs that facilitate marriage. First, they must be sure that their potential partners are suitable. Second, even when they are sure that their potential partners are suitable, they must also be sure that their potential partners will not leave the marriage in the future. The following interview with an unmarried African American father illustrates this point (DeParle, 1998, A1; emphasis added): "'I ain't really for all that marriage stuff, man,' said Sylvester Bradshaw, a 21-year old father of two. 'It's easy for a person to say "I love you," man. But you *got to really know somebody to marry* them.' Mr. Jones pushed back. 'How well do you have to know them to have kids?' he asked. Mr. Bradshaw answered with an embarrassed smile, as if to confess the *shortcomings of his relationship* with his children's mother."

Thus, the question becomes, Under the conditions of scarce search activity, how can people really know each other well enough to marry? The answer lies in confirmative beliefs emerging from social embeddedness. We argue that marriage is more likely to emerge from among those who are socially embedded because that social embeddedness increases the assurance that partners will not leave the marriage in the future as well as the belief that the potential partner is suitable. Therefore, the marriage model must incorporate social embeddedness around actors.

The preceding discussion can be summarized into several points. First, men and women employ a variety of sexual-matching strategies in their interactions with sex markets, including transactional, relational, and hybrid strategies. Second, there are two factors that lead individuals to choose among these different strategies—economic position and structural embeddedness. Third, sexual-matching strategies are likely to affect the decision to marry, which suggests that decisions in the sex market directly affect the marriage market.

## The Varieties of Sexual-Matching Strategies

We constructed several measures to assess the prevalence of sexual-matching strategies in the five samples of the CHSLS. These measures include the number of partners with whom our respondents expected to continue to have sex at the time of the interview, whether either partner had a concurrent sex partner during the course of the relationship, and the respondent's sexual-matching strategy during the twelve months prior to being interviewed. Sexual-matching patterns were broken down into four categories: relational; serial polygamous; short-term polygamous; and long-term polygamous.[8] People who had just one sex partner last year were assigned to the relational sexual-matching pattern. People who had multiple partners one after another were assigned to the serial polygamous pattern. People who had multiple partners at least two of whom were concurrent for less than six months were assigned to the short-term polygamous pattern. Finally, people who had multiple relationships with concurrency lasting more than six months were assigned to the long-term polygamous pattern. (See table 6.1.)

In Cook County, few men and women (between 4 and 6 percent) currently have concurrent sex partners. But, over the course of their relationships with their most recent partners, 35 percent of men and 30 percent of women reported that at least one partner had a concurrent partner, with the vast majority of cases being men having a secondary partner. If we look at our respondents' behavior over the twelve months prior to being interviewed, 17 percent of men and 9 percent of women had concurrent sex partners; however, it would appear that many of these cases were short-term polygamous relationships.

The other samples show marked variation. Both Westside and Erlinda show low levels of concurrent sex partners in the last year and at the time of the in-

8. These categories are based on up to five of the most recent partnerships in the twelve months prior to the interview. Even though all the relationships were present as of the last year, much of the overlap between relationships occurred before the last year.

Table 6.1 Measures of the Organization of Sexual Networks: Monogamous and Polygamous Relationships by Gender and Sample

| Variables | Cook County | | Westside | | Southtown | | Shoreland | | Erlinda | |
|---|---|---|---|---|---|---|---|---|---|---|
| | Men | Women | Men | Women | Men | Women | Men | Women | Men | Women |
| Number of sex partners whom respondent expects to continue sex with: | | | | | | | | | | |
| None (%) | 26 | 25 | 29 | 19 | 16 | 29 | 29 | 32 | 28 | 27 |
| 1 (%) | 68 | 71 | 71 | 81 | 62 | 65 | 64 | 66 | 68 | 72 |
| 2 (%) | 6 | 4 | 1 | 0 | 21 | 6 | 7 | 2 | 4 | 1 |
| N | 376 | 513 | 140 | 209 | 117 | 190 | 176 | 182 | 82 | 128 |
| Respondent's report of any concurrent partners with most recent partner: | | | | | | | | | | |
| No concurrent partner(s) (%) | 65 | 70 | 78 | 75 | 39 | 55 | 68 | 65 | 87 | 82 |
| Respondent had concurrent partner(s) (%) | 20 | 6 | 14 | 2 | 39 | 8 | 15 | 13 | 9 | 2 |
| Sex partner had concurrent partner(s) (%) | 5 | 14 | 7 | 21 | 5 | 21 | 3 | 12 | 4 | 13 |
| Respondent and sex partner had concurrent partner(s) (%) | 10 | 10 | 2 | 1 | 17 | 16 | 14 | 10 | 0 | 2 |
| N | 357 | 488 | 125 | 201 | 113 | 189 | 176 | 179 | 78 | 122 |
| Respondent's sexual networks in last 12 months: | | | | | | | | | | |
| No sex partners (%) | 14 | 19 | 18 | 16 | 9 | 15 | 5 | 14 | 15 | 20 |
| Relational (%) | 59 | 68 | 71 | 81 | 43 | 63 | 48 | 61 | 66 | 75 |
| Serial polygamy (%) | 10 | 4 | 6 | 2 | 8 | 5 | 20 | 16 | 8 | 2 |
| Short-term polygamy (< 6 months) (%) | 10 | 4 | 4 | 1 | 14 | 9 | 19 | 3 | 5 | 3 |
| Long-term polygamy (≥ 6 months) (%) | 7 | 5 | 1 | 0 | 27 | 7 | 8 | 5 | 5 | 0 |
| N | 362 | 498 | 136 | 206 | 117 | 183 | 173 | 178 | 74 | 122 |

*Note:* Results from samples are unweighted.

terview; however, the men are still more likely to have concurrent sex partners than are the women. Even more interesting, and in contradistinction to
the other CHSLS samples, both men and women in Westside and Erlinda are
more likely to suspect that their partners have had concurrent sex partners.
For example, in Westside, 14 percent of the men reported having had a concurrent sex partner during their relationships, while 21 percent of women
suspected that their partners had had another partner. Similarly, 2 percent of
women in Westside reported concurrent partners; 7 percent of men reported
that their female partners had other partners. One possible explanation is that
there is more underreporting of one's own behavior in these samples in comparison to the other samples. Alternatively, the Hispanic respondents in these
samples may be more suspicious. The answer to this question, however, cannot be determined here.

Finally, Southtown and Shoreland make for an interesting comparison since
both show high levels of nonmonogamous sex, but with important differences. In Shoreland, approximately 35 percent of men and women reported
a concurrent partner in their relationship, but few (7 percent of men and 2
percent of women) were actively maintaining two relationships at the time
of the interview. More important, only 8 and 5 percent of men and women,
respectively, exhibited a pattern of long-term polygamy, so the vast majority
of individuals who had two or more partners in the twelve months prior to
their interviews were engaged in multiple short-term relationships or short-
term polygamy. In Southtown, polygamy is even more prevalent; in fact, it is
the dominant pattern. Approximately 60 percent of men and 45 percent of
women experienced a concurrent partner in their relationship, and 21 percent of the men still had at least two partners at the time of the interview. In
sharp contrast to Shoreland, the dominant pattern of having multiple partners for men is in Southtown long-term polygamy. In fact, few men and
women, only 8 and 5 percent, respectively, reported having multiple short-
term partners.

Taken together, the CHSLS samples show three distinct patterns of sexual-
matching strategies. In general, men are more likely than women to engage
in nonmonogamous sexual-matching strategies. Respondents in our mostly
Hispanic communities reported the lowest levels of concurrency; however, it
is not clear whether this pattern is a result of underreporting. Our most striking finding is the prevalence of concurrent sexual-matching strategies in our
majority-black community of Southtown. Indeed, over the last year, 48 percent of the men in Southtown, compared with 22 percent of the women, had
multiple partners, with the majority of these men having concurrent partners
for six months or more. We believe that our study is one of the first to identify this pattern of long-term polygamy, and the fact that more than a quarter of the respondents in the Southtown sample used this sexual-matching

Table 6.2 The Distribution of Marital-Status and Sexual-Matching
Patterns by Race and Gender in Chicago (row %)

|  | Just One (%) | Multiple Short Term (%) | Serial Long Term (%) | Polygamous Long-Term (%) | N |
|---|---|---|---|---|---|
| **Men** | | | | | |
| Whites | | | | | |
| Dating (37%) | 46 | 21 | 24 | 9 | 70 |
| Cohabiting (8%) | 60 | 7 | 27 | 7 | 15 |
| Married (56%) | 97 | 0 | 1 | 2 | 106 |
| Blacks | | | | | |
| Dating (54%) | 21 | 21 | 33 | 24 | 42 |
| Cohabiting (14%) | 45 | 9 | 9 | 36 | 11 |
| Married (32%) | 97 | 0 | 1 | 2 | 25 |
| **Women** | | | | | |
| Whites | | | | | |
| Dating (29%) | 65 | 3 | 17 | 16 | 65 |
| Cohabiting (7%) | 93 | 0 | 7 | 0 | 15 |
| Married (64%) | 98 | 1 | 1 | 1 | 143 |
| Blacks | | | | | |
| Dating (60%) | 67 | 6 | 6 | 21 | 78 |
| Cohabiting (18%) | 96 | 0 | 4 | 0 | 24 |
| Married (23%) | 93 | 0 | 3 | 3 | 30 |

strategy is likely to have profound implications for family formation, STI transmission, and out-of-wedlock fertility.

As this overview suggests, there are important racial/ethnic and gender differences in sexual-matching strategies. Restricting our attention to the Cook County sample in table 6.2, we focus more specifically on how sexual-matching strategies vary with race/ethnicity and marital status. First, this table shows that African Americans are less likely to be married than are whites, a pattern consistent with prior research and attributed to lower likelihoods of ever marrying and staying married (Cherlin, 1992). More than half (54 percent) of the African American men in Cook County are currently dating, with 33 percent engaged in serial long-term relationships, 24 percent in polygamous long-term relationships, and about one-quarter in monogamous relationships. In sharp contrast to this pattern, of dating white men in Cook County, only 9 percent were in long-term polygamous relationships, 24 percent were in serial long-term relationships, and 46 percent were in monogamous relationships.

These racial differences have important implications for marriage rates in these two populations. Among whites, dating is a precursor to marriage.

The most popular sex-market strategies for single white men are the relational (monogamous) and the short-term polygamous patterns, both of which are much more likely to lead to marriage than is the long-term polygamous pattern. Single African American men, however, are more likely to be in long-term polygamous relationships, and we suggest that this strategy makes marriage less likely in most cases. Table 6.2 also reveals that African American women have sexual-matching strategies that are similar to those of white women. This is consistent with our argument that, in the African American population, polygyny might be an alternative to marriage, which supports the notion that the African American marriage rate is lower than that expected by the sex-ratio explanation because of the prevalence of polygamous relationships.[9]

This raises questions about what leads individuals to form long-term polygamous relationships. We believe that demographic associations with sexual-matching strategies and with marriage behavior among African Americans provide two important clues. Figure 6.3 (based on the NHSLS) shows sexual-matching strategies of black and white men by education level. Among the white men, there is no relation between the likelihood of having long-term polygamous relationships and education level. Among the black men, however, long-term polygamous partnerships are positively associated with education level. Figure 6.4 (again based on the NHSLS), in turn, shows a curvilinear pattern between the likelihood of marriage and age among African American men. Also, African American men are much more likely never to have married regardless of education level.

## Sexual-Matching Strategies and Marriage

We argue that a rational-choice model of sexual-matching strategies provides a suggestive explanation for these patterns. Figure 6.5 illustrates a sexual-matching game that includes marriage as an ultimate, possible outcome. Assume for the moment that there are two people who are considering forming a sexual relationship. If these two people are able to maintain a monogamous relationship, that relationship can lead to marriage. We assume that marriage emerges primarily when both partners are monogamous since sexual infi-

---

9. Even though observation numbers are not so large in table 6.2, the results of the log-linear analysis are consistent with the description given above. There is a systematic relation between sexual-matching patterns and marital status: e.g., people in long-term polygamous relationships are much less likely to be married. The results also confirm that African Americans are more likely to be in long-term polygamous relationships.

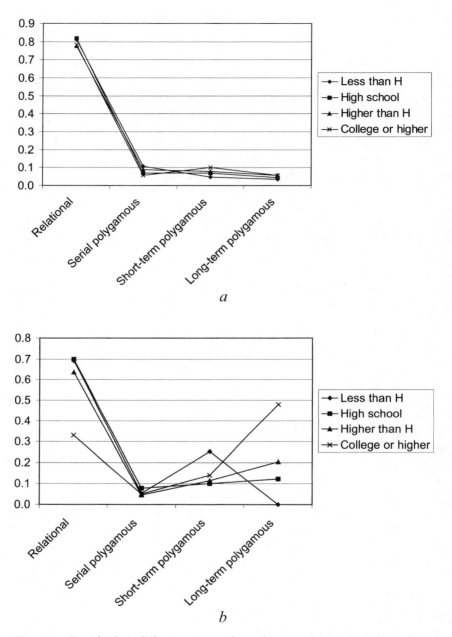

Figure 6.3. Racial/ethnic differences in sexual-matching strategies. *a*, Sexual-matching modes among whites. *b*, Sexual-matching modes among blacks.

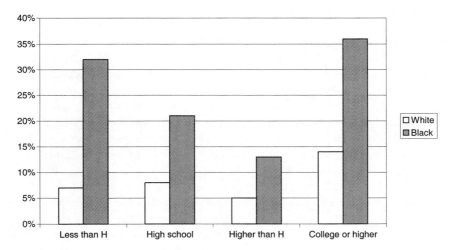

Figure 6.4. Proportion never married among men who are older than thirty-five.

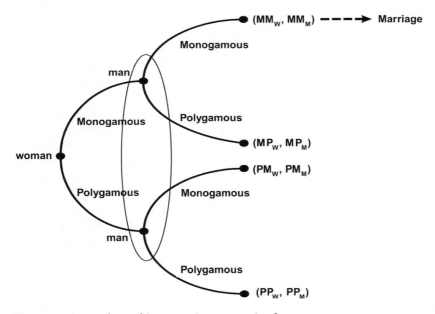

Figure 6.5. A sexual-matching game in an extensive form.

*Note:* See explanation in text.

delity is generally considered a violation of the marriage contract and few individuals plan to marry while in a polygamous relationship.[10] We also assume
that partners do not know each other's decision when they themselves decide.[11] Depending on each party's two possible actions, there are four possible
payoffs: MM; MP; PM; and PP. MM is the payoff when both are monogamous, PP when both are polygamous, MP when the woman is monogamous
and the man is polygamous, and PM when the woman is polygamous and the
man is monogamous. The subscript $w$ indicates the payoff for the woman, the
subscript $m$ the payoff for the man. All payoffs are represented in parentheses,
with the woman's utility given first.

The key factor affecting the decisions of these two actors is, we argue, relative supply and demand. On the basis of our previous discussion, we concluded that polygamy decreases the marriage rate. So let us see whether there
is any incentive for the woman to prefer MP to MM. Figure 6.6 illustrates the
supply (solid line) of men, where all the men are identical, and the demand
(dotted line) for women, where a woman's payoff from a relationship with a
man is represented as $Z_w$ on the z-axis. In panel *a*, a polygamous relationship
is not allowed, and the total number of men $(N_m)$ is smaller than the total
number of women $(N_w)$. Thus, every woman will have one partner if her $Z_w$,
the payoff from the relationship, is greater than $Z_{sw}$, her payoff when she has
no partner (the supply line will be vertical once $Z_w > Z_{sw}$). On the other
hand, every man will take one partner if the marginal product of having one
partner (the difference in payoff between having no partner and having one
partner, $MP_1$) is greater than the minimum amount of the payoff that he must
offer to that one partner, $Z_w$ (the dotted line will be vertical once $Z_w < MP_1$).
In this situation, every woman will have one partner, while some men will
have no partner. The circle shows the payoff to women at the equilibrium:
every woman will get $Z_{sw}$ from the relationship.[12]

This situation changes once we assume that there can be polygamous relationships and that men have different levels of resources. We now include
MP (the marginal product from one additional partner) in our hypothetical
example, and we further assume that there are three types of men, types A,
B, and C. Type A men have the greatest amount of resources and, thus, offer
their partners the greatest payoff. Type C men have the least amount of re-

10. It is possible for individuals to have polygamous relationships during marriage. However, we can assume that people start a marriage within a monogamous
relationship.

11. The circle drawn around the man's decision nodes represents the fact that the
man does not know the woman's choice when he makes a decision.

12. For the basic axiomatic proofs, see Becker (1991). For the same line of argument, see Grossbard (1978, 1980), Kanazawa and Still (1999), and Wright (1994).

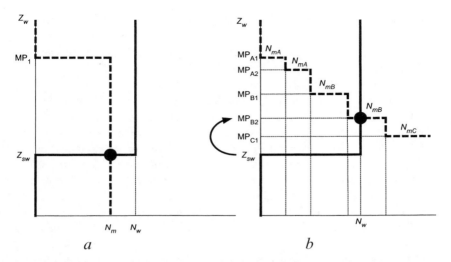

Figure 6.6. Polygamous relationship as preferable to both men and women. *a,* Polygamy not allowed. *b,* Polygamy allowed.

sources and, thus, offer their partners the least payoff. Type B men have middle-range resources. Resources include income, education, etc. $MP_{A1}$ is the payoff difference for type A men between having no partner and having one partner. $MP_{A2}$ is the payoff difference for type A men between having only one partner and having two partners. Let's assume that the maximum amount of payoff that type A men can offer a second partner ($MP_{A2}$) is greater than the maximum amount of payoff that type B men can offer a first partner ($MP_{B1}$), as illustrated in panel *b* of figure 6.6. A woman will, therefore, prefer being the second partner of a type A man to being the first partner of a type B man. As a result, in figure 6.6*b,* all type A men have two partners, some type B men have only one partner, and all type C men have no partner. As a result of polygamy, the equilibrium point changes, bringing higher income to women: the new payoff will be $MP_{B2}$ instead of $Z_{sw}$. This increase comes from the increased demand for women (current assumptions allowing men multiple partners). One consequence is that some men (i.e., those of type C) will be without partners even though they can offer higher payoffs than $Z_{sw}$.

In order to change the equilibrium, we must add one caveat here: the polygamous sexual relationship in panel *b* must be stable and long-term because the marginal product can be realized only by relationships based on long-run gains. In other words, if the relationship is transactional (i.e., a one-night stand), a woman will not gain in expected payoff by choosing a resource-rich man over a resource-poor one. When the sexual relationship is long-term,

184 )     Y. Youm and A. Paik

however, the gain will be substantial: the model suggests that a woman will prefer being the second partner of a resource-rich man to being the first partner of a resource-poor man. Hence, under certain conditions, both men and women will prefer polygamous relationships.

How would this deductive model play out in an actual population? If the African American sex market is more like the polygamous regime in panel *b* of figure 6.6, we would expect the marriage rate to be much lower than is predicted by the sex-ratio explanation. Further, if our expectation holds, we should also observe three empirical phenomena that are not explained by the sex-ratio explanation. First, African Americans will have a higher proportion of long-term polygamous relationships as an alternative to marriage than will whites. Second, and more important, more educated African American men will be more likely to have long-term polygamous relationships. This contradicts the marriageable-men explanation, which argues that more educated men are more likely to be married (and, thus, less likely to have polygamous relationships). Finally, the marriage rate must have a curvilinear pattern among African Americans. If we use education attainment as a proxy for men's resources, the most educated and the least educated men will have lower marriage rates than will those with moderate levels of education. The most educated men will have lower marriage rates because they are more likely to engage in long-term polygamous relationships (type A men in figure 6.6). The least educated men will also have lower marriage rates because the difference in marginal product between having no partner and having one partner is lower than the equilibrium price of having one partner (type C men in figure 6.6). Moderately educated men will have the highest marriage rate because they are most likely to have only one sex partner, which has the highest probability of leading to marriage (type B men in figure 6.6). As we showed in figures 6.3 and 6.4, these are patterns that we, in fact, observe in the African American population.

Our approach also allows us to explain the emergence of the racial gap in marriage rates after the 1970s. Various statistics have shown that serious racial/ethnic differences in terms of employment rates among men emerged only after the 1970s (Jaynes & Williams, 1989, 302–3). For example, among men aged sixteen to twenty-four, the relative odds ratio of employment (whites to blacks) was 1.4 in 1970 but increased to 2.0 in 1975 and to 2.4 in 1980. While since the 1940s black women have consistently attained higher levels of education than have black men (which had the effect of increasing $Z_{sw}$, the minimum amount of payoff that men must offer women), these changes in men's employment rates have worsened the situation by increasing the difference between the marginal product of a polygamous relationship with a man with greater resources and that of a polygamous relationship with a man with lesser resources.

## Structural Embeddedness

Even if a woman prefers monogamy to polygamy, forming a marriage is not a guaranteed outcome. In this section, we focus on how the structural embeddedness of a couple is a contingent factor in determining which of the payoffs shown in figure 6.5 results. Specifically, we examine how structural embeddedness can make monogamy, rather than polygamy, the preferred outcome. If we assume that MP and PM (one person, call him or her *ego*, is monogamous while his or her partner is polygamous) are worse than PP (both are polygamous), this is what in game theory is called a *coordination game*. And a coordination game has two Nash equilibria: MM and PP.[13] These outcomes are equilibria in the sense that, once the partner's choice is made, ego has no incentive to switch strategies. For example, as long as the partner chooses monogamy, ego will choose monogamy as well. Or, if the partner chooses polygamy, ego's best course of action will be to choose polygamy. The theory of Nash equilibrium in the original coordinated game is silent on which equilibrium will be selected. However, once we incorporate structural embeddedness into the model, we can produce insights about which equilibrium is plausible.

Structural embeddedness is conceptualized as a network characteristic of a given couple. For example, compare the two networks shown in figure 6.7. In panel *a* (showing *weak embeddedness*), both ego and partner have two friends apiece, but neither partner knows the other's friends (i.e., the two sets of friends do not overlap). In panel *b* (showing *strong embeddedness*), ego's two friends are also the partner's friends. Couples with this kind of overlapping social network are structurally embedded. Structural embeddedness facilitates the partners' commitment to each other through four mechanisms (cf. Coleman, 1988; Laumann, 1973, 83–130; Sandefur & Laumann, 1998). First, overlapping networks improve monitoring efficiency. In panel *b*, the partner can easily check what ego did last night by asking mutual friends. Second, overlapping networks also increase the effect of reputation (Frank, 1988). If ego betrays his or her spouse, he or she will lose face with mutual friends. Third, overlapping networks are more likely to elicit coordinated, shared attitudes or opinions that facilitate social commitment through mutual social support and shared activities. Finally, overlapping networks increase partners' emotional commitment to each other because there is greater social cohesion through more mutual reinforcement and sharing of attitudes and activities. Through these four mechanisms, strong embeddedness provides a couple with the network capacity to build mutual commitment and belief within the

---

13. Readers should note that only a brief proof has been provided here. However, the full proof can be worked on out the basis of the same logic employed in the text.

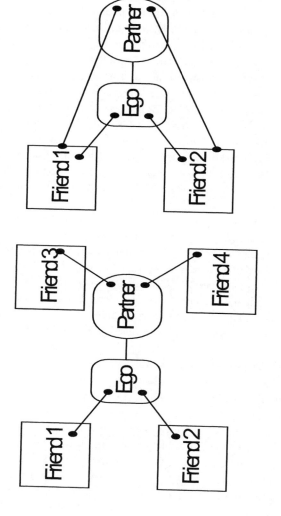

Figure 6.7. Structural embeddedness measured by social networks. *a*, Weak embeddedness. *b*, Strong embeddedness.

*a*

*b*

dyadic relationship itself.[14] The following analysis will show how this commitment induces monogamous relationships.

Under weak structural embeddedness, a polygamous relationship incurs no substantial costs (e.g., stigmatization, loss of reputation, emotional conflict). Thus, the likelihood that one partner will enter into a polygamous relationship is great, an incentive for the other partner to enter into a polygamous relationship as well. Under strong structural embeddedness, however, a polygamous relationship does, in fact, incur substantial costs. Thus, the likelihood that one partner will remain monogamous is great, an incentive for the other partner to remain monogamous as well.

In terms of structural embeddedness, African Americans' networks of friends tend to be smaller and segregated by gender. (On the basis of data from the General Social Survey, Peter Marsden [1987, 129] observed: "Whites have the largest networks [mean size 3.1], blacks the smallest [mean size 2.25]; Hispanics and others are intermediate.") We therefore hypothesize that, owing to this lack of structural embeddedness, African Americans are more likely to be in polygamous than in monogamous relationships. We would particularly expect marriage to be an implausible option for African American women, not only because so many of the partners available to them will be engaged in polygamous relationships, but also because they do not have the social resources (in terms of social networks) to guarantee that they have chosen the right partner.

Supporting this hypothesis are two related research findings. First, there are powerful relational and sexual scripts shared by inner-city African American men that delegitimate marriage and monogamy and, thus, indirectly encourage polygamy (see Wilson, 1996, 95–105).[15] Second, low-income African American women often expect to be single parents and are wary of entering into marriage with resource-poor men, who, according to the wisdom of the street, cannot be trusted to provide financially or emotionally (see Waller, 1999). Multivariate analysis with detailed social-network information from the CHSLS will confirm this hypothesis.

14. The terms *structural embeddedness* and *embeddedness* will be used interchangeably for the rest of the chapter. Temporal embeddedness (as found in a long-duration relationship) can produce the same results as structural embeddedness, as exemplified in various iterative game-theoretic models. We do not, however, consider temporal embeddedness in this model.

15. Wilson (1996, 99) notes: "There is a widespread feeling among women in the inner city that black males have relationships with more than one female at a time. And since some young men leave their girlfriends as soon as they become pregnant, it is not uncommon to find a black male who has fathered at least three children by three separate women."

The confirmation of our hypothesis about the effects of structural embeddedness will proceed in two steps. First, structural embeddedness must be a significant predictor of the choice between polygamous relationships and marriage. Second, after controlling for level of embeddedness, the racial difference must be reduced.

## Measuring Structural Embeddedness

Structural embeddedness, which encourages trust in a relationship and, thus, helps the relationship grow into marriage, has two dimensions: a relationship can be strongly embedded from the moment that people first meet, or it can develop into one that is strongly embedded as time goes by. CHSLS respondents were asked to enumerate up to six of their friends, including up to three free-time friends and up to three discussion partners, and to specify the relationship between each of these social-network intimates and the respondent's most recent and second most recent partner. The first dimension of structural embeddedness was measured from responses obtained to the question, "Did any of these (network intimates) know (most recent partner/second most recent partner) before you did?" The second dimension of structural embeddedness was measured from responses obtained to the question, "How would you characterize your relationship with (partner) at the time when you first had sex?" After trying out several categorizations, we dichotomized this dimension as having first sex before having established a dating relationship versus having first sex after having established a dating relationship. People who have sex before having dated have neither the time nor the resources (or perhaps do not wish) to embed the relationship in their social ties.

The data thus obtained allowed us to collapse the two dimensions into one measure of trust with three categories. (Note that we equated structural embeddedness with trust level although they are not the same concepts.) First, if the partners were unknown to each others' social intimates before the couple's first sexual encounter *and* that first sexual encounter occurred before a dating relationship was established, the trust level is designated as *low.* Second, if either of the partners was known to any of the other partner's social intimates before the couple's first sexual encounter *and* a dating relationship had been established before the first sexual encounter, the trust level is designated as *high.* Third, the trust level in all other cases (i.e., the partners were unknown to each other's social intimates *and* the first sexual encounter occurred after a dating relationship had been established; either of the partners was known to any of the other partner's social intimates *and* the first sexual encounter occurred before a dating relationship was established) is designated as *moderate.* The reader should note that measuring the level of embeddedness prevailing

before the first sexual encounter took place, not the current level of embeddedness, enabled us to perform regressions with causal inference. In the next
section, a multinomial logit analysis will show that people who are strongly
embedded before the first sexual encounter are much more likely to pursue
marriage than they are to engage in other sexual-matching strategies.

## Multinomial Logit Analysis of Sexual-Matching Patterns

In order to test whether a couple's level of embeddedness can significantly
predict the divergence between pursuing marriage and engaging in alternative sexual-matching strategies, we utilized a multinomial logit analysis to
predict the dependent variable, which has three categories: *currently married;
unmarried with only one partner;* and *unmarried with multiple partners.* Readers
should note that, owing to the very small number of people who engaged in
them, all three types of polygamous relationships (serial polygamous, short-
term polygamous, and long-term polygamous) were collapsed into the single
category *unmarried with multiple partners.* The effect of embeddedness can,
therefore, be underestimated.

The data come from the CHSLS representative sample of Cook County
and are limited to heterosexual, same-race couples. In addition, any nonmarital relationships started after the first marriage were dropped because, for
legal reasons, those relationships cannot develop into marriage. Table 6.3 displays the results of the multinomial logit analysis using odds ratios. The baseline category of the dependent variable is *currently married.*

In sum, older, more religious people are more likely to be married. Employment status is important only for men. For example, men who are working full-time are eight (= 1/0.13) times more likely to be currently married
(instead of unmarried with multiple partners) than are unemployed men.
The level of embeddedness is consistently significant in predicting the divergence between marriage and having multiple partners. Men who were
strongly embedded before first sex are nine (= 1/0.11) times more likely to
be currently married (instead of unmarried with multiple partners) than are
men who were weakly embedded. In general, table 6.3 reveals that the level
of embeddedness before first sex is an important predictor for the divergence
between marriage and alternative sexual-matching strategies (especially unmarried with multiple partners).

However, this multinomial logit model is not satisfactory, for various reasons. First, as mentioned earlier, the embeddedness effect might be underestimated because people who engaged in long-term polygamous relationships
(the extreme opposite case to marriage) are collapsed into the *unmarried with
multiple partners* category with other people who engaged in serial polyga-

Table 6.3 Multinomial Logit of Sexual-Matching Patterns (odds ratios)

| | Men | | Women | |
|---|---|---|---|---|
| | One Partner | Multiple Partners | One Partner | Multiple Partners |
| Age | .99 | .91*** | .96* | .90*** |
| Age * age | 1.00 | 1.00* | 1.00*** | 1.00*** |
| High school graduates | 8.03* | 1.34 | .55 | 3.65 |
| Some college education | 4.32 | 1.43 | .42 | 2.04 |
| African American | .68 | 3.15** | 6.33*** | 7.72*** |
| Church attendance | .98** | .98* | .98** | .96*** |
| Currently student | 7.46** | 4.03 | 1.51 | 2.21 |
| Medium embedded (vs. weakly) | .94 | .21** | .54 | .16*** |
| Strongly embedded (vs. weakly) | .52 | .11*** | .20** | .03*** |
| Part-time work (vs. no work) | .09** | .05** | .79 | 1.36 |
| Full-time work (vs. no work) | .11** | .13** | 1.09 | 1.17 |
| N | 173 | | 220 | |
| Pseudo-$R^2$ | .24 | | .24 | |

*Note:* Baseline category for the dependent variable is currently married. For education level, the baseline category is high school dropout. Church attendance was recorded as follows and treated as continuous: 0 for never; 0.5 for less than once a year; 5 for several times a year; 12 for about once a month; 30 for two or three times a month; 50 for nearly every week; 52 for once a week; and 100 for more than once a week. Part-time work is defined as working less than thirty-five hours per week.

*.05 < $p$ < .01.

**.01 < $p$ < .05.

***$p$ < .01.

mous and short-term polygamous relationships. Second, because we had to take the average of the embeddedness level for the two partners, the effects for each partner are mixed. Third, this multinomial logit does not properly handle right-censored cases, the people who have not yet married. Fourth, the hazard function for marriage might not be well captured by the simple square term for age. Thus, in the next section, event-history analysis is employed to solve these problems. However, in the event-history analysis, we cannot examine divergent sexual-matching strategies because we do not have enough information about how sexual-matching strategies changed during the risk period. We can examine only the probability that the partnerships ended in marriage.

## Event-History Analysis of Marriage

For the event-history analysis, we assume that the risk period for the marriage started with the first sexual encounter. Among the variables used in the pre-

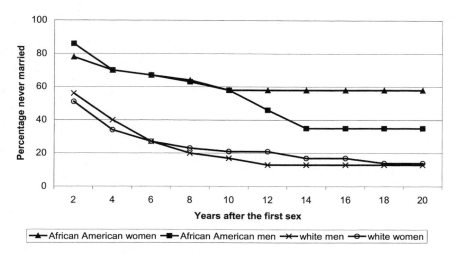

Figure 6.8. Kaplan–Meier survival estimates, by gender and race.

vious multinomial logit, *working status* and *currently a student* must be dropped because they can change during the risk period.[16] The unit of analysis is not the person but the partnership. Figure 6.8 shows the Kaplan–Meier survival estimates from the data set, with the data again limited to heterosexual, same-race relationships. We see that there is a strong racial/ethnic difference and that African American women are the least likely to marry. After testing that the risk of marriage is proportional over time,[17] the Cox proportional model with discrete time[18] is chosen because there are many tied failure times.

The results presented in table 6.4 confirm the embeddedness effect once again. For example, among men, the relationships that were strongly embedded before the first sexual encounter are seven times more likely to end up in marriage than are the relationships that were only weakly embedded. Furthermore, after controlling for the embeddedness level (the first model), the racial/ethnic difference lost its statistical significance among men: the absolute *t*-value decreases from 2.27 to 0.61. Although the embeddedness level is very significant among women as well, it only slightly decreases the racial/ethnic difference.

16. We keep *education* and *church attendance*, however. Even though these variables can change during the risk period, they are relatively stable for most people.

17. On the basis of Schoenfeld residuals, the *p*-value for the hypothesis of proportional hazard is .41 for the whole model after controlling for gender.

18. This is equivalent to conditional logistic regression where groups are defined by the risk sets and the outcome given by the marriage variable.

Table 6.4 Discrete–Time Cox Proportional Hazard Model of Marriage (odds ratios)

|  | Men | Men | Women | Women |
|---|---|---|---|---|
| Age | .98 | .96** | .97** | .96*** |
| Less than college, college | .79 | .82 | 1.57 | 1.44 |
| College, less than college | 2.65** | 2.38*** | .67 | .72 |
| College, college | 1.97** | 2.09** | 1.68** | 1.74** |
| Church attendance | 1.01** | 1.01*** | 1.02*** | 1.02*** |
| African American | .61 | .46** | .33*** | .33*** |
|  | (1.45) | (2.70) | (4.42) | (4.49) |
| Medium embedded (vs. weakly) | 3.35*** |  | 2.51*** |  |
| Strongly embedded (vs. weakly) | 7.32*** |  | 4.70*** |  |
| N | 646 | 646 | 1,258 | 1,258 |

*Note:* The baseline category for the couple's education is less than college, less than college: ego's education level comes first. Values in parenthesis shows the absolute value of *t*-statistics. Church attendance was
recorded as follows and treated as continuous: 0 for never; 0.5 for less than once a year; 5 for several times
a year; 12 for about once a month; 30 for two or three times a month; 50 for nearly every week; 52 for
once a week; and 100 for more than once a week.
*$.05 < p < .01$.
**$.01 < p < .05$.
***$p < .01$.

## Conclusion

In this chapter, we have identified several structural factors that lead individuals into nonmonogamous sexual relationships. In general, we have discovered that individuals' degree of social embeddedness is a critical factor in explaining the relationship outcomes of different populations. In particular, we
have focused on answering the question, Why are African Americans less
likely to marry than are members of the other racial/ethnic groups in our
study? Our analyses demonstrate that African Americans have a relatively
high proportion of polygynous relationships at equilibrium in the sexual-
matching market owing both to the disproportionally small number of marriageable men in the population, which makes a polygamous relationship
more attractive to both men and women, and to the lack of strong embeddedness as social capital, which makes marriage implausible in many circumstances. Although we have stressed structural factors, this chapter suggests
that the sexual and relational scripts of different groups and the nature of social networks may support hybrid matching strategies and polygamous relationships among some groups. We suspect that the causal relations among
social embeddedness, sexual cultures, and the availability of possible sex or
marriage partners in a given sex market are very complex. Future analyses

may be able to clarify these relations and help us further understand why a high degree of social embeddedness among some groups (e.g., Latinos, white gay men or lesbians) fails to discourage concurrent sexual relationships (i.e., serial polygamous and short-term polygamous relationships) but does not lead to long-term polygamous relationships, as among African Americans.

# 7 )

# Commitment, Jealousy, and the Quality of Life

Anthony Paik,
Edward O. Laumann,
and Martha Van Haitsma

Jealousy, the green-eyed monster, as Shakespeare called it, has long been of literary interest. In contrast, scientific attention to this social phenomenon only recently developed into an active area of research. Psychologists, therapists, and historians view jealousy as related to culture, gender, biology, and the dynamics of relationships, yet there is scant research about how jealousy

Earlier versions of this chapter were presented as "Sexual Jealousy, Violence, and Embeddedness in Intimate Relations: A Social Structural and Cultural Explanation" at the annual meeting of the Society for the Scientific Study of Sexuality, Orlando, 10 November 2000, and as "Sexual Jealousy and Intimate Partner Violence: The Importance of Commitment in Sexual Relationships" at the annual meeting of the Population Association of America, New York, 26 March 1999.

is actually distributed in populations.[1] We therefore attempt to provide in this chapter a social-epidemiological account of sexual jealousy that acts to complement existing research agendas, which are primarily psychological.

We also seek to update the sociocultural narratives about the organization of jealousy in American culture. A consistent theme in these narratives is that the rise of more companionate orientations, where equality and equity are highly valued, has displaced more "traditional" gender roles, the situation where the male is the breadwinner and the female is the center of domesticity. An important cultural consequence of this historical shift, the change from gender-role traditionalism to gender-role liberalism between intimate partners, is the suppression of sexual jealousy (Hansen, 1985; Stearns, 1989). In this view, jealousy, once the emotional signal of one's love, has become an inappropriate emotion signaling an inappropriate possessiveness. Specifically, the expression of jealousy indicates a fundamental lack of trust, trust being, supposedly, the basis on which modern relationships are founded. However, what happens to jealousy when there is substantial ambiguity about whether individuals are committed to one another in the first place? This is the situation in sex markets, which incorporate a diversity of sexual-matching strategies characterized by varying levels of commitment.[2] Thus, our purpose here is to examine, generally, how sexual jealousy is an important consequence of today's sex markets and, specifically, how it is a perceived breach of the commitment between sex partners.

Because cheating, shirking, and opportunism are all-too-common possibilities in intimate relations, people often seek committed sex partners. Youm and Paik (chapter 6 in this volume) argued that socially embedded sexual relationships were more likely to lead to committed partnerships like marriage. We, in turn, investigate commitment and jealousy in intimate relations in order to understand how sex markets affect the well-being of sexual relationships. With the appeal of nonmonogamous sexual-matching strategies among Chicagoans (see Youm & Paik, chapter 6 in this volume), we suggest that expectations about sexual exclusivity are frequently breached, resulting in conflicts over sexual jealousy, and making these events an important empirical concern. Thus, in what follows, we distinguish between those who are and those who are not committed (as indexed by expectations of sexual exclusiv-

1. Prominent, recent examples of research on jealousy include evolutionary-psychological arguments by Buss (2000), historical research by Stearns (1989), and therapeutic accounts by White and Mullen (1989).

2. On the terms *sex market* and *sexual marketplace* as they are used in this study, see the section "The Social Organization of Sexual Partnering and Sexual Relationships" in Ellingson, Laumann, Paik, and Mahay (chapter 1 in this volume).

ity), investigate the causes and the consequences of breaches of commitment (the conflicts over sexual jealousy), and address the relevance of sex markets for contemporary sexual relationships in Chicago.

We follow Parsons (1968) in defining *commitments* as symbolic acts signaling moral obligations or promises to promote and uphold a given social value. For example, in sexual relationships, the promise of sexual exclusivity and the marriage contract are two major commitments made by contemporary American couples (Davis, 1973). Committed relationships are important because they facilitate the development of relationship-specific capital and joint investments, which is advantageous for raising families (Frank, 1988; Laumann, Gagnon, Michael, & Michaels, 1994). They are also more durable (Bennett, Blanc, & Bloom, 1988; Thomson & Colella, 1992; Sprecher, 2001) and are associated with better relationship quality (Laumann, Gagnon, Michael, & Michaels, 1994; Waite & Joyner, 2001). Marriage, for example, produces better health and improved financial status in comparison to nonmarital relationships (Waite, 2000; Waite & Gallagher, 2000).

Yet what happens when commitments are not met or are breached? In this chapter, we focus on the expectation of sexual exclusivity and jealousy, both of which are important themes related to sex markets.[3] We present below a social-psychological model of commitment breaches and negative sanctions that has empirical importance as well: it shows how breaches mediate the association between commitment and the well-being of sexual partnerships. Hence, we seek to provide a solid empirical understanding of the consequences of commitment breaches in intimate relations while advancing the hypothesis that having extensive commitments confers risks in addition to rewards.[4]

As a classic breach of commitment, sexual jealousy is an increasingly important social-psychological factor in sex markets. In the United States, the expectation of sexual exclusivity is widespread and shared among sex partners, particularly heterosexual sex partners (Davis, 1973; Blumstein & Schwartz, 1983), and is closely linked to the formation of emotional attachments between partners (Swidler, 1980). However, recent research shows that the threat and the actual occurrence of sexual infidelity are common, more prevalent

---

3. Commitment breaches are also relevant in the other areas of social interaction where commitments are relevant, including formal organizations (Kanter, 1968; Brockner, Tyler, & Cooper-Schneider, 1992; Robinson, 1996) and groups (Lawler, 1992), social networks (Lawler & Yoon, 1993, 1996), as well as in other aspects of intimate relations (Johnson, 1973; Laumann, Gagnon, Michael, & Michaels, 1994).

4. An earlier study of organizational commitment by Brockner, Tyler, and Cooper-Schneider (1992) identified the basic relation between commitments and risk/rewards.

among nonmarried men and women (Forste & Tanfer, 1996; Treas & Giesen, 2000; Youm & Paik, chapter 6 in this volume), and important factors depressing relationship quality (Waite & Joyner, 2001). Approximately 11 percent of Americans with sex partners have had at least one concurrent sex partner during a one-year period, and 15 percent of married women and 25 percent of married men report extramarital affairs at some point during their marriages (Laumann, Gagnon, Michael, & Michaels, 1994). This dual aspect of American sexual expression—the centrality of sexual exclusivity and the prevalence of sexual infidelity—suggests that jealousy is a pervasive phenomenon related to participation in sex markets.[5] However, there are no population-based studies of sexual jealousy, so its prevalence among the general population and distribution across key demographic categories (i.e., marital status, race/ethnicity, and gender) are unknown.

Indeed, research investigating the social-organizational bases of sexual jealousy is still in its infancy. Prior research on sexual jealousy primarily focused on gender and cross-cultural comparisons to test evolutionary-psychological (Buss, Larsen, Westen, & Semmelroth, 1992; Geary, Rumsey, Bow-Thomas, & Hoard, 1995; Buss, 1998, 2000) and social-constructionist (Reiss, 1986; Zammuner & Fischer, 1995; Hupka & Bank, 1996; Pines & Friedman, 1998; Nannini & Meyers, 2000) hypotheses. Others found this emotion to be a major factor leading to intimate-partner violence (Daly, Wilson, & Weghorst, 1982; Stets & Pirog-Good, 1987; Block & Christakos, 1995; Wilson & Daly, 1993).[6] Most of these studies assume that jealousy occurs in the context of *valued* relationships, which raises an important but unexplored question about how the level of commitment and sexual jealousy jointly affect the likelihood of intimate-partner violence. Several other studies have found positive associations between jealousy and factors associated with commitment, including level of dependency (Barnett, Martinez, & Bluestein, 1995), relationship length (Aune & Comstock, 1997), and socioemotional distance (Dutton & Browning, 1988). These findings highlight the relevance of social-exchange concepts like commitment for explaining the social bases of jealousy (Hansen, 1985; Bringle & Buunk, 1991).

Unfortunately, all these studies rely on clinical or convenience samples, focus only on one marital status (typically, married couples), and fail to link

5. For a discussion of nonmonogamous sex, see Blumstein and Schwartz (1983). For reviews of sexual jealousy, see DeLamater (1991) and Bringle and Buunk (1991).

6. Indeed, Stets and Pirog-Good (1987) found that, among dating women, sexual jealousy increased the probability of using and being the object of physical violence by 240 and 225 percent, respectively. Block and Christakos (1995) found that 14 percent of all intimate-partner homicides in Chicago over a twenty-nine-year period could be directly attributed to situations involving sexual jealousy or love triangles.

the dynamics of sexual jealousy to the population at large. These limitations make their findings incomplete and less generalizable. Thus, we seek in this chapter to rectify this situation by providing a theoretical and empirical account that explains how commitment is linked to sexual jealousy and intimate-partner violence (one measure of the well-being of sexual partnerships) among the dating, cohabiting, and married Chicago Health and Social Life Survey (CHSLS) respondents.

## Conceptual Framework

The level of commitment indicates an individual's, a dyad's, and a culture's sense that social relationships can be scaled according to the relative irreversibility of promises made and obligations assumed, where greater commitment implies increased obligation enhanced through an affective bond (Laumann, Gagnon, Michael, & Michaels, 1994). Commitments are composed of cognitive, affective, and normative components (Parsons, 1951; Kanter, 1968, 1972; Lawler & Yoon, 1993, 1996), which are analytically separable but are likely to be coupled with one another, to varying degrees, in social relations. According to Kanter (1968, 1972), the cognitive component of commitments encompasses the perceived costs and benefits of staying in committed relationships (*continuance commitment*), the affective component the emotional gratification that binds individuals to social relationships (*cohesion commitment*), and the normative component the moral obligations and sanctions that uphold norms of conduct (*control commitment*).[7]

Applied to sexual relations, continuance, cohesion, and control commitments capture how sexual partnerships vary with regard to, respectively, degree of investment, emotional intimacy, and internalization of sexual and family values. The term *continuance commitment* refers primarily to the cognitive perceptions of partners, social networks, and social institutions about the perceived costs and benefits of staying, or the stakes, in relationships. We argue that marital status is a particularly important indicator of continuance commitments. Researchers, for example, argue that marital relationships typically involve the most sunk costs in terms of children, property, and social networks and the most relationship-specific capital (England & Farkas, 1986;

---

7. Traditionally, sociologists focused on the cognitive components of commitment, especially as they relate to intimate relations (e.g., Davis, 1973; Johnson, 1973; Vaughan, 1986; Kollock, 1994), but rational-choice (Frank, 1988, 1993) and social-exchange (Lawler & Yoon, 1993, 1996) researchers have recently spurred renewed interest in the emotional component by highlighting how positive emotions are crucial to the process of commitment formation.

Brines & Joyner, 1999; Treas & Giesen, 2000), making these relationships a source of emotional, physical, and material benefits and costly to dissolve. Marriage also entails public rites (e.g., weddings) and a legally binding contract that involves sacrificing some individual autonomy and incurring joint obligations. In comparison, dating and cohabiting relationships have lower exit costs, fewer joint investments, and less specialization. Dating and cohabiting relationships are also more heterogeneous in terms of the composition of committed individuals since they are necessarily less selective than marital relationships (Waite & Joyner, 2001). Thus, higher levels of continuance commitments are more likely to be found among the married than among the nonmarried, although these statuses are, to some extent, fuzzy sets.

The term *cohesion commitment* refers to the development of emotional bonds, intimacy, and love between sex partners. Two mechanisms facilitate the formation of this dyadic cohesion: renunciation of actual or potential competitors and communion between partners (Kanter, 1968, 1972). Renunciation involves prioritizing the partner over others, including other potential and actual sex partners, friends, family members, and groups. Communion involves engaging in social arrangements that place sex partners in close or continual proximity with another—for example, shared living arrangements, having the same set of friends, and spending considerable amounts of time with one another. Both processes produce or maintain higher levels of dyadic cohesion, which means that partners increasingly rely on one another as a primary, if not an exclusive, source of emotional intimacy. Some researchers argue that these positive emotions play a crucial role in group formation by reducing uncertainty and creating feelings of trustworthiness, thereby facilitating more risky investments like relationship-specific capital (Frank, 1988; Lawler & Yoon, 1993, 1996). Thus, high levels of dyadic cohesion are expressed as feelings of love and can even produce *dyadic withdrawal,* the situation prevailing when the sex partners spend time with one another and devalue social ties to friends, family, and the community at large (Slater, 1963). Although marital status may be closely associated with level of dyadic cohesion, the two are likely to be loosely coupled among some American couples.

The term *control commitment* refers to an individual's normative orientations toward beliefs, values, and attitudes about sex and family roles. Two important sexual attitudes relevant for sexual exclusivity are beliefs about extramarital permissiveness and gender roles. The former centers on the extent to which individuals approve of extramarital sex (Reiss, Anderson, & Sponaugle, 1980); the latter covers beliefs about how economic and childrearing roles within a family should be distributed by gender. Specifically, gender-role traditionalism is the belief that men, not women, should be the primary breadwinners for the family; gender-role liberalism indicates that the economic and childrearing roles should be more equally shared. Not surprisingly, researchers find that marriage is more selective of beliefs against extramarital permissiveness (Laumann, Gagnon, Michael, & Michaels, 1994, 509–40) and sex-role liberalism (Clarkberg, Stolzenberg, & Waite, 1995) than are non-married statuses. Taken together, marital status is an important factor related to all three kinds of commitments in sexual relationships, but dyadic cohesion and sexual attitudes may operate independently as well.

Commitments, then, are integral to the organization of sexual relationships and are socially organized by marital status, dyadic cohesion, and values related to sex and family roles. We seek to extend knowledge of commitments in sexual relationships by highlighting their negative side—specifically, the relations among commitments, breaches, and intimate-partner violence. As Parsons (1968) noted, negative sanctions are the central mechanism by which actors are induced to uphold promises made and obligations assumed. Our argument is that sexual jealousy is a sharp emotional experience that often leads to conflict in intimate relations. There are two parts to this model: the marking of a breach of commitment by a subjective emotional experience and the expression of this emotion, which varies with intensity of arousal and with socially constructed "feeling rules" (Hochschild, 1983). The former is essentially a cognitive process, while the latter encompasses the arousal and behavioral components of emotions.

As an emotion, sexual jealousy has these cognitive, arousal, and behavioral elements (DeLamater, 1991). *Sexual jealousy* has been defined as "a protective reaction to a perceived threat to a valued relationship or to its quality" (Clanton, 1990, 180). Here, we conceptualize *sexual jealousy* as a relational property derived from expectations of sexual exclusivity. Jealousy results, not only from actual cases of sexual infidelity, but also from instances where a partner's interactions or behaviors are perceived to conflict with the expectation of sexual exclusivity. An important distinction centers on whether sexual jealousy should be approached as a subjective phenomenon or as a dyadic property. While both approaches are valid, we focus on the dyadic dimensions of sexual jealousy: its interpersonal expression as an argument, a fight, or a conflict. As a consequence, sexual jealousy has behavioral concomitants as well. Prior research established a close connection between sexual jealousy and intimate-partner violence, so our fundamental question centers on how the different types of commitments, indexed by marital status, dyadic cohesion, and sexual attitudes, organize the elicitation of sexual jealousy and physical aggression.

With regard to the experience of sexual jealousy, we argue that the cognitive and normative dimensions of commitments (i.e., continuance commitments and control commitments) are influential. Because continuance commitments are primarily about profit and loss, individuals with lower expectations of continuance are simply more likely to adopt behaviors that elicit sexual jealousy and, therefore, are more likely to be approached by others who are seeking partners. Indeed, research shows that individuals in cohabiting and dating relationships are less likely to be sexually exclusive (Forste & Tanfer, 1996; Treas & Giesen, 2000). Continuance commitments are also relevant to the experience of sexual jealousy because of considerations of cognitive consistency. Psychological research shows that attention tends to be selective; that is, people focus on information that confirms their prior beliefs (Robinson, 1996). Individuals who are more highly committed to a relationship (those with, in this case, higher expectations of continuance) will tend to ignore disconfirming information, such as potential sexual infidelity; those who are less highly committed (those with lower levels of continuance) will tend to seek signals confirming breaches. Sexual jealously should, therefore, be more prevalent among the nonmarried because these couples are more likely to experience breaches in terms of actual sexual infidelity or perceived threats to the relationship.

Control commitments are relevant because they reflect an individual's attachment to the norm of sexual exclusivity. We argue that believing in gender-role traditionalism and extramarital permissiveness tends to amplify suspicions about sexual exclusivity, thereby generating more sexual jealousy. Prior research identified a positive association between gender-role traditionalism and sexual jealousy (Hansen, 1985). Since gender-role liberalism is associated with mutual trust between sex partners, couples with more traditional orientations should have lower thresholds of suspicion. On the other hand, beliefs about extramarital permissiveness, we argue, index the extent to which individuals are willing to accept the norm of sexual exclusivity. Although only a small percentage of Americans believe that there is nothing wrong with extramarital sex, individuals holding this belief should be the object of their partner's sexual jealousy because this position is likely to conflict with the attitudes and values of those partners.

Because cohesion commitments are primarily affective, we do not anticipate any effect on the elicitation of sexual jealousy, which we view as a cognitive phenomenon. However, the level of dyadic cohesion should influence the process by which sexual jealousy is aroused. Research on the arousal of emotions suggests that, as expectations and experience become more incongruous, the intensity of emotional reactions increases (Smelser, 1998; Turner, 1999, 2000). Thus, when perceived breaches occur, individuals with higher levels of cohesion will experience more intense emotional reactions than will those in less committed relationships. This argument is consistent with social-exchange perspectives on sexual jealousy (Berscheid, 1983; Bringle & Buunk, 1991) but goes further by providing an explicit theory of the emotional mechanism. Although the expression of sexual jealousy will be subject to feeling rules, the intensity of this emotion should follow a structural relation: the greater the intensity, the greater the likelihood of observing a cultural display of jealousy. While some researchers argue that Americans perceive sexual jealousy to be a personal defect, specifically, evidence of inappropriate possessiveness (Swidler, 1980; Stearns, 1989), the empirical research shows a strong association between jealousy and violence (Stets & Pirog-Good, 1987; Block & Christakos, 1995). Thus, we argue that jealousy is frequently expressed as interpersonal conflict, which often leads to violence.

We should note that our conceptual approach is dyadic in nature. While commitments, jealousy, and intimate-partner violence can all be treated from an individual perspective, we are interested primarily in the relational perspective. We believe that there are good reasons for adopting a relational approach. First, most commitments in sexual relationships occur at the dyadic level, with the most obvious being marital status. Dating, cohabitation, and marriage are mutually shared distinctions that differentiate relationships from one another. Second, the phenomena of interest are essentially pairings of interaction episodes, and pairing is a dyadic process (Huston & Robins, 1982). We assume that sexual jealousy generates a set of interactions between sex partners that conform to display rules. Sexual jealousy is typically expressed in dyads as arguments, fights, or conflicts (Bringle & Buunk, 1991). Moreover, these episodes sometimes lead to physical aggression, which may be instigated by the jealous partner, the accused partner, or both. We therefore hypothesize the following relations between dyadic measures of commitments, sexual jealousy, and violence: First, jealous conflict is positively associated with cohabiting and dating relationships as well as with attitudes of sex-role traditionalism and extramarital permissiveness and is an important predictor of intimate-partner violence. Second, the level of dyadic cohesion should, however, mediate the association between jealousy and violence.

## Data and Methods

The empirical work reported here is based on selected parts of the CHSLS, which is described in detail in Van Haitsma, Paik, and Laumann (chapter 2 in this volume). In the analyses presented below, we utilized only three samples—the Cook County sample and the Westside and Southtown neighborhood samples. The Westside and Southtown samples were overwhelmingly Hispanic and black, respectively, enabling us to provide comparative results for sexual jealousy and its links to intimate-partner violence. However, because the small sizes of the neighborhood samples limit their use to bivariate analyses, we use only the Cook County data for our multivariate models. We did not employ the Shoreland and Erlinda samples, both of which are composed of more heterogeneous populations—with respect to sexual orientation in the former case and race/ethnicity in the latter.

After excluding individuals who were not in any heterosexual sexual partnerships in the past twelve months, the effective sample sizes were 735 observations for Cook County, 301 for Westside, and 264 for Southtown. Only persons in current relationships were asked questions about intimate-partner violence. The question about jealous conflict, however, was posed with respect to respondents' most recent sex partners, regardless of time period. This meant that some respondents who had had a sex partner in the past twelve months but who had terminated the relationship prior to the interview were not asked about intimate-partner violence. In all, there were 154 cases across the three samples, or 12 percent of the total sample, that had had a relationship in the past twelve months but that were excluded from the questions about intimate-partner violence. While the argument could be made that these missing cases were on average more violent than those included in this study, our data showed that these respondents were overwhelmingly single—more than 93 percent were in dating, noncohabiting relationships—and less likely to have experienced jealousy within the relationship. In short, the exclusion of these cases makes, we believe, for a more conservative test in the analyses presented below because the excluded cases were likely to consist mostly of short-term dating relationships. Our effective samples, representing heterosexual couples in established, ongoing sexual relationships, were 647 cases in Cook County, 271 cases in Westside, and 228 cases in Southtown.

Because commitments are conceptualized as a relational property, we employed dyadic measures for our independent and dependent measures whenever possible. For the same reason, we measured sexual jealousy and intimate-partner violence as interpersonal behaviors, not as individual subjective experiences. Importantly, we lacked dyadic measures of sexual and family attitudes, so we were forced to rely on respondents' reports of their own attitudes for this commitment measure. We used several nondyadic control variables as well. Because of racial/ethnic, educational, and age homogamy between sex partners, we do not believe that this is problematic. However, there are critical questions regarding whether these dyadic measures reflect actual behaviors or respondents' perceptions of the dynamics within the dyad (Huston & Robins, 1982; Thompson & Walker, 1982) and whether they are systematically biased in some way. Our data-collection strategy sought to reduce bias as much as possible. The data were collected using a computer-assisted questionnaire, and sensitive questions about intimate-partner violence were self-administered to reduce social-desirability biases. We also expect relatively little recall bias since both jealousy and intimate-partner violence tend to be rare, vivid events, with the latter measured only for the last year.

Analyses performed in this study utilized logistic and ordered logistic regression. When assessing the likelihood of jealous conflict, we performed logistic regressions. Next, we estimated models predicting the likelihood of intimate-partner violence using ordered logistic regressions. The dependent and independent variables employed in these models are outlined in the following section.

## Dependent Measures

*Conflict over sexual jealousy.* All respondents in current partnerships were asked: "Which of the following are sources of conflict or things you and (partner) argue or fight about?" The following categories were provided: "jealousy"; "sex"; "money"; "drinking"; "children"; "partner's relatives"; "respondent's relatives"; "drugs"; "friends"; "household chores"; and "something else." And respondents were asked to code all that applied. A follow-up question asked about the frequency of jealous conflict over either the respondent or the sex partner paying too much attention to another person. Those reporting any jealous conflict in the relationship were coded with a dichotomous indicator.

*Intimate-partner violence in the last twelve months.* The questionnaire included an abbreviated, self-administered version of the Conflict Tactics scale, originally devised by Straus (1979). Respondents in current relationships were asked whether they, their partners, or both had engaged in a series of violent behaviors toward one another during the last twelve months. These behaviors included argued heatedly short of yelling, yelled at or insulted the other, sulked and refused to talk, threatened to hit or throw something at the other, threw something at the other, pushed, grabbed, or shoved the other, hit the other with a hand or fist, hit the other with something hard, beat the other up, threatened the other with a knife or gun, and used a knife or fired a gun. We constructed a Guttman scale for the physical-violence items, which scaled quite well (coefficient of reproducibility = 0.95; coefficient of scalability = 0.89). The best fit progressed in the following order: (1) no physical violence; (2) threatened to hit or throw something or pushed, grabbed, or shoved; (3) threw something; (4) hit with a hand or fist; (5) beat the other up or hit with a hard object; (6) threatened with or actually used a weapon. The results of the Guttman scale also indicated that a large break exists between item 4 (hitting) and the remaining items, a pattern fitting the distinction over the severity of violence. In the models presented below, we created a three-category ordinal variable, distinguishing between *no violence,* physical violence that stops short of hitting (*moderate violence*), and physical violence that involves or goes beyond hitting (*severe violence*). In the total sample, the probability of injury among those reporting moderate and severe violence was 9 and 27 percent, respectively.

As we mentioned before, violence is tapped as a dyadic rather than an individual characteristic. Because only one member of a partnership was interviewed, respondents' reports of their own and their partners' behavior are used as an indicator of violent conflict in a relationship. Reports of respondents' violence toward partner and partners' violence toward respondent were used to signal violence in a relationship without any presumption of direction. We should point out, however, that the literature has shown that women tend to be the victims of violence and that their own use of violence may be defensive in nature.

## Independent Measures

*Commitment measures.* To measure continuance commitments, we created a standard trichotomous measure of marital status for respondents vis-à-vis their current, most recent sex partner. Nonmarried couples were divided into two categories on the basis of whether they were cohabiting. We refer to nonmarried couples who were not cohabiting as *dating*. To measure cohesion commitments, we employed responses to the question: "About how much of your free time do you spend with (partner)? Was that all, most, about half, some, very little, or none?" After investigating the associations of dyadic cohesion with jealousy and intimate-partner violence, we dichotomized the measure, with respondents who spent less than half their free time with their partners characterized as exhibiting *low,* as opposed to *high, dyadic cohesion.* To measure control commitments, we employed responses to the following two statements: "A married person having sexual relations with someone other than their marriage partner—always wrong, almost always wrong, wrong only sometimes, or not wrong at all"; and "It is much better for everyone if the man earns the main living and the woman takes care of the home and family—strongly agree, agree, disagree, or strongly disagree." We dichotomized the former measure into those who believe that extramarital sex is not wrong at all and those who believe that it is wrong. We dichotomized the latter measure into those who strongly agreed with this statement and those whose responses fell in the other categories.

*Concurrent sex partner.* In order to ascertain whether a couple had experienced a situation where at least one partner had sexual relations with a third party, we combined the results from two questions: "To the best of your knowledge, how many people other than you did (partner) have sex with during the course of your relationship?" and, "How many people other than (partner) did you have sex with during the course of your relationship with (partner)?" We combined the results of these questions and dichotomized the answers to indicate if either of the sex partners had ever or never had a sexual relationship with a third party during the course of their relationship with each other.[8] This variable was employed in the logistic regressions predicting jealous conflict but was then integrated with the jealousy variable, described below, for the ordered logistic regressions predicting intimate-partner violence.

*Jealousy or concurrency in the partnership.* For the models predicting intimate-partner violence, we combined the dependent variable from the logistic regressions, *conflict over sexual jealousy,* with the indicator for concurrent sex partners to create a dichotomous indicator of jealousy and/or concurrency. This was an effort to more accurately operationalize jealousy as a perceived or an actual threat to a relationship. Jealousy may be induced by situations other than actual sexual infidelity; thus, an undercount of jealous situations will result if one considers only concurrent partners. Relying only on reports of jealous conflict, however, discounts those situations where a perceived threat is not translated into open conflict. Combining a more objective measure of infidelity with self-reports of jealous conflict seemed a more accurate indicator of the underlying construct of jealousy between sex partners than either measure taken alone.

*Control variables.* We included control variables for demographic characteristics such as gender, ethnicity, education attainment, and age. Respondents whose ethnic or racial affiliation was "other," the majority of whom were Asian American, were grouped into a *white/other* category. We also introduced control variables for other potential sources of intimate-partner violence. These included dichotomous indicators for whether the respondent was raised by a biological or an adoptive father, whether the respondent was ever incarcerated (included being detained or sent to reform school), and the relative options of the respondent and the partner outside the relationship. Respondents' and partners' options outside their partnership were based on three questions, using five-point scales, that asked about how their standard of living, happiness, and social life would be affected if the partnership ended.[9] These items were combined for both the respondent and the partner (Cronbach a = 0.76 and 0.70, respectively). Individuals whose options outside their current relationships were the same as or better than those in their current relationships were grouped together. This operation produced two

8. In some cases, respondents did not know whether their partner had had a concurrent partner. Such responses were recoded as not having had a concurrent partner since a "don't know" answer is likely to reflect lack of knowledge about the partner's fidelity. This is a conservative assumption with respect to our hypotheses. Reporting that one does not know about the sexual fidelity of one's partner could be taken as a lack of trust, an indicator of likely suspicion.

9. This approach is similar to Lennon and Rosenfield's (1994) strategy for tapping women's options.

dichotomous measures that reflected the economic and social options of the respondent and the partner.[10] Finally, we included a dichotomous indicator for conflicts over drinking alcohol or taking drugs, a known predictor of intimate-partner violence, as well as conflicts over money and friends.[11] Descriptive statistics of these control variables are listed in table 7.1.

## Results

Table 7.1 also provides tabulations for our measures of continuance, cohesion, and control commitments, showing distinct patterns among the three samples. Southtown, for example, has the highest percentage of couples with low levels of commitments: 65 percent of the respondents are unmarried; 36 percent have low dyadic cohesion; and more than half were in relationships with sexual infidelity. In contrast, Westside exhibits a more "traditional" pattern of commitments. The majority of respondents are married and sexually exclusive, and they report the highest level of approval for traditional gender roles. However, they also have the highest percentage of respondents in cohabiting relationships, suggesting that the organization of intimate relations in Westside does not conform neatly to the traditional ideal-type of sexual relations. Using Cook County as a baseline, these results suggest that the sex markets in Southtown tend to be more transactional or hybrid and those in Westside more relational. We should note, however, that, in all our samples, approval of extramarital permissiveness is extremely rare.

Table 7.2 presents the distribution of jealous conflict and intimate-partner violence in the Cook County, Westside, and Southtown samples. Overall, jealous conflict between current sex partners is remarkably widespread. Within Cook County, 23 percent of male and 31 percent of female respondents report experiencing jealous conflict at some point during their relationships. The prevalence in Westside and Southtown is markedly higher. Approximately one of three respondents in the Southtown sample reports

---

10. Because the likelihood of responding violently to jealousy is partly a product of how likely the wronged party is to think such a course will be effective, it is important to control for partner dependence. This measure of options outside the relationship is an important control to try to hold constant the relative power arrangements that affect the likelihood and direction of violence inside a relationship. The model presented here is an effort to look at the relationship as a whole.

11. We did not include indicators for other sources of conflict. Bivariate analyses indicated that these other sources of conflict did not increase the likelihood of severe intimate-partner violence. None of these other indicators have been theoretically identified as predictors of violence.

Table 7.1 Descriptive Statistics for Current Sexual Partnerships, CHSLS (%)

| Variable | Cook County | Westside | Southtown |
|---|---|---|---|
| Concurrent partner | 30 | 22 | 54 |
| Low dyadic cohesion | 25 | 22 | 36 |
| Extramarital permissiveness | 2 | 2 | 4 |
| Gender-role traditionalism | 16 | 35 | 15 |
| Married | 59 | 63 | 35 |
| Cohabiting | 11 | 19 | 11 |
| Dating | 30 | 18 | 54 |
| White/other | 64 | 8 | 0 |
| Black | 25 | 0 | 98 |
| Hispanic | 11 | 91 | 1 |
| Less than high school degree | 13 | 56 | 19 |
| High school to some college | 52 | 37 | 73 |
| College degree | 35 | 7 | 7 |
| Aged 18–31 | 37 | 50 | 36 |
| Aged 32–45 | 40 | 36 | 41 |
| Aged 46–59 | 23 | 14 | 23 |
| Women | 52 | 62 | 58 |
| Nonbiological or no father | 17 | 19 | 51 |
| Ever jailed | 9 | 6 | 15 |
| Respondent has options | 28 | 25 | 59 |
| Partner has options | 24 | 20 | 45 |
| Conflict over money | 37 | 38 | 36 |
| Conflict over friends | 24 | 25 | 16 |
| Conflict over drinking/drugs | 16 | 30 | 16 |
| Number of observations | 635 | 260 | 227 |
| Percentage missing | 2 | 4 | 0 |

*Note:* The Cook County sample estimates are weighted.

jealous conflict. There are also slight gender differences in reporting. In all three samples, men report lower prevalences of jealous conflict, and the spread between men's self-reports of jealousy and women's reports of their male partners' jealousy is wider than that between women's self-reports of jealousy and men's reports of their female partners' jealousy. For example, while 23 percent of women in Cook County report that their male partners were jealous, only 9 percent of men report that they were jealous of a third person, a 14 percent gap. In contrast, the gap in Cook County between women's self-reports of jealousy and men's reports of their female partners' jealousy is a mere 4 percent.

Table 7.2 also indicates that violence between sex partners during the last twelve months was also quite common, ranging from 14 percent to 41 percent across the three samples. In Cook County, 8 percent of the men report moderate violence (the category that aggregates reports of threatening to throw or hit, throwing things, pushing, or shoving). An additional 7 percent of the men report severe violence (hitting with hands or fists, hitting with a hard object, beating up a partner, or threatening to use or using weapons). Women in Cook County report higher rates of violence, with 13 percent reporting moderate violence and another 13 percent reporting severe violence. In both the Westside and the Southtown samples, the prevalence of intimate-partner violence is even higher: approximately 26 and 40 percent of respondents report violence, respectively. As with the self-reports of jealous conflict, there are gender differences in reporting violence as well. Men appear to be underreporting, although this seems to be restricted to the Cook County sample.[12] Despite these reporting differences, there appears to be a consistent relation between jealous conflict and violence. Samples with a high prevalence of jealous conflict tend to have a high prevalence of intimate-partner violence as well. Moreover, these data suggest that issues of jealousy and intimate-partner violence afflict many Chicagoans.

We calculated odds ratios (OR) for associations between the different types of conflict and intimate-partner violence. Table 7.3 shows that sexual jealousy significantly raises the odds of any violence in all three samples. It increases the odds of violence by more than three times in Cook County and by about four times in Westside and Southtown. Except for conflicts over drinking/drugs and over friends, few other types of conflict consistently elevate the likelihood of violence. Thus, not only is sexual jealousy a notable, consistent feature of the social organization of sexual relationships, but it also appears to be one of the most important motives for intimate-partner violence.

An important question centers on the conditions of sex markets that elicit

12. Other research presents evidence that male perpetrators are less truthful in self-reporting violence toward women than in reporting violence toward other men (Hilton, Harris, & Rice, 2000). In our data sets, we see evidence of this gender bias in reporting in the cross section but not in the Southtown and Westside samples. This may reflect different cultural norms attached both to class and to race/ethnicity. Men in working-class, ethnic communities may feel less social stigma associated with reporting violence than do middle-class white men and, thus, may report these behaviors more accurately. A limitation of these data is that there are not sufficient cases to run samples separately by gender. The gender variable is in the model to control for this sort of bias to the extent possible.

Table 7.2 Distribution of Jealous Conflict and Intimate-Partner Violence in Cook County, Westside, and Southtown (%)

| Variables | Cook County (N = 635) | | Westside (N = 260) | | Southtown (N = 227) | |
|---|---|---|---|---|---|---|
| | Male Respondent | Female Respondent | Male Respondent | Female Respondent | Male Respondent | Female Respondent |
| Conflicts over jealousy | 23.2 | 30.8 | 26.3 | 39.1 | 33.7 | 38.6 |
| Man was jealous due to a third person | | | | | | |
| Never | 90.9 | 77.0 | 87.9 | 79.5 | 79.0 | 72.0 |
| Rarely | 4.7 | 10.7 | 4.0 | 9.3 | 11.6 | 8.3 |
| Sometimes or more | 4.4 | 12.3 | 8.1 | 11.2 | 9.5 | 19.7 |
| Woman was jealous due to a third person | | | | | | |
| Never | 81.8 | 86.2 | 82.8 | 78.3 | 71.6 | 75.0 |
| Rarely | 7.8 | 8.0 | 8.1 | 9.9 | 6.3 | 10.6 |
| Sometimes or more | 10.4 | 5.9 | 9.1 | 11.8 | 22.1 | 14.4 |

| | | | | | | |
|---|---|---|---|---|---|---|
| Violent acts in the last 12 months | | | | | | |
| No violence | 85.6 | 74.3 | 73.7 | 74.5 | 59.0 | 59.9 |
| Threats, throwing things, pushing, shoving | 7.7 | 13.0 | 12.1 | 11.8 | 16.8 | 18.2 |
| Hitting, using hard objects, beating, weapons | 6.7 | 12.8 | 14.1 | 13.7 | 24.2 | 22.0 |
| Man was violent in the last 12 months | | | | | | |
| No violence | 87.6 | 80.8 | 76.8 | 78.9 | 65.3 | 69.7 |
| Threats, throwing things, pushing, shoving | 8.4 | 13.3 | 13.1 | 10.6 | 14.7 | 12.9 |
| Hitting, using hard objects, beating, weapons | 4.1 | 5.8 | 10.1 | 10.6 | 20.0 | 17.4 |
| Woman was violent in the last 12 months | | | | | | |
| No violence | 90.3 | 78.8 | 80.8 | 79.5 | 62.1 | 68.9 |
| Threats, throwing things, pushing, shoving | 4.9 | 10.0 | 10.1 | 11.8 | 16.8 | 18.9 |
| Hitting, using hard objects, beating, weapons | 4.8 | 11.2 | 9.1 | 8.7 | 21.1 | 12.1 |

*Note:* Cook County results are weighted; results from other samples are unweighted.

Table 7.3 Sources of Conflicts between Current Sexual Relationships and the Likelihood of Intimate-Partner Violence

| Sources of Conflict | Cook County (N = 635) | | Westside (N = 260) | | Southtown (N = 227) | |
|---|---|---|---|---|---|---|
| | Percentage Reporting | Odds Ratio of Violence | Percentage Reporting | Odds Ratio of Violence | Percentage Reporting | Odds Ratio of Violence |
| Jealousy | 27.2 | 3.13*** | 34.2 | 4.35*** | 36.6 | 4.00*** |
| Sex | 11.3 | 1.49 | 16.5 | 2.47** | 15.0 | 1.57 |
| Money | 37.4 | 2.72*** | 38.5 | 1.55 | 36.3 | 1.48 |
| Children | 22.4 | 1.63 | 21.5 | 0.95 | 19.4 | 1.44 |
| Drinking and or drugs | 16.3 | 3.09*** | 29.6 | 3.01*** | 15.9 | 2.07* |
| Relatives | 24.3 | 1.49 | 24.6 | 2.35** | 15.9 | 1.58 |
| Friends | 16.6 | 2.10* | 22.7 | 1.86† | 25.6 | 2.24** |
| Household chores | 32.9 | 1.03 | 22.7 | 1.36 | 17.6 | 1.25 |
| Something else | 9.3 | 1.26 | 6.9 | 1.93 | 5.7 | 1.77 |

Note: Odds ratios are bivariate estimates of the increased odds of any intimate-partner violence.

†$p \le .10$ (two-tailed tests).

*$p \le .05$ (two-tailed tests).

**$p \le .01$ (two-tailed tests).

***$p \le .001$ (two-tailed tests).

sexual jealousy. As social constructionists have shown, the production of jealousy is clearly related to cultural factors. However, there are also important structural differences in the motivations behind jealousy, and these are most clearly evident in ethnic and racial differences. Using the Westside and Southtown samples as illustrative cases of Hispanic and black sexual relationships, figures 7.1*a* and 7.1*b* show substantial behavioral differences regarding concurrent partnerships despite almost equal prevalences of jealous conflict. In Westside, a bare majority of sexual relationships, 54 percent, are sexually exclusive and do not involve jealous conflict. Among those relationships experiencing jealous conflict, the majority are also exclusive. In contrast, concurrent partnerships are much more common in Southtown, with 54 percent of the respondents reporting nonexclusive relationships. The significance of these behavioral differences is that the production of sexual jealousy among blacks is likely to be more closely associated with the prevalence of polygamous sexual-matching strategies (see Youm & Paik, chapter 6 in this volume). The expression of sexual jealousy among Hispanics, on the other hand, may be a normative behavior associated with traditional gender roles.

Table 7.4 presents maximum–likelihood estimates from logistic regressions predicting jealous conflict. Although the best-fitting model is model 7, models 1–6 provide a number of key results on different sets of predictors. Models 1–4 show bivariate associations between different commitment measures and the likelihood of jealous conflict. In general, most of these measures increase the likelihood of jealous conflict, although low dyadic cohesion and gender-role traditionalism are not significant at the 5 percent level. Model 5, which includes all the commitment measures simultaneously, confirms our hypotheses since it indicates positive associations of having a concurrent partner, extramarital permissiveness, gender-role traditionalism, and nonmarital statuses with the likelihood of jealousy conflict. Low dyadic cohesion has no effect in this model, suggesting that the positive association indicated in model 2 results from correlation with the other commitment measures. In model 6, two control variables are significant predictors of jealous conflict: age and race/ethnicity. There is a strong negative association between age and the likelihood of jealous conflict; older respondents are less likely to experience jealous conflict. In comparison to respondents categorized as white/other, black respondents are almost two times (= exp[0.67]) as likely to report jealous conflict, while Hispanics are more than three times (= exp[1.13]) as likely. However, the introduction of the commitment measures in model 7 causes the coefficient for black Americans to become statistically insignificant, which suggests that their higher rates of jealousy, in comparison to whites, result from differences in the organization of sex markets (i.e., lower levels of commitments and more sexual infidelity). The coefficient for Hispanics, however, remains significant and positive even with controls and commitment measures.

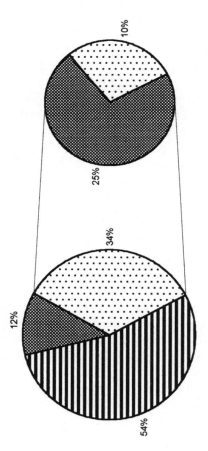

Figure 7.1*a*. Distribution of sexual exclusivity and jealousy among current sexual partnerships (Westside).

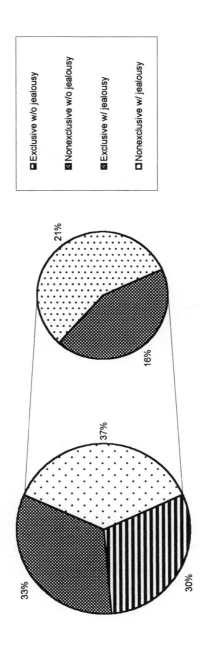

Exclusive w/o jealousy

Nonexclusive w/o jealousy

Exclusive w/ jealousy

Nonexclusive w/ jealousy

21%

16%

37%

33%

30%

Figure 7.1b. Distribution of sexual exclusivity and jealousy among current sexual partnerships (Southtown).

Table 7.4 Logistic Regression Predicting Jealous Conflict within the Relationship (log-odd coefficients)

| | Cook County ($N = 635$) | | | | | | |
|---|---|---|---|---|---|---|---|
| Variables | Model 1 | Model 2 | Model 3 | Model 4 | Model 5 | Model 6 | Model 7 |
| Commitment measures: | | | | | | | |
| Concurrent partner | 1.16*** | | | | 1.07*** | | .93** |
| Low dyadic cohesion | | .49† | | | -.01 | | .04 |
| Extramarital permissiveness | | | 1.98*** | | 1.34** | | 1.95** |
| Gender-role traditionalism | | | .81† | | 1.00* | | 1.07* |
| Married | | | | a | a | | a |
| Cohabiting | | | | 1.69*** | 1.68*** | | 1.21*** |
| Dating | | | | 1.28*** | 1.10*** | | .73* |
| Controls: | | | | | | | |
| White/other | | | | | | a | a |
| Black | | | | | | .67* | .33 |
| Hispanic | | | | | | 1.13** | 1.25* |

| | 1 | 2 | 3 | 4 | 5 | 6 | 7 |
|---|---|---|---|---|---|---|---|
| Less than high school degree | | | | | | [a] | [a] |
| High school to some college | | | | | | .44 | .33 |
| College degree | | | | | | -.53 | -.36 |
| Aged 18–31 | | | | | | [a] | [a] |
| Aged 32–45 | | | | | | -.64* | -.67* |
| Aged 46–59 | | | | | | -1.15** | -1.14** |
| Women | | | | | | .25 | .32 |
| No biological/adoptive father | | | | | | .54† | .33 |
| Constant | -1.39*** | -1.12*** | -1.18*** | -1.65*** | -2.18*** | -1.19* | -2.10*** |
| Log likelihood | -352.668 | -368.538 | -358.191 | -341.770 | -317.240 | -326.016 | -291.540 |
| Pseudo-$R^2$ | .051 | .008 | .036 | .080 | .146 | .123 | .215 |

*Note:* Models include design effects.

[a] Contrast category.

† $p \leq .10$ (two-tailed tests).

* $p \leq .05$ (two-tailed tests).

** $p \leq .01$ (two-tailed tests).

*** $p \leq .001$ (two-tailed tests).

The results from model 7 support our argument that continuance and control commitments are important factors organizing the elicitation of sexual jealousy. First, couples that have had at least one concurrent sex partner are about two and a half times (= exp[0.93]) more likely to experience jealous conflict. In addition, even after controlling for sexual infidelity, couples in dating (OR = 2.1) and cohabiting (OR = 3.4) relationships are still more likely to experience jealous conflict than are married couples. Because those involved in dating and cohabiting relationships are most often exposed to sexual infidelity, nonmarried couples are particularly vulnerable to jealous conflict and may have low thresholds of suspicion owing to cognitive consistency. Both our measures of control commitments are significant as well. Even though few Americans approve of extramarital permissiveness, respondents who did were seven times (= exp[1.95]) more likely to experience jealous conflict. On the other hand, individuals espousing gender-role traditionalism, a more widespread belief, were almost three times more likely to experience jealous conflict. The commitment measures also account for more than half the explained variance: model 5 has a pseudo-$R^2$ of 0.146, model 7 a pseudo-$R^2$ of 0.215. In sum, this analysis confirms our argument that continuance and control commitments play a central role in the social distribution of jealous conflict.

Table 7.5 presents maximum-likelihood estimates from ordered logistic regressions predicting intimate-partner violence. Model 7 is the best-fitting model overall; however, model 2 is more parsimonious than model 5, suggesting that continuance and control commitments are unrelated to the likelihood of intimate-partner violence. Model 1 shows that perceived breaches resulting from either jealous conflict or prior concurrency are strongly associated with intimate-partner violence. Model 2 shows that the level of dyadic cohesion mediates this relation. When breaches occur, individuals with low dyadic cohesion are significantly less likely to be violent than are those with high dyadic cohesion. Interestingly, the main effect of low dyadic cohesion is positively associated with intimate-partner violence. Except for extramarital permissiveness, models 3 and 4 indicate weak positive associations between the other commitment measures and intimate-partner violence. Model 5 indicates that these associations are largely a result of jealousy and dyadic cohesion. Once these factors are accounted for, the association between nonmarital statuses and violence turns negative. Models 6 and 7 show the significance of several control factors, which include women, family structure, options, conflicts over money, and conflicts over drinking/drugs. In model 7, the association between nonmarital statuses and violence becomes increasingly negative, although not significant, suggesting that the higher rate of violence observed among cohabiters results from jealousy and other factors. The effects of jealousy, dyadic cohesion, and their interaction remain significant, large, and in the predicted direction as well.

Table 7.5 Ordered Logit Predicting Intimate–Partner Violence within the Relationship (log-odds coefficients)

| Variables | Cook County (N = 635) | | | | | | |
| --- | --- | --- | --- | --- | --- | --- | --- |
| | Model 1 | Model 2 | Model 3 | Model 4 | Model 5 | Model 6 | Model 7 |
| Jealousy/concurrency | 1.11*** | 1.36*** | | | 1.39*** | | 1.40*** |
| Low dyadic cohesion | | 1.20*** | | | 1.21*** | | 1.05** |
| Low cohesion × jealousy/concurrency | | −.94* | | | −1.02* | | −1.49** |
| Extramarital permissiveness | | | 1.15* | | .79 | | .78 |
| Gender-role traditionalism | | | .21 | | .06 | | .27 |
| Married | | | | [a] | [a] | | [a] |
| Cohabiting | | | | .25 | −.14 | | −1.09† |
| Dating | | | | .37 | −.14 | | −.37 |
| Controls: | | | | | | | |
| White/other | | | | | | [a] | [a] |
| Black | | | | | | .48 | .54 |
| Hispanic | | | | | | .43 | .28 |
| Less than high school degree | | | | | | [a] | [a] |
| High school to some college | | | | | | −.43 | −.58 |
| College degree | | | | | | −.64 | −.64 |
| Aged 18–31 | | | | | | [a] | [a] |
| Aged 32–45 | | | | | | −.46 | −.62† |
| Aged 46–59 | | | | | | −.03 | −.18 |

continued

Table 7.5 *continued*

| Variables | | Cook County (N = 635) | | | | | |
|---|---|---|---|---|---|---|---|
| | Model 1 | Model 2 | Model 3 | Model 4 | Model 5 | Model 6 | Model 7 |
| Women | | | | | | .75* | .84* |
| Nonbiological or no father | | | | | | .71† | .76* |
| Ever jailed | | | | | | 1.00* | .90† |
| Respondent only has options | | | | | | 1.00* | 1.01** |
| Partner only has options | | | | | | .68 | .81† |
| Respondent options × partner options | | | | | | −1.07† | −1.34* |
| Conflict over money | | | | | | 1.03*** | 1.04*** |
| Conflict over friends | | | | | | .28 | .36 |
| Conflict over drinking/drugs | | | | | | .71* | .85* |
| Cut value (moderate violence) | 1.931 | 2.267 | 1.443 | 1.511 | 2.249 | 2.634 | 3.184 |
| Cut value (severe violence) | 2.808 | 3.155 | 2.297 | 2.359 | 3.142 | 3.658 | 4.272 |
| Log likelihood | −394.565 | −388.008 | −406.729 | −408.598 | −386.633 | −349.774 | −332.959 |
| Pseudo-$R^2$ | .038 | .054 | .008 | .004 | .057 | .147 | .188 |

*Note:* Models include design effects.

a Contrast category.

† $p \leq .10$ (two-tailed tests).

* $p \leq .05$ (two-tailed tests).

** $p \leq .01$ (two-tailed tests).

*** $p \leq .001$ (two-tailed tests).

To facilitate the interpretation of these results, we generated synthetic profiles by varying the occurrence of jealousy and the level of cohesion.[13] These results are presented in figure 7.2. There are two basic patterns to note: main and interaction effects. First, the main effect of sexual jealousy is powerful. Among those who are married with high cohesion (the first and second bars), the likelihood of violence for those without jealousy is only 5 percent. A breach increases the likelihood to almost 18 percent, a 249 percent increase. In addition, a slightly greater proportion of violence is severe among those with jealousy. Having low dyadic cohesion also raises the likelihood of violence. Comparing the first and third bars, low dyadic cohesion increases the probability of violence to a little over 13 percent, a 161 percent increase. However, there is no effect of jealousy when dyadic cohesion is low, which is shown by comparing the third and fourth bars: 12 percent of jealous couples with low dyadic cohesion experience violence, which is essentially the same rate as for the nonjealous couples but 31 percent lower (17.8 vs. 12.3 percent) than the rate for jealous couples with high cohesion. To summarize, sexual jealousy, dyadic cohesion, and their interaction are important covariates of intimate-partner violence.

## Discussion

A central finding of this study is that sexual jealousy is an important social-psychological dimension of sex markets. We estimate that one in four current sexual partnerships in Cook County, the third largest metropolitan area in the United States, has experienced a conflict over sexual jealousy at some point. For the vast majority of these couples, episodes of sexual jealousy are rare, but, for some, they are frequent and likely to be dangerous, which is a phenomenon that psychologists call *morbid jealousy*. Sexual jealousy is the most powerful predictor of intimate-partner violence in our analyses. In the bivariate analyses, sexual jealousy increased the likelihood of violence by more than 300 percent in Cook County and by 400 percent in the Westside and Southtown neighborhoods. Even after controlling for other covariates, sexual jealousy still increased the likelihood of violence by more than 250 percent.

Moreover, there are substantial differences in the distribution of sexual jealousy across racial/ethnic, age, and marital-status categories. Black and His-

---

13. These profiles assume the following values for the other covariates: married; disapproval of extramarital permissiveness; gender-role liberalism; marriage; white/other; high school degree/some college; ages eighteen to thirty-one; women; had a biological father; never jailed; both respondent and partner have poor options; and no other conflicts.

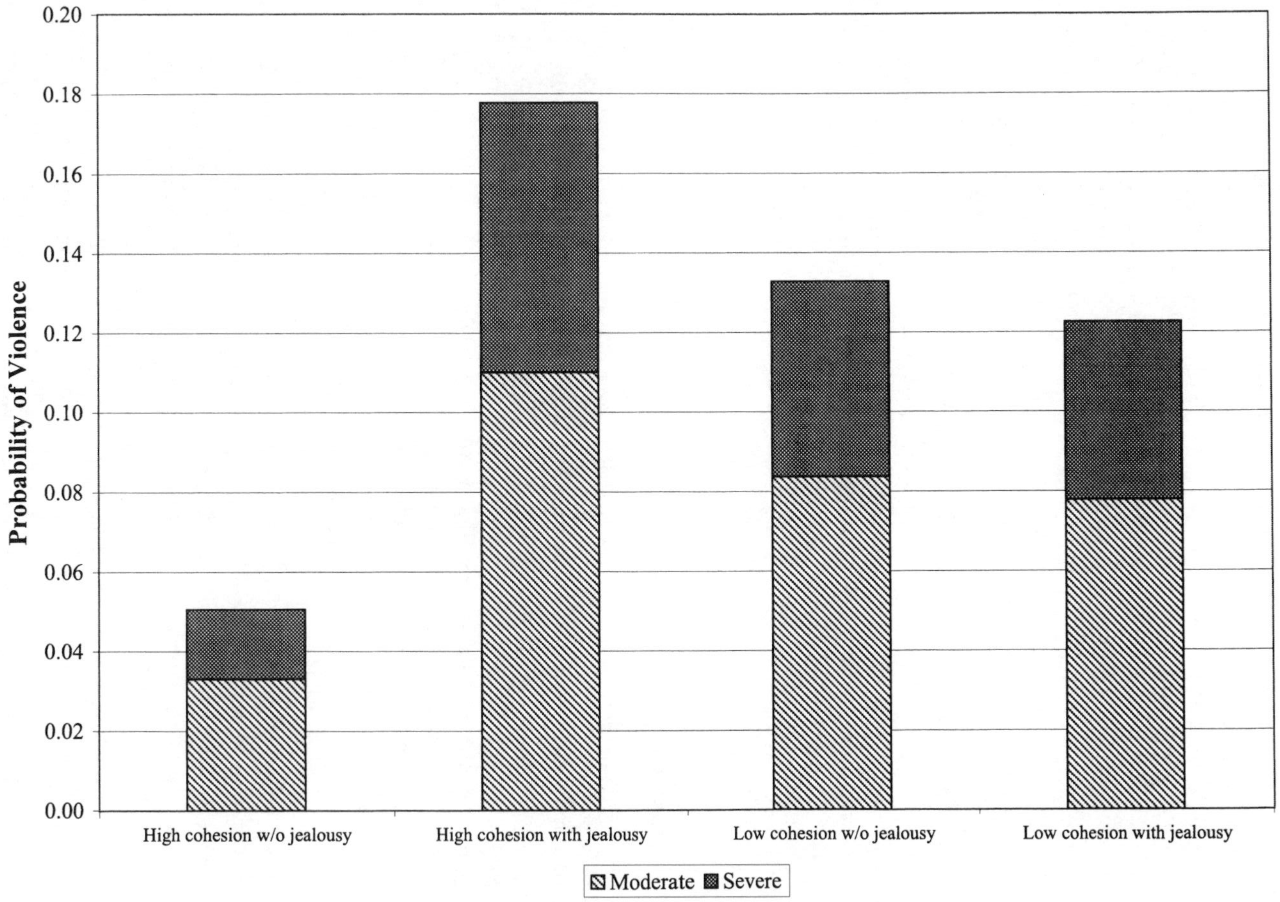

Figure 7.2. Predicted probability of intimate-partner violence.

panic Americans are more likely to report jealous conflict than are members of other racial/ethnic backgrounds, but the causes of their sexual jealousy are different. Because of structural factors related to lower marriage rates, higher numbers of sex partners, and imbalanced sex ratios, sexual jealousy among blacks appears to be tied to the prevalence of polygamous sexual-matching strategies. Hispanics, on the other hand, have low rates of concurrent sex partners. Future research on sexual jealousy should investigate what factors increase the likelihood of jealousy among Hispanics. Given the numerous controls in our models, we hypothesize that this racial/ethnic difference arises from more permissive display rules for expressing jealousy.

We also find that age is important; youth is associated with more sexual jealousy, which is a reasonable finding given that the competition for sex partners is highest among young adults. Likewise, dating and cohabiting relationships are more closely associated with sexual jealousy than are marital relationships. It also appears that sexual jealousy plays an important role in elevating the likelihood of intimate-partner violence among dating and cohabiting couples. Once we controlled for sexual jealousy, these relationships became less associated with violence, although these findings are not significant. Thus, this study goes beyond social-constructionist and evolutionary-psychological perspectives on sexual jealousy by showing how demographic factors like ethnicity/race, marital status, and age structure the social distribution of sexual jealousy.

Our findings also support our theoretical argument that sexual jealousy is primarily organized by commitments. Marital status and sexual attitudes play important roles in determining when breaches occur but are generally unrelated to the expression of sexual jealousy as violence. Instead, the level of dyadic cohesion mediates whether jealousy translates into violence. Men and women with high dyadic cohesion, we believe, experience more intense arousal, which leads to increased pressure to express jealousy, which leads ultimately to aggression. At the same time, high dyadic cohesion is associated with less violence when there is no jealousy at all. Thus, extensive commitments do shield individuals from the difficulties of sexual jealousy. If, however, jealousy does occur, even infrequently, the consequences are severe.

Although some may argue that sexual jealousy is a special emotion, the links that we have established to commitments suggest that jealousy is an aspect of the negative side of commitment formation. This raises interesting theoretical questions about the role of negative emotions and sanctions in social relationships. Indeed, Fehr and Gächter (2002) found that negative emotions play an important role in motivating the application of sanctions to "free riders" even when it is costly to do so, suggesting a close connection between social organization and negative emotions.

Besides being a contribution to the study of commitments, this chapter should be relevant to several areas in sociology. First, it is one of the few available studies of the epidemiology of emotional experiences as well as being one of the rare studies that treats emotions as an antecedent of social action. Second, this study should also be useful to researchers working on intimate-partner violence. We identify an important factor that produces intimate-partner violence and is tied to the structure of intimate relationships. Specifically, the relation between commitment and violence is more than a simple negative one. Commitments confer benefits in terms of less violence in the context of a jealousy-free relationship, but they carry substantial risks in the context of jealousy. This study also shows that differences in exposure to sexual jealousy may explain those prevalence studies that consistently show that nonmarital couples are more violent than married couples. We should stress that we did not focus on gender differences. Instead, we assumed that, in the majority of cases, women are victimized, regardless of who instigated the physical aggression. In addition, we also believe that sexual jealousy, as it is measured in our study, is a predictor of "common-couple violence," not the more severe forms of "patriarchal terrorism" (Johnson, 1995). Finally, this research suggests the importance of sexual expression for social behavior in general. Too often the study of human social relations has neglected the relevance of close relationships and sexual behavior.

There are, however, several issues that necessitate caution about these results. First, as we mentioned before, the dyadic nature of this analysis is vulnerable to biases in reporting, and, unfortunately, we observed gender differences in the reporting of jealous conflict as well as in the reporting of intimate-partner violence. Because of the small size of the sample available to us, we did not perform separate analyses by gender; we compensated for small sample size by controlling for gender, which was significant only in the models predicting violence. Although we did find some evidence that men are likely to be underreporting, we have no reason to expect that gender is relevant for our commitment measures. Our focus on the dyadic level also leaves issues about the direction of jealousy and violence unexplored. Future research should address these issues. Second, the cross-sectional nature of our study raises issues of reverse causality. To minimize this issue, we developed measures that were more likely to be causally prior. Our jealousy and concurrency measures tapped events at any time during relationships, whereas the violence measures were restricted to the twelve months prior to the interview. A third issue is that qualitative studies suggest that sexual jealousy may be less a causal factor than a proximate emotional process related to the violence process (Denzin, 1984), suggesting the possibility of unobserved heterogeneity. This is certainly a possibility, and future studies should focus on jealousy as an emotional process. Yet our approach does show how sexual jealousy varies with social organization, not just with violence. Fourth, although a strength of this study is its ability to integrate a wide set of control variables, many of them rare in probability samples, we rely primarily on single-item measures, raising issues of accuracy, validity, and reliability. Only future studies can resolve these issues, so our findings must be retested using other data.

This research shows that the expectation of sexual exclusivity, combined with the availability of partners in sex markets, yields widespread conflict over sexual jealousy among Chicagoans. The results from the CHSLS data indicate that the effect of sexual jealousy on intimate-partner violence has been underappreciated. We find that commitments have important implications for jealous conflict and violent outcomes because they focus attention on how sexual relationships are embedded in sex markets. With the link between sexual jealousy and intimate-partner violence established, the commitment in intimate relationships should be recognized as one that has risks and rewards.

# 8 )

## *Violence and Sexuality*

### Examining Intimate-Partner Violence and Forced Sexual Activity

Jennifer Tello Buntin,
Zohar Lechtman,
and Edward O. Laumann

Since Leticia is five months pregnant, her husband beats her about the face and on the back these days. She describes how he pushes her down on the bed, twisting her feet and hands, and hitting her repeatedly on the back. As she speaks, she covers her face to hide a busted lip and a knocked-out tooth. There are bruises on her hand. She wears a sweat suit that covers her entire body even though it is a hot day in early August. She said that her husband often beats her up and then expects her to sleep with him, "as if I were an animal without any feelings."

Leticia, a young woman in Westside, wants to leave her husband, but she has no family in Chicago. When asked whether she calls for help when he is beating her, she says that, if she saw a police car passing by, she would consider running out for help. She would not actually call the police herself, however. Her husband taunts her, telling her to call the police on him, prob- ably knowing that she would not do it. He tells her to go ahead and leave him, knowing that her only relatives are in California, too far away to provide any immediate support or assistance.

In Shoreland, a police officer describes the beautiful homes that she has seen destroyed as a result of violence between gay partners. An older sergeant warned her that gay domestic-violence calls are generally more violent than straight ones. In addition, police officers, she said, are often confused when it comes to identifying who the perpetrator is and who the victim is, and they may be uncomfortable in these situations as a result of their own attitudes to- ward or feelings about same-sex relationships.

Across town, a Southtown pastor describes the difficulty that she had in finding a shelter to take a battered woman in her congregation. She said that, after being beaten by her husband, the woman lost custody of her four chil- dren and now moves around between the homes of friends and family. The pastor feels that there are still not enough places for women who have been "kicked in the face" to seek help.

Finally, an Erlinda police officer describes a case that she had a few years ago in which she and her partner entered a home to find a severely beaten woman. "It was all I could do to keep from dragging the woman away with us!" They spent forty-five minutes talking with her, telling her she did not deserve such treatment. In the end, they had to leave because it was clear that she was not going to press charges. She would not even let them call for an ambulance. The officer was haunted by this case for several years, until she ran across the same woman during a routine traffic stop. The woman said, "Officer, I've been looking for you. You and your partner saved my life." Af- ter speaking with the officers that night many years before, the woman had found a friend to confide in and eventually left her husband.

These stories illustrate just a few of the ways in which violence can invade, organize, or dominate an intimate relationship. They also suggest how vio- lence and power pervade the processes of sex markets.[1] *Sexual violence* is a broad term, one encompassing a variety of situations and acts embedded across personal, interpersonal, and broader social contexts. Indeed, *intimate violence* has no consensual definition or meaning among individuals, social scientists, or institutions. Consider the problem of *domestic violence*. The legal system, law-enforcement agencies, and social-service organizations may address differ- ent aspects of the same phenomenon, address different phenomena, or attach

---

1. On the terms *sex market* and *sexual marketplace* as they are used in this study, see the section "The Social Organization of Sexual Partnering and Sexual Relationships" in Ellingson, Laumann, Paik, and Mahay (chapter 1 in this volume).

different meanings to the same phenomenon. For example, violence between spouses may be addressed through the legal system as a criminal activity. Alternatively, such violence may be addressed through marriage counseling as an interpersonal marital problem. Likewise, individuals attribute different meanings to *physical violence*. Even in what seem to be hard data, the prevalence estimates of these phenomena vary with the different meanings of *violence, sexuality,* and *intimacy* employed by researchers.

In this chapter, we examine two broad categories of sexual violence: *intimate-partner violence* and *forced sexual activity*. We use the Chicago Health and Social Life Survey (CHSLS) to address the meanings of intimate-partner violence and forced sexual activity from the perspective of victims and the organizations that assist them. This type of sexual violence takes many forms, and individuals, as well as researchers, frame this issue using a variety of perspectives. Although capturing all facets and perspectives of forced sex in one chapter, using one survey, is clearly impossible, the CHSLS offers quantitative and qualitative data, permitting us to address some of the issues from multiple perspectives. Specifically, we address how victims comprehend the sexual violence that they experience and how the institutions assisting them frame the problem.

We argue that understanding the social construction of intimacy in sex markets is central for understanding intimate-partner violence and forced sex. Paik, Laumann, and Van Haitsma (chapter 7 in this volume) demonstrate the links among intimacy, sexual jealousy, and the likelihood of intimate-partner violence. Similarly, while there is rising awareness of the fact that forced sex is commonly perpetrated by someone well-known to the victim, we suggest that intimacy still plays an important role in distinguishing criminal from noncriminal behavior in the perceptions of the victims as well as of society as a whole. We first address intimate-partner violence, describing typical acts of violence reported by respondents and the differences between men's and women's reports. We focus on these differences to discuss the variety of meanings attached to *violence* and offer possible explanations. Next, we describe the prevalence of forced-sex reports by victims, the majority of whom are women, and the patterns of forced sex, paying particular attention to how victims frame their experiences. We then present data on help-seeking behavior and discuss the institutional-interview data from social-service, religious, health, and law-enforcement organizations that tell us how these organizations understand and deal with the issue of intimate-partner violence.[2]

---

2. Unfortunately, limitations of the interview data do not allow meaningful analysis of service-provider perceptions of forced sexual activity.

## Intimate-Partner Violence

Sociological research on domestic violence generally follows one of two perspectives, the *family-violence* perspective or the *feminist* perspective (Johnson, 1995). The family-violence perspective, attributed originally to Gelles (1974) and Strauss (1971), examines intimate violence in terms of discrete, violent acts occurring in family conflict. Family-violence researchers rely mostly on quantitative analysis of large-scale surveys to estimate the prevalence of violence and to perform causal analyses. Theoretically, they are interested in finding commonalities among different aspects of family violence, such as frequency, the role of stress, and adherence to norms of violence within the family (Johnson, 1995). The feminist perspective (e.g., Kurz, 1989; Dobash & Dobash, 1979; Walker, 1984), on the other hand, looks at violence more in terms of a mechanism that organizes relationships of domination and control, primarily by men over their female partners. Feminists call attention to the context in which discrete acts of assault take place and to the fact that these are manifestations of ongoing abusive behavior toward a partner. They are also more likely to depend on qualitative research in particular settings, such as battered women's shelters. Theoretically, the emphasis is on patriarchal relations, constructions of gender roles, and structural constraints that make escape difficult for systematically beaten women.

The underlying differences in conceptualization of violence, relationships, and lines of investigation also yield different estimates of prevalence of domestic violence or intimate violence. The findings of each perspective have been so different that researchers on each side have long argued that the other perspective misunderstands the nature of family violence. Johnson (1995), however, stresses that these approaches actually analyze different phenomena. He suggests that the feminists focus on *patriarchal terrorism*. This term fits most of the experiences described in this chapter's introduction. It is "a product of patriarchal traditions of men's right to control 'their' women . . . a form of terroristic control of wives by their husbands that involves the systematic use of not only violence, but economic subordination, threats, isolation, and other control tactics" (Johnson, 1995, 284). Patriarchal terrorism is hard to uncover in large-scale samples of respondents and can be better studied through feminists' qualitative analyses of women in shelters and other help organizations. Victims of patriarchal terrorism are a relatively small group of women who experience extreme levels of both physical and psychological violence. The family-violence approach, Johnson argues, focuses on *common-couple violence*. Common-couple violence tends to be more moderate in nature, rarely escalating to the extreme levels associated with patriarchal terrorism. In addition, common-couple violence tends to be more gender balanced. In many cases, both partners are active and equal participants in the violence. As a result of these characteristics, large-scale surveys tend to be a more suitable source of information about this type of violence.

The CHSLS survey data follow primarily in the footsteps of the family-violence perspective.[3] They focus on violence in the context of conflicts between intimate partners rather than instances of unprovoked violence as a means of control. The survey asks about a variety of aggressive activities, beginning with verbal aggression (i.e., heated arguments, yelling, insults, sulking) and moving, ultimately, to physical violence (i.e., threatening to hit or throw something, pushing and shoving, hitting, beating up, and using a weapon). In addition, the respondent is asked who engaged in each activity: only the respondent; only the respondent's partner; or both. Finally, and perhaps most important, questions about violence in the last twelve months were presented only to respondents who were involved in current relationships that they expected to continue in the future. Thus, anyone leaving a partner because of violence in the relationship is not captured in this analysis. At first glance, this may appear to be a shortcoming. For example, by excluding those who left, we may miss violence occurring in relationships that have dissolved. However, we can get a very interesting, yet sobering, picture of the levels of violence that people experience in their ongoing relationships. The patterns of violence depicted here are those that do *not* lead to the relationship dissolving or cause one partner to flee, at least not yet. Thus, the persistence of moderate or even severe physical violence in the relationship is a factor that these couples negotiate as they continue to maintain the relationship over time. The violence shapes and is shaped by their experiences and positions in the sex market.

---

3. The reader may note that several of the stories presented in the introduction better fit the category of patriarchal terrorism while the survey data deal primarily with common-couple violence. This is true. These stories are drawn from the service-provider interviews collected along with the CHSLS survey data. These interviews target community organizations that are more like those with which feminist researchers might work (battered women's shelters, counseling centers, churches, etc.). Consequently, like the feminist researchers, these interviews tend to deal with patriarchal terrorism, the more systematic patterns of violence and control of women by men, while the survey data deal primarily with common-couple violence, or more gender-balanced and less extreme forms of intimate-partner violence. This distinction in the data will be discussed further below.

## Measuring Intimate-Partner Violence in Chicago

Table 8.1 shows the number and percentage of men and women who report physical violence in Cook County and in each of the four neighborhoods. These estimates are similar to those presented elsewhere in this volume (see Paik, Laumann, & Van Haitsma, chapter 7 in this volume, table 7.2). However, we slightly modify the categorizations and include results from Shoreland and Erlinda. Building on the category constructions introduced by Paik, Laumann, and Van Haitsma, we have summarized the physical-violence data into two categories of severity: *moderate* physical violence, including "threatened to hit the other or throw something at the other," "threw something at the other," and "pushed, grabbed, or shoved the other"; and *severe* physical violence, including "hit the other with a hand or fist," "hit the other with something hard," "beat the other up," "threatened the other with a knife or gun," and "used a knife or gun."[4] Since the CHSLS questionnaire allows respondents to report each type of violent conflict separately, these categories are not mutually exclusive. In our analysis, we maintain the categories separately. Thus, a respondent can report instances of both moderate and severe violence; reporting severe violence does not obscure accompanying events of moderate violence. Table 8.1 also distinguishes between violence perpetrated by the respondent only, violence perpetrated by the partner only, and violence perpetrated by both partners.

We analyze differences between men and women by comparing reports of their own and their partner's activities and by examining differences across

4. The CHSLS data also provide information on what we term *verbal aggression,* e.g., heated arguments, yelling, and sulking. We exclude this category, however, and focus directly on instances in which physical violence was threatened or occurred. We argue that this distinction is necessary because, although verbal aggression is often related to physical violence, it is likely to have a very different meaning and dynamic within the relationship. In Cook County, 75 percent of the women and 70 percent of the men reported that they argued, yelled, or sulked. Among the neighborhoods, Southtown had the highest prevalence of verbal aggression (68 percent of women and 67 percent of men), followed closely by Shoreland (64 percent for both men and women). Westside (60 percent of women and 51 percent of men) and Erlinda (49 percent of women and 39 percent of men) had the lowest rates. Also, the reader should note that specific threats of violence (threatening to hit or throw something and threatening to use a knife or gun) are included in the violence categories (moderate and severe, respectively) because we believe that these threats are qualitatively different than the other forms of verbal aggression and are more related to the acts of violence themselves. This is especially true for threats with a knife or gun since the weapon itself may be present during the interaction.

Table 8.1 Rates of Intimate-Partner Violence by Participant, Severity, Neighborhood, and Gender (%)

| | Cook County | | Westside | | Southtown | | Shoreland | | Erlinda | |
|---|---|---|---|---|---|---|---|---|---|---|
| | Women | Men | Women | Men | Women | Men | Women | Men | Women | Men |
| Any violence in relationship[a] | 29 (110) | 22 (61) | 36 (61) | 37 (38) | 58 (77) | 62 (61) | 18 (22) | 19 (17) | 23 (22) | 10 (6) |
| Respondent only:[b] | | | | | | | | | | |
| Moderate[c] | 9 (33) | 7 (18) | 9 (16) | 9 (9) | 17 (23) | 12 (12) | 8 (9) | 4 (4) | 4 (4) | 3 (2) |
| Severe | 6 (22) | 3 (8) | 4 (6) | 6 (6) | 8 (10) | 7 (7) | 4 (5) | 3 (3) | 4 (4) | 3 (2) |
| Any[d] | 11 (42) | 7 (20) | 10 (17) | 12 (12) | 19 (26) | 15 (15) | 8 (10) | 6 (5) | 6 (6) | 3 (2) |
| Partner only: | | | | | | | | | | |
| Moderate | 6 (22) | 5 (13) | 11 (19) | 8 (8) | 17 (23) | 14 (14) | 4 (5) | 7 (6) | 9 (8) | 3 (2) |
| Severe | 3 (11) | 4 (10) | 6 (10) | 6 (6) | 13 (17) | 11 (11) | 2 (2) | 1 (1) | 2 (2) | 2 (1) |
| Any | 7 (26) | 7 (18) | 11 (19) | 10 (10) | 19 (26) | 18 (18) | 4 (5) | 7 (6) | 9 (8) | 5 (3) |

Both:

| | | | | | | | | | | |
|---|---|---|---|---|---|---|---|---|---|---|
| Moderate | 10 | 9 | 15 | 15 | 16 | 26 | 6 | 7 | 9 | 2 |
| | (40) | (23) | (25) | (15) | (22) | (25) | (7) | (6) | (8) | (1) |
| Severe | 4 | 3 | 5 | 5 | 7 | 15 | 1 | 1 | 2 | 0 |
| | (14) | (7) | (8) | (5) | (9) | (15) | (1) | (1) | (2) | |
| Any | 11 | 9 | 15 | 16 | 19 | 29 | 6 | 7 | 9 | 2 |
| | (42) | (23) | (25) | (16) | (25) | 28 | (7) | (6) | (8) | (1) |
| N | 383 | 272 | 171 | 91 | 134 | 98 | 119 | 91 | 94 | 60 |

Source: CHSLS, 1997.

Note: N's are given in parentheses.

[a] Any level of severity (moderate or severe) and any participant (respondent only, partner only, or both).

[b] Respondent only, partner only, and both are mutually exclusive categories.

[c] Moderate and severe are not mutually exclusive categories.

[d] Moderate, severe, or both.

these categories. Because sex partners were not interviewed for the CHSLS, we depend on respondents to report their partner's violent acts. To capture differences between men's and women's perceptions, we compare the level of violence that men attribute to their female partners with the level of violence that women attribute to themselves, and vice versa. We also restrict this analysis to ongoing, heterosexual relationships.[5]

ESTIMATES OF VIOLENCE IN COOK COUNTY.    Table 8.1 shows that physical violence is a common feature of sexual relationships. In Cook County, about three of every ten women (29 percent) and one of every five men (22 percent) report at least one incident of moderate or severe violence in their intimate relationship in the past year.[6] Twenty-five percent of the women and 21 percent of the men reported moderate physical violence.[7] About 13 percent of the women and 10 percent of the men reported at least one instance of severe violence in the past year, making moderate violence more prevalent than severe violence. This suggests either that the severity of the encounter is relatively moderate for most couples or that people are more willing to report moderate than severe violence. Again, we discuss moderate violence and severe violence as separate acts, but that does not necessarily mean that they occur in separate events. Partners often engage in both moderate and severe acts of violence concurrently. In fact, about 70 percent of the respondents reporting instances of severe violence also reported concurrent instances of moderate violence. In other words, situations of severe violence,

5. The number of respondents involved in current same-sex relationships is small and of those reporting violence in these partnerships even smaller. In fact, the prevalence of violence among same-sex couples appears to be somewhat lesser (although differences between heterosexual and same-sex couples are not statistically significant). Of the sixty-six men who reported that they were involved in a same-sex relationship at the time of the survey, 11 percent (seven men) reported that violence had occurred in the past year. Of the seventeen women involved in same-sex relationships, 29 percent (five women) reported that some form of violence had occurred in the last year. The small absolute numbers limit our ability to provide a comprehensive analysis. Therefore, we limit our current analysis to heterosexual couples. Please note, however, that same-sex intimate-partner violence is a phenomenon that is increasingly coming to the forefront among researchers and in the gay and lesbian community. We consider this issue further later in this chapter.

6. These numbers include acts perpetrated by the respondent only, acts perpetrated by the partner only, and acts perpetrated by both.

7. These estimates are calculated by aggregating the reports of violence by the respondent only, by the partner only, and by both partners, for each level—moderate or severe violence. As mentioned previously, the categories of partner involved exclude each other.

such as hitting, beating, and using a weapon, are often accompanied by less severe violence, such as throwing things, pushing, or grabbing.

Although a conflict between partners inherently involves both partners, it does not necessarily mean that both of them also engage in violence. About 11 percent of the women in Cook County reported that both partners engaged in violence during conflicts in the past year, but 18 percent reported that only one partner engaged in either moderate or severe violence. Seven percent reported that their partner was the only one who engaged in violence, and 11 percent reported that they alone engaged in a violent act. Among the men, 9 percent of the men reported that both partners engaged in violence, in contrast to 14 percent reporting only one violent partner: 7 percent themselves and 7 percent their partner.[8] Thus, women reported slightly higher rates of violence than men did, and men attributed fewer violent acts to their female partners than women attributed to themselves.

INTIMATE-PARTNER VIOLENCE IN THE FOUR NEIGHBORHOODS. Overall, reports of violence varied across the CHSLS neighborhoods.[9] More respondents reported violence in Southtown than in any other neighborhood: the rates there were nearly twice as high as in Westside. The rates in the other two neighborhoods were about half the rates reported in Westside. The specific patterns in terms of level of violence, partner's identity, and gender also vary across these neighborhoods. Below, we present a detailed description of the patterns in each neighborhood. We should note, however, that the absolute numbers of respondents reporting each type of violence for each person involved within each community are small. In Erlinda, for instance, the numbers of respondents in general and the numbers of those reporting violence are much smaller than in the other communities surveyed.[10]

*Westside.* In Westside, 36 percent of the women and 37 percent of the men reported violence in their intimate partnerships during the year prior to the survey. Approximately 15 percent of the couples in Westside experienced physical violence involving both partners. In addition, there is symmetry in the reports by men and women about who perpetrated the violence. Eleven percent of women and 10 percent of men reported that they were exposed to their partner's violence, moderate or severe. The rates among the men correspond

8. Unfortunately, when both partners are involved in violence, we cannot identify who initiated the violence.

9. Overall estimates represent aggregated categories of violence: moderate and severe; respondent only, partner only, and both.

10. In Erlinda, the survey process faced several problems that led to a relatively limited number of respondents to begin with. For a more detailed description of the samples, see Van Haitsma, Paik, and Laumann (chapter 2 in this volume).

to the 10 percent of self-reports among the women; the 11 percent among the women correspond to the 12 percent of self-reports among the men. Thus, men and women in Westside report quite similar patterns of violent conflict.

*Southtown.* Residents of Southtown reported the highest percentages of intimate-partner violence. About 58 percent of the women and 62 percent of the men reported that at least one of the partners engaged in physical violence during the year prior to the interview. Men in Southtown were more likely to report violence that involved both partners (29 percent) than any other kind of violence and were more likely to report such violence than women (19 percent). On the other hand, men's self-reports (15 percent) were lower than were women's reports of their male partners in the overall estimate (19 percent). Specifically, men reported lower rates of their own severe violence (7 percent) than women attributed to their partners (13 percent). As for the women, although they reported lower rates of their own severe violence than men attributed to their female partners, the levels that men attributed to their female partners largely corresponded to the levels that women attributed to themselves. A report of violence in which both partners were involved can be seen as a self-report, but one in which the respondent shares responsibility with his or her partner. While women's self-reports largely corresponded to men's reports of their female partners, men's self-reports tended to differ from women's reports of their male partners, generally indicating lower levels of severe violence, and describing mutual participation when indicating higher levels of severe violence.

*Shoreland.* Overall, 18 percent of women and 19 percent of men reported intimate-partner violence during the year prior to the interview. This pattern is quite similar to that prevailing in Westside, although the estimates in Shoreland are lower in general. Women's and men's self-reports were slightly higher than were their reports about their partner: 7 percent of the men reported that their female partner was the only violent partner, but 8 percent of the women reported that they were violent; and 4 percent of the women attributed violence to their partner, compared to 6 percent of the men reporting their own violence. Reports of both partners' violence were higher among men than among women, a situation quite similar to that in Westside, but not a difference as extreme as that in Southtown.

*Erlinda.* Erlinda differs greatly from the other samples. Unfortunately, the number of respondents was much lower there than in the other neighborhoods, reducing the power of statistical tests to discriminate significant differences. We can say only that more women than men reported violence in almost every category.

To summarize, more violence was reported in Southtown than in any other neighborhood, followed by Westside and Shoreland. In Shoreland and Westside, there was some correspondence between men and women, whereas, in Southtown, men tended to underestimate violence in comparison to women, with one exception. Southtown men reported higher rates of mutual violence, resulting in men reporting higher overall rates of violence in the relationship. In the following section, we consider the prevalence of another form of sexual violence: forced sexual activity.

## Forced Sexual Activity

Since the 1960s, controversies over what qualifies as rape have increasingly come to the front of public-policy debates. Because of its social stigmatization, rape is widely recognized as an underreported violent crime. However, much has been done to facilitate the reporting of violent occurrences, as reflected in the recent increases in reports by law-enforcement agencies, health-care agencies, and help lines. Previous studies have investigated the prevailing perceptions of rape in the general population, noting variations by gender, age, race, and other social characteristics (for a review, see Bourque [1989]). Others have studied experiences of rape among women who seek help from social agencies (see, e.g., Dobash & Dobash, 1979; Martin, 1981; Roy, 1976; Walker, 1984). However, much less has been done regarding the experience of victims as a group, which would include those who did not seek help from a social-service agency and those who did. As a representative, population-based survey of Chicago, the CHSLS can capture, not only those victims who overcame social and institutional barriers and sought help, but also those victims who, for whatever reason, never spoke up, thus providing more accurate information about both the incidence of forced sex and victims' experiences and perceptions of the event. In this section, we describe the prevalence and patterns of forced sex, focusing on three elements: the forcer's relationship to the victim; the particular sex acts forced on the victim; and the method of force used (such as intimidation or actual physical force). We discuss these elements as part of an effort to understand the "sexual scripts" (Laumann, Gagnon, Michael, Michaels, 1994) involved in forced-sex experiences. Here, we refer to the respondents' answers to survey questions about their definition of what happened to them and whether they turned to others for help (e.g., friends, relatives, or institutions). Finally, we discuss these issues in relation to the victims' reports of help-seeking behavior.

CHSLS respondents were asked whether they had been forced to do something sexual since the age of thirteen.[11] Fourteen percent of women and 2

---

11. The questionnaire included two full sets of questions concerning forced sex—one for respondents whose first sexual experience was forced, another for those

percent of men in Cook County answered yes to this question. The greater likelihood of sexual victimization among women, as well as the higher rates of reports among educated whites as compared with other groups, is well documented in other studies as well (see, e.g., Browning & Laumann, 1997). The small number of men who were sexually forced does not allow for statistically reliable results. We therefore focus primarily on women's experiences and provide only a brief discussion of the rates and experiences reported by men. In this section, we focus only on the details of the most recent forced-sex event. However, for some, this could be just one event in a long history of sexual coercion. Fifty-three women—4 percent of the women in the total sample and 34 percent of the women who were sexually victimized—were forced at least twice. About half of them were forced by the same person at least twice.[12] In order to provide more detailed analyses, we focus only on the most recent forced-sex event.

Rates of reports of at least one forced sex event varied by neighborhood. The highest rates are found in Shoreland (20 and 8 percent of women and men, respectively). Comparably lower rates are found in Southtown (15 and 2 percent of women and men, respectively) and in the Cook County sample (14 and 2 percent of women and men, respectively) and even lower rates in Erlinda (9 and 1 percent of women and men, respectively). The lowest rates were reported in Westside (5 and 1 percent of women and men, respectively).

## Characteristics of Women's Forced-Sex Experiences in Cook County

Table 8.2 presents percentages of women who were sexually forced as well as the characteristics of and the definitions associated with these forced-sex experiences. Characteristics include the type of relationship between the forcer and the victim, the sex acts associated with the event, and whether physical force or weapons were used. The table also presents the percentages of victims who defined the event as a crime and those who defined it as rape, broken down by neighborhood.

*The forcer.* Respondents were asked what their relationship was to the person who forced them into sexual activity. They were able to choose among eleven categories: stranger; acquaintance; friend; relative; boyfriend; girlfriend; spouse; employer; someone they paid to have sex; someone who paid them to have sex; or "other." We combined these items into five categories

---

who experienced forced sex only later in life. The data that we use here are derived from both groups. The reader should note that a separate set of questions investigated respondents' sexual experiences prior to age thirteen. Those data are analyzed elsewhere (see, e.g., Browning & Laumann, 1997).

12. The same was true for ten of the men.

Table 8.2 Women's Forced–Sex Experiences by Neighborhood,
Characteristics, and Perceptions of the Event (%)

|  | Cook County | Westside | Southtown | Shoreland | Erlinda |
|---|---|---|---|---|---|
| Any forced sex | 14 | 5 | 15 | 20 | 9 |
| Relationship to forcer: | | | | | |
|   Stranger | 10 | 10 | 18 | 11 | 9 |
|   Acquaintance/friend | 32 | 10 | 46 | 47 | 22 |
|   Relative | 8 | 30 | 4 | 5 | 9 |
|   Intimate partner | 35 | 40 | 21 | 29 | 78 |
|   Other | 15 | 10 | 11 | 8 | 0 |
| Sex acts involved: | | | | | |
|   Kissed/body touched | 36 | 30 | 36 | 30 | 27 |
|   Genitals touched | 51 | 50 | 50 | 41 | 36 |
|   Forced to touch forcer | 18 | 60 | 25 | 16 | 18 |
|   Oral sex | 17 | 40 | 29 | 22 | 9 |
|   Vaginal sex | 63 | 80 | 71 | 54 | 64 |
|   Other penetration | 6 | 0 | 11 | 5 | 9 |
|   All penetrative acts | 65 | 80 | 71 | 57 | 89 |
| Physical force/weapon | 56 | 40 | 54 | 60 | 73 |
| Perceived as crime | 78 | 70 | 96 | 65 | 55 |
| Perceived as rape | 67 | 80 | 86 | 46 | 82 |
| N, forced-sex victims | 73 | 10 | 28 | 37 | 11 |
| N, all women | 513 | 209 | 190 | 182 | 128 |

*Source:* CHSLS, 1997.

according to the type of relationship and the level of intimacy expected: stranger; acquaintance or friend; relative; intimate partner; and other.[13] As has been found in other studies (see, e.g., Laumann, Gagnon, Michael, & Michaels, 1994), in most cases the perpetrator is not a stranger to the victim. In the Cook County sample, only 10 percent of the women who were sexually victimized reported that the perpetrator was a complete stranger. On the other hand, more than a third of the victims in Cook County (35 per-

13. *Acquaintance/friend* ranges from short-term relationship, to friendly nonsexual relationship, to a date. *Intimate partner* includes boyfriend, girlfriend, or spouse. *Other* includes employer and other. The categories representing paid or paying sex partners were not included because there were no instances to report.

cent) reported that they were forced by their intimate partner, and another third (32 percent) reported that they were forced by an acquaintance or a friend.[14] Only small percentages reported being forced by a relative, an employer, or some other type of person.

*Forced sex acts.* The respondents were also asked what happened sexually. Table 8.2 presents the estimates for six categories: respondent was kissed or her body was touched; respondent's genitalia were touched; the respondent was forced to touch the other's genitalia; vaginal sex; oral sex; anal sex or penetration by something other than a penis.[15] We also add a category representing any kind of penetration because of the importance of penetration for the victim's perception of the event as rape. As the table shows, vaginal intercourse is the most frequently reported act (63 percent in Cook County), followed by kissing and touching the body (36 percent).

*Method of force.* Fifty-six percent of the women in Cook County reported that the perpetrator used physical force or a weapon (or threatened to use one). The other 44 percent reported that the perpetrator used other forms of intimidation, such as blackmail or threatened physical force. This contrasts with the conventional image that sex is forced only if physical force or a weapon is used. At the same time, as we found elsewhere (Buntin & Lechtman, 2001), victims were more likely to define the event as a crime when physical force was involved than when it was absent.

*Differences between neighborhoods.* As we did in the previous section on violence between intimate partners, we also compared neighborhoods. The pat-

14. Since in the CHSLS the difference between *friend* and *acquaintance* is not clarified, we cannot tell what type of relations and what level of intimacy respondents attributed to these two categories. We cannot dismiss, however, the possibility that some sexual intimacy is involved—especially since the only other categories offered that clearly imply a sexual relationship were *husband/wife* and *boyfriend/girlfriend.* Given the limited choice of responses, it is possible that someone might call a partner in a casual or an uncommitted sexual relationship a *friend* or describe a dating partner as an *acquaintance.*

15. These categories represent combinations of the original categories included in the questionnaire. The questions presented to those whose first sexual experience was also forced were slightly different than those presented to all other victims of forced sex. The response categories offered to the former included kissing; respondent's genitals were touched; respondent touched other person's genitals; vaginal intercourse; respondent performed oral sex on other person; other person performed oral sex on respondent; fingers or other objects in vagina; respondent's vagina or anus penetrated with something other than a penis; something else, specify. The latter were offered an additional category—respondent's body was touched—while the two anal-sex categories were reduced to one—anal sex. We too combined the two anal-sex categories as well as *kissing* and *touching body.*

tern of coercion by persons known to the victim is replicated across all the neighborhoods. However, neighborhoods differed in terms of whether perpetrators are intimate partners or acquaintances/friends. More respondents living in Shoreland and Southtown reported that they were forced by acquaintances or friends than by intimate partners. The opposite was true for Westside and Erlinda. Since the categories *friend* and *acquaintance* may refer to a variety of sexual relationships, the differences may reflect variations in sexual scripts (Laumann, Gagnon, Michael, & Michaels, 1994) for dating and intimate relationships that are socially operative across racial and ethnic or socioeconomic categories. For example, sex between partners who are not married or not involved in a committed relationship is more common in Shoreland and Southtown than in Westside and Erlinda. In addition, forced vaginal sex was also the most common forced-sex act in all the neighborhoods, but the percentages vary across neighborhoods. Women in Southtown reported the highest rates, women in Shoreland the lowest.

## Victim's Perception of Forced Sexual Activity

The respondents who reported that they had been sexually forced were also asked whether they considered their forced-sex experience to be a crime and whether they defined it as rape. Cross-tabulating the characteristics of the event with the respondents' definitions provides an initial look at how the elements of the event shape its meaning for the victim. Table 8.2 presents the pattern of responses to these questions by neighborhood. The majority of victims, it turns out, do not consider forced sex as something that society legitimizes: 78 percent of the respondents in Cook County defined the event as a crime, and 67 percent defined it as rape. The difference between these estimates shows, however, that specific characteristics are required for a forced-sex act to be considered, not just a criminal act, but rape. The identity of the perpetrator and the use of physical force and weapons play a role in establishing the meaning of the event for the respondent.

## Perceiving Forced Sex as Rape

Rape is not a crime that exists as a "natural" act outside its economic, social, and political contexts (Madriz, 1997; Hengehold, 2000). To complicate matters further, the same event can be defined differently from different perspectives. For example, a victim of a forced-sex experience may not define the experience as rape even if a social-service or legal organization would, and vice versa. Thus, not only is community context important, but so are the perspectives of the persons involved (for the definition of rape within several institutional contexts, see Hengehold [2000]). Estrich (1986) distinguishes between two types of rape: "traditional" rape, which involves physical force and is perpetrated by a stranger; and "nontraditional" rape, a "less violent" rape committed by someone the victim knows. The traditional form matches the general societal perception of rape. This is the stranger lurking in the dark alley with a knife or a gun. The key components are the fact that the attacker is a stranger and the use of physical force or a weapon. Estrich (1986) and Basile (1999) both present this idea as the starting point for defining rape. They argue that these are the incidents about which there is broad consensus. There is little agreement about the nontraditional instances of forced sex, however.

Forced sex perpetrated by a spouse has only recently gained recognition as a form of rape and as an illegal activity (Basile, 1999). Thus, the type of relationship that existed between the victim and her forcer is an important element that shapes perceptions of the event. Forced sex involving a non–intimate partner was much more likely to be defined as a rape than was forced sex involving an intimate partner. In our data, all victims of forced sex involving strangers defined what they have gone through as a crime, and the vast majority also defined it as a rape (88 percent). In fact, the percentage of women defining the forced-sex event as a rape was the highest among victims of forced sex involving strangers. On the other hand, the lowest rates, for rape or crime, were among victims of forced sex involving intimate partners. Only half the women who were forced by their intimate partners defined the event as a crime, and a little more than half (54 percent) defined it as a rape. Intimate relationships, marriage, and even long-term romance are all characterized by, among other things, sexual intimacy. One might suspect, then, that different perpetrators are likely to force different sexual activities and that this plays into the different social understandings of these events. We show elsewhere (Buntin & Lechtman, 2001), however, that the identity of the perpetrator and the nature of the acts forced on the victim also play a role in the definition, each independently.

Penetrative sex acts, especially vaginal, are a central element influencing the perception of rape. Understandably, these acts are significantly related to the definition of an event as rape (Buntin & Lechtman, 2001). Here, the percentage of women defining what they have gone through as rape was much higher among those reporting forced vaginal intercourse or penetration in general than among those reporting only other forced acts. In contrast, penetrative sex acts were less central, in comparison with other acts, to the definition of the event as a crime. Here, most victims defined any kind of coercive act as a crime. These perceptions follow general and legal understandings of forced sex.

*Differences between neighborhoods.* Table 8.2 presents comparisons across the neighborhoods that reveal striking differences. Almost all the women in Southtown (96 percent) considered what they had gone through to be a crime, a much greater percentage than among women in Cook County (78 percent). The rates in Westside and Shoreland were somewhere in the middle, and Erlinda had the lowest rate. Even more interesting is the victims' perception of the event as rape. Here, although the rates in Southtown were still the highest, the differences between Southtown, Erlinda, and Westside were not great—the estimates all ranged between 80 and 82 percent. These rates were much higher than those in Cook County or Shoreland. In fact, not only was the rate in Shoreland the lowest, but it was much lower when it came to rape and very low when it came to defining the event as a crime.

PERCEIVING RAPE IN SHORELAND. The pattern in Shoreland is particularly intriguing. In this affluent, trendy neighborhood populated by young, mostly white, college-educated professionals, about one in five women report being forced into sexual activity at least once. However, when we look at the rate of perceiving the event as rape, we see a very different pattern. Of the four neighborhoods, women in Shoreland are the *least* likely to define the experience as rape (46 percent). This percentage is much lower than the Cook County rate (67 percent) as well as the rates in the other three neighborhoods (which range between 80 and 86 percent). In general, women in Shoreland are more likely to define their experience as a crime (65 percent) than as rape, but that rate is also quite a bit lower than that in the Cook County sample.

Previous studies suggest that certain demographic characteristics play a key role in shaping an individual's understanding of what constitutes rape. Bourque (1989) reviews the findings of several studies that show that gender, age, race, education, and sex-role attitudes are important determinants of one's definition of rape. Women, younger persons, whites, more highly educated persons, and those with nontraditional sex-role attitudes tend to have a broader definition of what constitutes rape (e.g., Williams & Holmes, 1981; Field, 1978; Klemmack & Klemmack, 1976; Krulewitz & Payne, 1981). On the basis of this research and Shoreland's demographic characteristics, we would expect that women there would be more likely to define a forced-sex experience as rape. However, the data show that the opposite is true. Shoreland women are much *less* likely to define the experience as rape.

It should be noted, however, that these previous studies refer to the perceptions of the population at large. For the majority of people, rape and sexual assault are hypothetical situations. They are scary possibilities, but not realities. How does living through the experience affect an individual's perception? Do women who report forced-sex experiences follow the same patterns of definition as those who have not? We argue that they do not. Instead, the lived experience of forced sexual activity is a mediating factor in the process of defining forced sex as rape. In fact, a national study of college students showed that, among women whose forced-sex experience would be legally defined as rape, only 27 percent considered themselves rape victims (Koss, 1988). This suggests that, while college-educated persons may have a broader definition of rape in theory, their perspective may be quite different when it is their own experience that they are considering.

Elsewhere (Buntin & Lechtman, 2001), we have employed the Shoreland data to analyze the relations between the identity of the forcer, the sex acts forced on the victim, and the method of force used as well as several socioeconomic variables and the victim's perception of the forced-sex experience as a crime or as rape. These analyses showed that, while characteristics of the forced-sex event were important in the labeling process, education was also an important and consistent factor. Controlling for the characteristics of the forced-sex event, women with a bachelor's degree or higher are 85 percent less likely to define their forced-sex experience as rape than are women with less than a bachelor's degree. In Shoreland, the low rate of defining forced sex as rape becomes much more understandable when we recognize this important effect of education. Nearly 85 percent of Shoreland women who reported at least one forced-sex experience have a bachelor's degree or higher, compared to 31 percent in Cook County as a whole. Westside, Southtown, and Erlinda have much lower rates of college completion (20, 11, and 9 percent, respectively).

How do these findings relate to the findings of previous studies that, in general, college-educated people have a broader definition of rape and, thus, should be more likely to define a forced-sex experience as rape? As suggested above, we argue that there is an important difference between the perceptions of people who have actually experienced forced sex and the perceptions of those who have not. The patterns of perception in Shoreland suggest that college-educated women may be more likely to perceive a forced-sex experience as "being forced to do something they didn't want to do." Recall that Shoreland has the highest rate of reported forced sex. Clearly, however, this labeling process is quite different from the process by which the event is defined as rape. College-educated women, like those in Shoreland, are much less likely to take the next step and define the experience as rape.

Higher education may, in general, lead to a broader definition of rape, but what happens when it comes to defining one's own experiences? We suggest that, for women, college education is likely to be associated with a personal identity of independence and freedom. Regarding sexuality, more educated women are likely to have a greater sense of shared responsibility and equal participation and enjoyment in their sexual interactions than their less educated counterparts. Defining one's experience as rape includes defining oneself as a rape victim. But social discourse commonly portrays a rape victim as being extremely vulnerable and powerless, a figure to be pitied. The victim identity may be difficult to adopt without challenging a woman's sense of independence and self-sufficiency. Women may also feel shame and embarrassment because they should have "known better," or "been more careful," or been able to avoid the vulnerable position in which they found themselves. Therefore, college-educated women may be less likely to accept the status of rape victim than are women with more traditional, less egalitarian gender-role expectations.

The negative relation between education and the perception of forced sex as rape is important because the victim's understanding of her experience plays a central role in determining what kind of support or assistance she seeks—if any. For example, if the victim of forced sex does not define the experience as rape or as a criminal act, she is unlikely to report it to the police and seek legal action against the perpetrator. She is also unlikely to call a rape-crisis hotline or to visit a rape-crisis center. Thus, many forced-sex experiences among college-educated women remain hidden from legal and social-service organizations and probably even from the victim's friends and family. In the light of these findings, we suggest that organizations that wish to reach victims of forced sex may want to reconsider the use of the terms *rape* and *rape victim,* particularly those working with college-educated populations. If college-educated women are resisting such labels, then perhaps a new vocabulary is necessary in order to reach these women successfully and provide meaningful services to them. A subsequent section further considers the help-seeking behaviors of women who have experienced forced sexual activity.

## Men's Experiences of Forced Sex

To this point, we have focused on women's forced-sex experiences. It is important to note that an overwhelming majority of respondents who reported at least one forced-sex experience were women. In fact, only 2 percent of men in Cook County reported forced sex. Since gender plays an important role in how both victims and nonvictims understand and label forced-sex events, it is important to examine men and women separately. Unfortunately, owing to the small number of men reporting forced sex, we can provide only estimates of the prevalence of forced sex among the men in each sample. As with the rate of forced sex among women, the rate of forced sex among men was highest in Shoreland. Eight percent of the men in Shoreland said that they had been forced into sexual activity at least once since the age of thirteen. This is much higher than the Cook County rate. Rates in the other three neighborhoods were also quite low, between 1 and 2 percent. More detailed descriptions of men's forced-sex experiences were precluded by the very small number of cases available for analysis.

## Seeking Help in Chicago

The preceding sections of this chapter have examined the nature and rates of intimate-partner violence and forced sexual activity in Chicago. We now examine where the victims of violence and forced sex go for help. We first present the CHSLS data on where respondents sought help after experiences of intimate-partner violence and forced sexual activity. Then, using the CHSLS institutional-interview data—which cover a variety of topics related to sexual behavior, including violence (see Van Haitsma, Paik, & Laumann, chapter 2 in this volume)—we examine the attitudes toward and approaches to dealing with violence in sexual relationships of religious, social-service, health-care, and law-enforcement and other legal organizations. Finally, we highlight issues of importance to each neighborhood regarding sources of assistance for women and men dealing with violence in their sexual relationships.[16]

### *Finding Help after Intimate-Partner Violence*

Respondents were asked whether they had sought help from anyone, formally or informally, as a result of conflicts with their partners. Informal sources of support included respondent's family, partner's family, and friends. Formal sources included the police, members of the clergy, social workers, mental-health professionals, staff at battered women's shelters, and medical practitioners. Table 8.3 specifies the proportion of respondents who approached the various sources of support in Cook County and each neighborhood, by gender. Entries in the row labeled *social-service worker* give the percentages of respondents who approached any of the various social-service workers listed above.

In general, when people seek help regarding conflicts with their partners, they are much more likely to approach family or friends than they are formal organizations. In all four neighborhoods, and in Cook County, the overall percentages of those seeking help from family or friends were persistently much higher than the percentages of those seeking help from a formal organization, although the rates did vary. In Southtown, for example, we find the highest rates both of approaching family or friends and of approaching formal organizations. In Westside, however, while we find rates of approaching formal organizations comparable to those in Southtown, we also find the lowest rates of approaching family and friends.

Gender differences between neighborhoods were also found. In Cook

16. For a more detailed discussion of religious, social-service, health-care, and law-enforcement and other legal organizations' approaches to risky sexual behavior, see Ellingson, Van Haitsma, Laumann, and Tebbe (chapter 11 in this volume).

Table 8.3 Respondent's Sources of Support for Intimate-Partner Violence by Gender and Neighborhood (%)[a]

| Respondent Approached: | Cook County | | Westside | | Southtown | | Shoreland | | Erlinda | |
|---|---|---|---|---|---|---|---|---|---|---|
| | Women | Men | Women | Men | Women | Men | Women | Men | Women | Men |
| Friends/family | 79 | 75 | 66 | 45 | 91 | 77 | 77 | 53 | 59 | 50 |
| Police | 7 | 8 | 12 | 8 | 21 | 12 | 9 | 0 | 0 | 0 |
| Clergy | 12 | 13 | 10 | 5 | 17 | 8 | 0 | 6 | 9 | 0 |
| Doctor | 5 | 12 | 5 | 5 | 8 | 5 | 0 | 12 | 0 | 0 |
| Social-service worker | 8 | 20 | 16 | 8 | 16 | 10 | 5 | 12 | 18 | 17 |
| N | 110 | 61 | 61 | 38 | 77 | 61 | 22 | 17 | 22 | 6 |

Source: CHSLS, 1997.
[a]Data shown include cases reporting either moderate or severe intimate-partner violence in the past year.

County as a whole, the percentages approaching friends and family were higher among women, whereas the percentages approaching formal agencies were higher among men. The pattern in Shoreland bears some resemblance to that in Cook County, with men reporting higher rates of seeking formal support and women reporting higher rates of seeking informal support, although none of the men talked to the police. In Westside and Southtown, however, women were more likely to approach any source of support, informal or formal. The major source of formal support in Southtown was the police, in Westside social-service workers.[17]

## *Finding Help after Forced Sex*

Victims of forced sex were asked whether they had approached anyone for help at the time the event happened. Those who responded affirmatively were further asked to identify those to whom they had turned for help. Again, the options included friends or relatives, a spouse or partner, the police, a doctor or some other medical professional, a member of the clergy, a telephone help line, a social worker or a rape victim's advocate, or someone else. Table 8.4 summarizes the estimates of help-seeking behavior. The table shows the percentage of women who approached these sources of help and support among victims of forced sex in general and broken down by residential area. The table is also broken down by whether the victims perceived the event as a crime, whether they perceived the event as rape, whether the event involved forced penetrative sex, and the victims' relationship to the perpetrator.

The data show that forced sex continues to remain hidden. Sixty percent of the women who reported that they were forced approached no one for help. Only 40 percent (sixty-three women) reported approaching anyone. Most of those who did seek help (sixty-two of the sixty-three) approached family or friends. Regarding institutional sources of support, the rates are much lower. Only 11 percent of the victims went to the police, and 10 percent sought help from a doctor or some other medical professional. Only 6 percent sought help from a social worker or a rape victim's advocate, a similar number approached a member of the clergy, and only 4 percent called a telephone help line.

The data also show that women's help-seeking behavior is shaped by certain central elements of the forced-sex event. For example, the proportions seeking formal sources of support were greater among women who defined the event as a crime or as rape than among those who did not. (Yet, even among women who defined the event as a crime or a rape, the great major-

17. Keep in mind, however, that the absolute numbers are very small here.

Table 8.4 Forced-Sex Victims' Sources of Support by Neighborhood, Perception of Event, and Aspects of the Forced-Sex Event (%)

| | Approached: | | | | | |
| --- | --- | --- | --- | --- | --- | --- |
| | Friends/Relatives | Police | Doctor | Clergy | Social Worker | N |
| All forced-sex victims | 39 | 11 | 10 | 6 | 6 | 158 |
| Neighborhood: | | | | | | |
| Cook County | 40 | 14 | 11 | 6 | 3 | 72 |
| Westside | 60 | 0 | 0 | 0 | 0 | 10 |
| Southtown | 46 | 21 | 18 | 11 | 18 | 28 |
| Shoreland | 32 | 3 | 8 | 3 | 3 | 37 |
| Erlinda | 18 | 9 | 0 | 9 | 9 | 11 |
| Perceived as crime: | | | | | | |
| Yes | 43 | 14 | 12 | 7 | 8 | 118 |
| No | 28 | 5 | 5 | 3 | 0 | 40 |
| Perceived as rape: | | | | | | |
| Yes | 44 | 15 | 12 | 7 | 8 | 105 |
| No | 31 | 4 | 6 | 4 | 2 | 53 |
| Penetration: | | | | | | |
| Yes | 39 | 15 | 14 | 8 | 9 | 104 |
| No | 39 | 4 | 2 | 2 | 0 | 54 |
| Relationship to forcer: | | | | | | |
| Stranger | 77 | 35 | 41 | 18 | 29 | 17 |
| Acquaintance/friend | 35 | 7 | 5 | 4 | 5 | 57 |
| Relative | 31 | 8 | 8 | 8 | 8 | 13 |
| Intimate partner | 26 | 6 | 2 | 6 | 0 | 53 |

*Source:* CHSLS, 1997.

ity—more than 80 percent—did not seek formal sources of support, further evidence that rape remains hidden.) Also, the percentages seeking any help at all, formally or informally, were highest among women forced by a stranger— 77 percent approached family or friends, 35 percent the police, 41 percent a doctor, 18 percent a member of the clergy, and 29 percent a social worker— and lowest among women forced by an intimate partner.

*Differences between neighborhoods.* In general, more women in Southtown and Westside than in Shoreland and Erlinda, or Cook County as a whole, re- ported seeking help after their forced-sex experience. Whereas women in Westside sought help only from family and friends, some women in the other neighborhoods did approach institutional sources of support. The proportion of women approaching institutional sources of support was highest in South-town and lowest in Shoreland.

## Sources of Assistance in the Four Neighborhoods

The survey data examined so far tell us that, in general, people dealing with either intimate-partner violence or forced sexual activity are unlikely to seek help from a community service provider. They are more likely to go to friends or family for support, although many approach no one about these violent experiences. Since some respondents did, however, report approaching a service provider, we briefly examine these organizations' perspectives on intimate-partner violence.[18] What do they perceive as the cause of intimate-partner violence in their neighborhood? Do they consider intimate-partner violence to be a serious problem in their community? The following discussion addresses these questions and focuses on what the data suggest is a key issue or challenge for each neighborhood. Finally, some issues relevant to all four neighborhoods are considered.

SHORELAND: SAME-SEX INTIMATE-PARTNER VIOLENCE. As mentioned earlier, Shoreland is home to Chicago's gay community. Therefore, same-sex intimate-partner violence is an important issue there (although violence among heterosexuals also occurs in Shoreland, as the survey data demonstrate). Violence in gay and lesbian relationships is becoming an increasingly recognized and studied phenomenon. Only a few short years ago, this problem went unrecognized within the gay community. Even today, the common portrayal in both the popular media and academic research of the domestic-violence victim as female and the perpetrator as male serves to obscure violence between same-sex partners. Nevertheless, more and more researchers, community organizations, and activists are beginning to recognize the importance of dealing with same-sex domestic violence (for a review of the relevant literature, see Renzetti [1992]).

Annie, a leader in the gay and lesbian community in Shoreland, describes intimate-partner violence as "a huge issue in the queer community. Most women don't believe it, though, so it is hard to bring pressure." She is concerned about the lack of services available to gay and lesbian victims of vio-

---

18. Unfortunately, owing to the scarcity of interview data regarding resources for people dealing with forced sexual activity, we must limit our discussion here to service providers' approaches to physical violence between intimates, which may, as Leticia's story suggests, include some form of forced sexual activity, although not necessarily.

lence. She feels that homophobia in women's shelters prevents lesbians from seeking and receiving help there. She also points out that there are no places for male victims to go at all. "Gays and lesbians are unlikely to use the court system. This is, in part, because of a sense of loyalty to 'the family' and a consciousness of the public image of the queer community." Others interviewed suggest that a fear of being outed also prevents gay and lesbian victims from making use of the court system.

Interviews with Shoreland police officers suggest discomfort and confusion regarding same-sex intimate-partner violence. Same-sex domestic-violence calls are perceived as more violent, and, therefore, more dangerous to the officers, than heterosexual domestic-violence calls. One female officer said that she had seen "beautiful houses destroyed due to gay and lesbian domestic violence, particularly gay [male] violence. In gay situations, both of the parties tend to stick around and fight it out and destroy furniture. In straight abuse cases, the man tends to leave after the abuse."

In addition to the perceived higher level of violence involved, same-sex domestic-violence calls are also challenging because the police officers often find it difficult to discern which party is the perpetrator and which the victim. In heterosexual incidents, there tends to be an underlying assumption that the man is the perpetrator and the woman the victim. But this shorthand approach cannot be applied to same-sex relationships. This uncertainty, the expectations of higher levels of violence, as well as varying levels of homophobia among police officers influence the officers' responses to same-sex violence. A male officer in Shoreland described gay domestic-violence calls as disorienting and unsettling, particularly if one or both of the parties is not fully clothed.

Nevertheless, the police response to same-sex intimate-partner violence appears similar to their response to heterosexual violence. They try to diffuse the situation by talking with both parties, make arrests if necessary, and provide some instruction to victims on how to obtain orders of protection, where to get help in the community, etc. Since, according to the male officer interviewed, income disparity tends not to be as great between same-sex partners as between heterosexual partners, the cause of same-sex domestic violence tends, he believes, less often to be financial matters, as with heterosexual partners, and more often to be emotional matters. This difference, he argues, also affects the outcome of the situation. In heterosexual relationships, the female victim often does not want the male perpetrator arrested because she is dependent on him economically. This is generally not true for gay and lesbian couples. Still, the officer believes, most of the time the officers "can talk it out with the couple." In general, however, the police officers appear to offer little in the way of referrals to community organizations providing services to gay and lesbian victims of intimate-partner violence.

In all fairness, there are very few organizations even in Shoreland, let alone elsewhere in Chicago, that deal specifically with gay and lesbian victims of intimate violence. And sometimes the relationship between gay and lesbian organizations and the police is ambivalent at best. Joe, who runs a legal-advocate program for a local gay and lesbian service organization, describes his program's relationship with the police as a "love/hate thing": "On the one hand, we are looking to get officers reprimanded and disciplined for anti-queer infractions, and, on the other hand, we couldn't do our work without them. Nothing happens if you don't have a police report."

The program that Joe runs is accessed primarily through a hotline. Gay and lesbian victims of violence can call the hotline for legal assistance as well as for medical and counseling referrals. When charges are brought, the advocates follow a caller's case through the legal system. The organization deals, not only with intimate-partner violence, but also with other forms of violence, such as gay-bashing and other hate crimes. Joe notes, however, that calls about intimate-partner violence have increased recently, perhaps because of an article in a lesbian community periodical about violence between women. "Many women started calling in and asking if what was happening in their relationship was abuse. Sometimes it was and sometimes not. In order to determine abuse [we] look for a pattern of power and control." He stressed that there does not have to be physical violence for it to be abuse. Callers deemed to be being abused are referred to a therapist and, sometimes, to a medical professional. Each case is dealt with on an individual basis.

As Joe's observations suggest, often gay and lesbian victims of intimate-partner violence do not even recognize the violence as abuse. Gay men may think that only women are domestic-violence victims. Lesbians may think that only men perpetrate domestic violence. One therapist interviewed, Barbara, called this latter perception *lesbian nirvana,* referring to the belief that all lesbians are sisters and no lesbian would ever hurt another. She also pointed out that, when violence does occur in lesbian relationships, it is often as a result of jealousy and anxiety. "This is no different from heterosexual couples. It is a power thing—power and control. There is a proprietary attitude, that one owns the other."

Barbara went on to elaborate gender differences in same-sex intimate-partner violence. According to her, our culture tends to sanction violence between men, whether it is on the playground, in the bars, or on television. Men are used to fighting and to resolving conflicts through the use of violence. Violence between male partners is, therefore, less traumatic and does less damage to the relationship than violence between female partners, who are not culturally prepared for physical violence.

These observations suggest that gay and lesbian relationships are not lacking in violent conflict and abuse. What *is* lacking is the support network (such

as it is) available to heterosexual victims of violence, even in a gay community as developed as Shoreland. For example, even those Shoreland churches
that are open to and supportive of gay men and lesbians had no programs to
assist victims of same-sex intimate-partner violence.[19] And, as noted above,
programs at gay and lesbian social-service organizations are limited in number and in scope. In addition, lesbians may feel unwelcome at battered women's
shelters, while gay men really have nowhere to go for help. Thus, gay men
and lesbians are left to deal with intimate-partner violence largely on their
own and in secret.

Because same-sex intimate-partner violence has only recently been "outed,"
much work remains to be done, not only among theorists and researchers,
but also among service providers. Same-sex intimate-partner violence seems
at first glance to challenge the feminist perspective on violence, which focuses on the negative effects of patriarchy on women's lives, although some
researchers are beginning to address this theoretical problem (see, e.g., Renzetti, 1992). In addition, because of small sample sizes, estimates of prevalence
are still difficult to arrive at and generally unreliable. However, researchers
such as Renzetti (1992) have begun utilizing qualitative methods with small
samples to gain insight into same-sex intimate-partner violence. Future research will, one hopes, build on these studies, and perhaps someday a more
reliable approach will be developed.

WESTSIDE AND ERLINDA: CULTURE AND VIOLENCE. The two
Latino neighborhoods in our study, Westside and Erlinda, deal with a different sort of issue in that intimate-partner violence is generally perceived by
service providers as an established part of the culture. For example, many of
the service providers interviewed perceived violence against women as an
important aspect of Latino masculinity and women's acceptance of this behavior as a sign of their docility and low self-esteem. One Methodist pastor
in Westside described a "culture of abuse," in which the wife is expected to
respect her husband regardless of the way he treats her. And a Catholic priest
there described violence as "the dark side of Mexican culture." According to
an Erlinda community leader, "Hispanic men generally direct a lot of abuse
toward women, like hitting their girlfriends, giving them a slap in the face.
Many girls learn to accept this type of behavior." And a Catholic church

---

19. It should be noted that Shoreland churches had limited services even for heterosexual couples dealing with intimate-partner violence. And few of those churches
that did provide counseling were connected to, and, thus, could offer referrals to, the
neighborhood network of social-service organizations through which more material
forms of assistance could be obtained. The lack of connection between community
organizations will be further discussed later in this chapter.

worker in Erlinda reported: "Domestic violence is so much a part of the culture that people lack a vocabulary to identify it."

Ellingson (chapter 10 in this volume) discusses health-care and social-service organizations' use of cultural causal stories to explain risky sexual behavior among Latinos, and intimate-partner violence also follows this pattern. Service providers often explain what they perceive to be a higher rate of violence among Latinos, and a lower rate of reporting incidents of violence and of seeking help, in terms of "the culture of machismo" and "the culture of silence." There are, however, structural and economic factors at play as well, even if they are often obscured by the perception of cultural causes. For example, the priest who described violence as "the dark side of Mexican culture" went on to describe the immigration experience and economic instability as contributing to that violence: "When a man comes up to the United States, he is suddenly much richer in absolute terms than he was in Mexico, but much poorer in relation to the wider population. He feels inadequate, belittled. Often he will require his wife to stay at home and not work. But even if this is not the case, the only person he can push around is his wife, or the kids when he is in his castle. So there is a very high incidence of domestic violence in [Westside]."

Another example of culture obscuring other factors can be seen in discussions of the culture of silence and the submissive nature of Latinas. Many service providers told us that women were unwilling to report their husband's abuse because Latinas, particularly Mexican immigrant women, are socialized to be submissive and to show respect to their husband regardless of his treatment of them. Several service providers perceive Mexican women to be more submissive than Puerto Rican women in general because "they are more traditional . . . willing to put up with more abuse for the sake of the family." Puerto Rican women, on the other hand, are often perceived as putting up with abuse because of low self-esteem.

However, other providers note important social and economic factors that may keep Latinas silent about abuse and prevent them from leaving their violent partners. For Mexican immigrant women, fear of deportation can play a major role. If their legal residency in the United States is linked to their marriage (or if they perceive it to be), they may put up with a violent partner in order to stay in the country. If they are undocumented immigrants, they may feel that they cannot seek help because they may be deported. In addition, many Latino families in the United States are economically unstable. Thus, a woman may fear that she cannot provide for herself and her children without the financial contributions of her husband.

As one social-service provider puts it: "Abused women go back to violent relationships because they have no other alternatives. For women who are undocumented aliens, the alternatives are even fewer." A battered women's shelter worker concurs: "The barriers to intervention and treatment for Hispanic victims of domestic violence include a lack of information, illiteracy, . . . a language barrier, racism, and economic dependency."

These contrasting points of view suggest that cultural explanations of intimate-partner violence may be obscuring more than they are explaining. While we would not suggest that culture is irrelevant to the Latino experience in Chicago (and elsewhere), what counts as culture often depends on the observer's point of view. Often, stereotypes at play in the larger society shape people's understanding of an ethnic group's culture: "Buttressed more by negative and ethnocentric stereotypes than by research, the Anglo gaze casts the Chicano family—and by extrapolation, the Mexican family—as a static, homogeneous entity where patriarchy and pathology reign" (Hondagneu-Sotelo, 1994, 9).[20] These perceptions result in a cultural emphasis that may hide important structural and economic situations that shape an individual's behaviors and attitudes. For example, Latinas who hide intimate-partner violence and stay with their violent partners are described as being socialized into submissiveness and silence by Latino culture. However, many people from many cultural backgrounds who have abusive partners suffer in silence, a silence that is not always explained culturally.

The contradictions evident in the interviews also attest to the power of cultural stereotypes and point to the possibility that, like beauty, culture is in the eyes of the beholder. For example, consider the contradictions in the following discussions of the cultural causes of intimate-partner violence in Mexican and Puerto Rican families. While one Erlinda health worker describes Puerto Rican women as having low self-esteem because they have been socialized to become wives and take care of the household rather than to work outside the home, another describes them as more assertive than Mexican women (and Puerto Rican men as less macho than Mexican men) and argues that, as a result, violence is less prevalent in Puerto Rican homes. Some service providers consider intimate-partner violence to be a huge problem for Latino families; others find it to be less of a problem because Latinos, particularly Mexicans, are more family oriented. And, although a Methodist church worker described Mexican women as submissive and, therefore, willing to put up with more abuse than Puerto Rican women were, she also said that "Mexican women place a higher value on their families. They are there for their children and carry out the daily tasks such as cooking. Mexican men are also more involved with their families than Puerto Ricans. Because of these complementary roles, the Mexicans are better able to keep their families together than the Puerto Ricans."

20. For more on this issue, see Hondagneu-Sotelo (1994), Ybarra (1983), and Zinn (1979).

In addition, there are differing perspectives on whether Latinos or African Americans are more violent. Some service providers consider Latinos to be more violent (a product of the culture of machismo), some less. However, one police officer said that, in general, black men push their wives around more and that black couples have more violent physical fights than do Latino couples. Clearly, cultural stereotypes are being used in ways that may confuse and obscure the real dynamics of these situations. The inconsistencies and contradictions described here suggest that culture is being used as a blanket explanation for a number of different and conflicting patterns of behavior, perhaps making it difficult for many service providers to recognize other kinds of influences and situations. Structural and economic factors such as immigrant status, English proficiency, and economic instability are often hidden behind stories of machismo, female submissiveness, and Hispanic culture generally.

Regarding Puerto Ricans, there is an additional causal story that appears along with or in place of the cultural explanations: the persisting negative consequences of colonialism (for a more extended discussion, see Ellingson, Van Haitsma, Laumann, and Tebbe [chapter 11 in this volume]). One community leader argues that incest and intimate-partner violence are both consequences of colonialism: "For a man who has no power, the family domain becomes the last place in which to assert a lost sense of power and control."

Often, the postcolonial approach manifests itself in an emphasis on individual or psychological issues, although economic issues are important as well, as the remarks of the community leader quoted in the previous paragraph suggest.[21] Puerto Rican women are perceived by service providers as having low self-esteem, which explains their reluctance to leave an abusive partner. This argument represents a slight variation on the cultural approach, in which this behavior is perceived to be a result of gender-role socialization (submissiveness). As a result of this individual/psychological perspective, adherents of the postcolonial approach tend to focus on building self-esteem and on education rather than on addressing structural and economic problems directly.

Our purpose in reviewing these various perspectives and cultural explanations here is not to debunk some and support others. We do not wish to put forth the idea that some are true while others are not. It would be remiss to suggest that culture plays no role in the experiences of Latinos (or of any

---

21. For a classic example of the psychological consequences of the colonial experience, see Fanon (1967). Subsequent authors have argued that the lingering effects of colonialism affect contemporary minority groups, e.g., Puerto Ricans. For further discussion of this issue, see Ellingson, Van Haitsma, Laumann, and Tebbe (chapter 11 in this volume).

other racial/ethnic group, for that matter). Rather, what we question in this chapter is the extent to which purely cultural perspectives and explanations of behavior—in this case, intimate-partner violence—obscure more complicated relations between cultural, structural, and economic influences. We argue that more research is needed to unearth a more satisfying understanding of these relations and their influence on intimate-partner violence as well as other aspects of sexual and social behavior.

We turn next to the example of two service providers who do attempt to base their approaches on more complex explanations. But, before we do so, we should emphasize that our point here is the consequences of simplified cultural explanations. If violence is culturally determined, then escaping violence means, at least to some degree, renouncing one's culture. And this is a step that many in the Latino community will be loathe to take. Thus, few in the Latino community are likely to seek help from institutions whose approach is based on a simplified cultural explanation, and institutions that use such an approach often have little to offer those who want help but also want to maintain cultural traditions and beliefs.

Two social-service organizations in Erlinda, the Welcome Home Shelter and Casa de Vida, illustrate alternative understandings of intimate-partner violence and of Latino experiences. These organizations utilize more structural and economic approaches, which allows them to work with Latinas in a way that does not challenge their cultural heritage.

Ana, of Casa de Vida, described intimate-partner violence as prevalent in all ethnic groups and income brackets. She emphasizes economic barriers to escaping violence, pointing out that many women have few alternatives for themselves or for their children. Similarly, Susanna, of the Welcome Home Shelter, argues: "Violence is a social and not a cultural issue. There are no barriers to domestic violence. It exists in all communities. . . . It is not a cultural issue. Rather it is about power and control." Thus, Susanna teaches Latinas to be "bicultural" rather than to acculturate. And she tries to help immigrant women maintain their existing cultural values while learning to negotiate culture and life in the United States. Rather than using such cultural explanations as machismo and female submissiveness, Susanna contends that "there are a number of social, economic, and cultural constraints that are built into the immigrant marriage contract that make it difficult for immigrant women to escape a violent relationship."

Such more complex models, ones that move beyond culture (emphasizing, e.g., illiteracy, language barriers, and economic dependency) while still considering its influence, may provide more avenues for assisting immigrant women who are dealing with intimate-partner violence. The Welcome Home Shelter also encourages women to form communities among themselves, thus creating their own support networks. In this way, they can receive assistance in more informal ways, which seems like a productive approach considering CHSLS data suggesting that people are more likely to talk to friends and family about violence than to approach formal service providers.

SOUTHTOWN: MORALITY, DENIAL, AND INTIMATE-PARTNER VIOLENCE. Gathering data in Southtown proved to be challenging for several reasons. In general, most service providers, particularly church workers, do not perceive intimate-partner violence to be a serious problem in their community. One Baptist minister stated that intimate-partner violence is "not a problem in my church." Other providers acknowledged that intimate-partner violence is an issue in their community but did not consider it a significant problem, at least not more so than in any other neighborhood.

These responses left open several avenues of interpretation. First, intimate-partner violence may not be a significant problem in Southtown. If this is, in fact, the case, the limited discussion of the topic by service providers seems appropriate. However, the survey data analyzed above suggest that intimate-partner violence occurs at a higher rate in Southtown than in any other neighborhood and Cook County as a whole. In addition, one pastor told us that the "black church" is in denial about a number of issues, including intimate-partner violence and sexual abuse. He had little to say on the topic but gave it as his opinion that violence is more common than people in the church are willing to admit. His comments suggest that violence is occurring but that neighborhood residents and service providers are unwilling to acknowledge it as a problem. Few church programs were prepared to deal with the issue, and those that were operated on an informal, case-by-case basis and were not likely to refer people to other service organizations.

Another interpretation of the limited interview data is that intimate-partner violence is occurring but that people are not coming to community organizations for help and that service providers therefore see no evidence of it. One health-care worker/community leader described intimate-partner violence as "elusive": "People have a tendency to hide it. However, it is a problem." This interpretation of the data follows the survey findings that very few victims of intimate-partner violence seek help from community service providers.

However, observations made by service providers and other researchers, as well as our own research experience, suggest the likelihood that the providers whom we interviewed may simply be unwilling to share their thoughts and perspectives fully with our research team. One Southtown health-care provider told us point-blank that we were likely to meet with resistance in the black community. Why? Because people in the black community feel that undue research attention has been directed toward them and that they have gained little, if anything, from their participation in such efforts. A Presbyterian minister and academic scholar voiced a similar position:"The answer to someone coming from the University of Chicago asking about domestic violence would be, 'It's none of your business whether my church members beat each other up, and frankly I'm a little offended that you would even ask.'"

We suggest that the proper interpretation of these data takes account of all three possibilities. It is likely that some service providers were reluctant to discuss this issue with us. Several CHSLS interviewers reported that some interviewees seemed uncomfortable discussing the topic. It is also likely that many service providers legitimately do not consider intimate-partner violence to be a serious problem, perhaps because, in their professional capacity at least, they see no evidence of it. A Presbyterian minister in Southtown referred to a "theology of endurance," according to which the most noble achievement is to survive stoically, suggesting that many people may, indeed, be unwilling to ask for help when they need it. Or perhaps service providers are unwilling to admit—even to themselves and their fellow community workers—that intimate-partner violence is a problem, as has been suggested. This question must necessarily remain a mystery to us, at least as long as we are working with the currently available data. We will, therefore, discuss explanations of intimate-partner violence offered by Southtown service providers only briefly, keeping in mind these limitations.

Although the data are limited, there does appear to be a clear pattern—especially among those affiliated with religious organizations—of violence being interpreted primarily in terms of "moral choice" and only secondarily in terms of such structural and economic factors as poverty, racism, and lack of education.[22] The comments of a medical practitioner at a Christian health clinic exemplify this perspective: "Domestic violence is not a resource problem but a problem of moral choices. People do not take into account the implications of their actions. . . . There is too much self-seeking behavior and not enough emphasis on family." Similarly, a Southtown Catholic priest argues that there is too much "feel-good" theology being preached: "There is a war going on between the flesh and the spirit in every person. . . . Truth and knowledge are what people need." He sees the primary cause of intimate-partner violence as "a lack of spiritual rootedness and understanding," followed by a lack of self-love and self-belief and, finally, such social conditions as unemployment, racism, etc.

These perspectives, like the cultural explanations operative in Westside and Erlinda, may serve to discourage people from seeking what little help is available. And it is unclear how organizations taking an approach based on

22. For a discussion of morality as a causal story in the black community, see Ellingson (chapter 10 in this volume) and Ellingson, Van Haitsma, Laumann, and Tebbe (chapter 11).

moral choice can effect change except by continuing to preach the virtues of moral strength. In the face of many of the structural constraints experienced by Southtown residents (financial instability, racism, etc.), however, individuals may feel that these moral choices are too difficult to negotiate and may, therefore, hide their difficulties, such as intimate-partner violence, from community service providers.

CHALLENGES ACROSS NEIGHBORHOOD BOUNDARIES. Finally, we want to address several important issues that reach across neighborhood boundaries and appear relevant for service providers throughout Chicago. First, several service providers voiced concerns that there are very few services available for men and for abusers (who are, from the organizations' perspectives, generally men). It was noted above that abused gay men would not be welcomed at battered women's shelters and have few other options for seeking help. Sandra, a counselor at a Catholic church in Westside, argues that, while organizations that deal only with female victims and their needs are important, "since nobody is dealing with the men, the underlying problem is still there." Also, even if a woman leaves a relationship because of abuse, other social and personal factors often force her to return. Sandra said that she tries to counsel as many men as possible because she feels that this is an important aspect of dealing with violence. The director of a Westside organization that helps women who are dealing with domestic violence and sexual assault said that she would like to see more programs directed toward abusers, instead of just the abused.

These comments lead to a second issue relevant to all four neighborhoods. Earlier in the chapter, we made the conceptual distinction between *common-couple violence* and *patriarchal terrorism* (Johnson 1995), noting that the survey data primarily uncover common-couple violence. It is clear from the interview data, however, that service providers generally approach intimate-partner violence from the perspective of patriarchal terrorism. This is not surprising considering the nature of many social-service organizations as well as the general tone of social discourse on "battered women" and "wife beating." In many cases, Johnson argues, these organizations are likely to be interacting with people dealing with a completely different form of violence than the survey data depict. Thus, their emphasis on "victims of domestic violence" and "the abused" is logical.

However, the CHSLS survey data, combined with Johnson's theoretical contributions, suggest that this second form of violence, "common-couple violence," is going unaddressed by many community organizations. According to the survey data, many couples in all four neighborhoods are dealing with this more gender-balanced form of intimate-partner violence. However, the interview data suggest that service providers focus mainly on men's abuse of women (or patriarchal terrorism) and may perceive violence in that way even when confronted with an instance of common-couple violence. The different meanings and dynamics of the two forms of violence suggest that different approaches to intervention and assistance are appropriate.[23] Thus, this theoretical insight may prove useful to organizations dedicated to reducing the overall level of intimate-partner violence in their communities.

Finally, the institutional-interview data suggest that, in each community, there is relatively little connection across institutional boundaries. And, when there are interactions across institutional boundaries, they are often ambivalent and, occasionally, antagonistic. Ellingson (chapter 10 in this volume) discusses the four institutional perspectives and approaches in greater detail. Here, we simply point out the challenges that organizations face when trying to create coalitions across institutional boundaries.

For example, a Southtown pastor shared her frustration with and disappointment in social-service organizations that make arrangements to work with churches in the community: "Oftentimes, social-service agencies will seek out churches to house them because of the church's natural constituencies, and then, when their funding runs out, they pull out at once. This leaves the pastors holding the bag when people come around looking for the services." She does feel that churches should house multiple services for their congregations and the community, but she thinks that social-service organizations are often not stable enough to make such an arrangement work. She wants to find new ways in which clergy and social-service providers can work together, without leaving church leaders feeling exploited.

Clearly, the survey data suggest that many people dealing with intimate-partner violence are receiving inadequate support, if any, from service providers. Perhaps more effective coalitions between organizations in all four institutional categories (social service, religious, health, and law enforcement) would have more success in reaching these people. There are organizations working toward this goal, and one hopes that more will join in the effort. In addition, the survey data suggest that people are much more likely to go to friends and family for assistance in dealing with intimate-partner violence (as well as forced sexual activity). Thus, organizations trying to tap into these social networks and build on them may find that they are better able to reach people with whom they might otherwise not connect. Churches, as the Southtown pastor suggests, often provide a strong connection to community mem-

---

23. Churches often included marriage or couple counseling as a primary part of their approach to dealing with intimate-partner violence, which suggests that the problem is being dealt with as a dynamic of the relationship. However, it is unclear whether the violence is perceived as mutual at times (common-couple violence) or whether the assumption of violence being directed by men at women persists.

bers. In addition, creating informal networks, like the Welcome Home Shelter's "communities of women," is an interesting strategy for making use of people's comfort with and preference for informal social support.

## Concluding Comments

Ultimately, this chapter argues that the connections between sex markets, intimacy, and sexual violence are important to tease out. The narratives and data presented here demonstrate some of the ways in which violence can invade, organize, or dominate an intimate relationship. Leticia pinpoints this connection when she describes how her husband beats her up and then expects her to sleep with him, "as if I were an animal without any feelings." Her experiences of violence at her husband's hands influence her feelings about sexual intimacy with him (and, perhaps, with anyone else in the future). Her decisions as a wife, as a sexual being, and, if she seeks a new partner, as a participant in the sex market will be powerfully shaped by the violence in her current relationship. Conversely, her current situation was constructed out of her initial location in a sex market, which had implications for her individual sexual opportunities, available partner choices, and bargaining position vis-à-vis potential sex partners. Thus, her story serves to illustrate these key connections between sexuality and violence.

However, it is important to note that the connection between sexuality and violence is not found only in extreme cases like Leticia's. *Sexual violence* is a broad term encompassing a variety of situations and acts embedded across personal, interpersonal, and broader social contexts. The survey data show that, for many people, violence is intimately linked to sexual partnering. Roughly three of every ten women in Cook County and one in five men experienced at least one incident of moderate or severe violence in their sexual relationship during the past year. In some neighborhoods, the rates were even higher. In addition, about 14 percent of women in Cook County have experienced some form of forced sexual activity since age thirteen. This chapter described the prevalence of two forms of sexual violence (intimate-partner violence and forced sexual activity) and attempted to uncover some patterns and meanings behind these behaviors in Cook County as a whole as well as in the four sample neighborhoods. It also explored respondents' help-seeking behaviors and the approaches and perspectives of the organizations striving to assist people with issues of violence in relationships.

One of the main observations arising out of the combination of the CHSLS survey and interview data is how very little real support is available to individuals dealing with intimate violence. The survey data show that very few people who report moderate or severe intimate-partner violence or any type of forced sexual activity seek help from community organizations. The vast majority seek help only from friends and family or tell no one of the problem. Thus, sexual violence is an issue that remains hidden, despite recent movements to focus public attention on it. Individuals continue to confront violent situations within their intimate relationships with very little support from the community. Whether this violence is considered moderate or severe, rape or forced sex, it is an issue intricately connected to sexuality. Just as sexuality itself is an "institutional stepchild" (see Ellingson, Laumann, Paik, & Mahay, chapter 1 in this volume) with no institutional sphere directly concerned with it, the relation between sexuality and violence is also often hidden or distorted. It is our hope that future research will continue to investigate this key relation as well as its implications for individuals' sexual, social, and emotional well-being.

# 9 )

# Social Networks and Sexually Transmitted Diseases

Yoosik Youm and Edward O. Laumann

Sexually transmitted diseases (STDs) are a serious social problem in the United States. Rates of curable STDs are the highest in the industrialized world and are even higher than those in some developing regions (Aral, 1999). Half the most commonly reported infections in the United States are STDs (Division of STD Prevention, 1997), and STDs accounted for 87 percent of the cases reported for the ten leading notifiable diseases in 1995 (CDC, 1996). The Cen-

This chapter is based on Yoosik Youm and Edward O. Laumann, "Social Network Effects on the Transmission of Sexually Transmitted Diseases," *Sexually Transmitted Diseases* 29, no. 11 (2002): 689–97. An earlier version was presented as "Social Network Effects on the Transmission of Sexually Transmitted Diseases" at the Sunbelt XXI International Social Network, Budapest, 27 April 2001.

ters for Disease Control estimated 15.3 million new cases in 1996 (Alexander, Cates, Herndorn, & Ratcliffe, 1998), and the annual costs of selected major STDs, excluding HIV infections, are estimated to be $10 billion (Eng & Butler, 1997). In addition, various STDs may lead to cancer, infertility, ectopic pregnancy, spontaneous abortion, stillbirth, and low birth weight for infants and increased risk for acquiring HIV (Devanter, 1999).

Historically, the main focus of STD epidemiology has been on the attributes and behaviors of individuals, this being consistent with the dominant perspectives in clinical medicine, chronic-disease epidemiology, and psychology (Aral, 1999). Since the late 1980s, however, many researchers have recognized the important role of sexual networks in sustaining the extraordinarily high infection rates in the United States. Whereas with chronic diseases the odds of being infected are determined by individual-level factors, the odds of being infected by (and also infecting others with) STDs are also determined by factors above the level of the individual; that is, they depend, not only on the individual person's risk factors, but also on that person's sex partners' risk factors. Thus, sexual-network effects on the dynamics of STDs have steadily gained research attention (Aral, 1996; Aral et al., 1999; Garnett & Anderson, 1993, 1996; Laumann & Youm, 1999; Potterat et al., 1985; Potterat, Rothenberg, & Muth, 1999; Rothenberg & Potterat, 1988; Rothenberg, Potterat, & Woodhouse, 1996; Rothenberg et al., 1998). In sharp contrast to the increasing attention devoted to *sexual* networks, research on *social*-network effects on STD transmission has rarely been emphasized, and empirical research is limited owing to the lack of pertinent data in the United States, with a few notable exceptions (Wasserheit & Aral, 1996; Morris, Zavisca, & Dean, 1995; Rosenberg et al., 1999). In Europe, although some research—based on the pooling of sixteen population surveys across eleven countries undertaken by the project European Concerted Action on Sexual Behaviour and Risks of HIV Infection (Van Campenhoudt, Cohen, Guizzardi, & Hausser, 1997; Hubert, Bajos, & Sandfort, 1998)—has succeeded in revealing that social factors are critical to the spread of HIV, most research has focused on social relationships in general instead of probing the specific features of social networks that mediate these effects.

Without paying closer attention to social networks, research on the spread of STDs is necessarily incomplete because risk factors are socially constructed, as confirmed in many European research studies (e.g., Aggleton, O'Reilly, Slutkin, & Davis, 1994; Bajos, 1997; Delor & Hubert, 2000). Although sex has a biological substrate, sexual behavior is one of the most socially diverse of human activities. As a direct result of this fact, risk factors regarding sexual behaviors are rooted in and consistently affected by the social environments in which those behaviors are found. For example, the same person bears quite different levels of risks or different odds of changing her sexual behavior depending on whether the sexual relationship in which she is engaged is defined in her social milieu as short-term and casual or regular and ongoing, voluntary or forced, and supported or unsupported by her and her partner's social peers.

Research on the effects of social networks is vital for establishing effective primary prevention—intervention that prevents infection from occurring in the first place. Improved diagnostic tests for STDs have recently revealed both that asymptomatic infections are much more prevalent than symptomatic diseases are (Sparling & Aral, 1991; Parish et al., 2003) and that most STDs result from contact, not with clinically apparent diseases, but rather with unnoticed and frequently subclinical infections (Judson & Paalman, 1991). Given this situation, primary prevention is crucial for curbing STDs (Eng & Butler, 1997). However, reaching a population targeted for primary prevention—those who are at risk but not yet infected—with the necessary information about avoiding STDs is not a straightforward process because most people do not get their information about STDs from the public media. Instead, people obtain and transmit information about STDs primarily through their informal social networks, especially their friends.[1]

Using data from the Chicago Health and Social Life Survey (CHSLS), which includes information about both sexual behavior and social relationships, we will attempt to determine whether there are any social-network effects on STD transmission after controlling for other risk factors. We will also probe for the underlying mechanisms by which social networks could exert their effects.

## Methods

### Data

For this analysis, we shall use only the representative sample of 890 Cook County residents. Respondents were asked to enumerate up to six of their friends, including up to three free-time partners and up to three discussion partners (excluding their sex partners). Respondents were asked to provide detailed information about their friends as well as their sex partners.

---

1. The National Health and Social Life Survey (NHSLS) found that about 40 percent of the adult population relied primarily on close informal nonkin networks (friends or sex partners) for learning about sexual matters when they were growing up while only 8 percent relied primarily on school instruction (and only 1 percent on television or medical clinics) (Laumann, Gagnon, Michael, & Michaels, 1994).

## *Measures*

CONTROL VERSUS INFORMATION. Social networks can change STD transmission dynamics through their effects, first, on the social control exercised by social-network members over the focal individual's choice of sex partners and behaviors and, second, on the flow of pertinent information about the risks posed by particular sex partners and behaviors. Let us elaborate on these alternative pathways of social influence (Friedkin, 1998).

First, people's sexual behaviors are shaped and controlled by various stakeholders in the sexual relationship (Laumann, Gagnon, Michael, & Michaels, 1994). Social control or influence over sex partners' behavior can be exerted directly by the two immediate stakeholders, that is, by the sex partners themselves, or via third parties, such as parents or friends, who constitute the sex partners' informal social networks and, therefore, have a stake in maintaining (or disrupting) the relationship. The stronger the control exerted either by the sex partners themselves or by certain third parties (such as parents), the less likely either partner will be to engage in risky behavior (especially having multiple, nonexclusive sex partners). Conversely, strong social control exerted by social peers such as friends or neighbors, however, can have the opposite effect. If, for example, a young man is tightly embedded in a circle of young men who regard having large numbers of sex partners as normal and even desirable (enhancing one's social standing or reputation in the group), he is likely to have more partners than he would otherwise.

Second, people typically obtain and transmit pertinent sexual information through their social networks (Sprecher & McKinney, 1993). From general knowledge about safe sex or techniques to avoid STDs to specific information about locales in which one is likely to find safe partners for casual sex, people rely heavily on their informal social networks because information drawn from such social ties is more likely to be available, credible, trustworthy, timely, and specific. (For example, in Bangladesh, a social-network approach that utilized local influential persons was five times more efficient in transmitting modern contraceptive practices than was a traditional approach that sent field-workers on home visits [Kinkaid, 2000].) The public media are poor sources for such information because the material that they present is overly general and neither timely, trustworthy, nor reliable; in short, the media lack credibility and immediacy of access to locally relevant information. This is important because people with timely, accurate information are less likely to be infected with STDs.

Although information pertinent for orchestrating sexual purposes can, in principle, flow through either third parties or the dyadic relationship itself, we believe that most sexual information (especially information regarding potential new sex partners) flows mainly through third-party connections and not through the dyadic sexual tie itself. Needless to say, third-party mechanisms and dyadic mechanisms interact in many ways. For example, strong support from a third party can increase self-esteem or bargaining power in the dyadic exchange itself. Unfortunately, we cannot analyze this interaction effect separately owing to the small number of cases at hand.

FRIENDSHIP NETWORKS.  We characterize friendship networks in terms of the two dimensions of range and density in order to distinguish the network mechanisms of information and control. We shall treat five or six friends as constituting a *large* friendship network and fewer than five friends as constituting a *small* friendship network. Further, we shall assume that, if people talk to their friends every day on average, they have a *strong* friendship network and that if they talk to their friend less frequently than once a day they have a *weak* friendship network. Thus, four types of friendship networks are distinguished: *no friends; strong, small networks; weak, large networks;* and a combination of *strong, large networks* and *weak, small networks.* (The final categorization was made after evaluating various criteria for measuring the friendship effect in the multivariate regressions.)

Strong, intensive ties are believed to produce greater mutual commitment and social control, while weak ties provide more information than control (Burt, 1992; Sandefur & Laumann, 1998). In general, having many social ties will lead to the provision of more information, having few ties to the provision of less information. Few and strong ties are more likely to produce social control and influence, while many and weak ties are more likely to produce useful information. Thus, we make the following assumptions: The category *no friends* will manifest strong dyadic control (only the sex partner is present to exercise control) without third-party integration (no extrarelational ties exist). The category *strong, small networks* will manifest strong third-party control through a small clique of friends who can communicate with one another about the matters at hand. The category *weak, large networks* will produce larger flows of information among third parties (friends) who have access to different sources of information. The combined category *strong, large networks* and *weak, small networks* is not easy to interpret because we cannot specify a priori whether the control or the information effect is dominant without more detailed knowledge of the social networks surrounding the respondent.

DYADIC CONTROL/INFORMATION.  As discussed above, social networks exert social control or influence and disseminate information in two ways: through the sexual dyad itself and through third parties. Dyadic control will be measured by four variables: *shared free time* (the amount of free time spent with the most recent partner); *jealous conflict* (conflict with the most recent partner arising from sexual jealousy); *ever having forced sex* (as either perpetrator or victim); and *ease of talk about sexual topics* (with the most recent partner).

We shall assume that spending free time with one's sex partner provides more opportunities to exert influence over one another as well as indexing tighter control over one another. We utilize the incidence of jealous conflict to indicate the failure of strong dyadic control. Also, if sex was forced, it is apparent that there is a considerable disparity in power between the partners. Unlike the previous forms of dyadic control, this expression of strong control over a victimized partner will, we believe, have a positive effect on the probability of having been infected because of the intrinsic nature of forced sex. Effective negotiations regarding safe sexual activities during intercourse (e.g., condom use) might simply be impossible under these circumstances. We also assume that the easiness of talking about sexual topics with the partner can be a proxy measure for the power relationship between the partners (Ferrand, Marquet, & Van Campenhoudt, 1998): a very unequal relationship does not allow sexual topics to be discussed. Although we do not anticipate that information exchange about STD risk factors is especially likely to occur within the dyad itself, *shared free time* and *ease of talk about sexual topics* can be related to diffusion of information within the partnership. The easier it is to talk about sexual topics, and the more people share their free time, the greater the information flow is likely to be.

THIRD-PARTY CONTROL/INFORMATION. Not much of the survey data is pertinent to the issue of third-party embeddedness, which makes it difficult to distinguish between control and information effects.

To see how difficult it is to distinguish the control effect from the information effect, recall the example of the young man tightly embedded in a social circle of very sexually active men. It is highly probable that his peers exert a powerful social influence over him and, at the same time, that they provide him useful information about the potential risks of his sexual activities. When two people who have many mutual acquaintances begin a sexual relationship, it is likely that the mutual acquaintances, as stakeholders, will work both to provide information about the partners' respective strengths and weaknesses and to persuade them that they are a good (or a bad) match, thus affecting the duration of the relationship (Krane, 1977; Lewis, 1973; Parks, Stan, & Eggert, 1983). As indicators of third-party influence (without being able to distinguish between the effects of control and those of information), we shall use *mutual acquaintances at the beginning* (i.e., number of mutual acquaintances when respondent met most recent partner) and *acquaintance with current neighbors* (i.e., whether respondent was acquainted with more or fewer than half the people living in the same building or on the same street).

One kind of third-party control is, however, explicitly measured, namely, *partner knows both respondent's parents* (i.e., whether the partner knows both of the respondent's parents). If the partner knows both of the respondent's parents, we assume that the couple is strongly integrated in an overlapping kinship network and, thus, that risky behavior is decreased through the mechanism of social control (rather than information exchange).

## Analyses

*Logistic regressions.* Below, we present two sets of regressions in order to answer two broad questions: Can we observe effects of friendship networks on the likelihood of ever having been infected with an STD, even after controlling for other risk factors? Can we demonstrate that social-network effects operate through two distinct mechanisms, either dyadic control/information or third-party control/information? Preliminary log-linear results strongly suggested that we should divide the sample into two subgroups because there is strong evidence that social networks work on the likelihood of ever having been infected with STDs in opposed directions, depending on whether a respondent has had many lifetime sex partners (more than twelve) or relatively few. Thus, all the logistic regressions are examined separately for these two subgroups.

*Dependent variable.* The dependent variable, *STDs ever* (i.e., whether the respondent has ever been infected with any STDs), is measured on the basis of the following question: "There are several diseases or infections that can be transmitted during sex. These are sometimes called venereal diseases or VD. We will be using the term *sexually transmitted diseases* or STDs to refer to them. [At this point, before the interviewer continued, the respondent was given a card listing each STD (sometimes including the vernacular term, e.g., *clap* or *drip* for *gonorrhea*).] As I read each STD, tell me whether you have *ever* been told by a doctor that you had it."

*Control variables.* Demographic attributes, including age, gender, marital status, racial/ethnic group, and education level, are included in the logistic regressions as control variables. Other control variables measuring the respondent's other risk factors for STDs include *ever same-gender sex* (ever experiencing same-gender sex), *ever injected drugs* (ever injecting nonprescribed drugs), *number of sex partners over lifetime,* and *having concurrent partners* (i.e., during the most recent partnership).

Readers should note that, although the partner-related network variables all refer to the most recent sex partners and both the neighborhood-related and the friend-related variables are current (they refer to current neighbors or current friends), the dependent variable refers to lifetime experiences with STDs. This undesirable reversal in the time order of the dependent and independent variables was necessitated because the current (or last year's) STD prevalence is too low (only 1.9 percent) to sustain statistical analysis. (In contrast, the lifetime prevalence is 19 percent, providing a much more substantial case base to sustain analysis.)

We contend that this reversal of time order is not fatal to our purposes because individuals' patterns of organizing their informal social ties tend to be relatively stable over the life course (Laumann, 1973; Blieszner & Adams, 1992; McCall, McCall, Denzin, Suttles, & Kurth, 1970; McCall & Simmons, 1978), especially once demographic characteristics such as gender, age, education, and especially marital status are controlled (Huang & Tausig, 1990; Kurth, 1970; Moore, 1990; Wellman, Wong, Tindall, & Nazer, 1996). In short, the measure of the respondent's current social network can be regarded as a proxy measure of the adult respondent's lifetime structure of informal social ties.

In a study of the friendship ties of 1,013 white men living in Detroit, for example, Laumann (1973) found that the men characterized themselves as either "having just one or two really close friends" or as "having a large number of people they felt really close and friendly with" (96–97) and that whether they had few or many friends was associated with a basic personality need for affiliation as well as the actual number of friends they presently had. There is also an extensive literature in social psychology that links various measures of extraversion and sociability with actual patterns of socializing with others that strongly imply stability in the structuring of a person's social network with respect to size and density over the adult life course, especially in the research on attachment styles (Baldwin & Fehr, 1995; Collins & Read, 1990; Feeney, Noller, & Hanrahan, 1994; Keelan, Dion, & Dion, 1994; Scharfe & Bartholomew, 1994; Senchak & Leonard, 1992; Shaver & Brennan, 1992).

All the variables in the logistic regression are summarized in table 9.1.

## Results

### Existence of Friendship-Network Effects

Table 9.2 reveals, not only that friendship networks do have effects on the transmission of STDs, even after controlling for other risk factors, but also that friendship networks have different effects, depending on the number of sex partners that the respondent had. Regression 1 (R1) is the logistic regression for people with few lifetime sex partners (one to twelve partners), and regression 2 (R2) is the logistic regression for those with many lifetime sex partners (more than twelve). Among the people with few lifetime partners, those with no close friends (*no friends*) are only roughly 0.4 times as likely to be infected as people with one or more friends. Among people

Table 9.1 Summary Description of the Independent and Dependent Variables

| | Summary | N |
|---|---|---|
| Categorical variables: | | |
| STDs ever[a] | Ever (19%), never (81%) | 887 |
| Number of sex partners over lifetime | 1–2 (52%), 3–12 (32%), 13 or more (16%) | 827 |
| Gender | Male (42%), female (58%) | 890 |
| Ever married | Never (37%), ever (63%) | 890 |
| Racial/ethnic group | White (55%), black (28%), other (18%) | 890 |
| Education | Less than high school (15%), high school (35%), more than high school (50%) | 890 |
| Ever same-gender sex | Never (94%), ever (6%) | 880 |
| Ever injected drugs | Never (97%), ever (3%) | 880 |
| Having concurrent partners[b] | No (80%), yes (20%) | 886 |
| Ever traded sex for drugs | Never (94%), ever (6%) | 846 |
| Talk about sexual topics[b] | Very easy (61%), not very easy (39%) | 846 |
| Jealous conflict[b] | Never (74%), ever (26%) | 844 |
| Spend free time together[b] | All free time (15%), not all free time (85%) | 848 |
| Ever having forced sex | Never (84%), ever (16%) | 880 |
| Partner knows both respondent's parents[b] | Both parents (57%), not both (43%) | 835 |
| Mutual acquaintances at the beginning[b,c] | Less than 5 (63%), 5 or more (37%) | 843 |
| Acquaintance with current neighbors | More than half (74%), less than half (26%) | 888 |
| Friendship network[d] | None (12%), strong/small (23%), weak/large (10%), others (55%) | 890 |
| Continuous variables: | | |
| Age | 36.8 (mean), 10.8 (standard deviation) | 890 |

[a]The list includes gonorrhea, syphilis, herpes, chlamydia, genital warts, Hepatitis B, NGU (male only), vaginitis (not yeast infection, female only), and PID (female only).
[b]Items refer to the most recent sex partners.
[c]Number of mutual acquaintances at the beginning of the most recent sexual relationship.
[d]Items refer to the current friends (up to six).

who had many lifetime sex partners, those with many friends but weak ties to them (*weak, large networks*) are only roughly 0.2 times as likely to be infected when compared to those with either fewer friends or stronger ties to their friends.

Consistent with previous research, both R1 and R2 show that women in general and African American men and women in particular are much more likely to have had an STD sometime during their lifetime. Having concurrent partners during the most recent partnership has opposite effects de-

Table 9.2 Existence of Friendship–Network Effects
(odds ratios on ever any STDs for lifetime).

|  | R1[a] | R2[b] |
|---|---|---|
| Demographic variables: | | |
| Age | 1.00 | 1.04 |
| Women | 1.81** | 2.83** |
| Ever married | .95 | 1.40 |
| African American[c] | 3.17*** | 2.55* |
| Other racial groups[c] | .97 | 1.80 |
| High school[d] | .73 | 3.57 |
| More than high school[d] | .99 | 3.03 |
| Risky behavior: | | |
| Ever same-gender sex | 1.06 | 1.80 |
| Ever injected drugs | 1.12 | 1.05 |
| Ever traded sex for drugs | 1.25 | 5.03* |
| Having concurrent partners | 1.85** | .38** |
| 3–5 lifetime sex partners[e] | .67 | |
| More than 5 sex partners[e] | 2.61*** | |
| 20–40 sex partners[f] | | .71 |
| 41 or more sex partners[f] | | 1.71 |
| Friendship network: | | |
| No friends[g] | .37** | |
| Weak, large network[h] | | .18** |
| Number of cases | 683 | 129 |
| Pseudo-$R^2$ | .11 | .18 |

[a]Regression among the people who had one to twelve sex partners over lifetime.
[b]Regression among the people who had thirteen or more lifetime sex partners.
[c]Compared to whites.
[d]Compared to less than high school.
[e]Compared to one to two lifetime partners.
[f]Compared to thirteen to nineteen partners.
[g]Compared to the rest of the people who have one or more friends.
[h]Compared to the rest of the people who have no friends at all or who have only small number of friends
(fewer than five friends) or who have large but strong (talking every day on average) friendship circle.
*Significant at 10 percent alpha level.
**Significant at 5 percent alpha level.
***Significant at 1 percent alpha level.

pending on the number of lifetime sex partners the respondent has had. Con-currency increases the odds of having been infected among those with few lifetime partners while it decreases the odds of having been infected among those with many lifetime partners.

The decreasing effect among people with many sex partners is counterin-tuitive and, thus, requires explanation. Our speculation is that concurrency may imply longer and, thus, less risky relationships among people with many sex partners. If one has, say, twenty partners none of whom were concurrent, most of the partnerships are likely to have been short-term and, thus, highly risky. If, however, one has twenty partners some of whom were concurrent, more of the partnerships are likely to have been long-term and, thus, less risky. Other things being equal, concurrency should decrease the risk of in-fection. This effect will not be found among people with few lifetime sex partners because, in this case, concurrency does not imply long-term and, thus, less risky relationships.

## Social-Network Effects

In order to probe mechanisms producing the effects of social networks on the differential likelihood of having had STDs, we ran four logistic regressions for each of the two subgroups defined in terms of the number of lifetime sex partners (i.e., *moderate number of partners* and *many partners*). Table 9.3 summa-rizes eight logistic regressions. The first group of regressions (model 1 [M1] for *moderate number of partners* and model 5 [M5] for *many partners*) tests for the existence of an effect of friendship networks. The second group of regres-sions (model 2 [M2] and model 6 [M6], respectively) examines whether there are effects of dyadic control/information exchange in addition to the effect of friendship networks alone. The third group of regressions (model 3 [M3] and model 7 [M7], respectively) checks whether there are effects of third-party control/information exchange in addition to the effect of friendship networks alone. The fourth group of regressions (model 4 [M4] and model 8 [M8], respectively) takes all the effects into account. For the purpose of com-parison across regressions, each regression includes exactly the same set of observations; that is, the number of observations is the same for all regressions run on a given subgroup ($N = 664$ for *moderate number of partners,* and $N = 126$ for *many partners*).

PEOPLE WITH FEW LIFETIME SEX PARTNERS. M1 in table 9.3 shows the same regression as R1 in table 9.2 except that M1 contains fewer obser-vations in order to be strictly comparable to M4. As R1 showed, apparent risk reduction for *STDs ever* associated with having no current friends still per-sists even when we control for the other demographic and risk factors. Per-

Table 9.3 Different Social-Network Effects (odds-ratios on ever any STDs for lifetime)

| | Moderate Number of Partners (1–12 partners since age 18) | | | | Many Partners (13 or more since age 18) | | | |
|---|---|---|---|---|---|---|---|---|
| | M1 | M2 | M3 | M4 | M5 | M6 | M7 | M8 |
| Demographic variables: | | | | | | | | |
| Age | 1.00 | 1.01 | 1.00 | 1.00 | 1.05 | 1.05 | 1.06* | 1.07** |
| Women | 1.64* | 1.20 | 1.73** | 1.26 | 3.29** | 3.03* | 3.36** | 3.28* |
| Ever married | .90 | .99 | 1.09 | 1.15 | 1.42 | 1.67 | 1.20 | 1.34 |
| African American[a] | 3.14*** | 3.25*** | 3.17*** | 3.23*** | 2.28 | 2.87* | 2.86* | 4.05** |
| Other racial group[a] | 1.01 | .96 | .98 | .91 | 2.09 | 2.28 | 2.65 | 2.76 |
| High school[b] | .72 | .66 | .72 | .66 | 4.55 | 3.59 | 4.23 | 2.79 |
| More than high school[b] | .99 | .97 | 1.09 | 1.03 | 2.80 | 2.41 | 2.71 | 1.92 |
| Risky behavior: | | | | | | | | |
| Ever same-gender sex | 1.10 | .83 | .98 | .78 | 2.25 | 2.32 | 2.29 | 2.55 |
| Ever injected drugs | 1.13 | .94 | 1.06 | .93 | .85 | 1.04 | 1.36 | 1.51 |
| Ever traded sex for drugs | 1.11 | .99 | 1.22 | 1.08 | 7.16** | 5.87* | 12.85** | 11.86** |
| Having concurrent partners | 1.86** | 1.62* | 1.86** | 1.61 | .35* | .29** | .41* | .35* |
| 3–5 lifetime sex partners[c] | 1.00 | .85 | 1.01 | .87 | | | | |
| More than 5 sex partners[c] | 2.67*** | 2.30*** | 2.61*** | 2.26*** | | | | |
| 20–40 sex partners[d] | | | | | .62 | .58 | .88 | .79 |
| 41 or more sex partners[d] | | | | | 1.38 | 1.37 | 1.59 | 1.62 |
| Friendship network: | | | | | | | | |
| No friends | .40* | .43 | .39* | .41 | 2.48 | 2.30 | 2.53 | 2.70 |
| Weak, large network[e] | .65 | .54 | .66 | .55 | .14** | .12** | .19* | .15* |
| Other[e] | .97 | .96 | .99 | .96 | .66 | .60 | .75 | .59 |

*continued*

Table 9.3 *continued*

| | Moderate Number of Partners (1–12 partners since age 18) | | | | Many Partners (13 or more since age 18) | | | |
| --- | --- | --- | --- | --- | --- | --- | --- | --- |
| | M1 | M2 | M3 | M4 | M5 | M6 | M7 | M8 |
| Dyadic information/control: | | | | | | | | |
| Ease of talk about sexual topics | | 1.06 | | 1.05 | | 1.14 | | 1.15 |
| Jealous conflict | | 1.84** | | 1.76** | | 1.57 | | 1.58 |
| Shared free time | | 1.45 | | 1.36 | | 3.21 | | 4.46 |
| Ever having forced sex | | 3.19*** | | 3.02*** | | 1.07 | | .86 |
| Third-party information/control: | | | | | | | | |
| Partner knows both respondent's parents | | | .53*** | .59** | | | .69 | .79 |
| Mutual acquaintances at the beginning[g] | | | .74 | .75 | | | .44 | .36 |
| Acquaintance with current neighbors[h] | | | .93 | .97 | | | .22** | .19** |
| Number of cases | 664 | 664 | 664 | 664 | 126 | 126 | 126 | 126 |
| Pseudo-$R^2$ | .11 | .16 | .13 | .16 | .20 | .22 | .26 | .28 |

[a]Compared to whites.

[b]Compared to less than high school.

[c]Compared to one or two lifetime partners.

[d]Compared to thirteen to nineteen partners.

[e]Compared to strong, small friendship circle (having fewer than five friends and talk everyday on average).

[f]Compared to people for whom it is not very easy (somewhat easy, somewhat difficult, or difficult) to discuss sexual topics with partner.

[g]Compared to less than five mutual acquaintances when the respondent met the most recent partner.

[h]Compared to knows half or less of the current neighbors who live in the same building or on the same street.

*Significant at 10 percent alpha level.

**Significant at 5 percent alpha level.

***Significant at 1 percent alpha level.

sons in the category *no friends* are only 0.4 as likely to be infected as those in the category *strong, small networks* (the reference group) (the *p*-value increases because of the smaller number of observations).

Four variables pertaining to dyadic control/information were added in M2 to examine its effect. Two of these—*jealous conflict* and *ever having forced sex*—seem to be very effective. Reports of jealous conflict—assuming that jealous conflict implies a failure of strong dyadic control—increase the odds of being infected almost two times. Having forced sex—the respondent being either the perpetrator or the victim—increases the odds of being infected about three times (i.e., a serious power discrepancy between partners, and, thus, no room for negotiation regarding safe sex, increases the odds of being infected). However, the other two—*ease of talk about sexual topics* and *shared free time*—seem to have little effect.

In M3, we tested for the effects of third-party control/information exchange. Only the effect of *partner knows both respondent's parents* is significant: respondents whose partners know both their (the respondents') parents are only half as likely to be infected. (This is regarded as third-party control rather than third-party information because parents rarely give sexual information to their adult children.) *Mutual acquaintances at the beginning* and *acquaintance with current neighbors,* however, do not exert significant effects.

Once we take dyadic control (measured by *jealous conflict* and *ever having forced sex*) into account, the friendship effects are weakened, as shown in M2 (the statistical significance of friendship effects changes from less than 10 percent to more than 10 percent). This implies that part of the effect of *no friends* comes from dyadic control as measured in M2.

In M4, we included all the variables, and still two measures of dyadic control (*jealous conflict* and *ever having forced sex*) and one of third-party control (*partner knows both respondent's parents*) are significant.

PEOPLE WITH MANY LIFETIME SEX PARTNERS. M5 in table 9.3 is the same regression as R2 in table 9.2 except that it has fewer observations in order to be comparable to the other models in table 9.3 (from M6 to M8). People in the category *weak, large networks* are only 0.1 times as likely to be infected as people in the category *strong, small networks.*

M6 reveals that neither dyadic mechanism (control or information exchange) is operative among people with many lifetime sex partners.

M7 shows that, among third-party control/information mechanisms, *acquaintance with current neighbors* is a very effective measure of STD avoidance. The fact that, once we take the neighborhood effect into account, the statistical significance of friendship network changes from less than 5 percent to less than 10 percent implies that part of the effect of *weak, large networks* comes directly from *acquaintance with current neighbors.*

The last model, M8, contains all the variables, but only the effect of *ac-quaintance with current neighbors* is observed to be significant.

## Conclusion

We have found that there is, indeed, an important effect of friendship net-works on the likelihood of having had STDs, even after controlling for other risk factors. Furthermore, depending on the number of lifetime sex partners, different friendship patterns exert different effects. Among the people with few lifetime sex partners, those falling in the category *no friends* most effec-tively avoided STDs, while, among the people with many lifetime sex part-ners, those falling in the category *weak, large networks* most effectively avoided STDs. As far as the former effect is concerned, we speculate that people who are socially isolated are likely to focus their energy and social resources on their sex partners, resulting in strong mutual control and influence and, thus, a reduction in risk. As far as the latter effect is concerned, we suspect that information (rather than control) is the critical factor. That is, when people have many sex partners, because their attention cannot be adequately focused on each relationship, and because they cannot legitimately demand sexual ex-clusivity of partners who are not themselves assured of it, dyadic control is unlikely to be strong. Thus, they must rely on third-party embeddedness to mitigate risks.

These accounts gain further support from the results obtained in the logis-tic regressions reported in table 9.3. Among the people with few lifetime sex partners, dyadic control is an especially effective measure of STD avoidance (from M2 to M4). Specifically, the most effective measures are *jealous conflict* and *ever having forced sex*. Also effective was *partner knows both respondent's parents*. In sharp contrast, only *acquaintance with current neighbors* is an effective measure of STD avoidance among people with many lifetime sex partners. Perhaps knowing many of one's neighbors provides critical information about poten-tial partners or a good place to meet safe partners. Also, neighbors may func-tion as stakeholders, encouraging stable and norm-complying relationships, although we believe that this is not as important as information exchange.

Although the CHSLS is rare in having a representative data set that con-tains such a comprehensive inventory of both people's sex lives and their so-cial networks, our models all suffer from a fundamental inconsistency in the time order between the dependent variable (which references the acquisition of STDs over the adult lifetime) and some of the independent variables (which reference only a narrowly defined, recent period). Even though we firmly believe that an individual's informal-social-network pattern tends to be stable over time, reflecting his or her social competence, social position, and ability to sustain ties with others, and, thus, that the current network may be treated as a proxy for past networks, only a data source that provides longitudinal network information as well as time-ordered information about sexual activities will allow us to test our hypotheses definitively. Granting this limitation in our data, we nevertheless believe that the CHSLS provides highly suggestive evidence for the strong and consistent effects of informal social networks on STD transmission dynamics.

To summarize, network mechanisms affecting the vulnerability to STDs of persons with many sex partners contrast sharply with those that are operative for persons with more moderate numbers of sex partners. Dyadic control (as measured by *jealous conflict* and *ever having forced sex*) and parental integration (as measured by *partner knows both respondent's parents*) are especially effective for people with few sex partners, while third-party embeddedness (measured by *acquaintance with current neighbors*) is highly effective for people with many partners. These differences imply the need for developing preventive-intervention strategies that appropriately target different population subgroups and that take full account of the distinctively different roles that informal social networks play in guiding and regulating individual partner choice and sexual behavior. For example, we need to develop extensive programs for those who have many sex partners but, at the same time, have only a small number of friends, to whom they are, nevertheless, strongly tied (i.e., the category *strong, small networks*). These are people who have a high risk of contracting and no appropriate resources for avoiding STDs. Successful programs would reach their informal social networks and disseminate necessary information. To take another example, programs targeting those with many partners falling in the category *weak, large networks* are most likely to be effective if they work through the mass media (say, through television ads). Future research must focus on more localized sex markets since concrete social-network mechanisms are also typically specific to particular regions and racial/ethnic groups.[2]

2. On the terms *sex market* and *sexual marketplace* as they are used in this study, see the section "The Social Organization of Sexual Partnering and Sexual Relationships" in Ellingson, Laumann, Paik, and Mahay (chapter 1 in this volume).

Part Four )

*Institutional Responses and Silences*

# Constructing Causal Stories and Moral Boundaries

## Institutional Approaches to Sexual Problems

Stephen Ellingson

Institutional control of sexual behavior and identity is a common theme in histories and contemporary accounts of sexuality. Many studies suggest that institutional actors exert strong control over sexuality by outlawing certain practices and identities, restricting access to potential partners or at least raising the costs of access, and, more generally, defining what kinds of partners and activities are legitimate. According to Foucault (1990), for example, the institutions of religion, medicine, education, the police, and the family powerfully channel sexuality into particular forms (i.e., heterosexual, monogamous marriage) through the practices of surveillance, stigmatization, and socialization (see also Chauncey, 1994; D'Emilio, 1983). Institutional control is often exercised more indirectly as individuals internalize norms regarding sexuality and become self-regulating. Academic and popular treatments of the medicalization of AIDS and the rise of safe-sex interventions suggest that the work of public-health organizations has altered gay men's sexual repertoires, scripts, and meanings (see Murray, 1996, 99–142; Aveline, 1995; Ostrow, Beltran, & Joseph, 1994; Davidson, 1991; Shilts, 1987).

At the same time, many studies identify the inefficiencies of institutional control and suggest that individuals and groups often circumvent the norms and restrictions that are intended to govern sexual relationships and activities. This is clearly evident in the literature on gay and lesbian communities (especially regarding gay men's resistance to the safe-sex paradigm), in accounts of the Sexual Revolution, and in studies of teen pregnancy (see Murray, 1996; Beemyn, 1997a; Duberman, Vicinus, & Chauncey, 1989; D'Emilio & Freedman, 1988; Bailey, 1988; Nathanson, 1991). Consistently high rates of premarital sex and the liberalization of attitudes toward sexuality suggest that the surveillance and socialization power of religion and family has declined (e.g., Laumann, Gagnon, Michael, & Michaels, 1994; Joyner & Laumann, 2001). Rubin (1999, 161) summarizes the limitations of institutional control over sexuality in the following manner: "The sexual system in not a monolithic, omnipotent structure. There are continuous battles over the definitions, evaluations, arrangements, privileges, and costs of sexual behavior."

The extant record offers competing evidence and explanations about the power of institutions to regulate sexuality, and we are left with unanswered questions about the nature, scope, and meaning of institutional control. To what extent is institutional control over sexuality strong or weak, direct or indirect, complete or partial? How do regulatory organizations create and deploy mechanisms meant to control sexual behavior, and how are these mechanisms shaped by the social context of the organizations and the responses of their clients? Can institutional actors overcome the embeddedness of individuals in local sexual cultures, spaces, and networks to move them away from sexually risky situations? How and to what extent do the intervention strategies of health-care workers and social workers affect sexual-marketplace activities and redefine the contours of sex markets?[1] What do institutional efforts to control sexuality tell us about the cultural politics, interpretive battles, and moral boundaries surrounding sex in the United States? In this chapter, I suggest answers to these questions through an analysis of the interpretive stories and intervention strategies employed by health-care and social-service organizations in Chicago.

---

1. On the terms *sex market* and *sexual marketplace* as they are used in this study, see the section "The Social Organization of Sexual Partnering and Sexual Relationships" in Ellingson, Laumann, Paik, and Mahay (chapter 1 in this volume).

## Theoretical Background

At the most general level, institutions transmit values about good and bad so-cial relationships as well as expectations about their legitimate ordering (see Bellah, Madsen, Sullivan, Swidler, & Tipton, 1991, 287–93). They also con-strain and enable social action by providing models or scripts for behavior and identity (see Clemens & Cook, 1999, 445–47). DeLamater (1987, 238) notes that institutions provide scenarios or scripts that specify "the kinds of sexual behavior that can occur, the type(s) of persons appropriate as partners for that behavior, and the time(s) and place(s) in which that form of sexual expression is appropriate." Moreover, institutional actors are often positioned to mete out rewards and punishments as a means of ensuring conformity with the scenarios. In short, institutional actors regulate sexuality by defining norms and wielding sanctions.

However, this control is constrained or tempered by the operational bound-aries of the institutional sphere in question. A common premise in recent work on institutions is that each institutional order (e.g., family, politics, medicine) has a central logic, framework, or organizing principle that orders reality, "defines ends, and shapes the means by which interests are determined and pursued" (DiMaggio & Powell, 1991, 10; see also Friedland & Alford, 1991; Haveman & Rao, 1997). In other words, each institutional sphere has a primary goal or set of goals and a set of rules and practices by means of which to realize those goals. Moreover, these frameworks serve as lenses through which institutional actors see the world—helping them identify so-cial problems and their causes—and as guides for acting in the world. For ex-ample, the central goal within medicine is to preserve health and prolong life, and actors follow a biomedical model of disease and treatment.[2] This can lead health-care practitioners to minimize or ignore the social, cultural, and eco-nomic causes of disease (e.g., poverty) and focus their attention on treating the immediate biological symptoms. Thus, institutional actors have a model for "how to do something," but that model constrains opportunity and action because it focuses attention on a narrowly defined imperative (see Clemens & Cook, 1999, 445). Any area of social life that falls outside the mandate of an institutional sphere likely will be treated as an externality—something that demands attention only when it begins to impinge on the resources of a particular institutional actor.

2. The model starts with the assumption that disease is fundamentally biological and that the social, psychological, and behavioral dimensions of illness are irrelevant, or, at best, secondary, to understanding its causes and determining treatment (see En-gel, 1977).

Sexuality is one of those areas. There is not one institutional sphere that is primarily concerned with sexuality (the family may be the closest), nor do most institutional actors make strong claims for ownership. As a result, sexuality is an institutional stepchild and tends to be acted on only when it threatens to disrupt the institutional order or when clients bring sexual concerns to institutional actors. Once sexuality is placed on the agenda of some organization, that organization becomes a stakeholder with a set of interests and goals to protect or advance and deals with sexuality according to its institutionally specific framework. Institutional actors draw on a preexisting set of symbolic resources that they employ in order to articulate a specific normative understanding of sexuality, identify what constitutes a sexual problem, and then determine how to resolve that problem (see, e.g., Nathanson, 1991).

While institutional actors primarily rely on an institutionally specific lens and resources to address sexuality issues, they also draw on broad cultural understandings about human agency, sexual risk, and sexual values. Since the nineteenth century, those working within health care, social work, and law enforcement have increasingly relied on the assumption that human beings are rational actors. This assumption of rationality is part of a larger neoliberal political ideology in which citizens are understood to be autonomous and self-regulating. With regard to sexuality, individuals are assumed to act in their own self-interest and, hence, to avoid risky sexual behaviors and situations. Lupton (1999, 90–91) notes: "In late modern societies, not to engage in risk avoiding behavior is considered a failure of the self to take care of itself—a form of irrationality, or simply a lack of skillfulness. Risk avoiding behavior, therefore becomes viewed as a moral enterprise relating to issues of self-control, self-knowledge and self-improvement." However, once an individual becomes "at risk" or falls into a high-risk category, that person's agency is called into question. On the one hand, the at-risk individual may no longer be seen as able to exercise effective (i.e., rational) agency. On the other hand, the at-risk individual may be seen as an overactive sexual agent—as in the case of the biomedical discourse about men with AIDS in which they are described as being "sexually potent" (Treichler, 1999, 371) or as being "adventuresome" or on the "sexual fast-track" (Weeks, 2000, 149, 151). Lupton (1999, 114) notes: "The 'at-risk' label tends either to position members of these social groups as particularly vulnerable, passive, powerless, or weak, or as particularly dangerous to themselves or others." Institutional actors engage in a variety of strategies to persuade or empower at-risk persons to become self-conscious risk monitors and risk calculators (see Crook, 1999, 171; Dean, 1999, 145–49; Treichler, 1999, 362; Lupton, 1999, 87–91).

Health care and social services tend to understand risk as an objective and measurable hazard and, hence, avoidable by changing behaviors, attitudes, or environments. However, many scholars of risk note that expert and lay understandings of risk often contradict one another and that individuals at risk may use different criteria to assess risk. Lay risk assessment may be powerfully shaped by material resources, embeddedness in social networks, cultural meaning systems, past experiences with helping professionals, or social location. When individuals use these criteria rather than a strict rational calculation of costs and benefits, they may be considered by institutional actors as ignorant and in need of education. Lupton (1999, 111), however, warns: "What is considered to be 'ignorance' on the part of experts may be thought of by lay actors as a deliberate ignoring or avoidance of expert knowledge because it is regarded as essentially peripheral to the key issues at stake, or at worst inaccurate or misleading. 'Ignorance' on the part of laypeople becomes a positive and agential choice in these cases, not a passive deficit requiring access to expert knowledges." Thus, for a homeless teenager, exchanging unprotected sex for a night off the street in a warm, clean hotel room may be the rational choice despite the health risks attending such behavior. The question for this chapter is, To what extent are health-care and other service providers aware of the alternative risk-assessment criteria that their clients use, and does such knowledge inform their diagnostic tasks and intervention strategies?

Historically, institutional actors have helped create and reinforce explicitly moral claims about sexual identity, behaviors, and outcomes, even as some actors—health-care and social-service providers—adopt an explicitly morally neutral, nonreligious discourse grounded in science or psychology. This official moral neutrality may hide the moral assumptions on which actors rely. Rubin (1999) argues that medical and social-service workers, among other institutional agents, tend to view sexuality through a variety of ideological lenses all of which regard sexuality as inherently dangerous and categorize sex acts, sexual relationships, and sexual identities in a hierarchy of value. She notes that "virtually all erotic behaviour is considered bad unless a specific reason to exempt it has been established" (150) and identifies the exception as monogamous, heterosexual, reproductive marriage. Other relationships and behaviors fall under this ideal with varying degrees of institutional approval or disapproval (e.g., sexually monogamous but unmarried heterosexual couples are morally superior to stable, long-term gay or lesbian couples, who, in turn, are morally superior to "bar dykes and promiscuous gay men" [151]). The following analysis will attend to the moral assumptions and claims of health-care and social-service providers in Chicago and seek to learn whether this "creeping moralism" (Watney, 1999, 411) limits their effectiveness or undermines their interventions.

Health-care organizations address sexuality in terms of how sexual behavior affects personal and public health and attempt to organize sexual behaviors, relationships, and identities in order to minimize the health risks of sexual activity (e.g., by promoting sexual scripts that require individuals to use condoms or by defining certain types of potential partners, such as prostitutes, as "unsafe" and, hence, illegitimate). Following the general biomedical model (see Ellingson, Laumann, Paik, & Mahay, chapter 1 in this volume), health-care actors understand sexual risk in epidemiological terms. That is, illness and disease in particular populations are linked to somatic and environmental causes with the goal of predicting health outcomes for these populations and reducing health risks. Thus, sexuality is problematized as an illness, and practitioners aim to treat the symptoms (e.g., prescribing penicillin for gonorrhea) or to induce behavioral change through education and media campaigns (e.g., safe-sex campaigns). In recent years, health-care practitioners have begun to identify risks attached to particular "lifestyles" and have focused their efforts on targeting groups in high-risk categories. The goal is to make individuals in such groups aware of their risk factors and, thus, more self-regulating and empowered to take the actions that will minimize risks (see Lupton, 1999, 96–97). This diagnostic and intervention strategy relies on the assumption that individuals are rational actors noted above.

Organizations within the sphere of social service also rely on education as a means to control sexual activities, but they reach that intervention strategy from a different starting point. Social-service providers take on the mandate of "regulating social dependence" (Reid, 1992, 35). That is, they aim to move individuals from a state of being unproductive in society to one in which they have a useful and self-sustaining role in family, work, and/or community. At a minimum, the social-service mandate aims to protect individuals from the consequences of dependence. The institutional framework advances the values of autonomy, empowerment, self-determination, and self-improvement, while institutional action to realize those values focuses on reform, rehabilitation, and reintegration (see Hartman, 1994, 15).

Thus, for social-service organizations, sexual problems arise from the social or community context (e.g., gangs, a sense of fatalism arising from poverty, high rates of alcohol or substance abuse). Decisions to engage in unprotected sex as part of a gang initiation or to trade sexual intercourse for drug money are coded as *bad* or *dysfunctional* because they threaten to undercut individuals' independence and ability to function in society as well as their future life chances (e.g., the teen who becomes pregnant may be forced to drop out of school, which in turn affects her occupational chances and may affect her ability to care for her child). Educational interventions focus on teaching individuals how to recognize and escape from the contexts or situations that will lead them to make bad decisions (e.g., counseling a woman to leave an abusive relationship and go to a shelter).

The nature and scope of institutional actors' control over sexuality are also constrained by the interpretive repertoires available for use. An important tool within the repertoires of institutional actors is the causal stories used to make sense of the sexual behaviors of their clients and justify institutional action. Causal stories are accounts that "describe harms and difficulties, attribute them to the action of other individuals and organizations, and thereby claim the right to invoke governmental [or some other institutionally based power] to stop the harm" (Stone, 1989, 282). The import of causal stories is illustrated in Nathanson's (1991) work on adolescent sexuality. She identifies three causal models of teen pregnancy. The first identifies teen pregnancy as an outcome of social, political, and medical barriers that limit teenagers' access to contraception and abortion services; the second sees it as the outcome of the state's legitimization of sexual permissiveness through subsidizing family-planning services; and the third views it as an outcome of deeply rooted cultural and social problems (e.g., the culture of poverty).

Nathanson goes on to note how the causal stories inform and justify particular interventions or solutions on the part of different institutional actors. For example, some health-care organizations rely on the first model to advocate for federal funding of family-planning services, condom distribution in public schools, and safe-sex education campaigns, while some political actors, adhering to the second model, promote abstinence as the appropriate solution and work to end federal or state funding of family planning. At the same time, certain causal stories about teen pregnancy define heterosexual marriage as the only legitimate relationship in which sexual behavior can be expressed. Such a story upholds, at least implicitly, the sexual double standard that marks virgins as *good girls* and delegitimates a set of behaviors (e.g., extramarital intercourse) and relationships (nonmarried unions). Thus, causal stories become a key means of constructing particular normative definitions of moral sexual expression (*moral* meaning here coded as safe or risky, legal or illegal, functional or dysfunctional). These stories often draw on and reinforce the widely held cultural scenarios about sexuality in the United States and, thus, indirectly shape sexuality by setting standards for appropriate behaviors, partners, and venues for partner searches.

In the following section, I describe the causal stories created and used by institutional actors in Westside, Erlinda, and Southtown.[3] Then I discuss the

---

3. I have omitted the white gay enclave of Shoreland because the interviews there tend to focus on broader issues surrounding the gay and lesbian communities (e.g., politics and community organizing, racism in the gay community) rather than on the ways in which health-care and social-service organizations understand the causes of sex-related health problems and how they attempt to ameliorate them. At best a few interviewees provided a thin explanatory account that stressed misinformation or a sense of fatalism that propelled individuals to make sexual decisions that result in infection with HIV or some other STD.

intervention strategies and the relation between causal stories and interventions. I end with some summary comments about moral boundaries and institutional attempts to control sexuality.[4]

## Causal Stories as Interpretive Tools

The causal stories created and deployed by health–care and social–service organizations followed the same generic model (see figure 10.1). Workers in both types of organizations identified sexually risky behavior (e.g., sex without a condom) and its consequences (e.g., sexually transmitted disease [STD] or unintended pregnancy) as the problem that they were trying to prevent and/or repair. I found five different causal stories that actors used to make sense of high–risk sexual behavior and justify particular interventions. The stories most commonly identified some set of structural (e.g., poverty) or cultural (e.g., patriarchal gender roles) obstacles that prevented individuals from having safe sex or from abstaining from sex altogether. In these interpretive stories, the structural and cultural barriers led to some individual-level cause, such as inadequate information about sex or poor decisionmaking skills, which, in turn, resulted in some unhealthy sexual situation or outcome.

### *Westside and Erlinda: The Use of Cultural Stories to Explain Sexual Problems*

Social–service and health–care organizations in Westside and Erlinda relied on one of three different causal stories. Two of the stories identified cultural causes for teen pregnancy, STDs (including HIV/AIDS), and domestic violence. Health–care providers and social workers noted that a pervasive "culture of silence" surrounding sexuality and the culture of machismo were the deep-seated causes of many sexual problems. These two fundamental causes give rise to a number of surface or more easily identifiable causes, such as lim-

4. For this chapter, I use the interviews with fifty-eight persons who represent fifty-one medical and social-service organizations. The analysis of the interview transcripts followed an analytic model based on work from the construction-of-social-problems literature (e.g., Gusfield, 1981; Best, 1990; Stone, 1989; Schneider & Ingram, 1993; Rochefort & Cobb, 1994). For each transcript, I identified the interpretive and intervention repertoire for each organization. For each organization's interpretive repertoires, I identified the populations targeted, the definition of the problem, and the causal stories created. For each organization's intervention repertoires, I identified treatment and education programs and the rationales for them. I also looked for linkages, or the lack thereof, between the causal stories and the interventions.

| Underlying Cause → | Proximate Cause → | Sexual Problem → | Outcome |
|---|---|---|---|
| Structural or cultural barrier to safe sex | Individual-level barrier to safe sex | High-risk behaviors | Disease or pregnancy |

Figure 10.1. Generic causal stories.

ited or erroneous knowledge about sexual diseases. In turn, these proximate causes lead to the primary sexual problem—unprotected sexual intercourse—reported by workers in both institutional fields. Figure 10.2 summarizes these three causal stories.

The following excerpts from interviews illustrate how health-care and social-service providers construct these causal stories. The stories highlight the complex causal pathways from sex act to negative outcome and demonstrate how institutional actors are able to break from the institutional models and attend to the meaning systems, norms, and life experiences that mark residents of the two neighborhoods. The first story emphasizes the Hispanic culture of silence as the fundamental cause of sexually risky behavior and negative sexual outcomes. It is illustrated by the comments of Felecia Sanchez, director of an AIDS-outreach social-service agency in Westside. The interviewer asked her to describe some of the main concerns about health and sexuality in Westside, and she replied: "Sexuality itself is not widely accepted in Westside because of Latino culture. Premarital sex is simply not permissible, so young people often don't receive proper education about birth control or protection against disease. For example, a young woman can't usually go on the pill or even buy condoms for fear that her parents will find out." She followed this comment with an example from her own family life. Her mother accepts the fact that her twenty-one-year-old brother is sexually active and even buys him condoms. Meanwhile, Felecia, who is twenty-six, cannot even bring up such topics with her mother. In this account, the social worker identifies several sexual problems facing young Latinos that flow from the cultural taboo against speaking about sex: inadequate knowledge to prevent unwanted pregnancies or STDs; a sexual double standard that demands celibacy for young women but tacitly sanctions male sexual activity outside marriage; and an unwillingness to take preventive action.

Two employees of neighborhood health clinics also identified the culture of silence as a key cause of sexual problems. The director of one clinic spoke about some of the cultural barriers to teaching about sexuality in Westside:

> In Mexico it is acceptable for a young woman to date an older man; such behavior gives the young woman respectability because her partner is older and more established. For this reason many mothers don't object when their teenage daughters see older men, and then these girls often end up sexually active and pregnant. In Mexican culture many people don't talk about such issues and try to pretend they're not occurring. The language barrier also restricts communication and dialogue about issues of sexuality. Sexuality is often a taboo subject for this community. Many young people refuse to use birth control because that would mean admitting their sexual activity.

| Underlying Cause → | Proximate Cause → | Sexual Problem → | Outcome |
|---|---|---|---|
| Culture of silence → | Limited knowledge & education about sex/body → | Unprotected sex → | Teen pregnancy or STDs |
| Machismo/gender roles → | Limited knowledge about sex, powerlessness and sexual double standard, traditional sex roles and low self-esteem for women → | Unprotected sex → | pregnancy or STDs, abuse |
| Colonialism → | Destruction of Puerto Rican culture and society, leading to fatalistic worldview → | Unprotected sex & high risk behaviors → | Pregnancy, STDs |

Figure 10.2. Causal stories in Westside and Erlinda.

Another health educator noted: "There is a huge stigma attached to talking about sex and condom use. Because of the low level of education, people only think about pregnancy prevention. Mostly people don't talk about condom use because of culture and religion."

The second causal story emphasizes the role of machismo in Hispanic sexuality. Machismo is implicated in a field-worker's notes recording the comments of Maria Perez, a county public-health official, during a conversation about domestic violence and AIDS among women in Westside: "Maria said that domestic violence tends to occur as a result of machismo. The men feel that their wife is their property, and the women are submissive. As a result of the submissiveness, there are many housewives with AIDS. Maria said that a 'good' Mexican woman only has sex in the missionary position—anything else and her husband would consider her dirty. As a result, the men cheat so that they can experiment. This experimenting ranges from having sex with prostitutes to having sex with other men." Maria continued by claiming that Catholic teachings about birth control, virginity, abortion, and female submission have a pervasive influence over the thinking and behavior of women, especially among recent immigrants. Similarly, a field-worker's notes reveal how a health educator at a private clinic also stressed the way in which machismo and the culture of silence create the conditions that foster sexual-health problems: "She explained that in the Mexican community women are assumed to be virgins when they marry. They should be pure, or they are sinning. So they don't seek help or advice from outside agencies or their families. It's a 'hush-hush' topic, especially in households with a *machista*[5] figure. This is why her job of educating young women about birth control is so important."

The third causal story includes structural as well as cultural factors and stresses the long-term destructive consequences of colonialism among Puerto Ricans. Social-service providers in Erlinda were the only agents to construct this causal account (six of fifteen social-service agencies in the neighborhood used it). Several interviewees spoke at length about how the experience of U.S. colonialism has created economic dependence among Puerto Ricans, destroyed Puerto Rican culture, and created severe identity problems for many. The lack of identity and/or economic opportunities, the argument

---

5. A man is *machista* if he enforces a particular order in the home. The wife should be home and not working outside the home; she should take care of the children, cook, clean, and perform all other household tasks. The husband should be the breadwinner and have the authority, and, thus, the wife should not do anything without his permission. Daughters should not see boys in unchaperoned situations. Thus, what Maria means is that having in a household a father (or grandfather) who holds such views and such authority makes it unlikely that a girl would get information about birth control.

runs, has led to a fatalistic view of the world and, thus, to escapist behaviors such as intravenous drug use or exchanging sex for drugs. These informants also noted that the combination of the colonial legacy, machismo, and the culture of silence have exacerbated the transmission of STDs.

This third causal story emerged during an interview with the director and the community organizer of an HIV/AIDS social-service agency in the neighborhood. The two informants noted that, among Puerto Ricans, HIV transmission tended to be related to intravenous drug use rather than sexual activity. When pressed to account for this, they responded with the colonialism story. High-risk behaviors, such as needle sharing, having multiple sex partners, or the failure to use condoms, are the product of a weak national identity owing to the legacy of colonialism. Puerto Rican identity is "shot by colonialism" and "stifled by a history of economic control," argued Jimmy Cruz, the community organizer. He noted that the Puerto Rican experience of being economically dependent on the United States, the lack of work opportunities in the United States, and the sense of not belonging has led to a "crazy mentality" in which individuals "jump into any behavior because they might get some sense of meaning from it. There is such an overwhelming sense of fatalism among this group that, for many of them, HIV is not an important issue."

These two informants also link teen pregnancy and unprotected sex to colonialism and, in doing so, suggest that one of the cultural causes arises from a structural issue. Machismo is the result of the "destroyed self-esteem" of Puerto Rican men. Controlling sexual relationships is one way of compensating for the loss of identity and power and is manifest in the "use of multiple partners" and having fathered babies. Jimmy said: "Guys don't just want sex but a baby as well because it provides them with status. In some circles, the more babies that a guy is able to have with different women, the higher his ranking."

The three causal stories outlined above emphasize cultural causes of high-risk sexual activity and their outcomes. In effect, they claim that the system of sexual meanings and norms in two Hispanic populations creates the possibility for high-risk behaviors. Familial and religious barriers to sexual communication and education result in erroneous information about sex. In turn, this low level of education or access to information gives rise to a fear of using protection and a reluctance to challenge traditional sex roles. Even the structural barriers, such as colonialism, poverty, and unemployment, are given a cultural spin as they are perceived as creating a fatalistic attitude or worldview that pushes many residents of these two neighborhoods toward high-risk behaviors.

The emphasis on culture among health-care organizations departs from the expected traditional biomedical model. One clinic director explicitly criticized the biomedical model, claiming: "It [the biomedical model] is not enough, nor it is effective. . . . The physiological component of health is small, and the environment may be much more important." While the health-care interviews provided little direct information about why these organizations moved away from the biomedical model, they suggest two possible reasons. First, nearly all the interviewees are Mexican or Puerto Rican and have inside knowledge of and experience with the sexual cultures of the two neighborhoods (several interviewees spoke about how their particular Hispanic sexual culture shaped their own sexual histories). Second, interviewees seem very attentive to their clients, as evinced in their reports of how their clients talk about why they think they got pregnant or why they will not use condoms.

Thus, the interpretive repertoires of the social-service and health-care organizations are anchored in neighborhood-specific causal stories about sexual problems. They reflect a familiarity with the people and the sexual norms and meaning systems of each neighborhood. Despite the cultural sensitivity evinced, these causal stories are based on the assumption that sexual problems can be solved by rational risk assessment and the application of safe-sex knowledge and practices. None of the interviewees acknowledged the legitimacy of these alternative risk-assessment criteria used by residents of the two neighborhoods or tried to develop interventions that work within the culture of silence, machismo, or the legacy of colonialism to lessen their negative impact.

These stories also shift the blame away from individuals and toward impersonal social forces (i.e., sexual meaning systems, the family, colonialism) in what may be a strategy to present the organizations as morally neutral. This strategy may be critical for reaching at-risk populations for whom church and family set the moral boundaries around sexuality. Yet the implicit moral message within these stories is that at-risk individuals are passive victims and that their current sex practices are bad, unhealthy, or dangerous.

## Southtown: The Breakdown of Institutions

The causal stories employed in Southtown lack the complexity and coherence of those in the two Hispanic neighborhoods. This may be a result, in part, of the research process in both neighborhoods, but it may also be a result of different social contexts and clientele.[6] Southtown has experienced a

6. The research team experienced significant difficulty securing interviews in Southtown, and there was a general reluctance to talk about any problems in the community with the interviewers. In part, this seemed to be a white-interviewer effect, but even paired black interviewers ran into considerable resistance. This may

more severe and prolonged economic collapse, and the African American leaders we interviewed commonly offered structural arguments to explain sexual problems facing the community (see Cohen, 1996). The lack of complexity or coherence is evident in several interviews in which the interviewees identified a set of structural problems—endemic unemployment and the loss of commerce, substandard housing, environmental pollution, drugs, and gang violence—but did not explicitly connect these structural problems to sexual behaviors. In addition, two interviewees spoke about proximate causes, such as exchanging sex for drugs or patriarchal sex roles that allow men to reject using condoms, but did not discuss how these causes are related to broader cultural or structural features of Southtown. However, two related causal stories did emerge from the interviews. One story stressed the breakdown of social institutions like the family as the underlying cause of sexual problems. The other focused on structural issues such as unemployment and poverty. In both stories, these structural or institutional causes give rise to several proximate causes such as drug use or fatalism, which in turn impair sexual decisionmaking.

In Southtown, the causal stories articulated by health-care and social-service agents started with structural rather than cultural causes, as illustrated in figure 10.3. The underlying cause of the main sexual problems affecting residents of the neighborhood (i.e., unprotected sex often arising from the drug trade, increasing rates of STDs and HIV/AIDS, teen pregnancy, domestic violence) is some structural or institutional failure. The specific causes ranged from the lack of jobs and the ensuing poverty to the breakdown of the family. For example, John Singleton, the executive director of a Shoreland youth and family agency, argued that "between the hours of 3:30 and 5:30 is when most teen pregnancies occur." When pressed to explain, he noted that these are unsupervised hours for teens and that his job is to create a place where teens can be watched after school. A counselor at a mental-health clinic also stressed the breakdown of the key institutions in the neighborhood that are tied to teenage sexual problems: "The moral message [about drug use and sex] is supposed to come from the nuclear family, but that is not the case

---

have been related to the strained relationship between Southside communities and the University of Chicago, which is perceived as studying these communities but not providing anything in return. The field period also spanned the O. J. Simpson trial and a statutory-rape trial of a black, Southside congressman, both of which may have put informants on the defensive. One informant pointed out that there were already "black poster boys" for domestic violence and sexual promiscuity—they did not really need to be adding fuel to the fire. The general feeling was that African Americans are negatively portrayed by both researchers and the press and that there is no need to further air the community's dirty laundry in public.

| Underlying Cause → | Proximate Cause → | Sexual Problem → | Outcome |
|---|---|---|---|
| Institutional breakdown → | Breakdown of community, leading to involvement with drugs or inadequate moral instruction | → Unprotected sex → | Disease and pregnancy |
| Economic depressions → | Involvement with drugs, fatalism → | Unprotected sex → | Disease |

Figure 10.3. Causal stories in Southtown.

in today's society. Church and community organizations are not as consistent as they used to be. Kids are turning to gangs, drugs, and sex to obtain what they're not getting at home."

These two comments constitute almost the entire causal story articulated in these two interviews. The second interviewee also spoke about the lack of sound information about sexuality, pregnancy, and disease transmission, but she did not link it to institutional breakdown explicitly. Neither interviewee outlined the intervening actions and attitudes that lead from institutional failures to STDs but implied that, without adequate supervision and moral socialization, young people will make unhealthy or bad sexual decisions. Two other health-care interviewees blamed the church and the school system—the former for its refusal to acknowledge AIDS in the African American community and, hence, for not making it a priority issue, the latter for teaching safe-sex strategies, not abstinence, in sex-education classes.

This causal story, which blames current sexual problems on widespread institutional breakdowns in the African American community, draws more explicit moral boundaries than do the stories used by care providers in Erlinda and Westside. In the accounts presented above, the interviewees identify teenagers as illegitimate sexual actors whose sexuality is unruly and, if left unchecked by social institutions, must lead to negative outcomes such as pregnancy.[7] More striking in the institutional-breakdown story is the attack on the community's allegedly traditional guardians of sexual virtue and chastity. The key institutional powers of the African American community—family, church, and school—are blamed for the sexual problems. The interviewees complain that, if only they would do their job, then unwanted pregnancies, HIV/AIDS, and the sex-for-drugs trade would disappear. Moreover, health-care and social-service agents exhibit a reluctance to take responsibility for these sexual problems. It is as if they are saying, Isn't it enough that we have to deal with the problems associated with unemployment, poverty, and welfare, and now you want us to repair all the damage created by the unruly sexuality of our clients?

The other variant of the structural causal story begins with the economic context of Southtown. In her discussion of drugs and the routine trading of sex for drugs, the director of a church-based community-development organization blamed the increase in both on the "severe economic depression" afflicting the South Side of Chicago (closures and layoffs in the steel industry and the collapse of Southtown's commercial district). She also noted that the lack of economic opportunity has created a sense of isolation and fatalism

7. This view of sexuality is based on the ideology of "essentialism" or "nativism," in which sexuality is considered to be presocial, often dangerous, and, thus, something that must be checked, molded, and channeled into socially appropriate relationships and actions (see Rubin, 1999, 149; Connell & Dowsett, 1999, 179–83).

among some residents, calling one area of the neighborhood "a valley of de-
spair." A city health worker at a Southtown clinic also stressed this linkage of
sexual problems with a fatalistic worldview that stems from the poverty of the
neighborhood: "I was advising a man from the neighborhood that he needed
to take more precautions when it comes to sex because he was in a high-risk
category. He said to me, 'Why should I worry about something [i.e., AIDS]
that will take ten years to happen? It's so far in the future. Even if I do become infected, I'm not going to get sick for a long time.'" This clinician continued by noting that practicing safe sex seems impossible to many of the
clinic's patients, for whom just getting through the day—finding work,
housing, food—is the top priority. According to some health-care workers,
this sense of fatalism that accompanies the lives of many African American
men in the neighborhood limits the effectiveness of both the education
efforts and the treatments offered by area clinics.

## Intervention Strategies

These various interpretive accounts justified the particular interventions on
which the agencies or clinics relied in the three neighborhoods. Recall that,
according to one narrative, the fundamental cause of sexual problems is the
culture of silence surrounding sexuality that pervades Hispanic communities.
A collective unwillingness or inability to speak about sexuality with one's
partner creates a social context in which individuals, especially girls and
women, lack the basic biological facts about conception and disease transmission. Individuals are, therefore, unaware of what constitutes high- and
low-risk behaviors or relationships. This causal story leads health-care clinicians and social workers to create basic sex-education programs for young
people and women in which they learn how conception and disease transmission occur or how to put on a condom. The goal is to help them make
better decisions and, thus, avoid the dependency problems that can arise from
the unintended effects of sexual activity. According to one health educator,
the goal of her HIV-prevention program is "to change behavior through
knowledge" and "[to make] youths think twice before they engage in high-
risk forms of social and sexual behavior."

Thirty-three of the thirty-eight organizations in Westside and Erlinda
spoke about some form of sex education as their primary intervention.[8] These
programs range from providing basic information about disease transmission

8. Nine of thirteen organizations in Southtown also identified education as their
primary strategy. Those organizations that did not report about education also did
not discuss interventions or spoke only about medical treatment.

and birth control to offering "self-esteem" classes for women trying to get free from the power of machismo; from teaching Puerto Rican young people about their cultural heritage as a way of fostering a strong sense of identity and, thereby, combatting the fatalistic attitudes that lead to unsafe sex; to training teens to teach one another about using condoms. Nancy Sanchez, leader of a Hispanic health-care-advocacy organization, summarized an approach that combines sex education and self-esteem training to combat the culture of machismo: "A large part of what we do is try to provide information to pregnant teens. We encourage safe sex, birth control, and, most importantly, hope. They must know that they will not be slaves forever, that they can study and start work and move ahead." Her organization urges young women to get off public assistance and finds some of them scholarships for business school.

Yet there is a disconnect between the causal story and the interventions. While the causal story identifies deeply held sexual meanings and norms within Hispanic cultures, the interventions focus on changing the behaviors and attitudes of clients. Both health-care and social-service organizations fall back on the institutional logic or mandate of restoring individuals to health or autonomy. This disconnect may be a result of several factors. First, while institutional actors recognize the complex causes that determine sexual behavior, they are constrained by institutionally imposed limits on their action. Health-care workers can do little more than treat the disease and provide education about and training in safe sex. They possess neither the skills nor the authority to change an entire sexual culture. The institutional limitations are heard in the comment of a city public-health clinician as he responded to a question about his ideal solution to STDs: "Stealth protection for women. It would be a gel that women could use to protect themselves from STDs, HIV, and pregnancy without having to talk to the man about it. This way women would not have to negotiate condom use, and it would empower women in sexual ways." His response reflects a health-care approach to problem solving. The "stealth technology" would prevent disease, but it would not improve the economic conditions of individuals in Southtown or change sexual norms regarding communication, condom use, and sex roles. At best, it would bypass the cultural and structural causes of sex-related health problems.

Some informants openly acknowledged that the cultural or structural problems are intractable and that their organizations can do very little to remedy the situation. One Erlinda social worker complained that, despite her organization's education programs, there was little that could be done to prevent teen pregnancy or the transmission of STDS from "polygamous husbands" to their wives given the submissive sex roles deeply ingrained in women. Another spoke about the "overwhelming sense of fatality" among Mexican and Puerto Rican youths and concluded: "There is no way of teaching behavior." A health-care counselor in the same neighborhood noted that, because the culture of silence prevents teenagers from talking about sex, her clinic is forced to practice "guerilla medicine." That is, when a teenager comes into the clinic complaining about some health problem, for example, a sore throat, a clinician will ask if that person practices oral sex. If he or she answers yes, then they can prescribe a medicine that will combat both the relevant STD and strep throat. At the end of the interview, the counselor wondered how much longer she could continue doing this type of work. She said that, not only have they been unable to reverse (through medical intervention) the "collapsed life cycle" of many young Mexican Americans and Puerto Ricans (i.e., the rush to sexual adulthood by young men and women born out of the expectation that street violence and/or substance abuse will kill them before they reach twenty-five or thirty years of age), but things are actually getting worse: "Kids are functioning at a primitive survival level, and unfortunately they are using sex and violence as a means of survival."

Second, the strategy of creating complex causal stories and linking the cause to deep-seated and seemingly intractable cultural and structural problems within the community may allow organizations to shift the blame away from the individual (see Stone, 1989, 292). This strategy may allow service providers to appear morally neutral to their potential clients and those who refer people to the organizations. Many organizations in Erlinda and Westside distanced themselves from the sexual ethics advocated by the Roman Catholic or Pentecostal churches since two key interventions—teaching about safe sex and distributing condoms—are not sanctioned by either religious group. A health counselor in Erlinda claimed that his outreach program promotes a "value-free approach to sex," in which he and his coworkers "preach that there is not good sex and bad sex." The basic message is simple: "Cover your dick." An HIV-outreach worker in Erlinda spoke about how her organization combats the "abstinence-only" stance of most churches by marking clear institutional boundaries: "Your business is saving the soul; my business is saving the body."

Yet social-service and health-care providers do make moral claims and judgments about their clients and their sexual problems. Their educational-intervention strategies are premised on the assumption that people can act rationally if they desire and that rational action regarding sexual risk will prevent unwanted pregnancies and STDs. While acknowledging the specific cultural meanings that lead to a different way of assessing risk among some populations (e.g., the fatalism of some African Americans born of racism and poverty), they tend to dismiss an approach that takes account of these meaning as irrelevant or wrong in the end. The goal is to inform the clients about sexual risks and their negative outcomes and then to persuade them to give up the behaviors and culture- or context-bound beliefs that undergird those risky behaviors; and, to accomplish this, clients must act rationally. The comments of Jorge Carballo, a health educator and researcher in Erlinda, illustrate how institutional actors rely on the rational-action presumption and make moral claims despite the attempt to be morally neutral. Carballo described his intervention program as an "empowerment model" of sexual education and behavior modification. He said that the program aims to empower at-risk Latinos to overcome "various barriers that keep individuals from putting knowledge into practice." In order to overcome these barriers (e.g., the culture of silence or poverty), Carballo said, his clients must first link cultural beliefs to sex acts and then link those acts to negative health outcomes. In other words, empowerment implies gaining a complex set of skills: the ability to identify the causal sequencing of sexual behaviors and their outcomes and the ability to assess the costs and benefits of those actions.

This educator's comments also contain the moral framing shared by many of his colleagues. In general, other health-care and social-service providers are reluctant to pass moral judgment on the sexual behaviors of their clients but quick to judge the thinking of at-risk individuals. Thinking rationally will lead to rational (i.e., nonrisky) sexual behavior, which is good. Rationality, especially rational thought, is the moral standard by which institutional actors evaluate sexuality. Carballo advances the moral claim that the deep cultural and structural conditions that give rise to sexual risk taking are not legitimate excuses for the failure of many Latinos to practice safe sex. Thus, while explicitly blaming the cause of his clients' sexual problems on larger sociocultural forces, he implicitly blames individuals for not acting rationally in the sexual arena, for failing to assess sexual risk correctly, and for engaging unnecessarily in risky behaviors.

The accounts provided by health-care and social-service clinicians speak loudly about their goals for changing sex-market behaviors and redefining what constitutes a legitimate market for their clients. The bottom-line goal for most social-service and health-care workers is for their clients to abandon high-risk behaviors such as exchanging sex for drugs and having sex without a condom (a few organizations in Southtown favored abstinence as the solution). Implicit in their educational efforts are claims about which people are legitimate sex partners (e.g., those who use condoms or those who will wait for marriage before having intercourse). If adopted, such behavioral changes could potentially alter the makeup of some sex markets by eliminating certain categories of potential partners or by shifting individuals out of transactional into relational markets.

Unfortunately, we do not have direct evidence with which to assess the effectiveness of clinicians' diagnoses and intervention strategies. However, it may be fair to conclude that health-care and social-service organizations in these three neighborhoods have a limited impact on sex markets. Several informants admitted that they have had little success in changing the behaviors of their high-risk clients, and a few wondered aloud how long they would be able to continue doing this seemingly impossible job. Moreover, the misfit between their identification of the deep-seated cultural and structural causes of risky sexuality and their individualist or "bandage" interventions suggests that their impact on sex markets is not great. In order effectively to help individuals adopt low-risk sex practices and redefine the goals of sexual activity toward long-term monogamy, health-care and social-service organizations would need to engage in a program of major social reengineering (e.g., help individuals escape from the economic conditions that engender fatalism and a disregard for one's sexual health; change gender attitudes and roles among groups that keep women in a sexually subordinate position and, thus, unable fully to control their sexual relationships). In short, the institutional logics that define sex as an externality and limit interventions to those who fit within institutional mandates make it difficult for health-care and social-service organizations to affect sex markets significantly.

## A Note on the Police

As this chapter was originally conceived, the police were to have been included as a third institutional actor. Yet an examination of the police interviews made it clear that they were very different than the health-care and social-service interviews and not very comparable. First, the causal stories of the police were partial at most and more often absent. In the accounts generated during the police interviews, sexual activities and identities were characterized, not as sexual problems, but as legal or social-order problems. Thus, informants did not discuss such topics as sexual risk or unprotected sex, STDs, unwanted pregnancies, and inadequate knowledge to act in a sexually responsible manner, as did the health-care and social-service interviewees.

Second, the police had an extremely limited repertoire of interventions, and their interventions did not include efforts to ameliorate, fix, or eradicate sexual problems (except by way of arrest). The police officers whom we interviewed identified a small range of sexual issues that officers encountered in their daily patrols. Prostitution, exchanging sex for drugs, and domestic violence were the most common. Their accounts reveal how the institutional logic of policing provides a limited language, one that stresses social order and connects sexual issues to those issues identified as common in their neighborhoods (e.g., drugs, poverty, violence).

For example, when we asked about prostitution in the neighborhood, most of the officers identified the social location, often naming streets and local bars where the transactions occurred, and then some blamed the continued existence of prostitution on their beat or in their district on either drug addiction or an overwhelmed court system, one that cannot handle its case load or help prostitutes exit their occupation. One officer in Erlinda claimed that "the majority are addicted to narcotics" and that, "when a girl is busted, the courts don't take it seriously. Their attitude is that prostitution is something that has been around for centuries, so what can they do to stop it?" An officer in Shoreland echoed these comments in his description of prostitution in the neighborhood: "There is street prostitution in Shoreland but no red-light district per se. There are streetwalkers who work for themselves, not for pimps in organized houses. We usually know who these women are because they've been arrested before. Right now they mostly walk along Michigan Avenue. Sometimes we crack down, and it pops up somewhere else. It's like a balloon—if you push it down one place, it pops up somewhere else. You can't really eradicate it. Most live around the area. Most of the prostitutes are drug addicts, and they don't look very healthy."

Unlike their counterparts in other institutional spheres, police officers did not identify any cultural or structural underlying causes matching the proximate causes that they did identify, nor did their accounts connect proximate causes to sexual outcomes (e.g., risky sexual behavior). Instead, the outcomes that they spoke about were grounded in the institutional logic of policing—that is, getting busted for breaking the law in the case of prostitution or resorting to violence to settle a dispute with a spouse. Since sexuality becomes a concern for police only when actions violate the law or public order, it is no surprise that their interventions rely primarily on legal means. Arresting johns and prostitutes or persons who use violence against spouses or gay men is the most common intervention strategy employed by the police. A few officers spoke about "community policing" as one way to prevent law breaking and public disturbances caused by gangs or drug trafficking, but rarely were such preventive measures connected with problematic sexual behavior. Some officers refer battered women to shelters or clinics, some are willing to hear the stories of victims, and some said that responsibility for care or prevention lies with the courts. In short, our police interviewees had little to say about the institutional strategies in use to prevent, repair, or end any of the sexual problems that they encounter.

The police interviews reveal how institutional actors are severely limited in their abilities to address issues involving sexuality when those issues are far removed from the mandates of law enforcement. Many such issues (e.g., pregnancy, STDs) neither fall within the purview of the police nor fit into the logic of maintaining public order and enforcing laws. When coded as victimless crimes, certain issues (e.g., prostitution) are not considered to be as important as other criminal activities and, thus, are given less attention. Most important, the police do not become as morally invested in their clients because they are not charged with helping individuals resolve sexual problems, as social-service and health-care workers are, and they do not, therefore, maintain ongoing relationships with their clients. Thus, they have not developed, nor do they need to develop, more complex understandings of the causes of sexual problems.

## Causal Stories, Social Control, and the Construction of Moral Boundaries

Seidman (1999) argues that two moral logics guide public discourse about sex in the United States. One assumes that certain sex acts are inherently good, normal, or moral and that others are inherently bad, abnormal or immoral. The other moral logic, what he calls a *communicative sexual ethic,* rejects the notion that particular acts are intrinsically good or bad, assuming instead that sexual morality is based on the nature of the relationship and the interactive context (i.e., the consensual, mutual, caring nature of the sexual relationship or exchange is used as the basis on which to judge sexuality morally). Seidman notes that this second logic "breaks from the logic of natural/unnatural and normal/abnormal [advanced by the first logic] . . . [and] permits a wide range of sexual choice, tolerance, and affirmation of intimate differences while also producing fewer deviant identities" (168). Seidman and others (e.g., Rubin, 1999; Weeks, 2000) contend that the second logic has pushed back or opened up the moral boundaries around sex at the same time that it has engendered intense social conflict over such issues as homosexual rights, family values, and cohabitation.

The analysis of the Chicago interviews reveals that service providers mix these two logics in their causal stories. On the one hand, many interviewees argue that sex without condoms is inherently bad and reflects bad decision-making on the part of individuals. On the other hand, many (except for church-based organizations) refuse to condemn multiple partners or non-marital sexual activities. The mixed moral messages offered by our interviewees are driven in part by the interviewees' various institutional mandates and logics. In their causal stories, health-care and social-service providers make clients responsible for their own sexual problems. Their clients, they believe, work out of a logic that defines sexual risk in terms of behaviors that defy rational (i.e., good) thought and action that, in turn, threatens the health, welfare, or autonomy of the individual. At the same time, they are reluctant to condemn certain behaviors and relationships (such as same-sex relationships and activities) because of their institutional mandate to treat symptoms and because of a growing sensitivity to the social and cultural contexts that shape the sexual beliefs and actions of their clients. Thus, institutional actors in Chicago give permission for a variety of sex acts and relationships, often by their silence or refusal to judge, while, at the same time, they condemn some forms of sexual expression and sexual actors through their calls for safe-sex or abstinence. The interview data suggest that institutional actors provide their clients with a fluid and shifting understanding of what it means to be a moral sexual actor and which sexual boundaries they should not cross and that this may undermine intervention.

The data also suggest that health-care and social-service providers are caught between two competing understandings of agency. The causal stories employed by these actors tend to define at-risk populations as unable to exercise agency. Individuals who have contracted STDs or who find themselves pregnant are understood as being misguided, irresponsible, or caught within cultural and institutional webs that make it difficult, if not impossible, to escape risky sex. They are "sexual dopes"—seemingly incapable of avoiding sexual situations that might endanger their health or well-being—and, thus, in need of education. At the same time, these providers are institutionally bound, and often personally motivated, to define their clients as fully empowered agents, as evinced in their educational interventions. By receiving new knowledge, once-passive clients will be able to overcome the social and cultural forces that led them into sexually risky situations in the first place.

This conclusion about agency dovetails with Watney's (1999, 411) argument that the emphasis in health care on treating illness as a result of harmful habits and lifestyles has led to an intervention strategy founded on "a highly voluntaristic picture of individuals taking charge of their lives and rejecting many previous unhealthy and irresponsible lifestyles." This strategy "assumes that individuals possess unqualified powers to shape their lives, with their future well-being their priority. This also involves a virtual suppression of any consideration of the many powerful contingent circumstances that may inform [sexual] decision-making. It is also a particularly inadequate approach in relation to questions of sexual behaviour, which comes to be seen as a simple arena of conscious choice, rather than as a complex arena of intense commercial and cultural pressures."

While the Chicago Health and Social Life Survey (CHSLS) data reveal that Chicago health-care and social-service providers demonstrate a contextually nuanced understanding of the different neighborhoods and subpopulations, that knowledge is subordinated to the overarching ideologies and interpretive lenses of their respective institutions. In other words, the causal stories that they create to diagnose the sexual problems of their clients do not inform and shape their interventions. Instead, their interventions are guided by the institutional logic of health care or social work. This disconnect between causal story and intervention severely limits their ability to help their clients overcome the social and cultural embeddedness that leads to high-risk behavior and negative sexual-health outcomes.

In the end, this analysis raises questions about the nature of institutions' control over sexuality. The CHSLS data suggest that the institutions charged with the responsibility of regulating and controlling sexuality often fail or, at best, exercise partial control. Local cultures, familial and peer relationships, and economic hardship appear to be the more powerful shapers of sexual expression. Institutional control is weakened by an articulation problem between diagnosis and intervention, and, thus, the causal stories of health-care and social-service actors may unintentionally undercut the legitimacy and authority of their efforts. What kind of social control can be exercised when institutions deny the likelihood of behavioral change because deep-seated cultural norms and social structures render individuals helpless while, at the same time, they expect these same individuals to overcome the very barriers that placed them at risk? It appears that the arguments about strong institutional control offered by Foucault and Freud are more illusory than empirically grounded. The Chicago study suggests that sexuality simply may be too unruly, too difficult to contain for institutions in a democratic society. Without the power to enforce safe-sex practices, institutional actors must depend on the persuasiveness of their stories to compel voluntary compliance. Yet, if there is one thing that frustrates our informants, it is that even the threat of disease and death that they report in their causal stories is not capable of persuading individuals to stop risky sexual activities. Sexuality, it seems, has a plasticity and variegated logic of its own that defies efforts to educate and control it.

11 )

# Religion and the Politics of Sexuality

Stephen Ellingson,
Martha Van Haitsma,
Edward O. Laumann,
and Nelson Tebbe

Buntin, Lechtman, and Laumann (chapter 8 in this volume) and, to a lesser
extent, Ellingson (chapter 10 in this volume) documented the limited control that health-care, social-service, and legal organizations exert over sexuality. In this chapter, we examine how religious organizations understand and
attempt to regulate sex markets.[1] Like organizations in other institutional
spheres, national and local religious organizations tend to treat most arenas of

An earlier version of this chapter appeared as Stephen Ellingson, Nelson Tebbe,
Martha Van Haitsma, and Edward O. Laumann, "Religion and the Politics of Sexuality," *Journal of Contemporary Ethnography* 30, no. 1 (February 2001): 3–55.
    1. On the terms *sex market* and *sexual marketplace* as they are used in this study, see
the section "The Social Organization of Sexual Partnering and Sexual Relationships"
in Ellingson, Laumann, Paik, and Mahay (chapter 1 in this volume).

sexuality as an externality. However, over the past decade, the topic of sexuality, and that of homosexuality in particular, has generated fierce controversy within American Christianity. In particular, debates over homosexuality have been fueled by official statements and teaching documents released by a number of denominations (see Fulkerson, 1995; Gilson, 1995, 37–63). In some churches, the controversy swirls around the issue of ordaining gay and lesbian ministers or performing same-sex-union ceremonies. In others, the affirmation of homosexuality or even the open discussion of human sexuality pushes the limits of tolerance. These issues are not merely philosophical. They have practical consequences. Members of the clergy have been defrocked, congregations have been expelled from denominations, and many denominations have been internally split by conflict over homosexuality.

While media attention has been focused on theological and political wrangling in the church hierarchy, working arrangements at the congregation level are the result of many interacting forces, of which official church doctrine is only one. Moreover, disjunctures between official teaching and local practice are common. Social norms regarding sexual behavior have been strongly challenged over the past four decades by a variety of other changes (e.g., the reliability and availability of birth control, the advent of AIDS, increased delays between sexual maturity and the end of schooling/economic independence/social adulthood). Yet churches must maintain moral authority with respect to right belief and behavior as they adapt to outside changes. Congregations' leaders find themselves on the front lines of this struggle as they seek to promulgate religious doctrine in ways that at once provide needed direction to members and potential members and are acceptable to them.

Using data from open-ended interviews with clergy and lay leaders of congregations in three Chicago neighborhoods, this chapter explains how congregations' leaders devise policies and practices to address the sexuality issues facing members and how they attempt to channel sexual identities, behaviors, and relationships into religiously sanctioned expressions. We describe how clergy and lay leaders take into account local social forces such as the demographic makeup of particular neighborhoods and the sexual cultures of residents as they negotiate between, on the one hand, the doctrines and rules of the larger denominations that lend them legitimacy and authority and, on the other hand, the needs and beliefs of the community on which they depend for survival. We argue that congregations' responses to sexuality are a matter of negotiation at several social levels as clergy and lay leaders attempt to reconcile official teachings with local concerns about sexuality under a variety of organizational constraints and in a variety of social and institutional environments. Religious institutions both react to and try to shape local sexual attitudes and behaviors. However, the power to define certain sexual beliefs, identities, relationships, and practices as moral does not necessarily translate into the power to prevent individuals from engaging in what are considered to be immoral sexual behaviors or to regulate sex markets effectively.

## The Problem of Sexuality for the Church

Historically, the Christian church has held an essentially negative or, at best, suspicious view of sexuality and has advanced a sexual ethic of control by which the church attempts to channel the sexual behaviors and attitudes of clergy and laity toward some ends and away from others (see Brown, 1988; Countryman, 1988; Monti, 1995). Traditionally, there have been two moral and, hence, legitimate avenues of sexual expression for Christians: celibacy and heterosexual marriage. However, changes in sexual mores and practices since the 1960s have led religious bodies, as well as individual members of the clergy and the laity, to question the traditional ethic of control. This questioning and the perceived challenge to traditional teachings on sexuality have created significant tensions within religious organizations.

The difficulties surrounding sex and the church rest on several tensions or conflicts experienced by clergy and laity. First, early-twenty-first-century Christians who try to affirm the goodness of sex find themselves in organizations that have strong and still operative beliefs about the dangers and immorality of sexual behavior. Second, traditional norms regarding and scriptural prohibitions on sexuality may seem outdated and difficult to apply to many congregations given the changes in American sexual culture (e.g., movements to accept alternative sexualities, delayed marriage coupled with the early onset of sexual maturity, prolonged periods of adult singlehood, widespread access to effective birth control). These changes have weakened the authority of official teachings, tradition, and the Bible for some church members, especially those from younger generations (see, e.g., Roof & McKinney, 1987, 203–17). At the same time, these developments have compelled others to hold tenaciously to the norm of heterosexual marriage (see Countryman, 1994; Monti, 1995, 1–6, 17–74).[2] Current conflicts within congregations and denominations over sexuality are often polarized around those who adhere to and those who reject the norm of heterosexual marriage and the ethic of control. Finally, the high degree of autonomy in American churches at the

---

2. On the liberalization of sexual attitudes and practices among mainline Protestants and Roman Catholics, see Beck, Cole, and Hammond (1991), Cochran and Beeghly (1991), Greeley (1989, 87–94), Greeley (1994), and Hertel and Hughes (1987).

local level makes uniform interpretation and implementation of official doctrines or teachings on sexuality problematic. Clergy and lay leaders are often caught between denominational or national church policy and the concerns, pressures, and interests of individuals within a particular local religious environment and community setting.

Hartman's (1996) recent account of conflict over homosexuality (e.g., performing same-sex-union ceremonies) within several North Carolina churches illustrates the complex process of negotiating between ambiguous scriptural teachings on sexuality, congregations' concerns about preserving their autonomy, and crosscutting social and political pressures. For example, in one chapter, Hartman documents how a Southern Baptist church eventually allowed its minister to perform a same-sex-union ceremony for two church members. This unlikely event occurred because the congregation resisted regional and national efforts by the denomination to undermine its local autonomy and because the process of studying Scripture, praying, and discussing the issue in small groups changed many minds and hearts (see Hartman, 1996, 25–49). Thus, its autonomy as a congregation and an internal process of discovery led one conservative church to move away from an outright rejection of homosexuality and a sexual ethic of control and to adopt a more tolerant ethic and set of practices regarding homosexuality.

As suggested by Hartman's account, we should not expect to find a direct relation between a congregation's theological orientation or polity type and its positions on and programs regarding sexuality. Instead, the relation between religion and sexuality at the institution level is a complex and negotiated phenomenon. It rests on an interrelated set of organizational, ideological, cultural, and demographic constraints and resources that flow from the local community and from regional (i.e., synod, diocese, conference) or national religious bodies. We contend that religious leaders and congregations must negotiate among multiple and often countervailing constraints and draw on different resources in order to develop a collectively sanctioned understanding of sexuality and specific interventions (e.g., sex-education classes, marriage counseling). In this chapter, we develop a model of how and why congregations address sexuality and sexual problems and use it to explain the particular positions and programs in place at six congregations in three Chicago neighborhoods.

## Theoretical Framework

Recent work on the relation between religion and sexuality provides macro- or individual-level explanations but offers limited help in understanding the relation at the organization or congregation level. Studies of changes in American religion since the 1960s have identified a broad liberal-conservative denominational split regarding changes in sexual attitudes and practices. This body of work suggests that mainline denominations tend to support or at least tolerate more liberal attitudes and policies while more conservative and/or sectarian bodies tend to support more conservative positions (e.g., Glock, 1993; Hunter, 1991). However, many congregations, like those in Hartman's (1996) study, do not fit the denominational pattern, and, as Wuthnow (1988) points out, denominations and congregations are often internally divided over moral issues. Thus, simply knowing the general stance and/or official position of a given denomination provides limited help in understanding how a local congregation will address sexuality issues.

Micro-level explanations provide insights about how individuals from different demographic categories compare on a range of sexual attitudes and practices (Beck, Cole, & Hammond, 1991; Cochran & Beeghley, 1991; Fischer, Derison, Polley, Cadman, & Johnston, 1994; Hertel & Hughes, 1987; Sherkat & Ellison, 1997; Thornton & Camburn, 1987). However, congregations often articulate policies and teachings on moral issues that diverge from the beliefs and preferences of individual members. Further, demographic categories are merely proxies for socially meaningful statuses, processes, and structural constraints and resources. Mid-level, organizational explanations that illuminate the process through which social norms are constructed, by which institutional control is exerted, and through which social change occurs are absent from most studies of religion and sexuality. We develop an organization-level explanation that draws on neoinstitutionalist and cultural theories as well as recent studies of congregations.

Religious organizations, like organizations in other institutional fields, must address two basic problems—adapting to the external environment and promoting internal integration. Sexuality, in particular, heightens routine problems of environmental adaptation and internal integration for congregations. In addition, congregations that fail to address challenges to the traditional ethic of control may be faced with the loss of members, resources, and/or legitimacy.[3] Clergy and/or lay leaders develop a congregation's response to problems with and concerns about sexuality by negotiating between cultural and structural constraints, between bottom-up and top-down pressures. A critical outcome of these negotiations is the normative frameworks about sexuality (i.e., sets of evaluatory ideas, beliefs, and images) that local religious leaders develop.

3. A liberal stance on social and moral issues is not a direct cause of membership decline in mainline Protestant congregations, but it is often part of a larger, interrelated set of organizational features that collectively lead to decline (see Smith, 1998; Roof & McKinney, 1987).

These frameworks are used to understand sexuality and the causes of the sex-related problems facing congregations, to define solutions to these problems, and to both organize and justify particular programs and policies that address sexual issues.[4] Fundamentally, these normative frameworks help clergy and laity define which sexual behaviors, identities, and outcomes are normal and, hence, moral and which are marginalized and, hence, immoral. These frameworks sanction the purpose of sexuality, often in terms of the procreational or the relational ends of sexuality, and identify the morally legitimate sexual unit (self, couple, or family).[5] They also identify the underlying authority of particular claims—commonly the Bible, but also psychology and other social sciences.

Historically, the church has tried to channel sexuality toward either heterosexual marriage or celibacy and prohibit all other forms of sexual expression. This framework of control is still in use, especially in conservative Protestant and some Roman Catholic congregations. Since the 1960s, more liberal congregations and denominations have created a framework of acceptance that welcomes and, in some cases, even celebrates alternative expressions such as homosexuality or single parenthood. The most common framework among mainline denominations is one of accommodation, in which practices and identities that challenge the norm of heterosexual marriage are allowed, especially if kept private. Many of our informants used the phrase *don't ask, don't tell* as a shorthand way to describe this framework.

Religious leaders are not free to create normative frameworks de novo; rather, they must work within the limits of the particular structural and cultural constraints and resources of their religious environment. These constraints and resources shape how religious leaders understand sexuality, how they determine what count as sexual problems, and what kinds of solutions they will offer. There are two broad sets of constraints and resources that shape how religious organizations address sexuality: organizational features, such as polity and existing canons of belief and practice, and features of neighborhoods and the wider institutional environments, such as the demographic

---

4. Scholars working within the neoinstitutionalist paradigm note that organizations develop frameworks of meaning to help organizational actors diagnose and resolve problems as well as to provide them with sets of rules, identities, and activity scripts to guide behavior (see, e.g., Becker, 1999; Friedland & Alford, 1991; Jepperson, 1991; Schein, 1991; Sherkat & Ellison, 1995).

5. A third orientation, recreational, or sex for pleasure, is generally rejected from the Christian viewpoint as the sinful and worldly construction against which a morally appropriate and Christian purpose of procreation or of maintaining a marital commitment is defined (see Fulkerson, 1995, 53).

composition or the sexual culture of a neighborhood's population. Figure 11.1 maps the relation between constraints, normative frameworks, and church responses to sexuality.

## Organizational Features

### Polity

*Polity* refers to the form of church governance. Polity may powerfully shape the manner in which policy, dogma, and religious practice are communicated and enacted (McMullen, 1994, 712). Polity types range from episcopal, which is hierarchical and centralized, to congregational, which is relatively democratic and decentralized. Church polity affects normative frameworks and organizational policies and programs in terms of the degree of local autonomy allowed to congregations, the power of national or regional church bodies to enforce official doctrine and policies, and the nature of resources available for congregations. First, congregational churches may have greater freedom than episcopally based churches to construct their understandings of and actions toward sexuality on the basis of local needs and the theological/ideological orientation of the congregation. Second, congregations within more centralized and hierarchical denominations have a clearer set of instructions about how to address sexuality issues as well as a greater set of resources (e.g., creedal documents, bishops) on which to draw. However, such congregations run the risk of incurring disciplinary action if they do not follow official teachings.[6] Specifically, hierarchical church bodies have the power to remove clergy from congregations and even expel congregations from the national organization if they violate church teachings and policies. While church bodies do not commonly exercise this power and seem reluctant to do so given the divisiveness of the process, the threat of this power may constrain how local congregations address sexuality, especially if there are recent or local instances of disciplinary action by a governing church body. However, polity does not always have the expected effects. In the Southern Baptist case from Hartman's book, the national denomination expelled the congregation from membership in the Southern Baptist Convention (SBC) even though the authority structure of the SBC does not make any national teach-

6. The latter event is illustrated by the case of two California Lutheran churches that ordained gay or lesbian ministers in defiance of the Evangelical Lutheran Church of America (ELCA) policy prohibiting this action. The congregations had their membership in the ELCA rescinded. They are now independent Lutheran congregations.

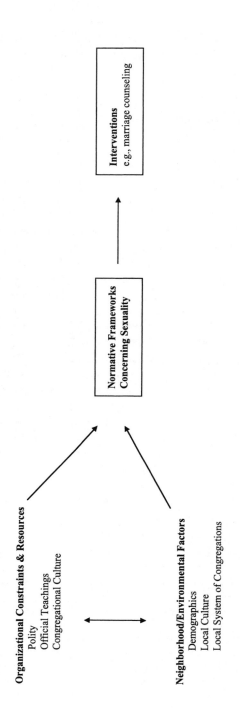

Figure 11.1. The relation between constraints, normative frameworks and church responses to sexuality.

ings or doctrine binding at the local level and its polity authorizes a congregation's independence.

## Official Teachings

Roman Catholicism and most Protestant denominations—especially those with episcopal polities—have official teachings on sexuality that are understood as authoritative and that carry proscriptions. Although there are often significant discrepancies between official teachings and the actual practices of local congregations, such teachings minimally serve as guideposts for local churches by outlining the boundaries of moral and immoral sexual behavior, by suggesting appropriate responses to particular issues, and by providing justifications for those responses. Official teachings within hierarchical denominations vary in terms of enforceability, with the result that some teachings are more closely adhered to than others (e.g., a ban on performing same-sex marriages vs. a directive to withhold the sacraments from Catholic couples who use birth control). Although official teachings within congregationally based denominations are often nonbinding, they may carry great moral weight in some communities. Congregational churches within fundamentalist and evangelical traditions often lack authoritative teachings from a centralized national office but typically follow a general set of guidelines abstracted from a literalist reading of the Bible. Following the work of Chaves (1997), we expect local congregations to be loosely coupled with denominations in terms of teachings regarding sexuality, although we expect the loose relationship to be an outcome of internal, congregational, and community pressures rather than pressures from the wider denominational environment.

## A Congregation's Culture

Becker (1999, 7) notes that a congregation's culture is the means by which members determine and understand their collective identity (in her terms, "Who we are") and mission ("How we do things here"). We expect that a congregation's culture—the collection of stories and language, rituals and patterns of interaction, symbols and beliefs—shapes how and why that congregation addresses sexuality issues. In particular, our data suggest that several aspects of a congregation's culture are resources for addressing the moral difficulties surrounding sex. First, theological orientation and how one applies the Bible are often the starting points for identifying what counts as a sexual problem and how to deal with it. For example, if a congregation follows the belief that the Bible is literally the word of God, it may decide that homosexuality is sinful because God condemns it in a few scriptural passages.

This belief may be used to mobilize members to take public action in protest of homosexuality such as holding a prayer vigil in front of a gay bar. Second, many congregations develop particular identities based on value commitments and/or understandings of how the congregation should relate to secular society. Thus, a collective commitment to seek justice for oppressed groups may lead a congregation to allow same-sex-union ceremonies.[7]

## Neighborhood/Environmental Factors

The wider institutional environments in which congregations are located also shape them. Some neighborhoods are heavily dominated by a single denomination, as is our Westside neighborhood by the Catholic Church, and others by a general type of church, as is our Southtown area by Protestant churches of a fundamentalist bent. Recent theoretical and empirical work that treats local religious systems as *markets* indicates that congregations may use neighboring congregations as reference groups.[8] In other words, a congregation may define its mission and identity in contradistinction to those of others in the neighborhood or look for help to those among its neighbors who are more successful at recruiting or retaining members. This suggests that congregations may develop policies and programs around sexuality issues in order to define themselves differently from neighboring congregations or to model themselves after congregations that appear to be growing or more connected to the community.

A second environmental feature that affects congregations' responses to sexuality issues concerns the role of nonreligious organizations in the neighborhood. Some areas have numerous social services provided by local secular agencies, while others are lacking in programs beyond those offered by churches and religious organizations. For example, one physician in Southtown, a predominantly poor African American neighborhood lacking in city resources, told us: "Churches have a mandate to care for the poor, and they are

---

7. We do not have complete data on the culture of each congregation in our sample, given the nature of the data-collection method that we employed. However, we have some information about congregations' theological and ideological positions, stories, and rituals. For more on the culture of congregations, see Becker (1999), Ammerman (1997), and Ammerman, Carroll, McKinney, and Dudley (1998, 78–104).

8. In this chapter, we treat the three Chicago neighborhoods, not as markets, but as settings in which congregations define themselves in relation to one another. An excellent empirical study of how congregations model themselves after or define themselves against other congregations in their neighborhood is Eiseland (1997). For theoretical work on religious markets, see Finke and Stark (1992) and Young (1997).

vital institutions in the black community." The emphasis on the church as a service provider carried across institutions in this neighborhood. Churches may work closely with each other or with secular groups, giving them options for referring members with problems to outside agencies. In Chicago, some political wards have more pull with City Hall in obtaining publicly funded services, while others are more dependent on local private groups. These factors affect the degree to which individual churches are called on to deal with certain types of problems and their ability to address them.

The demographic characteristics of the local population strongly organize the issues that become of particular concern to a given church. For example, Westside and Southtown have young population profiles, and religious leaders identify teenage sexuality as one of their pressing concerns. Conversely, in Shoreland, where a very small percentage of the total population is in the teenage range and gay residents form a visible local minority, clergy rank issues related to adult homosexuality as more important. In addition, given their long-standing concern with marriage and family, congregations in our study tend to be aware of the family concerns and dynamics of members and those within the larger neighborhood. In Southtown, this is reflected in efforts to reinforce the centrality of marriage in a community marked by low marriage rates and relatively high rates of single parenthood. In Westside and Erlinda, Catholic priests work within strong family networks and reinforce the centrality of families even as they try to resolve family or sexual problems arising from patriarchal gender roles and the culture of silence.[9]

As suggested in the examples above, the mores and cultures of particular groups within a neighborhood may profoundly shape sexual attitudes and behaviors. Local culture can compete with or reinforce religious understandings of and proscriptions regarding sexuality. For example, patriarchal attitudes toward gender dovetail with some conservative church teachings about marriage, but they may also encourage male promiscuity, the early onset of male sexuality, or the abuse of women (see Anderson, 1989). Shoreland's more liberal attitudes about sexual identity and partnering are reflected in many of its congregations' acceptance of and service to gay and lesbian persons. At the same time, these congregations seek to move people away from the dominant transactional market and toward the relational market. Clergy and lay leaders must attend to the sexual cultures and practices of community residents in order to understand the potential causes of sexual problems and to devise policies or interventions that are salient to church members and, thus, more likely to be effective.

9. On the culture of silence in Hispanic communities, see, e.g., Ellingson and Schroeder (chapter 4 in this volume).

## Shoreland: Acceptance and Accommodation within Mainline Protestantism

### *Overview*

Given their politically liberal constituency, particularly the concentration of openly identified gay persons, it was not surprising that the religious leaders in Shoreland articulated very tolerant positions on sexuality. Sexuality is confirmed as a good gift from God within the context of a committed, monogamous relationship. Rather than seeing some forms of sexuality as inherently sinful, many of these churches locate sin in the nature of the sexual relationship. Respondents emphasized that the purpose of sex is to develop love, intimacy, and wholeness in committed relationships. Thus, promiscuity, hedonism, and abuse are rejected. Paraphrased field notes from an interviewer illustrate this approach: God made people to love and things to use; our sin is using people and loving things; when you have sex to make yourself feel good and do not love your partner, then you are abusing God's gift; if you love someone and have sex, God does not condemn you, regardless of your partner's orientation. In general, the normative frameworks articulated by those members of the clergy whom we interviewed are anchored in the values of tolerance or acceptance and are based on a critical reading of Scripture. Church leaders in Shoreland intend such frameworks to be clear alternatives to a powerful gay sexual culture in the neighborhood that is characterized by the absence of commitment and a high degree of sexual leniency or freedom.[10] Their more inclusive understanding of normal or moral sexuality is one of the key differences between Shoreland congregations and those from other neighborhoods.

A second important difference is the lack of attention to marriage and the family. Individuals or couples are defined as the primary sexual unit, and Shoreland leaders rarely discuss the long-standing Christian ideology linking sexual behavior and procreation. Not only does the more accepting normative frame mitigate against such a discussion, but, more important, the demographic reality of significant numbers of singles (gay and straight) in these congregations makes the issue of procreation less relevant and potentially offensive.[11]

The final important difference between the Shoreland congregations and

---

10. On Chicago's gay sexual culture, see Herdt (1992a). On gay culture more generally, see Murray (1996).

11. When they occurred, discussions of the family were framed in terms of the church operating as a surrogate family—logical in a neighborhood where most residents are transplants. Family was also discussed in terms of reconciling gay and lesbian members with their estranged parents and/or siblings (especially in cases of AIDS).

those in the other neighborhoods was that all the leaders interviewed in Shoreland reported homosexuality as the most pressing sexual issue facing their congregation. Many of these congregations are open about and affirming of homosexuality, and a handful take even more politicized positions—calling openly gay pastors, conducting same-sex-union ceremonies, and getting involved in the fight to secure civil rights for gay and lesbian persons. Even congregations within hierarchical denominations that officially condemn homosexual behavior and reject same-sex unions and the ordination of gays and lesbians (i.e., Lutheran and Episcopal) welcome gays and lesbians. One Lutheran pastor spoke with pride about his congregation's decision over twenty years ago to be the first Lutheran congregation in the neighborhood "to ignore the church's teachings and embrace gays and lesbians." Yet many of the congregations in more hierarchical polities struggle with the conflict between official teachings and sexual practices that violate those teachings. Members of a Roman Catholic gay and lesbian para–church group claimed that they turned to a Catholic tradition that encourages individuals to rely on their own consciences to resolve moral dilemmas instead of on doctrine. Two informants called this a *cafeteria-style* approach to religion, saying that they reject some doctrines (e.g., masturbation as sin or official bans on birth control) that seem "absurd" but follow others that make sense for their lives. "Come on," said one, when asked about reconciling Roman Catholic teaching on homosexuality with the existence of this congregation, "Americans take a cafeteria-style approach to religion. You pick and choose what you want. Many heterosexuals use birth control even though they're Catholic. When I was a teenager, masturbation was a mortal sin. If you ask today, very few priests would subscribe to that view. So things change, and that lessens the power of a seemingly absurd doctrine. A lot is left to individual conscience in Catholicism."

Thus, some ministers and congregations more aggressively depart from denominational teachings on homosexuality, while others promulgate a "don't ask, don't tell" approach. Several congregations specialize as places where gays and lesbians can safely come out, find support, or cope with HIV/AIDS. Three congregations (one Roman Catholic, one Protestant, and one Reform Jewish) were established specifically to serve gay and lesbian populations that had no publicly recognized place within other congregations in their respective traditions. For example, the president of Congregation Shalom described the founding of her congregation in these terms: "Twenty years ago a group of gay men began to meet in each other's homes because they wanted a place where they could reconcile their gay identities with memories of Jewish life, and, at the time, it was impossible to be openly gay and Jewish."

These more tolerant positions on sexuality should be understood as responses by religious organizations to several interrelated pressures stemming from the demographic and religious environment of Shoreland. First, the population of Shoreland is less religious than is that of the greater metropol-itan area or our other two neighborhoods. Almost one-quarter of Shoreland residents report having no religious affiliation, compared to fewer than 10 percent of residents in the other neighborhoods. Shoreland residents also re-port much lower church-attendance rates than do residents of the other neigh-borhoods (fewer than 15 percent attend at least once per month, whereas over 35 percent of the men and 50 percent of the women in the other two neighborhoods attend at least once per month). Moreover, our informants noted that many gay and lesbian members have a history of being rejected by the religion of their childhood because of their sexual orientation; thus, re-turning to formal religion is difficult (see Gray & Thumma, 1997; Dillon, 1999). As one pastor noted: "People want to go back to the churches in which they were raised and be accepted there. . . . [B]ut change there [in mainline Protestant churches] has not happened as quickly as I had envisioned." Thus, traditional denominations and formally institutionalized religion are still viewed with suspicion by some gay and lesbian Shorelanders.

Second, marital status and education level are two important predictors of religiosity. So the fact that Shoreland residents are overwhelmingly single (over 80 percent of men and women) and highly educated (over half have a college degree, and a fifth have advanced degrees) suggests that neighborhood churches face a small pool of potential members (see Wuthnow, 1988, 171–72; Roof, 1993, 156–58; Marler & Hadaway, 1993). Shoreland is also a "tran-sition" neighborhood where young, single, white professionals live for a few years before marrying and moving away, further reducing the pool of resi-dents most likely to join a religious organization.

Third, mainline Protestant churches in the neighborhood attract only 17 percent of Shoreland residents—a pool that grows slowly or not at all, ac-cording to recent scholarship documenting the decline of mainline Protes-tantism (see Greeley, 1989; Roof & McKinney, 1985; Warner, 1994; Wuth-now, 1988). Shoreland congregations must approach issues of sexuality with great care in order to avoid alienating current members or deterring prospec-tive ones. In short, churches and synagogues in Shoreland must contend with a small pool of potential members and a general population that views reli-gion with indifference or suspicion. They must also offer services or pro-grams that can compete with those offered by secular organizations and the weekend leisure activities of neighborhood residents (from people watching at sidewalk cafés to playing softball in the neighborhood's main park).

## Case Study: Water Street UCC

Water Street United Church of Christ (UCC) is the archetype of the liberal, activist church. For over thirty years, the congregation has been involved in controversial social-justice issues facing mainline Protestants—racism, home-lessness, the sanctuary movement, gender equality, and gay rights. It is a con-gregation loaded with "Alinsky"-style community organizers, and, histori-cally, members have pushed the congregation to take action on behalf of oppressed populations—from fighting the ward machine over homelessness in Shoreland to engaging in civil disobedience in support of the sanctuary movement in the 1980s. The congregation's journey toward becoming an open and affirming congregation (i.e., welcoming of gay and lesbian persons) is illustrative of how Pastor Charmot and Water Street approach sexuality.

In 1974, a group of gay men from the neighborhood approached Charmot about using the church building to hold their own service because they had been expelled from another mainline Protestant church where they had been worshiping. Charmot noted: "This was the beginning of our consciousness of gay and lesbian issues." Later in the year, the gay group invited the con-gregation to share a Thanksgiving dinner, and Pastor Charmot claimed that this "opened up a lot of people to the humanity of gays and lesbians." In 1975, Water Street was short of church schoolteachers, and several men from the gay parish volunteered. According to Charmot, some people from the con-gregation "flipped out" when the offer was accepted, and, as a result, several members left the church.[12] However, those who stayed remained committed to being an inclusive and just church.

The next step came in the late 1980s during the AIDS crisis: "A member of their parish who works in an AIDS hospice started bringing one of the men to church. They [i.e., members of the congregation] worked through his dying with him. One powerful moment came during communion, when they stand in a circle and pass a common cup. The issue was not whether he would give them AIDS but rather whether they would give him something else that would kill him. Another man stood up in front of the congregation and announced that he was HIV positive. It was the first time he had told anyone. In fact, his parents didn't even know was gay. He told the parish, 'You are my family.'"

For many, the transformation into an open and affirming congregation was complete, and it was driven by a fundamental value commitment of both clergy and laity. According to Charmot, "if your doctrine is about inclusive-ness, you must act on that belief," and this accounts for both the membership decline and the appeal of the congregation to white liberals. Charmot also discussed how the congregation has carved out a niche in Shoreland: "We are fighting to retain a radical understanding of the church. Our radicalism is

12. The congregation's membership has declined from 200 in 1970 to 140 at the time of the interview, most people leaving, according to Charmot, because of the lib-eral and politicized actions of the congregation.

smart marketing in a way because not many churches have what we have. There is a clear reason to choose to join Water Street if you have certain commitments. But this has created conflict in the congregation as we need large numbers of volunteers to do the kind of work that makes us radical but we may need to relax in order to get more people into the church. There is always a temptation to compromise on some issues in the hope of raising membership."

In many ways, the movement toward becoming an open and affirming congregation was made possible by the value commitments of both laity and clergy within the context of a congregational polity. Water Street UCC sees its mission as one of pursuing social justice, and it is guided by the twin values of tolerance and inclusiveness. Moreover, its local autonomy within the United Church of Christ has allowed it to forge a position on human sexuality that is, it claims, more radical and truer to the gospel than is that of other neighborhood churches. Thus, like other local liberal Protestant churches, Water Street UCC affirms the goodness of human sexuality and welcomes gay and lesbian persons. However, unlike some of the more quietistic congregations in the neighborhood, Water Street seeks to live out these value commitments—even if it means losing members. Thus, it is willing to conduct same-sex-union ceremonies openly rather than sub rosa, as in the case of some area Episcopal churches. This combination of liberal policies and actions is the church's way of creating a niche among other Protestant churches in the neighborhood. Water Street offers a clear alternative to the "all talk but no action" styles of many of the other congregations in the neighborhood.

The normative framework at Water Street UCC is organized around inclusiveness, acceptance, and justice. The minister and the lay leader whom we interviewed claim that many people inside and outside the church have a profoundly flawed understanding of sexuality because it is based on fears of difference, prejudice, and an incorrect reading of the Bible. In educational programs as well as in worship, the congregation attempts to help members and other congregations think about sexuality in ways that overcome stereotypes, fears, and selectively literal readings of the Bible. Elizabeth, a volunteer educator who described the church's sex-education course, notes that the general goal is to help people and churches understand that "everything God created is good. There is nothing intrinsically wrong with the body, and there is nothing intrinsically bad about sexual behavior, [whether it is] masturbation, homosexuality, or intercourse. We make these things bad by treating them the wrong way."

Elizabeth continues by placing sexuality in the context of love for God, self, and others. When sexual behavior is divorced from a loving, committed relationship in which both partners put the other ahead of their own pleasure or needs, then it is bad. Her comments identify two other features of the Water Street framework. First, sexuality is explicitly linked to love relationships, and the only judgment of sexual behavior arises when sex is used for selfish purposes. Second, there is a strong therapeutic undercurrent. Both leaders place sexuality in a larger context of promoting self-love, self-acceptance, and self-respect and encouraging people to think or act sexually in ways that will result in these psychological ends.

The church's reliance on psychology and therapy as the means to understand sexual problems and develop solutions for them is another identifying characteristic of the normative frame employed by many churches in Shoreland. Counseling and therapy are seen as part of a normal and healthy life, and the neighborhood has a dense network of private counselors and social-service agencies available for ministerial referrals. Most clergy conduct a small number of counseling sessions with their parishioners—almost like intake interviews—and then refer them to private therapists or any number of mental-health clinics. In the other neighborhoods, the therapeutic frame is less salient. Clergy in predominantly Hispanic congregations suggest that many members, especially Mexican immigrants, distrust secular mental-health professionals. Immigrants often do not go to the secular therapist to whom they have been referred, preferring to consult their priest or parish counselor. In the African American neighborhood, there are few private therapists or mental-health services available. Instead, many churches develop counseling ministries for staff and lay members alike.

Water Street's normative framework is most evident in its educational work. The church offers workshops for other Chicago-area churches on becoming an open and affirming congregation. The curriculum is set up to debunk misreadings of the Bible on homosexuality, teach participants to read Scripture more critically, and help them integrate contemporary scholarship on sexuality with Christian understandings of the subject. According to Elizabeth, workshop leaders begin by challenging the legitimacy of common interpretations and applications of biblical passages on homosexuality. Biblical proscriptions are placed in the context of ancient Jewish society and the broader set of purity codes—most of which modern Western societies do not follow. The problem, she points out, is that U.S. Christians often claim that Old Testament or Pauline prohibitions on homosexuality are universal but that other purity laws are not, a practice that defies sound logic and threatens to undermine scriptural authority. Leaders urge class members to replace the selective application of Old Testament laws with a more critical and principled hermeneutic—that is, thinking about the Bible as providing universal principles about how humans are to interact and build just societies. Jesus' teachings about liberation, love of neighbor, and leaving judgment in the hands of God are cited to support the view that gays and lesbians should be treated with respect and loved as equal members in the family of God.

Water Street's approach to sexuality may be summarized in the pastor's favorite phrase (repeated several times during the interview and on a sign at the church entrance): "God is not mocked." In other words, the rejection and even hatred of gays and lesbians in other Christian churches, based on claims of piety, morality, and biblical purity, are false, evil, and at odds with the life of Jesus. Just as Yahweh rejected the disingenuous burnt offerings of the ancient Israelites, so today will God reject the pious diatribes against homosexuality made by many Christians.

## Case Study: Saint Pontain's Episcopal

Saint Pontain's normative framework regarding sexuality is similar to that of Water Street UCC, but without an activist orientation.[13] Its identity is, rather, as a community of worship and refuge. Father Downing notes that most people attending are looking for a home or a place of relief from the weight of their lives. Prayer and the Episcopal liturgy, rather than politics, are the focus of the congregation's collective life. Father Downing notes that the congregation intentionally does not follow the same tack as Water Street: "They [Water Street] are mainly concerned with 'Christian socialism' and are not interested in Christian liturgy and prayer. . . . On this we don't see eye to eye." In short, Saint Pontain's aims to serve a particular pool of potential members—middle-class liberals who want a supportive, contemplative community rather than the pace and commitment of an activist church—and it accomplishes this by capitalizing on its denominational traditions. This identity as a refuge or haven church and its membership in the Episcopal Church are key factors that shape how Saint Pontain's addresses sexuality.

Father Downing initially talked about his congregation in broadly therapeutic terms. He described the members of his church as people in search of a community who come from dysfunctional family backgrounds. Father Downing estimated that upward of 80 percent of his members were "emotionally disabled" and, thus, came to Saint Pontain's "as people with burdened lives looking for relief." When we asked about the sorts of things with which members struggle, he launched into a discussion of sexuality. In particular, he identified several issues surrounding homosexuality and members' struggles with their sexual orientation. He noted that people are trying to resolve sexuality issues; they want to be told that they are not crazy. He sees a lot of married men who are realizing that they are gay, and men who are sexually inactive but gay, and who believe that it is immoral to have sexual relationships

13. Saint Pontain's is active in a coalition of neighborhood organizations that runs a food pantry and a homeless shelter, but it rejects the political action and politicization of religion favored by Water Street.

with other men. He tries to reassure them that God does not condemn people for being homosexual or engaging in homosexual behavior if they love their partner. He also tries to create a religious community where gay men are accepted and affirmed and can come to accept their sexuality as good and valued by God and their fellow parishioners. Yet the members are not interested in a community in which sexuality is politicized, and they fear taking public stands that could damage the community. Thus, Saint Pontain's strives to be a place where one can safely be out or, just as safely, remain in the closet.

Saint Pontain's has a significant number of parishioners with HIV or AIDS. Father Downing sees his ministry and the mission of the congregation as, first, to welcome these people into the church. Then, the church's role is to help those suffering from the illness come to terms with disease and death, rediscover their faith, and answer fundamental questions about self-identity, God, and the afterlife. In the end, those who move beyond the phase of anger about having contracted the disease "discover a well of faith they didn't know they had," and they do this through the liturgical life of the congregation and individual counseling. Father Downing focuses his energies on providing the rich liturgical and spiritual experience of worship but taps into neighborhood resources and refers members to local AIDS support groups and therapists for long-term counseling and health care.

One of the few political activities of the congregation is its fund-raiser during the annual Pride Day. Unlike Water Street UCC, Saint Pontain's remains in the background, quietly working to alleviate suffering (through its donations to AIDS nonprofits), rather than trying to change the structures and social attitudes that marginalize AIDS as a gay disease. Like Water Street, Saint Pontain's relies on the tools of biblical criticism to interpret scriptural passages on sexuality and justify its normative frameworks and decisions to take public action on sexuality issues. Father Downing argued that, in the rare instances where the Bible mentions homosexuality, abusive relationships and inhospitality are denounced, not homosexuality per se. In addition, Father Downing reports that his congregation locates its understanding of Christianity in the fundamental truth claim that God loves all people, as revealed by Scripture and experience. This hermeneutic was evident during a recent conflict during a Pride Day event. Members from a nearby fundamentalist church complained about the strawberry daiquiris that Saint Pontain's was selling. The argument about the moral legitimacy of a church selling alcohol was finally settled when a fundamentalist's challenge to the sale of alcoholic beverages—"Don't you believe in the Bible?"—was met by Saint Pontain's reply: "No, we believe in God, but we find the Bible helpful."

Despite its welcoming stance on homosexuality, Saint Pontain's follows official Episcopal doctrines on sexuality. The church will not perform same-sex-union ceremonies, although Father Downing will offer a formal blessing at one if asked. When asked why he would not marry gay or lesbian couples, the priest offered a rationale that he said reflected the official position of the Episcopal Church: "Doctrinally, a marriage is a sign of a relation between God and humanity; it is meant for creative purposes. People of the same sex can't procreate. It's the possibility of doing so that is important because it is a sign of God's creation, an outward sign of inward grace." Father Downing acknowledges that the teaching authority of the national church constrains how he and the congregation deal with sexuality. He also said that the specter of a conservative backlash against priests and congregations for being too radical on homosexuality (here he referred to the disciplinary action against an East Coast bishop, prompted by a hostile conservative laity) also shapes the difference between the public and the private identities of Saint Pontain's. His advocacy of an ethic of tolerance and the relational framework described above may be understood as an attempt to distance the congregation from the more intolerant official position that he abides by in public and to signal to the neighborhood residents looking for a church home that Saint Pontain's actually holds liberal positions on sexuality.

For many members, Saint Pontain's is their family. In its worship, pastoral care, and social life, the church seeks collectively to affirm the dignity and worth of its members—many of whom are struggling to accept their sexual orientation, cope with rejection by their family of origin, or face the realities of being HIV positive. Saint Pontain's message of God's unconditional love trumps the message of God's judgment and damnation that members hear from conservative church neighbors. In a language rooted in modern psychology and a centuries-old liturgical tradition, Saint Pontain's welcomes everyone, without question.

These cases identify the two common approaches to sexuality of liberal and moderate religions in the neighborhood: public advocacy and inclusivity, on the one hand, and private acceptance, on the other. Polity allows some congregations great freedom with regard to sexuality issues, as is evident at Water Street, while it sets limits on other congregations, as is evident at Saint Pontain's. At the same time, different value commitments—inclusivity and political action for Water Street, compassion and conflict avoidance at Saint Pontain's—lead these congregations toward different normative orientations and practices. The case studies also reveal how each congregation tailors its approach to sexuality to fit the needs and interests of its core members and the significant gay and lesbian population of the neighborhood. In general, none of the congregations in Shoreland condemn members engaging in sexual practices that have been defined as immoral. Instead, through education, counseling, and ritual, these congregations attempt to channel individuals toward monogamous, committed, and egalitarian sexual partnerships.

## Southtown: Empowering the Community and Rebuilding the Family in the Black Church

### *Overview*

Historically, Southtown has worn the sobriquet *a community of churches*. From the late nineteenth century until the 1960s, Dutch Reform, Lutheran, Methodist, and Presbyterian churches dotted the neighborhood and served a predominantly white, immigrant, working-class population. Today, the neighborhood still houses numerous church buildings, but the composition of neighborhood churches has switched from mainline to more conservative Protestantism. Nearly 73 percent of religious adherents in Southtown belong to conservative Protestant churches that range from small storefront Pentecostal churches, to aging churches within the historically black denominations (e.g., African Methodist Episcopal), to large Baptist or nondenominational churches that characterize similar urban African American neighborhoods (see Jones, 1993; Gilkes, 1995). Not surprisingly, 58 percent of churchgoers identify themselves as "born again," and nearly 31 percent attend church at least once a week.[14]

The demographic, economic, and political changes that have transformed the neighborhood have also reshaped the composition and mission of religious organizations in Southtown. The population of Southtown shifted from predominantly white to nearly all African American between 1960 and 1980. This shift was accompanied by the deindustrialization of the entire South Side, a concomitant loss of commercial and retail businesses, and a relatively steady decline in city services, health-care institutions, educational facilities, and housing stock. Informants repeatedly stressed unemployment, inadequate housing and schools, the general lack of social and health services, and increasing gang violence and drug use as critical problems facing their neighborhood.

Informants also claimed that the problems arising from three decades of social and economic decline are the primary causes of the most frequently reported sexual problems: sexually transmitted diseases (especially AIDS); teen pregnancy; and domestic violence. Unlike the clergy in Shoreland, who rely on a therapeutic or psychological frame to understand and address the sex-related problems of their parishioners or neighborhood, many Southtown clergy locate the cause of sexual problems outside the individual, in

14. In Westside, 33.9 percent report being born again, while only 26.2 percent of the respondents in the countywide sample and 17.5 percent of the Shoreland sample make this claim. Weekly attendance in the other neighborhoods ranges from a high of about 25 percent to a low of 6 percent.

external social forces. A biblical interpretive lens often undergirds this interpretive scheme.

In general, the black church has taken a relatively conservative stance on sexuality, publicly advocating an ethic of control. Jackson (1983, 206–10, 204) reports that the church has upheld strong taboos against premarital and extramarital sex and opposed divorce and abortion. She qualifies this claim by noting that it is Pentecostal churches that are more likely to enforce these taboos and that churches within mainline Protestantism and the historic black churches tend to denounce but tolerate sex outside marriage, as long as it is conducted discreetly. A Presbyterian informant, the Reverend Townsend, agreed with this assessment, noting that the entire range of black churches—from mainline, to Baptist, to storefront Pentecostal—upholds strict moral teachings: "They don't believe in people living together unless they're married and are opposed to divorce, abortion, and homosexuality. The foundation of the church is family, so any deviation from that paradigm is wrong." At the same time, he said, many churches also allow for deviations as long as they are not discussed or made known in a public manner. For example: "No one talks about abortion, even though everyone knows it takes place. It's a thing not to do because African Americans think of themselves as a family who will help raise a child."

Similarly, most congregations are aware that gays and lesbians are active members of their churches, and they follow an implicit norm of tolerating the behavior as long as individuals do not publicly identify themselves as gay or lesbian. As one minister noted, church members can accept someone being gay "as long as he or she doesn't talk about it."[15]

This conservative ethic is embodied in a variety of programs sponsored by Southtown churches—marriage counseling, singles' ministries, and youth education. These programs were described as efforts to teach young men and women biblically sanctioned views of marriage, dating, and gender relations while raising the dangers (moral and physical) of promiscuity and premarital sex. Several ministers noted that, on matters of sexuality, the church's role is to teach members to live according to the principles of the Bible, not society,

15. Black gay men contribute to the practice of hiding a gay identity in order to secure the space to be gay (Peterson, 1992, 150–51; see also Cohen, 1996). Moreover, African Americans openly identified as gay or lesbian may have their identities as African Americans and their commitment to the African American community questioned by neighbors, church members, or others (Cohen, 1996). One black informant told us that he was stunned when a friend told him he was gay and that he responded, in effect: "How can you be gay? You're black!" A gay identity is considered a "white thing." Thus, gays and lesbians in Southtown face strong pressures to keep their sexual identity and behavior private.

as the values and forces of the latter may cause sexual deviance. One hope is that, by reintegrating black men into the family and the church, area churches may ameliorate the numerous sex-related problems facing the neighbor-hood's young people.[16]

The centrality of marriage and the family and the belief in the naturalness and morality of heterosexuality are key reasons behind the rejection of ho-mosexuality and the publicly acknowledged failure of black churches to re-spond to AIDS (see Comstock, 1996, 189–92; Morris, 1990).[17] Few churches have ministries that specifically target people with HIV or AIDS. Several min-isters whom we interviewed denied the existence of homosexuality or AIDS in their congregations and even in the neighborhood itself. However, three ministers and several informants from health-care and social-service agencies disagreed. In the words of the Reverend Samuel: "Homosexuality is deep up in the black church, . . . [but many ministers] are in denial." He and others listed several explanations for area churches' response to homosexuality.

First, there is strong opposition to homosexuality in the community. Ho-mosexuality is condemned as "always wrong" by 80 percent of the men and 72 percent of the women in the Southtown sample, a rate that is 20 percent higher than among respondents in the overall Cook County sample. Fear of publicly violating this communal norm may contribute to the relative silence of neighborhood churches on the topic of homosexuality.

Second, as the moral centers of the community, ministers and churches may feel compelled to present themselves as morally pure.[18] Officially toler-ating homosexuality, which has been defined as a sin in these biblically ori-ented churches, may be seen as a mark of contamination, not only within the neighborhood, but also among white observers. The black church is one of the few black institutions respected by whites, and anything that could mar its integrity and bring disgrace to the community must be avoided. More-over, Southtown leaders from various institutional spheres made an explicit

16.  This emphasis on men and families is not unique to Southtown, being found in other urban black churches. Gilkes (1995, 186) notes that many of the new mega-churches are aggressively recruiting men between the ages of twenty and sixty. She quotes a leader from a large New York City church who provides the rationale for this strategy: "When you build black men, you build strong families and strong com-munities" (see also Taylor, Chatters, Tuckers, & Lewis, 1990).

17.  Lack of response to HIV/AIDS in the black community is also partly a legacy of the infamous Tuskegee syphilis study, allowed to run for forty years (1932–72). That experience left black communities wary of public-health programs, particularly those related to sexually transmitted disease (Thomas & Quinn, 1991).

18.  On the problems experienced by the research team in its attempts to secure interviews in Southtown, see Ellingson (chapter 10 in this volume, n. 6).

effort to depathologize black sexuality and present it as normal. This strategy is also meant to defuse racism in the white community and to build up members of the African American community.

Third, for churches that hold to a literal reading of the Bible and strongly adhere to an ethic of control, homosexuality must be condemned. Moreover, since members of more conservative congregations have been born again and presumably live sanctified lives (i.e., lives that are morally pure), they would not engage in homosexual behavior. Thus, homosexuality could not exist in these churches, and ministers' denials of the existence of homosexuality can be seen as authentic.

The institutional silence surrounding homosexuality carries over to church responses to other problematic sexual issues. Most ministers also denied that abortion, domestic violence, and sexual abuse were problems, and those that did not maintained that these problems are no more prevalent in black than in white congregations. Breaks with the norm of heterosexuality, the ethic of sexual control, or the integrity of the family are understood as threats to the church and the African American community. However, many informants acknowledged that churches are aware of the slippage between a conservative sexual ethic and the more liberal practices of neighborhood residents.[19] In public, churches deny the existence or importance of these problems while trying to address them through particular educational or social ministries that operate out of public view.

## Case Study: Saint Sebastian Church

Saint Sebastian's is a large Roman Catholic parish. It serves about nine hundred families and has an average Sunday attendance of eighteen hundred to two thousand people. It generally follows Catholic doctrine on sexuality: it condemns abortion and sex outside marriage and affirms the official positions on homosexuality and divorce. Yet how Saint Sebastian's justifies its stance on sexuality and goes about teaching, counseling, and enacting its sexual legislation resembles the practices of its conservative Protestant neighbors more than those of other Catholic parishes in the city.

According to Father Felner, Saint Sebastian's ministries rely on the Bible

19. For example, 17 percent of Southtown households are headed by single mothers, compared with fewer than 10 percent in Westside and only 2 percent in Shoreland. Similarly, Southtown adults reported higher rates of having ever cheated on a spouse (31 percent vs. 20 percent countywide, 21 percent in Shoreland, and 7 percent in Westside) and of either having had an abortion themselves or having had a woman they got pregnant have an abortion (27 percent vs. 21 percent countywide, 23 percent in Shoreland, and 17 percent in Westside).

to help their members form moral templates that will guide behavior and develop a set of values to counteract the hedonistic (or, in his words, "the feel-good") values of secular society. The Bible provides universal truths about right and wrong behavior and identifies the goals and priorities that ought to direct Christians. Father Felner places the Bible over church teachings when the two conflict on sexuality issues. For example, he defended the congregation's permissive stance on birth control for couples who are not emotionally or financially ready to start a family by arguing: "If the Catholic Church has a teaching that is contrary to the Bible, they reserve the right to disagree with that teaching. Clearly the institutional Catholic Church has a problem with this issue. Honoring the authority of the church is a must, but we must also be allowed to disagree." Yet Father Felner upholds church teachings on divorce and marriage, and it seems that the compromises are driven in part by an effort to make the congregation's teachings and practices relevant to the context of Southtown.

As one of a few Catholic churches in a Southside sea of Protestantism, Saint Sebastian's has "indigenized" its style of worship, teaching, and devotional life to attract African Americans who may feel more at home in Protestant congregations. Placing the Bible at the center of preaching and teaching—a practice common among most African American churches—is perhaps the clearest means of meeting the spiritual and cultural needs of its audience.[20] The importance of using the Bible as the central authority for moral education is suggested by the comments of another local minister, who noted that most of the independent black churches in the neighborhood neither talk about sexuality nor take anything but a conservative stance on the issue because to do so would be to "go against Scripture" and, therefore, would not "be in tune with the values of the community."

Thus, Saint Sebastian's normative framework regarding sexuality also echoes the conservative position on sexuality that operates in most Protestant African American congregations. It is grounded in a literalist reading of the Bible and a Manichaean view of the world. Father Felner claimed that there is an ongoing war between the spirit and the flesh within every person and organization. Either the spiritual or the sinful will shape society's values, which in turn will shape the values of individuals. He continued by arguing that most

20. For a fuller example of an African American parish that has adopted the style and practices of black Protestantism, see Laudarji and Murphy (1996). Lincoln and Mamiya (1990, 159) note that the growing numbers of Catholic African Americans may be due in part to middle-class parents joining the Catholic Church after placing their children in parish schools. Saint Sebastian's operates an elementary school, and this resource may be another means by which the church attracts new members in this overwhelmingly Protestant neighborhood.

people will act according to the values of society unless they are given the knowledge about how to act morally, and that comes only from the Bible. This normative frame places moral sexuality in the context of heterosexual marriage and family formation, which is consistent both with Catholic doctrine and with the ethic of control dominant in the black church.

The centrality of the Bible, and an almost evangelical Protestant concern with "getting one's relationship right with God," is evident in how the church teaches young people about sexuality and marriage. The church runs separate educational and social ministries for young men and women. One of the first questions raised in these meetings is: "What does the Bible have to say about living as a single man or woman?" In these ministries, Father Felner teaches that young people must first learn how to live according to biblical principles and establish a relationship with God—only then can they develop dating and marriage relationships. The priest noted that, because the Bible (not Rome) affirms sex only within the bounds of marriage, cohabitation and premarital sex are sinful. During premarital counseling, the first step is to question the couple about whether they are sexually active. If they are, he demands that they put a stop to it. Then the couple is assigned same-sex mentors from among the older married parishioners. This strict moral code may be a strategy to combat the perceived sexual dangers surrounding Southtown young people: an environment characterized by seemingly high rates of teenage pregnancy, premarital sex, cohabitation, and drug use.[21]

Repeatedly, Father Felner used the Protestant trope of *the transforming power of the Word* as the organizing principle of Saint Sebastian's approach to sexuality. This belief in the power of the Bible to change individual behavior is evident in how the congregation addresses homosexuality (and other forms of sexual deviance). Father Felner notes that the Bible clearly identifies homosexuality as sinful. However, like other Catholic churches, Saint Sebastian's "loves the sinner but hates the sin." Felner said that he tries "to plant the seed" that homosexuality is a sin that can be stopped by repentance and a change of heart. The church must welcome homosexuals and provide opportunities for them to change. As an interviewer's log reports: "He knows there are homosexuals who come to his church, just as there are people who are living out of wedlock. People have all kinds of problems, and the church cannot require them to solve them before they come to worship. The church is like a hospital; you don't have to be well to come. He will never get up in the pulpit and say, 'Homosexuals are going to hell.' The Word is what should

21. We asked nine health-care and social-service providers to identify Southtown's major problems and their causes. All reported sexually transmitted diseases and teen pregnancy as the top problems and identified (in rank order) the following as causes: drug use and sex that is traded for drugs; gangs; bad schools; and unemployment.

heal you." This approach to homosexuality mirrors the stance taken by some of the more conservative Protestant congregations in the neighborhood, for whom the family is the foundation of the church and society and any deviation from that position is morally wrong.

In sum, the normative framework and educational/counseling programs of Saint Sebastian's emphasize control in an environment perceived as advocating tolerance and promiscuity. Situational ethics is rejected in favor of the universal truths about sexuality and gender relations that are clearly stated in the Bible. The church has developed its framework and programs in response to official church teachings (some of which have no relevance to the lives of members) and problems stemming from a poor, inner-city environment. First, by sounding conservative themes that are anchored in the Bible, the framework aligns the church with official Catholic positions on sexuality while at the same time offering a mode of teaching and preaching that is appealing to and resonant with the neighborhood's African American population. Second, the normative frame and programs directly address the social and sexual problems facing young African Americans living in Southtown.

## Case Study: Third Avenue UCC

While Saint Sebastian's seeks to empower its members morally, Third Avenue seeks to produce a more comprehensive set of social ministries. The church has roughly eight thousand members and a staff of seven ministers, two M.S.W.'s (an M.S.W. is a master's of social work), and twenty-one full-time and forty-two part-time volunteer support personnel. Third Avenue houses sixty-five ministries ranging from sexual issues such as HIV/AIDS, domestic violence, marriage counseling, and divorce to social problems such as drug and alcohol abuse, legal aid, and housing. Separate ministries have been established for men, women, grandparents, singles, and couples. Like other megachurches in African American communities, Third Avenue has stepped into the social-service vacuum and marshaled its financial and human resources to meet the needs of members and nonmembers alike.[22]

Third Avenue's approach to sexuality focuses on liberation over condemnation and institutional control. The goal of its marriage-counseling ministry, for example, is to liberate the individual and the couple from any number of intra- and interpersonal obstacles that might hinder a successful marriage (e.g.,

22. For example, Third Avenue Church stocks the food bank at a nearby storefront church and has been involved in trying to defuse gang violence in the city. On the social-service role of the black church, especially the new generation of large, neo-Pentecostal churches, see Gilkes (1995), Jones (1993, 238), and Lincoln and Mamiya (1990, 196–273).

unrealistic expectations about marriage). The associate minister whom we interviewed summarized the liberating goals and rationale that structure Third Avenue's marriage counseling and, more generally, the church's normative framework regarding sexuality: "The ideal [of marriage] is not to negate the other person but rather to get inside of them and try to understand them. At Third Avenue, we try to stress the whole issue of difference. Each person has a background completely different from that of his or her own mate. We stress the unconditional acceptance of a person. . . . If you could get inside the other person and understand them, you would not be so hard on them."

While Third Avenue affirms the goodness of marriage and upholds biblical teaching on the practice, its pastoral staff allows for alternative forms of sexual relationships. They do not judge members who cohabitate or have been divorced. Pastor Jones sounded the themes of tolerance and empowerment during his discussion of homosexuality. Third Avenue is one of the few black churches in the neighborhood not condemning homosexuality. The church follows the UCC's open and affirming policy and justifies its position with reference to the biblical model of Jesus. Pastor Jones explained that, because Jesus did not sit in judgment over the outcasts of his day but embraced those who were different or were judged immoral by society, the church today has the same responsibility. Third Avenue welcomes gays and lesbians into its collective life and challenges members and the African American community to reflect on which set of norms (divine or human) guides their response to homosexuality.[23]

Third Avenue is also one of the few neighborhood churches publicly to acknowledge the threat of AIDS and to challenge the community, especially other churches, to address the problem. The senior pastor preached a sermon entitled "Good News for the Homosexual," in which "he challenged other churches who would sit in judgment: who says yours is the norm?" According to Pastor Jones, the central message of the sermon demonstrated the power of the Bible to help Christians and the church come to grips with homosexuality and the problem of AIDS in the black community: "Homophobics will turn to passages in Paul and Leviticus [but forget] that Jesus dined with the homosexuals of his day—the tax collectors, the sinners, the sick. And then, on Calvary, Jesus said, 'Father forgive them for they know not what they do.' Does dogma bring people into the church or turn them away? This should be the litmus test. Who are we to turn people away? Gays and lesbians will not be turned away from this church."

23. Several informants from other institutional arenas claimed that Third Avenue tolerates gays and lesbians but does not necessarily accept them. Their description of the church suggests that it is not as liberal as the minister whom we interviewed would have us believe.

The congregation's AIDS ministry was established after this sermon. Pastor Jones continued on this theme and argued that ministers who claim that homosexuality or AIDS does not exist in their churches are more concerned with protecting the moral reputation of the institution than with dealing effectively with the disease. He rejected the argument that the African American community is so overburdened with the problems of racism, poverty, and unemployment that it cannot deal with AIDS and concluded: "The problem with this attitude is that AIDS exists in the community. Ignoring it won't change that. It's here. Somebody's got to break the silence. Our people need AIDS awareness."

Scripture guides the congregation's position on AIDS and homosexuality, Pastor Jones noting that the church takes it from Jesus' example. Just as Jesus did not judge the social outcasts of his day but accepted them as they were, so too should the church accept the social outcasts of today. Pastor Jones ended this part of the discussion with the simple declarative phrase: "I don't sit high enough to judge." This does not mean that the congregation is saying that it is OK to be gay, only that it has no right to judge and that gays and lesbians are people who need help from the church. In this biblically centered way, Third Avenue hopes to empower the community to address one of its more deadly social problems.

With its willingness to talk openly about homosexuality and its use of a biblically based ethic of tolerance to diagnose and redress problems, Third Avenue resembles other UCC congregations more than it does the other black churches in the neighborhood. However, these more liberal views are delivered via the familiar mechanisms of charismatic preaching, an appeal to the life and words of Christ rather than academic debates about the social and historical context of biblical writings, and self-help ministries based in the congregation itself. While Third Avenue may break from the dominant conservative position on sexuality espoused by other churches, it does so on the basis of arguments about facing up to the problems of the neighborhood and the broader black community rather than on the basis of claims that homosexual relationships are moral in and of themselves, as do such white UCC congregations as Shoreland's Water Street. Third Avenue's position and programs on sexuality reflect a judicious blending of liberal theology, a realistic assessment of the social-sexual problems facing Southtown residents, and traditional forms of preaching and self-help.

As the two case studies presented in this section illustrate, the congregations in Southtown attempt to channel sexual expression toward heterosexual marriage and family formation, whether pursuing a traditional or a more tolerant line. Although there is a recognition that alternative sexual expressions exist—for example, cohabitation, adultery, and homosexuality—these are clearly identified as deviations from the moral standard. Such activities are often tolerated and left unmarked, although they are sometimes actively discouraged. Compared to the congregations in Shoreland, Southtown congregations play a more active role in attempting to legitimate a narrowly defined sexual norm—one that promotes only heterosexual marriage and the formation of families. At the same time, within the fundamentalist Protestant tradition, these churches accommodate what is understood to be the common human condition of falling from grace before finding renewed salvation in a recommitment to biblical principles. Thus, while alternative lifestyles are not supported in Southtown as they are in Shoreland, neither are their adherents turned away from the church.

## Westside: Progressive Institutions Serving Conservative Immigrants

### Overview

Westside is predominately Catholic. Over 80 percent of Westsiders interviewed, white ethnics and Mexicans alike, identified as Catholic, only 8.5 percent as Protestant, and the remainder as professing either some other or no religion. This is a very traditional and very religious population. It is characterized by high rates of both church attendance and reports of being born again—44 percent for the latter, compared with 10 percent of Catholics in the countywide cross-section, a statistic that likely reflects the more emotional and magical character of the rural Mexican Catholic religion that immigrants bring with them.[24]

The practices of the local Catholic churches reflect the changing demographics of Westside over the past four decades, with most now offering Spanish masses, but several still offering mass in languages such as Polish and Lithuanian. All Catholic priests with whom we spoke were non-Hispanic whites. However, many were familiar with at least one Latino culture and spoke Spanish. In these cases, the experience that qualified them to serve a Mexican community came from having lived somewhere in Latin America, generally not Mexico. As a result, many of them had affinities with the liberation theology of Nicaragua, El Salvador, or Brazil.[25]

24. One parish counselor whom we interviewed noted that she keeps certain items of magical significance on her desk to reassure her clients and open the door to discussions of "witchcraft," which is often intermingled with, or practiced alongside of, more standard Catholic rituals in rural Latin America.

25. Others, however, did not have this kind of background and were not as progressively minded. Rather, they had served the Westside area before it was predom-

The local institutional environment in Westside is strongly organized by the liberation-church model. One multiparish consortium has established a system of small "base communities" for Bible study, patterned after the liberation-church structure in Brazil; another consortium (with overlapping members) focuses on social issues and community organizing. The activities of these two groups are part of an overall strategy on the part of Westside Catholic churches devised to meet the problems of the local populace while attending simultaneously to their own organizational concerns. Fundamentalist Protestants have been highly successful in recruiting Hispanics to their ranks, a trend that has the Catholic Church concerned (see Hurtig, 1996). The archdiocese has put pressure on local churches to attend more carefully to the concerns of Mexican Americans. Practically, this means training more priests in Latin American culture and the Spanish language and incorporating the more expressive spirituality of religious Mexicans into the life of the parishes (e.g., incorporating popular rituals like the Stations of the Cross [see Puente & Quintanilla, 1997]). Base communities more directly involve Westside Catholics in the church, and they create strong nonkin social ties that provide needed support to Mexican families that have lost their extended-kin networks through immigration (Hurtig, 1996).

Westside religious organizations must also contend with a number of problems that arise from the organization of sexuality in the neighborhood. The sexual culture is conservative. Traditional gender roles and family formation are highly valued.[26] There is strong opposition to homosexuality and, more generally, a taboo against talking about sexuality, not only in public, but also in private. While women are expected to be virgins at the time of marriage and to remain faithful to their partners during marriage, men are allowed, and in some cases encouraged,[27] to engage in sex outside marriage,

---

inantly Mexican, tended to be much more conservative on sexual issues across the board, and were not generally networked with progressive social-service agencies. Their claim to legitimacy was longevity in the community.

26. Family is highly valued among Mexican Americans in Westside; however, immigration to the United States puts a severe strain on traditional gender roles and the patriarchal family structure. Strong extended-family ties and *compadrazco* (ritual godparenthood)—important elements of traditional Mexican social structure—are often lost or attenuated as a result of migration. Many residents look to the Catholic Church for help and to reinforce the traditional family ideal. Family-related issues are key sources of difficulties among Westside immigrants and points at which they may look to the church for help. On the cultural importance attached to strong families by Mexicans, see Bean and Tienda (1987) and Horowitz (1983).

27. Various informants told us that Mexican-origin men might be expected to seek outside partners for activities deemed inappropriate with a legitimate wife. Such activities might simply be positions other than the missionary or might include

with either women or other men, so long as they continue to support their wife and children financially and spend time with their families.

Homosexuality poses particular institutional problems for Westside Catholic leaders. They must negotiate among a variety of cultural and religious understandings in such a way that they neither legitimize the practice whereby straight-identified men are allowed to have same-sex partners, condone homophobic attitudes and practices, nor legalistically apply church teachings out of context. Some local priests interpret the organization of homosexuality in Westside through the lens of liberation theology. For instance, on the basis of his nine years in Peru, Father O'Connell extends the teachings of the liberation church regarding economic emancipation to sexuality. Oppression is not only economic, he explained, but also psychological, gender based, and sexual. His response to homosexuality—opposition to the patriarchal structures that denigrate gay men—is an instance of this strategy. To him, Mexican sexual culture is one of "oppression, suppression, and homophobia," an admission that there is a religious aspect to this condemnation.

When asked how this might relate to the official Catholic teaching on homosexuality, Father O'Connell admitted that it is a "sticky issue." The official distinction between act and person is impossible to uphold in practice since people are not divisible in this way. The Vatican is trapped in "medieval models of the person." Instead, he tries to tell a Mexican lesbian who comes into his office that she is "loved by God": "If you experience these desires, then perhaps this is where God wants you to be." Problems arise when the community holds homophobic values and sees them as religiously sanctioned. In this case, he reported, the whole family needs to experience something like a "faith conversion" in order to accept a lesbian daughter or a gay son. The case studies presented below illustrate how religious leaders must balance conservative pressures of doctrine "from above," community norms of morality "from below," the pastors' theological stance on sexuality, and the disjuncture between behavior and the dominant ethic of control.

## Case Study: Saint Philomena's Catholic Church

Saint Philomena's is one of the Catholic churches in Westside with a leaning toward liberation theology. Father Gates, like other priests in this group, had spent several years in Latin America. Saint Philomena's has an identity as a place of safety, similar to the identity of Saint Pontain's, despite the priests' best efforts to push it in a more activist direction. The Catholic Church, Father

---

oral sex. Sex with a male partner was conceived of in this same manner: as a deviant *act,* not as a distinct sexual *orientation,* and, thus, as not threatening a marriage in and of itself.

Gates reported, is seen by Westsiders as a safe haven, a place where they can find help from people who speak Spanish and who will not ask them for legal papers. Other informants reported that most residents take their personal or family problems to the church first despite the neighborhood's impressive array of social-service agencies (most of them run by or tailored to the needs of local Hispanics). Many residents are unwilling to speak with secular counselors or social workers even if they have been referred by priests or church staff. Sexuality issues in particular are kept quiet and, if possible, left unspoken.

Father Gates seems more in tune with liberation theology's appeal to radical equality than to doctrinal positions taken by the Catholic Church. He expressed the opinion that the church's teaching on homosexuality was "fairly uncompromising" and that, instead, it should embrace all people as children of God. In private, he "feels free to move people toward attitudes of love." That is, he tries to open people's minds to the possibility that, for example, Jesus loves their daughter, who is a lesbian. However, in public, he is much more careful and feels constrained to follow church teachings, or at least to remain silent. We might guess that this reluctance results from knowledge that people in the community know the teachings of the church and believe in them. To deny them in public would be to alienate the majority of churchgoing Mexicans. Such an open stance on homosexuality flies in the face of the community's beliefs about family and sexuality. Father Gates said that families often refuse to accept that a son or daughter is homosexual and described a difficult counseling situation: "A mother with a lesbian daughter can't handle it. She thinks her daughter is going to hell and won't let her in the house."

Father Gates describes homosexuality in Westside in a manner congruent with the distinction between active and passive sex roles outlined in Ellingson and Schroeder (chapter 4 in this volume). He states that, while homosexuality is, doubtless, as prevalent in Westside as anywhere, nobody in his community would self-identify as gay. He relates this to the general trend among Mexicans to treat anything that threatens family relationships as sin. In order to preserve the family, it is easier to ignore problems, facing up to them only when they become unavoidable. Even then, neighborhood residents avoid dealing with the underlying causes of the problems, such as the sexual double standard and the machismo that mark Westside's sexual culture, and, instead, focus on the proximate causes. Homosexuality therefore gets scripted as an event rather than as an identity, an episode that passes or, more commonly, can be blamed on drinking. Father Gates noted that men often use the excuse "Father, I was drunk" to explain why they had sex with another man. Discussions about the deeper causes of homosexuality or sex outside marriage, such as Hispanic ideas of masculinity or the exercise of sexual power, are avoided. Father Gates tries to get people to deal with the underlying causes of sexual issues in the family—especially domestic violence and the abuse of children—but he is confronted with a real reluctance to deal with the issues as anything but momentary aberrations. Child sexual abuse, domestic violence, gang activity, alcoholism, teen pregnancy, and the like are understood to be problems, he said, only to the extent that they disrupt family relationships. Moreover, counseling, a preferred intervention from the church's perspective, is avoided because "it is seen as something that will further disrupt the family structure." Father Gates feels that this reflects the "downside" of Mexican familism.

The leaders of Saint Philomena's, like other area leaders from churches in the liberation-theology group, take a more liberal and activist stance than do members of their congregation. Father Gates tries, with local institutional support, to move his congregants (like the Good Shepherd) "toward attitudes of love," which in practice means moving them toward more tolerant and egalitarian ideas and practices even where these conflict with official church doctrine. The starting place for this is, he says, for the church to be "a welcoming station"—a place where people do feel supported, loved, and at home. Then they can be moved on to other things. His goal is to help people develop "attitudes of love" that will guide their thinking and action regarding homosexuality, marriage, and family relationships. Although Father Gates believes that he is clear on church doctrine, he says that he must begin from where people are. Around him, he sees people who are completely beaten down and need to be helped up again. This stance provides justification both for parting with official church doctrine (as an ostensibly interim measure) and for moving further from the practical mandates of radical social action prescribed by liberation theology and closer to the provision of immediate services most desired by church members.

## Case Study: Church of the Divine Word

Hispanics who feel alienated from the Catholic Church are turning more and more to the Pentecostal and evangelical churches for a viable alternative. While this is more common among Puerto Ricans, it is evident among Mexicans as well. While still a very small presence in Westside relative to the Catholic Church, Pentecostal churches are enjoying some growth.[28] Church of the

28. Only 6 percent of Westside residents could be considered Type II Protestants of any stripe; presumably, only a fraction of these are Pentecostal. Only 2 percent of our entire sample said that they were raised Pentecostal, and, of the 20 percent who do not follow the religion in which they were raised, only 7 percent became Pentecostal. Most members of Pentecostal and evangelical churches located in Westside are not area residents (Hurtig, 1996).

Divine Word is relatively small, with a total membership of about 200 former Catholics, including perhaps 125 children and young people. The building in which it is housed is small and dilapidated, evidence of the poverty of its membership. Although the Reverend Diaz is reluctant to characterize his congregants in any particular way, a mainline Protestant minister at a nearby church reports that Reverend Diaz's church, like similar churches, tends to attract the poor, the powerless (women and children), and social outcasts (drug addicts, indigenous people,[29] alcoholics). The strict rules of such churches, the observing pastor noted, serve to help people with serious problems pull their lives back together. Reverend Diaz does stress that he and his congregants do not try to hold themselves apart from gang members, drug users, and the like but instead try to befriend them and teach them that they can change. This approach is distinct from that of the Westside Catholic churches, which try to prevent their young members from mixing with gang-bangers in hopes of keeping them out of gangs.

Church of the Divine Word was once affiliated with the Pentecostal church but broke with it and is now aligned with the Church of God. Diaz characterizes his church as "conservative" and says that there was a time when it was the policy of the church to refuse to talk openly about sex. He cites two reasons for this: first, the Church of God generally considers speaking about sex to be evil; second, the Mexicans and Central Americans who attend his church believe that such things should remain unspoken. The cultural preference for silence on sexual issues remains, he says, and one must be cautious in the Westside community when talking about sex. If, for example, sexual issues are introduced to young people too quickly, their parents are likely to get angry. But, Diaz said, lack of education resulted in many problems in the community, and, ultimately, the church has to recognize the need to talk about these issues.

Reverend Diaz pointed to the general social environment as the reason that a change in policy was needed. He was adamant that his congregation was not troubled by problems such as teen pregnancy, domestic violence, and AIDS, echoing the claims of Southtown ministers (and suggesting that the congregation has an identity as a community of saved sinners). Rather, the problems were in the surrounding community and brought in by people of other faiths. The congregation tried to educate members, especially young people, so that they would not engage in forbidden activities, and, just like Father Felner at Saint Sebastian's, Reverend Diaz believes that fidelity to the Bible will enable

29. In Mexico, the class gradient tends to mirror the physical gradient of darker skin/more Indian features to lighter skin/more European features. More indigenous-looking people are widely looked down on, while those with lighter skin and more European features are admired.

church members to control their sexuality. When asked what the church teaches about premarital sex, divorce, domestic violence, and homosexuality, Reverend Diaz consistently invoked the Bible and often noted that a particular teaching reflects the doctrine of his denomination, which he referred to as *the church* throughout the interview. For example, we asked him about the congregation's view of premarital sex, and he replied that, if a young man has intercourse, he is in "fornication" according to the apostle Paul and Moses. "The church" urges him to get married in order to "solve the problem."

Like most conservative Christians, Reverend Diaz holds the patriarchal family up as the model for Christian living. Homosexuals are "respected," but they cannot hold office in the church. He teaches that gays and lesbians should strive to change or, in his argot, to get "an amendment of life." He bases this teaching on a literal interpretation of the Bible. There were homosexuals in biblical Corinth, but Paul said to them: "You were unclean, but now you have been cleansed by the blood of Christ." If homosexuals "repent," they will be allowed to hold office in the church. The ability of gays and lesbians to change is key to Diaz's approach; in support of this position, he offered the example of a man in Guatemala who was "like that" but repented and is now a famous priest. Because God gives such opportunities (i.e., to repent and change), so must the church.

Not only does Reverend Diaz seem reluctant to deviate from official Church of God teachings on sexual issues, but he also serves a constituency that may, in fact, need the order and guidance provided by the framework of control and biblical literalism more urgently than members of Saint Philomena's do. According to one informant, Church of the Divine Word, like other Pentecostal churches in the neighborhood, encourages members, especially the men, to "improve themselves" by becoming sober, learning how to keep a job, and renouncing their sexual promiscuity. The church's culture emphasizes a rule-based morality and expects that, once members learn the rules, they will no longer engage in improper behavior. Thus, Reverend Diaz stresses the need for educating members about right and wrong with respect to sexual behavior rather than dealing with underlying problems related to the behavior, as advocated by Father Gates at Saint Philomena's. Yet, like that of the Catholic parish, Church of the Divine Word's response to sexuality is informed by the local culture and the concerns of the neighborhood as well as by polity and dogma. Both Catholic and conservative Protestant congregations are embedded within a culture/social setting that is organized to move individuals into heterosexual marriage, and that strongly condemns homosexuality, but that simultaneously condones the sexual double standard that winks at men's nonmarital sexual activity, including homosexual activity.

These Westside congregations' attempts to regulate sexuality resemble those in Southtown: a mix of tolerance and the traditional ethic of control, both of which are used to channel individuals toward heterosexual marriage. These congregations also try to minimize the problems of abuse and disease transmission caused by men's drinking and the sexual double standard. The Catholic Church sets the tone for older members, particularly women, but it has been less successful with influencing the next generation of American-born and -raised children. Traditional Mexican sex roles are seldom challenged since these bolster strong families. However, behavioral change is the explicit goal of Church of the Divine Word, which, through it requirement of obedience and regular church attendance, appears to be effective in persuading men to abandon their promiscuous ways, or at least in keeping them away from sexual marketplaces. Paradoxically, despite the strong support for traditional sex roles among fundamentalist Protestants, the rigid demands and time requirements of such congregations can provide women with a measure of control over their husbands' unwanted outside behavior.

## Conclusion

In this chapter, we have identified a set of constraints and resources that shape the ways in which religious leaders address sexuality issues in their congregations. Clearly, polity, doctrine, and theological orientation are not the most powerful determinants of the different responses described in the case studies. Instead, these factors are balanced by local culture, the composition of membership pools, the particular identities and missions of congregations, and how each congregation positions itself vis-à-vis other neighborhood congregations in terms of its stance on sexuality and morality issues. Church leaders negotiate among these constraints to develop a normative framework regarding sexuality, whether that be control, accommodation, or tolerance. In turn, that framework enables a church to address sexuality in ways that are sensitive to the needs and concerns of its members, that resonate with neighborhood culture and religious sensibilities, and that further organizational goals of survival and competitiveness. Not only do churches react to, but they may also institutionalize, the local sexual culture by facilitating and legitimating some forms of sexual partnering, ignoring others, and forbidding yet others.

However, congregations' ability to legitimate certain sexual behaviors and relationships does not necessarily translate into significant control over their neighborhoods' sex markets. Like organizations in other institutional spheres, many of these religious organizations are guided by an internal logic that works against control efforts. When a congregation minimizes doctrine or official teachings on sexuality, it they may also lose its ability to punish nonconforming behaviors. Only the more conservative congregations in our sample—Saint Sebastian's in Southtown and Church of the Divine Word in

Westside—reported rules and programs requiring members to change illegitimate sexual behaviors. The other congregations exercise only indirect and, therefore, relatively weak control over sex markets and sexual-marketplace activities by providing services to or advocating for at-risk groups. This is most evident in the congregations in Southtown and Shoreland that are attempting to address the sociosexual problems associated with HIV/AIDS.

The Shoreland case studies illustrate how two liberal Protestant churches hold similar normative frameworks but champion different policies and programs. Both congregations rely on normative frameworks that are anchored in the values of tolerance and inclusion, and both rely on a therapeutic model to understand and remedy sex-related problems. Yet one church, Water Street UCC, takes a radical and politicized stand on sexuality and self-consciously avoids the temporizing positions prevalent in other mainline denominations. This position results from a decades-long history of social activism, an identity as a justice church, and membership in a denomination that allows great local freedom in addressing social issues. Conversely, Saint Pontain's is constrained by its membership in the Episcopal Church and by its identity as a refuge church. While the parish quietly welcomes gays and lesbians and offers them a place to simply be themselves, it refuses to perform same-sex-union ceremonies. The church has created an accommodating framework: it publicly and officially follows church doctrine while privately affirming all forms of sexual identity and all loving, committed sexual relationships.

In Southtown, different polities, congregational identities, and resources are the critical determinants of two alternative normative frameworks and programs that address sexuality. Additionally, the neighborhood's widespread social and sex-related health problems and lack of secular agencies to meet the needs of community residents place pressures on area churches not experienced by churches in Westside or Shoreland. Saint Sebastian's, one of the few Roman Catholic parishes in the area, has adopted a framework of control and intervention programs based on a literal reading of the Bible that closely resembles approaches used at nearby conservative Protestant churches. This approach to sexuality allows Saint Sebastian's to frame its moral message and programs in a familiar religious style and still remain faithful to church doctrine.

Third Avenue UCC struggles to fashion a version of its denomination's more liberal stand on homosexuality that will be acceptable to the neighborhood's morally conservative residents. To do so, this congregation emphasizes other long-standing themes within the black church—social activism and self-help. Its framework of tolerance, its judicious blending of professionally run but in-house social ministries with biblical teachings, and its willingness to address homosexuality openly when most churches in the neighborhood ignore the issue help Third Avenue carve out a unique niche in the neighborhood and attract a more liberal, middle-class audience. The "just say no" approach of Saint Sebastian's is rejected by the leaders of Third Avenue, who have mobilized its extensive resources to develop an array of ministries that address sexuality issues.

The Westside case studies provide clear evidence of the constraints that local culture places on church leadership. Local sexual culture plays a central role for two churches with very different institutional structures, one hierarchical and the other congregational. Both churches are forced to attend to familism, taboos against talking about sexuality (especially with outsiders), and an expressive spirituality, whether or not doing so coincides with the individual proclivities of the pastor or church teachings. However, opposing church identities, polities, and theological orientations of ministers led clergy to develop different normative frameworks and policies. At Saint Philomena's, Father Gates's approach to sexuality was strongly informed by liberation theology (and supported by like-minded priests in the area), but it was tempered by official doctrines and members' resistance to liberal positions on homosexuality that might threaten the family. The Church of the Divine Word advances a framework of control that is based on a literal and patriarchal reading of the Bible. Like Saint Sebastian's in Southtown, the Pentecostal storefront church is primarily concerned with saving souls; conversion and right belief are the remedies for sexual problems such as promiscuity. However, despite the fit between his message and his congregation's existing norms of morality, the pastor found that, in this Hispanic neighborhood, he was forced to contend with strong local pressure not to speak about private sexual behavior at all, an expectation quite different from that found at Saint Sebastian's in an African American context. As with local priests, Westside families wanted their pastor to deal privately and individually with the consequences of less-than-ideal sexual behavior and to do so in ways that maintained existing family relationships.

In this chapter, we have identified patterns of articulation between institutional actors, organizational structures, and local social environments that affect social change and social control. In order to discover how an institution like the church affects changing sexual behaviors and mores, it is important to pay attention, not only to denominations' official positions or individual members' attitudes, but also to the negotiated ways in which congregations and their leaders formulate overarching normative frameworks regarding sexuality, which in turn provide the rules, interpretive lenses, and action scripts that guide the congregation as a whole and members of the congregation individually. At the same time, we have shown how local sexual norms and practices shape congregations' responses to sexuality issues—in some cases limiting the voice of a congregation, in others driving the congregation toward a more public and politicized position. The case studies reveal that local norms regarding sexual behavior and identity and congregations' identities and histories are usually more salient than polity, official teaching, or denominational affiliation. These latter factors often serve as foils or negative references for congregations' leaders as they address sexuality issues in their churches and communities. It has been said that "all politics is local," and religious politics is no exception, especially where sexuality is concerned. The case studies have shown how local cultures, structures, and concerns—from the identities and traditions of each congregation to the demographics and institutional infrastructure of each neighborhood—drive congregations' approaches to human sexuality.

# 12 )

# *The Cultural Economy of Urban Sexuality*

Stephen Ellingson,
Jenna Mahay,
Anthony Paik,
and Edward O. Laumann

The existence of commercialized vice in the central business district is an inevitable part of the flux and flow of the region. Besides being a market place for thrill, the downtown district is a region of anonymity, where conduct either remains uncensored or is subject merely to the most secondary observation and regulation. Under such conditions personal taboos disintegrate and appetites become released from their sanctioned moorings.

—*W. C. Reckless, "The Distribution of Commercialized Vice in the City" (1926)*

Characterized as a place where sexuality is loosened from the constraints of family, religion, and education, the city is where all manner of sexual activities and subcultures flourish (see Knopp, 1995). As is suggested by the epigraph—taken from Walter Reckless, a student of the first Chicago school—the city's size, density, heterogeneity, and anonymity are alternately praised and blamed for sexual license. Reckless's summary of urban sexuality prefigures several of the themes in our study of the sexual organization of the city of Chicago: the role of urban space in providing opportunities for different types of sexual activity; the limited institutional regulation of sexuality; and the centrality of culture in organizing sexual relationships and identities. Although the first Chicago school tended to see aspects of urban sexuality—the illegitimate or illegal sexual activities occurring in the "zone in transition"—as indicators of social disorganization, the genius of these early sociologists was to identify and theorize the patterned, structured nature of the urban experience.

Likewise, in this study we uncovered the highly structured nature of urban sexual expression by highlighting the role of sex markets.[1] We learned how some sex markets are organized for short-term thrills, others for long-term relationships. We identified the sexual strategies of singlehood—the search and organizational decisions of sexual partnering. We saw how the social and institutional embeddedness of individuals shaped sexual decision-making, sometimes leading to unintended consequences, like sexually transmitted infections (STIs) and intimate-partner violence. In short, we uncovered the cultural economy of urban sexuality (i.e., the set of meanings that organize sexual identities, sexual relationships, and participation in a sex market) and the variety of ways in which social and institutional structures channel sexuality.

In this final chapter, we review the key findings about the cultural economy and the social structure of urban sexuality. At the same time, we wish to place our study in conversation with larger, enduring themes in American society, such as individualism and choice, the patterning of concomitant outcomes, particularly by race and ethnicity, the Sexual Revolution, and the institutional politics surrounding sexuality.

## The Disembeddedness of Sexuality

Institutional control over sexuality is a common thread that unites the historical, policy, and sociological literatures on sexuality, marriage, and family. One perspective suggests that institutions exert a high degree of control over sexual identities and expressions. Perhaps the best example of this approach is the work of Michel Foucault (1990). The early Chicago school and the more recent subcultural theory of urbanism imply strong institutional control over sexuality for the majority but weak control over certain urban populations owing to the heterogeneity, the size, and the density of urban spaces. The early Chicago school focused on single, transient men; subculturalists study lifestyle enclaves tolerating unconventional behaviors and beliefs (Wirth, [1938] 1956; Fischer, 1975, 1995). Thus, research in critical theory and urban sociology assumes that, for most Americans in most places, sexuality is channeled into safe, legitimate expressions (e.g., heterosexual monogamy) by the

1. On the terms *sex market* and *sexual marketplace* as they are used in this study, see the section "The Social Organization of Sexual Partnering and Sexual Relationships" in Ellingson, Laumann, Paik, and Mahay (chapter 1 in this volume).

family, religion, the state, and education while acknowledging that institutional surveillance and control fail for some special populations in the anonymous city. A second perspective, often advanced in historical studies of marriage, family, and sexuality, argues that the major changes associated with the course of the twentieth century and most evident in the Sexual Revolution (e.g., younger ages at first intercourse, widespread acceptance of nonmarital sexual relationships, the growing legitimacy and commonness of cohabitation) weakened institutional controls over sexuality (Joyner & Laumann, 2001; Laumann, Mahay, & Youm, 2002).

One aim of our study has been to investigate the nature of organizational control over sexuality and offer an explanation for it. As set out in part 3, organizational actors tend to exercise indirect, partial control over sexuality. There, we argued that three factors limited organizational capacities to affect sexual expression. First, sexuality is an externality to many organizations, and, as a result, few organizations have strong interests in addressing sexuality. Organizational actors are guided by a primary logic that helps them determine what sexual issues fall under their mandate and how they should intervene. In the case of the police, for example, their organizing principle of maintaining social order and upholding laws severely narrows the range of sexuality issues that they address to instances in which sexual behaviors (e.g., prostitution or child abuse) break existing laws. Similarly, health-care workers rely on a medical model of illness, which treats disease and fertility but does not resolve the underlying cultural and structural factors (e.g., poverty). Second, we demonstrated that there is a misfit between organizations' diagnoses of sexual problems and the programs or the practices that they implement to solve the problems. Organizational actors in the study tend to rely on person-specific interventions to repair problems with deep structural or collective roots. Third, we saw how institutions (especially religious congregations) adopting highly contextualized responses to sexuality abandon more strict ideological positions and intervention strategies; as a consequence, they limit their power to hold some practices in check.

Larger social forces also minimize the power and the effectiveness of organizational actors. A number of scholars have charted the growing disembeddedness of individuals in institutions. Bellah, Madsen, Sullivan, Swidler, and Tipton (1991) argue that American individualism has long minimized trust in and commitment to institutions. Similarly, the Chicago Health and Social Life Survey (CHSLS) respondents expressed in a number of ways a suspicion of institutions. For example, most respondents rely on family and friends for help, instead of consulting professionals like clergy or social workers. In Westside, the strong culture of familialism and the fear of deportation discouraged the neighborhood's Mexican and Mexican American residents from regularly using secular institutional services, although they often turned to the Catholic Church for help with everything from domestic violence to paying bills.

More recently, scholars investigating the breakdown of civic engagement among Americans describe how declining participation in social institutions of various sorts (e.g., voluntary organizations)—whether by choice, as in the case of dropping out of a church, or by compulsion, as in the case of downsizing—lowers public trust in institutions and, thus, institutional effectiveness (see Wuthnow, 1998, esp. chap. 3). In a recent essay, Ann Swidler (2002, 45, 50) argues: "Americans are undergoing a period of social, institutional, and cultural disinvestments. The effect is to place greater burdens on selves increasingly unsupported by institutions." Swidler continues by noting how U.S. citizens are less vested in everything from work, to religion, to politics. In particular, she identifies marriage as an institution in which we have "disinvested." That is, "individual marriages now survive insofar as they meet the needs of the partners, not because the marriage itself carries powerful institutional sanctions." The CHSLS data support Swidler's claim: individuals between the ages of eighteen and fifty-nine spend about 50 percent of their lives as singles as the trends toward cohabitation, divorce, and remarriage continue (see Mahay & Laumann, chapter 5 in this volume).

Moreover, according to Wuthnow (1998), institutions have become "porous." Today, social institutions operate with more permeable boundaries, allowing individuals to move in and out of them easily, further disconnecting individuals from institutions.

The data from our key-informant interviews support the findings of this research. For sex-related problems, the individuals in our study turn to religious organizations, health-care providers, social workers, and the police on a short-term, ad hoc basis. However, their ties to these organizational actors are tenuous, and organizations are, therefore, less able to establish binding obligations between themselves and individuals. In our data, we saw numerous signs of the weak relationship between individuals and organizations when it comes to regulating sexual behavior. For example, most health educators spoke about their inability to change the attitudes and sexual practices of at-risk populations regarding condom use, especially where sexual cultures (e.g., those found among Hispanic men and gay men) strongly oppose the practice. Some health-care clinicians lamented the lack of ongoing relationships with their clients, who move from one STD (sexually transmitted disease) clinic to another. Such ongoing relationships would help the clinicians track the patients and allow them to move toward more effective interventions. Similarly, the culture of silence and suspicion of the state kept many residents of Westside and Erlinda from reporting abuse or violence, except to priests.

Yet the effects of institutions regaining only partial control are not all negative. Our analyses suggest that the institutional dimensions of sex markets still exercise significant power to direct and shape sexual relationships, identities, and behaviors. We saw this most clearly in cases in which individuals are most deeply embedded within local religious organizations, families, communities, and group-specific gender and sexual norms. For example, in the two Hispanic neighborhoods, we discovered that deeply held beliefs about gender roles and the culture of silence discourage the adoption of homosexual identities and participation in same-sex sex markets. More specifically, lesbianism is not a culturally acknowledged possibility in Erlinda and Westside (see Ellingson & Schroeder, chapter 4 in this volume), and, thus, there are few public or marketplace spaces where Latina lesbians can gather in these neighborhoods. Even support of political groups for Latina lesbians is short-lived in these communities. Congregations' and denominations' common "don't ask, don't tell" position regarding homosexuality (see Ellingson, Van Haitsma, Laumann, & Tebbe, chapter 11 in this volume) can also powerfully shape sexual identities and institutional responses. In particular, we show how this position in black and white Protestant congregations and Roman Catholic parishes can stop gay men from publicly identifying as gay, send contradictory religious messages (which may undercut the legitimacy of the church body in the eyes of both liberals and conservatives), and prevent congregations from promoting safe sex, providing HIV/AIDS education, or even offering counseling to homosexual persons.

We also learned that residents of different neighborhoods are more likely to trust and, hence, follow the sexual prescriptions of certain institutional actors rather than others. In Westside, it is the Roman Catholic Church; in Erlinda, it is organizations that combine a particular institutional agenda (especially health education) with Puerto Rican nationalism; in Shoreland, it is organizations offering counseling or psychotherapy along with those religious organizations that accept gays and lesbians; in Southtown, it is the black church, not only for historic reasons, but also because health-care and social-service provision is not well developed. This institutional selectivity appears to be based on historic experiences unique to particular populations (e.g., a suspicion of the police and the legal system among African Americans in Southtown can be traced to the history of discrimination and police brutality in the city) or sexual cultures (e.g., the strong emphasis on female virginity and families closely articulates with Roman Catholic teachings).

Thus, the world of urban sexuality that we uncovered in Chicago does not resemble Foucault's world of strong institutional control over sexuality. Chicago's organizational actors, in general, do not exercise extensive or authoritative power (see Mann, 1986, esp. chap. 1). Instead, they exercise intensive, partial power (i.e., local and group specific) to constrain or channel sexuality. Individuals are largely disembedded or disinvested from most traditional institutions that operate as complex organizations, but, as noted above, they are selectively embedded in institutional dimensions of sex markets.

An important insight to be derived from the analysis presented in Ellingson (chapter 10 in this volume) is that contradictory diagnoses, interventions, and claims about moral agency tend to undercut the credibility and the effectiveness of organizational efforts to control sexuality. The multiple, conflicting messages create a situation of moral heterogeneity and confusion around sexuality. Health-care and social-service agencies go to great lengths to avoid the language and the appearance of judging or blaming their clients, yet they often end up treating at-risk individuals as if they are morally deficient. Specifically, organizational actors consider individuals with STIs or unwanted pregnancies to be victims of poverty, deeply rooted cultural norms, or historical experiences (e.g., the colonization of Puerto Rico or the enslavement of African Americans), therefore concluding that they lack the moral capacity to overcome these structural forces. Thus, by casting their clients in the role of victim, organizational actors minimize their clients' moral agency to avoid risky sex. At the same time, the diagnostic work and the interventions of practitioners often contradict. The common intervention of education rests on the assumption that high-risk individuals are capable of receiving new knowledge and acting on it, but, at the same time, these individuals are told repeatedly that they are incapable. In other words, many at-risk clients are first told that they are incapable of exercising any moral agency yet then told that the only solution to their sexual problems is to become fully empowered moral agents and to act on safe-sex information. This may be a situation that erodes the credibility of health-care and social-service agencies and, thus, their clients' trust in the help or remedies that they provide.

Finally, the condition of moral heterogeneity is a result of limited, institutional ownership of sexuality. By treating sex as an externality and addressing it primarily in terms of each organization's dominant logic, organizational actors do not develop a holistic approach to sexual behaviors, sexual relationships, or their consequences. Indeed, the interpretative frameworks and intervention strategies of religious, health-care, and social-service organizations feed into a "morality of the sex act," where certain behaviors, such as premarital sex, unprotected sex, or gay sex, are defined as immoral (see Seidman, 1999). We saw this in Saint Sebastian's approach to marriage counseling and veiled attack on homosexuality as a spiritual illness (see Ellingson, Van Haitsma, Laumann, and Tebbe, chapter 11 in this volume). We also saw this act-oriented morality in the approaches of health-care workers and social workers. Many of our informants claimed that they have a "value-free" approach to sex, insisting that there is no good or bad sex; but, by pushing condom use and safe-sex practices, they implicitly define some sexual activities as good and others as bad. Moreover, as individuals are referred to or interact with workers in different institutional spheres, they are exposed to countervailing moral perspectives on sexual identities and sex practices. And, given the lack of mandate over sexuality on the part of institutions, there is no one institution adjudicating among competing moral claims. In short, the numerous, incomplete responses of organizations to sexuality have fostered a situation of moral heterogeneity, and possibly atomization, in which individuals are forced to rely on themselves or personal networks for moral guidance on sexual matters, from risk to health, from identities to relationships.

## Sexual Choice, Sexual Constraint

If the urban world of sexuality that we uncovered is not organized along Foucauldian lines, then perhaps we should be looking for the opposite sexual world: namely, one organized by individual choice. Our theory of sex markets seemingly would lend itself to an individualistic, voluntaristic explanation of sexual partnering, identity formation, and behavior. Culturally, Americans favor individualism as the critical value or trait driving choices in matters of love and marriage. In her most recent book, Ann Swidler (2001, 111–24) argues that voluntarism or personal choice is both the foundation of the American myth of love and the dominant framework for understanding actions in the sex market. She notes that a "bourgeois love myth" surrounds choices about sex partners and sexual relationships, where decisions are made in defiance of family, work, or religious forces. However, she shows that choices about love are fundamentally contingent on the institutional and social relations in which individuals are enmeshed.

As sociologists working with ideas about markets from the field of economics, we were suspicious of the individualistic assumptions underlying economists' approaches, so, using insights from economic sociology, we developed a structural theory of sex markets that emphasized structural and cultural constraints on sexual choices. In particular, we argued (see Ellingson, Laumann, Paik, & Mahay, chapter 1 in this volume) that sex markets are embedded in group cultures, social networks, institutions, and social space. The analyses of heterosexual and same-sex markets presented by Mahay and Laumann and by Ellingson and Schroeder (chapters 3 and 4 in this volume) highlight the important role that group culture and space play in limiting personal choice. For example, strong profamily, antihomosexual attitudes in Westside and Erlinda make it difficult for Latino gays and lesbians to create the commercial and nonprofit infrastructure (e.g., bars, bookstores, rights groups) necessary to support a gay ghetto in these neighborhoods. At the opposite end of the spectrum, space in Shoreland's gay and straight sex markets is organized more commonly to facilitate short-term relationships or one-night stands, which in turn bolsters a sexual culture characterized by cruising, not by long-term monogamous relationships.[2]

We also showed how the conditions of sex markets affected individual decisionmaking. Our analyses, especially those presented in part 2, support the notion that sexual choices depend on and are shaped by familial and personal networks, by the social conditions and the sexual culture of a given group (i.e., race/ethnicity, sexual orientation), and by master statuses such as gender, marital status, and age. As shown in Mahay and Laumann (chapter 5 in this volume), the structure of opportunities and constraints in sex markets varies tremendously over the life course. Older individuals are differentially located in social networks, institutions, and geographic space, and are also likely to hold different cultural beliefs about sexuality, than are their younger counterparts. Together, these elements interact with sex markets to structure search and partnering patterns. In several chapters, we investigated the significance of embeddedness for sexual choices like family formation (Youm & Paik, chapter 6 in this volume) and for its consequences, such as sexual jealousy (Paik, Laumann, & Van Haitsma, chapter 7) and the transmission of STIs (Youm & Laumann, chapter 9). For example, we found that personal networks were much more important for women under age thirty regarding union formation and that individuals with larger social networks were less likely to contract an STD. In these cases, social networks serve either as a source of information or as a source of control.

In short, we have discovered that the sexual choices of Chicago residents may be best characterized in terms of a "bounded individualism." While the evidence suggests greater personal choice about union formation (with increasing numbers of adults between the ages of eighteen and fifty-nine moving between singlehood, dating, cohabitation, and marriage), fertility decisions, and the onset of sexual activity, sexual choices are neither wholly autonomous nor wholly independent. The sexual worlds of Chicago reflect, not the rampant individualism depicted in *Habits of the Heart* (Bellah, Madsen, Sullivan, Swidler, & Tipton, 1985), but the choice within constraints of Simon's *Administrative Behavior* (1957). That is, individuals' sexual choices are limited by their social network and institutional embeddedness and by the availability of sexual-marketplace space in which to conduct specific partner searches. For example, Ellingson and Schroeder (chapter 4 in this volume)

---

2. Note that we were unable to identify the specific pattern of causation between space and culture but, nevertheless, consistently found that the two were interrelated.

showed how the culture of machismo among Hispanic men creates high costs for adopting a public identity as a gay man, severely limiting the possibility for being out in Westside and Erlinda. As a result, openly gay men often act out the identity of the queen (the effeminate gay man), take the passive role in sexual exchanges, live their gay identity outside their neighborhoods, or remain closeted. This group-specific sexual norm, then, limits the market-place space (in terms of both number and type) available for same-sex en-counters. Similarly, several chapters documented how different stakeholders (from congregations, to families and friends) exercise some control but more often provide information that shapes the choices of individuals.

## Debunking Myths of the Sexual Life Course

The bounded individualism characterizing sex in the city of Chicago stands in sharp contrast to cultural myths of sexuality. As noted by Ellingson, Lau-mann, Paik, and Mahay (chapter 1 in this volume), quoting Park ([1929] 1967, 18), in the city "all suppressed desires find somewhere an expression." Thus, urban sexuality is about the variegated ways of organizing sexual networks and conducting searches for potential partners. The sheer density of different kinds of people, combined with the loosening of moral strictures regarding premarital sex and homosexuality, makes the city the locus for diverse modes of sexual expression. At the same time, the sexual lives of Chicagoans remain firmly embedded within concrete spaces, cultures, social relations, and insti-tutions. In short, the metropolis offers, even pulls individuals into, an im-mense array of sexual choices not available in rural parts of the country, but the sex markets are highly structured. However, a large disjuncture between the on-the-ground sexuality described in this collection and the cultural myths of sexuality exists, suggesting the need for new cultural spaces.

There are two major cultural myths of sexuality. The first, which empiri-cally has been in decline for some time now but still weighs heavily as a so-cial ideal, is the myth of the unitary nature of the sexual life course. This myth emphasizes true love over social position, sometimes with tragic conse-quences (epitomized in *Romeo and Juliet*), but, generally, love conquers all, leading to marriage and children. The second is actually an updated, post–Sexual Revolution version of the original that incorporates all manner of social change—cohabitation, divorce, remarriage. Here, the emphasis is on making the companionate bond work, but the myth still integrates these added stages—cohabitation and remarriage—as part of a natural history of the sexual life course (see Swidler, 2001). In the first, original version, sex and the family are securely bound. In the second, revised version, the bonds are broken, leaving individuals free to pursue sexual pleasure wherever they choose. This is the realm of singles on the prowl, one-night stands, and endless, urban sexual possibilities.

The emerging picture—which is based on our findings as well as on prior research—is more complex than either of these two myths, a result of two major demographic shifts that led to dramatic changes in the sexual life course in recent decades. First, owing to delayed marriage, divorce, and the decline in remarriage, Americans are spending a larger proportion of their lives as singles today than at any other time in the past hundred years (DaVanzo & Rahman, 1993). Second, sexual activity is no longer coupled with marriage (e.g., Axinn & Thornton, 2000). Sexual partnering has been transformed from what was once typically an early, one-time-only event resulting in (or beginning with) a lifelong marriage into a process that now often occurs over the entire life course and in a variety of patterns, potentially involving any combination of types of sexual relationships and numbers of partners, either concurrently or sequentially. Thus, both myths depict aspects of urban sexual expression—the swinging singles and the dysfunctional families—but they fail to represent at all how many of the singles and the cohabitors in the CHSLS negotiate sex markets.

Indeed, a core theme of this book is that, for many Chicagoans, sex is neither tightly coupled nor completely decoupled from family institutions; instead, it is loosely coupled. In chapter 6, Youm and Paik identified a pattern of long-term polygamy specific to the black population of Chicago. This issue has received scant scholarly attention and is a poor fit with popular myths about sexuality. However, Youm and Paik did find that long-term polygamy is an important factor affecting family formation. Similarly, in chapter 7, which examined marital status, concurrent sexual partnerships, and sexual jealousy, Paik, Laumann, and Van Haitsma discovered that being committed to a sex partner has benefits as well as risks. Their analyses showed that cohabitation has particular risks because, while it is in many ways similar to marriage (in terms of shared living spaces and expectations of sexual exclusivity), it is in other ways similar to a dating relationship (in terms of the likelihood of concurrent sex partners). Thus, cohabiting relationships may be particularly vulnerable to sexual jealousy and are exemplars of how family institutions are loosely coupled with sex markets.

These findings are striking, perhaps even disturbing. But they also highlight the fact that there are few narratives, stories, or myths to describe the variety of modes of sexual expression in singlehood. One approach is to characterize this social change as social pathology, to call for rebuilding the family and the marital commitment, and to tightly couple sex and the family again. Another approach is to recognize that the pluralism of American society also extends to sexuality. There is not one moral code to govern sexuality but many; the various modes of sexual expression are tied to the particular norms and moral codes of different populations. While we do not engage this debate directly, we hope that this book serves to open discussion about the rise of sex markets and the many singles populating them.

We hope that this book serves as a corrective to both academic and popular explanations of sexuality and, in particular, sex in the city. We have argued that sex-market activities are neither overwhelmingly controlled by institutions and organizations nor completely the product of individual choice. Instead, we have demonstrated how market choices—from search strategies to sexual-relationship formation—are differently constrained by culture, structure, space, and social networks. Thus, robust explanations must attend to both the cultural economy and the social structuring of sexuality. At the same time, we have provided empirical evidence that calls into question a few of our most enduring sexual myths: the unitary sexual life course, the city as a place of sexual license, and the singles' life of one-night stands. We have also demonstrated the ways in which sex in Chicago has been fundamentally reshaped by the Sexual Revolution. This is evident in the sexual search strategies of older women, the continued decoupling of sex and marriage, the weakening hold of family and religion over sexuality, and the more visible and legitimate same-sex sex markets in the white gay and lesbian neighborhoods. Finally, we hope that this book will spur new lines of inquiry into sexuality and theoretical work to refine our notion of *the sex market*.

# References

Adler, S., & Brenner, J. (1992). Gender and space: Lesbians and gay men in the city. *International Journal of Urban and Regional Research, 16*, 24–34.

Aggleton, P., O'Reilly, K., Slutkin, G., & Davis, P. (1994). Risking everything? Risk behavior, risk change, and AIDS. *Science, 265*, 341–45.

Ahuvia, A., & Adelman, M. (1992). Formal intermediaries in the marriage market: A typology and review. *Journal of Marriage and the Family, 54*, 452–63.

Alexander, L. L., Cates, J. R., Herndorn, N., & Ratcliffe, J. F. (Eds.). (1998). *Sexually transmitted diseases in America: How many cases and at what cost?* Research Triangle Park, NC: American Social Health Association.

Almaguer, T. (1991). Chicano men: A cartography of homosexual identity and behavior. *Differences: A Journal of Feminist Cultural Studies, 3*, 75–100.

Alonso, A., & Koreck, M. T. (1993). Silences: Hispanics, AIDS, and sexual practices. In H. Abelove, M. A. Barale, & D. V. Halpern (Eds.), *The lesbian and gay studies reader* (pp. 255–73). New York: Routledge.

Ammerman, N. (1997). *Congregation and community.* New Brunswick, NJ: Rutgers University Press.

Ammerman, N., Carroll, J. W., McKinney, W., & Dudley, C. (1998). *Studying congregations.* Nashville: Abingdon.

Anderson, E. (1989). Sex codes and family life among poor inner-city youths. *Annals of the American Academy of Political and Social Science, 501*, 59–78.

Anderson, E. (1999). *Code of the street: Decency, violence, and the moral life of the inner city.* New York: Norton.

Angel, R., & Worobey, J. L. (1988). Single motherhood and children's health. *Journal of Health and Social Behavior, 29*, 38–52.

Aral, S. O. (1996). The social context of syphilis persistence in the Southeastern United States. *Sexually Transmitted Diseases, 23*, 9–15.

Aral, S. O. (1999). Sexual network patterns as determinants of STD rates: Paradigm shift in the behavioral epidemiology of STDs made visible. *Sexually Transmitted Diseases, 26*, 262–64.

Aral, S. O., Hughes, J., Stoner, B., Whitington, W., Handsfield, H., Anderson, R.,

& Holmes, K. (1999). Sexual mixing patterns in the spread of conococcal and chlamydial infections. *American Journal of Public Health,* 89, 825–33.

Aune, K. S., & Comstock, J. (1997). Effect of relationship length on the experience, expression, and perceived appropriateness of jealousy. *Journal of Social Psychology,* 137, 23–31.

Aveline, D. T. (1995). A typology of perceived HIV/AIDS risk-reduction strategies used by men who "cruise" other men for anonymous sex. *Journal of Sex Research,* 32, 201–12.

Axinn, W., & Thornton, A. (1996). The influence of parents' marital dissolutions on children's attitudes toward family formation. *Demography,* 33 (1), 66–81.

Axinn, W., & Thornton, A. (2000). The transformation in the meaning of marriage. In L. J. Waite, C. Bachrach, M. Hindin, E. Thomson, & A. Thornton (Eds.), *The ties that bind: Perspectives on marriage and cohabitation* (pp. 147–65). New York: Aldine de Gruyter.

Bailey, B. (1988). *From front porch to back seat: Courtship in twentieth-century America.* Baltimore: Johns Hopkins University Press.

Bajos, N. (1997). Social factors and the process of risk construction in HIV sexual transmission. *AIDS Care,* 9, 227–37.

Baker, W. E. (1990). Market networks and corporate behavior. *American Journal of Sociology,* 96, 589–625.

Baker, W. E., Faulkner, R. R., & Fisher, G. A. (1998). Hazards of the market: The continuity and dissolution of interorganizational market relationships. *American Sociological Review,* 63, 147–77.

Baldwin, M. W., & Fehr, B. (1995). On the instability of attachment style ratings. *Personal Relationships,* 2, 247–61.

Barber, J. S., & Axinn, W. G. (1998). Gender role attitudes and marriage among young women. *Sociological Quarterly,* 39, 11–31.

Barnett, N. G., Bloom, D. E., & Craig, P. H. (1989). The divergence of black and white marriage patterns. *American Journal of Sociology,* 95, 692–722.

Barnett, O. W., Martinez, T. E., & Bluestein, B. W. (1995). Jealousy and romantic attachment in maritally violent and nonviolent men. *Journal of Interpersonal Violence,* 10, 473–86.

Barnhart, E. (1975). Friends and lovers in a lesbian counterculture community. In N. Glazer-Malbin (Ed.), *Old family/new family* (pp. 90–115). New York: Van Nostrand.

Basile, K. C. (1999). Rape by acquiescence: The ways in which women "give in" to unwanted sex with their husbands. *Violence against Women,* 5 (9), 1036–58.

Baumann, K. E., & Wilson, R. R. (1976). Premarital sexual attitudes of unmarried university students: 1968 vs. 1972. *Archives of Sexual Behavior,* 5, 29–37.

Bean, F. D., & Tienda, M. (1987). *The Hispanic population of the United States.* New York: Sage.

Bearman, P. S., & Bruckner, H. (2001). Promising the future: Virginity pledges and first intercourse. *American Sociological Review,* 106 (4), 859–912.

Beck, S. H., Cole, B. S., & Hammond, J. A. (1991). Religious heritage and premarital sex: Evidence from a national sample of young adults. *Journal for the Scientific Study of Religion,* 30, 173–80.

Becker, G. S. (1973). Theory of marriage. *Journal of Political Economy,* 81, 813–46.

Becker, G. S. (1981). *A treatise on the family.* Cambridge, MA: Harvard University Press.

Becker, G. S. (1991). *A treatise on the family: An enlarged edition.* Cambridge, MA: Harvard University Press.

Becker, G., Landes, M., & Michael, R. T. (1977). An economic analysis of marital instability. *Journal of Political Economy,* 85, 1141–87.

Becker, P. E. (1999). *Congregations in conflict: Cultural models of local religious life.* New York: Cambridge University Press.

Beemyn, B. (Ed.). (1997a). *Creating a place for ourselves.* New York: Routledge.

Beemyn, B. (1997b). A queer capital: Race, class, gender, and the changing social landscape of Washington's gay communities, 1940–1955. In B. Beemyn (Ed.), *Creating a place for ourselves* (pp. 183–209). New York: Routledge.

Bell, R. R., & Chaskes, J. B. (1970). Premarital sexual experience among coeds, 1958 and 1968. *Journal of Marriage and the Family,* 31, 81–84.

Bell, R. R., & Coughey, K. (1980). Premarital experience among college females, 1958, 1968, 1978. *Family Relations,* 29, 353–57.

Bellah, R. N., Madsen, R., Sullivan, W. M., Swidler, A., & Tipton, S. M. (1985). *Habits of the heart.* Berkeley and Los Angeles: University of California Press.

Bellah, R. N, Madsen, R., Sullivan, W. M., Swidler, A., & Tipton, S. M. (1991). *The good society.* New York: Knopf.

Bennett, N. G., Blanc, A. K., & Bloom, D. E. (1988). Commitment and the modern union: Assessing the link between premarital cohabitation and subsequent marital stability. *American Sociological Review,* 53, 127–38.

Bennett, N. G., Bloom, D. E., & Craige, P. H. (1989). The divergence of black and white marriage patterns. *American Journal of Sociology,* 95, 692–722.

Benson, M., Larson, J., Wilson, S., & Demo, D. (1993). Family of origin influences on late adolescent romantic relationships. *Journal of Marriage and the Family,* 55, 663–72.

Bernard, J. (1972). *The future of marriage.* New Haven, CT: Yale University Press.

Berscheid, E. (1983). Emotion. In H. H. Kelley, E. Berscheid, A. Christensen, J. H. Harvey, T. L. Huston, G. Levinger, E. McClintock, L. A. Peplau, & D. R. Peterson (Eds.), *Close relationships* (pp. 110–68). New York: Freeman.

Best, J. (1990). *Threatened children.* Chicago: University of Chicago Press.

Binnie, J. (1995). Trading places: Consumption, sexuality, and the production of queer space. In D. Bell & G. Valentine (Eds.), *Mapping desire* (pp. 182–99). New York: Routledge.

Binson, D., Michaels, S., Stall, R., Coates, T. J., Gagnon, J. H., & Catania, J. A. (1995). Prevalence and social distribution of men who have sex with men: United States and its urban centers. *Journal of Sex Research,* 32, 245–54.

Blau, P. M. (1964). *Exchange and social life.* New York: Wiley.

Blau, P., Beeker, C., & Fitzpatrick, K. (1984). Intersecting social affiliations and intermarriage. *Social Forces,* 62, 585–605.

Blau, P., Blum, T., & Schwartz, J. (1982). Heterogeneity and intermarriage. *American Sociological Review*, 47, 45–62.

Blieszner, R., & Adams, R. G. (1992). *Adult friendship*. Newbury Park, CA: Sage.

Block, C. R., & Christakos, A. (1995). Intimate partner homicide in Chicago over 29 years. *Crime and Delinquency*, 41, 496–526.

Blumstein, P., & Schwartz, P. (1983). *American couples: Money, work, sex*. New York: Morrow.

Booth, A. D., Brinkerhoff, D. B., & White, L. K. (1984). The impact of parental divorce on courtship. *Journal of Marriage and the Family*, 46, 85–94.

Bourdieu, P. (1991). *Language and symbolic power* (G. Raymond & M. Adamson, Trans.). Cambridge, MA: Harvard University Press.

Bourque, L. B. (1989). *Defining rape*. Durham, NC: Duke University Press.

Bowser, B. P. (1994). African-American male sexuality through the early life course. In A. Rossi (Ed.), *Sexuality across the life course* (pp. 127–150). Chicago: University of Chicago Press.

Brines, J., & Joyner, K. (1999). The ties that bind: Principles of cohesion in cohabitation and marriage. *American Sociological Review*, 64, 333–55.

Bringle, R. G., & Buunk, B. P. (1991). Extradyadic relationships and sexual jealousy. In K. McKinney & S. Sprecher (Eds.), *Sexuality in close relationships* (pp. 135–53). Hillsdale, NJ: Erlbaum.

Brinton, M. C., & Nee, V. (Eds.). (1998). *The new institutionalism in sociology*. New York: Sage.

Brockner, J., Tyler, T. R., & Cooper-Schneider, R. (1992). The influence of prior commitment to an institution on reactions to perceived unfairness: The higher they are, the harder they fall. *Administrative Science Quarterly*, 37, 241–61.

Brown, P. G. (1988). *The body and society: Men, women, and sexual renunciation in early Christianity*. New York: Columbia University Press.

Browning, C. R., & Laumann, E. O. (1997). Sexual contact between children and adults: A life course perspective. *American Sociological Review*, 62 (4), 540–60.

Bumpass, L. L. (1990). What's happening to the family? Interactions between demographic and institutional change. *Demography*, 27, 483–98.

Bumpass, L., Sweet, J., & Cherlin, A. (1991). The role of cohabitation in declining rates of marriage. *Journal of Marriage and the Family*, 53, 913–27.

Bumpass, L., Sweet, J., & Martin, T. C. (1990). Changing patterns of remarriage. *Journal of Marriage and the Family*, 52, 747–56.

Buntin, J. T., & Lechtman, Z. (2001). Crime and sexuality: Definitions of forced sex as rape or a crime in four Chicago neighborhoods. Paper presented at the annual meeting of the American Sociological Association, Anaheim, CA, 19 August.

Burgess, E. (1943). Homogamy in social characteristics. *American Journal of Sociology*, 49, 109–24.

Burt, R. S. (1992). *Structural holes: The social structure of competition*. Cambridge, MA: Harvard University Press.

Buss, D. M. (1998). Sexual strategies theory: Historical origins and current status. *Journal of Sex Research*, 35, 19–31.

Buss, D. M. (2000). *The dangerous passion: Why jealousy is as necessary as love and sex.* New York: Free Press.

Buss, D. M., Larsen, R. J., Westen, D., & Semmelroth, J. (1992). Sex differences in jealousy: Evolution, physiology, and psychology. *Psychological Science, 3,* 251–55.

Butler, J. (1990). *Gender trouble.* New York: Routledge.

Byrne, D. (1971). *The attraction paradigm.* New York: Academic.

Cahn, S. K. (1996). From the "muscle moll" to the "butch" ballplayer: Mannishness, lesbianism, and homophobia in U.S. women's sports. In M. Vicinus (Ed.), *Lesbian subjects* (pp. 41–65). Bloomington: Indiana University Press.

Carrier, J. M. (1989). Sexual behavior and the spread of AIDS in Mexico. *Medical Anthropology,* 10, 129–42.

Carrier, J. M. (1995). *De los otros: Intimacy and homosexuality among Mexican men.* New York: Columbia University Press.

Cassell, E. J. (1997). *Doctoring: The nature of primary care medicine.* New York: Oxford University Press.

Catania, J. A., Binson, D., Dolcini, M. M., Stall, R., Choi, K. H., Pollack, L. M., Hudes, E. S., Canchola, J., Phillips, K., Moskowitz, J. T., & Coates, T. J. (1995). Risk factors for HIV and other sexually transmitted diseases and prevention practices among U.S. heterosexual adults: Changes from 1990 to 1992. *American Journal of Public Health,* 85 (11), 1492–99.

Centers for Disease Control and Prevention (CDC). (1996). Ten leading national notifiable infectious diseases, United States, 1995. *Morbidity and Mortality Weekly Report,* 45, 883–84.

Chauncey, G., Jr. (1994). *Gay New York: Gender, urban culture, and the making of the gay male world, 1890–1940.* New York: Basic.

Chaves, M. (1997). The symbolic significance of women's ordination. *Journal of Religion,* 77, 87–114.

Cherlin, A. (1978). Remarriage as an incomplete institution. *American Journal of Sociology,* 84, 634–50.

Cherlin, A. (1992). *Marriage, divorce, remarriage.* Cambridge, MA: Harvard University Press.

Cherlin, A. (2000). Towards a new home socioeconomics of union formation. In L. J. Waite, C. Bachrach, M. Hindin, E. Thomson, & A. Thornton (Eds.), *The ties that bind: Perspectives on marriage and cohabitation* (pp. 126–44). New York: Aldine de Gruyter.

Christopher, F. S., & Sprecher, S. (2000). Sexuality in marriage, dating, and other relationships: A decade review. *Journal of Marriage and the Family,* 62, 999–1017.

Clanton, G. (1990). Jealousy in American culture, 1945–1985: Reflections from popular culture. In D. D. Franks & E. D. McCarthy (Eds.), *The sociology of emotions: Original essays and research papers* (pp. 179–93). Greenwich, CT: JAI.

Clarkberg, M. (1999). The price of partnering: The role of economic well-being in young adults' first union experiences. *Social Forces,* 77, 945–68.

Clarkberg, M., Stolzenberg, R. M., & Waite, L. J. (1995). Attitudes, values, and entrance into cohabitational versus marital unions. *Social Forces,* 74, 609–34.

Clemens, E. S., & Cook, J. M. (1999). Politics and institutionalism: Explaining durability and change. *Annual Review of Sociology,* 25, 441–66.

Cochran, J. K., & Beeghley, L. (1991). The influence of religion on attitudes toward nonmarital sexuality: A preliminary assessment of reference group theory. *Journal for the Scientific Study of Religion,* 30, 45–62.

Cohen, C. J. (1996). Contested membership: Black gay identities and the politics of AIDS. In S. Seidman (Ed.), *Queer theory/sociology* (pp. 362–94). Cambridge, MA: Blackwell.

Coleman, J. S. (1988). Social capital in the creation of human capital. *American Journal of Sociology,* 94 (suppl.), S95–S120.

Coleman, J. S. (1990). *Foundations of social theory.* Cambridge, MA: Harvard University Press.

Coleman, M., Ganong, L., & Fine, M. (2000). Reinvestigating remarriage: Another decade of progress. *Journal of Marriage and the Family,* 62, 1288–1307.

Collins, N. L., & Read, S. J. (1990). Adult attachment, working models, and relationship quality in dating couples. *Journal of Personality and Social Psychology,* 58, 644–63.

Comstock, G. D. (1996). *Unrepentant, self-affirming, practicing: Lesbian/bisexual/gay people within organized religion.* New York: Continuum.

Connell, R. W., & Dowsett, G. W. (1999). The unclean motion of the generative parts: Frameworks in Western thought on sexuality. In R. Parker & P. Aggleton (Eds.), *Culture, society, and sexuality: A reader.* New York: UCL.

Countryman, L. W. (1988). *Dirt, greed, and sex: Sexual ethics in the New Testament and their implications for today.* Philadelphia: Fortress.

Countryman, L. W. (1994). New Testament sexual ethics and today's world. In J. B. Nelson & S. P. Longfellow (Eds.), *Sexuality and the sacred: Sources for theological reflection* (pp. 28–53). Louisville: Westminster/John Knox.

Creith, E. (1996). *Undressing lesbian sex.* London: Cassell.

Crook, S. (1999). Ordering crisis. In D. Lupton (Ed.), *Risk and sociocultural theory* (pp. 160–85). New York: Cambridge University Press.

Daly, M., Wilson, M., & Weghorst, S. (1982). Male sexual jealousy. *Ethology and Sociobiology,* 3, 11–27.

Darity, W. A., & Myers, S. L. (1987). Public police trends and the fate of the black family. *Humboldt Journal of Social Relations,* 14, 134–64.

Dasgupta, P. (1988). Trust as a commodity. In D. Gambetta (Ed.), *Trust: Making and breaking cooperative relations* (pp. 49–72). New York: Blackwell.

DaVanzo, J., & Rahman, M. O. (1993). American families: Trends and correlates. *Population Index,* 59 (3), 350–86.

Davidson, A. G. (1991). Looking for love in the age of AIDS: The language of gay personals, 1978–1988. *Journal of Sex Research,* 28, 125–37.

Davis, M. S. (1973). *Intimate relations.* New York: Free Press.

Davis, M., & Kennedy, E. L. (1989). Oral history and the study of sexuality in the lesbian community: Buffalo, New York, 1940–1960. In M. B. Duberman, M. Vicinus, & G. Chauncey Jr. (Eds.), *Hidden from history: Reclaiming the gay and lesbian past* (pp. 426–40). New York: Penguin.

Dean, M. (1999). Risk, calculable and incalculable. In D. Lupton (Ed.), *Risk and sociocultural theory* (pp. 131–59). New York: Cambridge University Press.

DeLamater, J. (1981). The social control of sexuality. *Annual Review of Sociology,* 7, 263–90.

DeLamater, J. (1987). A sociological approach. In J. H. Greer & W. T. O'Donohue (Eds.), *Theories of human sexuality* (pp. 237–55). New York: Platinum.

DeLamater, J. (1991). Emotions and sexuality. In K. McKinney & S. Sprecher (Eds.), *Sexuality in close relationships* (pp. 49–70). Hillsdale, NJ: Erlbaum.

DeLamater, J., & MacCorquodale, P. (1979). *Premarital sexuality: Attitudes, relationships, behavior.* Madison: University of Wisconsin Press.

Delor, F., & Hubert, M. (2000). Revisiting the concept of "vulnerability." *Social Science and Medicine,* 50, 1557–70.

D'Emilio, J. (1983). *Sexual politics, sexual communities: The making of a homosexual minority in the United States.* Chicago: University of Chicago Press.

D'Emilio, J. (1989). Gay politics and community in San Francisco since World War II. In M. B. Duberman, M. Vicinus, & G. Chauncey Jr. (Eds.), *Hidden from history: Reclaiming the gay and lesbian past* (pp. 456–73). New York: Penguin.

D'Emilio, J., & Freedman, E. B. (1988). *Intimate matters: A history of sexuality in America.* New York: Harper & Row.

Denzin, N. K. (1984). Toward a phenomenology of domestic violence. *American Journal of Sociology,* 90, 483–513.

DeParle, J. (1998). Welfare overhaul initiatives focus on fathers. *New York Times,* 3 September, pp. A1, A20.

Devanter, V. N. (1999). Prevention of sexually transmitted diseases: The need for social and behavioral science expertise in public health departments. *American Journal of Public Health,* 89, 815–18.

de Vaus, D., & McAllister, I. (1987). Gender differences in religion: A test of the structural location theory. *American Sociological Review,* 52, 472–81.

Diaz, R. M. (1998). *Latino gay men and HIV.* New York: Routledge.

Dillon, M. (1988). Rome and American Catholics. *Annuals of the American Academy of Political and Social Sciences,* 558 (July), 122–34.

Dillon, M. (1999). *Catholic identity: Balancing reason, faith, and power.* Cambridge: Cambridge University Press.

DiMaggio, P., & Mohr, J. (1985). Cultural capital, educational attainment, and marital selection. *American Journal of Sociology,* 90, 1231–61.

DiMaggio, P. J., & Powell, W. W. (1991). Introduction. In W. W. Powell & P. J. DiMaggio (Eds.), *The new institutionalism in organizational analysis* (pp. 1–38). Chicago: University of Chicago Press.

Division of STD Prevention. (1997). *Sexually transmitted diseases surveillance, 1996.* Atlanta: Centers for Disease Control and Prevention.

Dobash, R. E., & Dobash, R. P. (1979). *Violence against wives.* New York: Free Press.

Drexel, A. (1997). Before Paris burned: Race, class, and male homosexuality on the Chicago South Side, 1935–1960. In B. Beemyn (Ed.), *Creating a place for ourselves* (pp. 119–44). New York: Routledge.

Duberman, M. B., Vicinus, M., & Chauncey, G., Jr. (Eds.). (1989). *Hidden from history: Reclaiming the gay and lesbian past.* New York: Penguin.

Dutton, D. G., & Browning, J. J. (1988). Concern for power, fear of intimacy, and aversive stimuli for wife assault. In G. T. Hotaling, D. Finkelhor, J. T. Kirkpatrick, & M. A. Straus (Eds.), *Family abuse and its consequences: New directions in research* (pp. 1–10). Newbury Park, CA: Sage.

Duyves, M. (1994). Framing preferences, framing differences: Inventing Amsterdam as a gay capital. In R. G. Parker & J. H. Gagnon (Eds.), *Conceiving sexuality* (pp. 47–66). New York: Routledge.

Eggert, L. L., & Parks, M. R. (1987). Communication network involvement in adolescents' friendships and romantic relationships. In M. L. McLaughlin (Ed.), *Communication yearbook 10* (pp. 283–322). Newbury Park, CA: Sage.

Eiseland, N. (1997). Contending with a giant: The impact of a megachurch on ex-urban religious institutions. In P. E. Becker & N. Eiseland (Eds.), *Contemporary American religion* (pp. 191–219). Walnut Creek, CA: Alta Mira.

Ellingson, S., & Schroeder, K. (1999). Race and the construction of same-sex markets in four Chicago neighborhoods. Paper presented at the annual meeting of the American Sociological Association, Chicago, 8 August.

Ellingson, S., Tebbe, N., Van Haitsma, M., & Laumann, E. O. (2001). Religion and the politics of sexuality. *Journal of Contemporary Ethnography, 30*, 3–55.

Ellwood, D. T., & Crane, J. (1990). Family change among black Americans: What do we know? *Journal of Economic Perspectives, 4*, 65–84.

Eng, T. R., & Butler, W. T. (Eds.). (1997). *The hidden epidemic.* Washington, DC: National Academy Press.

Engel, G. (1977). The need for a new medical model: A challenge for biomedicine. *Science, 196*, 129–36.

England, P., & Farkas, G. (1986). *Households, employment, and gender: A social, economic, and demographic view.* New York: Aldine de Gruyter.

England, P., & Kilbourne, B. S. (1990). Markets, marriages, and other mates: The problem of power. In R. Friedland & A. F. Robertson (Eds.), *Beyond the marketplace: Rethinking economy and society* (pp. 163–88). New York: Aldine de Gruyter.

Espenshade, T. J. (1985). Marriage trends in America: Estimates, implications, and underlying causes. *Population and Development Review, 11*, 193–245.

Espin, O. M. (1987). Issues of identity in the psychology of Latina lesbians. In the Boston Lesbian Psychology Collective (Ed.), *Lesbian psychologies* (pp. 35–55). Urbana: University of Illinois Press.

Esterberg, K. G. (1996). A certain swagger when I walk: Performing lesbian identity. In S. Seidman (Ed.), *Queer theory/sociology* (pp. 259–79). Cambridge, MA: Blackwell.

Esterberg, K. G. (1997). *Lesbian and bisexual identities: Constructing communities, constructing selves.* Philadelphia: Temple University Press.

Estrich, S. (1986). Rape. *Yale University Law Journal, 95*, 1087–92.

Faderman, L. (1992). The return of butch and femme: A phenomenon in lesbian sexuality of the 1980s and 1990s. *Journal of the History of Sexuality, 2*, 578–96.

Fanon, F. (1967). *Black skin, white masks.* New York: Grove.

Faulkner, R. R., & Anderson, A. B. (1987). Short-term projects and emergent careers—evidence from Hollywood. *American Journal of Sociology*, 92, 879–909.

Feeney, J. A., Noller, P., & Hanrahan, M. (1994). Attachment style and romantic
love: Relationship dissolution. *Journal of Social and Personal Relationships*, 8,
187–215.

Fehr, E., & Gächter, S. (2002). Altruistic punishment in humans. *Nature*, 415, 137–40.

Feld, S. (1981). The focused organization of social ties. *American Journal of Sociology*,
86 (5), 1015–35.

Fenstermaker, S., West, C., & Zimmerman, D. (1991). Gender and inequality: New
conceptual terrain. In R. L. Blumberg (Ed.), *Gender, family, and economy: The
triple overlap* (pp. 289–307). Newbury Park, CA: Sage.

Fernandez, R. M., & Gould, R. V. (1994). A dilemma of state power: Brokerage
and influence in the national health policy domain. *American Journal of Sociology*,
99, 1455–91.

Ferrand, A., Marquet, J., & Van Campenhoudt, L. (1998). Social networks and
normative context. In M. Hubert, N. Bajos, & T. Sandefort (Eds.), *Sexual behaviour and HIV/AIDS in Europe: Comparisons of national surveys* (pp. 303–27). London: UCL.

Field, H. S. (1978). Juror background characteristics and attitudes toward rape. *Law
and Human Behavior*, 2, 73–93.

Finke, R., & Stark, R. (1992). *The churching of America, 1776–1990: Winners and los-
ers in our religious economy.* New Brunswick, NJ: Rutgers University Press.

Fischer, C. S. (1975). Toward a subcultural theory of urbanism. *American Journal of
Sociology*, 80 (May), 1319–41.

Fischer, C. S. (1982). What do we mean by "friend"? An inductive study. *Social
Networks*, 3, 287–306.

Fischer, C. S. (1995). The subcultural theory of urbanism: A twentieth-year assessment. *American Journal of Sociology*, 101 (November), 543–77.

Fisher, R. D., Derison, D., Polley, C. F., III, Cadman, J. & Johnston, D. (1994). Re-
ligiousness, religious orientation, and attitudes towards gays and lesbians. *Journal
of Applied Social Psychology*, 24, 614–30.

Fitch, C., & Ruggles, S. (2000). Historical trends in marriage formation: The
United States, 1850–1990. In L. J. Waite, C. Bachrach, M. Hindin, E. Thomson, & A. Thornton (Eds.), *The ties that bind: Perspectives on marriage and cohabitation* (pp. 59–88). New York: Aldine de Gruyter.

Forste, R., & Tanfer, K. (1996). Sexual exclusivity among dating, cohabiting, and
married women. *Journal of Marriage and the Family*, 58, 33–47.

Fossett, M. A., & Kiecolt, K. J. (1991). A methodological review of the sex ratio:
Alternatives for comparative research. *Journal of Marriage and the Family*, 53,
941–57.

Foucault, M. (1990). *The history of sexuality.* 3 vols. in 1. New York: Vintage.

Frank, R. H. (1988). *Passions within reason: The strategic role of the emotions.* New
York: Norton.

Frank, R. H. (1993). The strategic role of emotions: Reconciling over- and under-
socialized accounts. *Rationality and Society*, 5, 160–84.

Frey, B. S., & Eichenberger, R. (1996). Marriage paradoxes. *Rationality and Society*, 8, 187–206.

Friedkin, N. E. (1998). *A structural theory of social influence*. New York: Cambridge University Press.

Friedland, R., & Alford, R. R. (1991). Bringing society back in: Symbols, practices, and institutional contradictions. In W. W. Powell & P. DiMaggio (Eds.), *The new institutionalism in organizational analysis* (pp. 232–63). Chicago: University of Chicago Press.

Fulkerson, M. M. (1995). Church documents on human sexuality and the authority of Scripture. *Interpretation*, 49, 46–48.

Gale, D., & Shapley, S. L. (1962). College admissions and stability of marriage. *American Mathematical Monthly*, 69, 9–15.

Garnets, L. D., & Kimmel, D. C. (1993a). Cultural diversity among lesbian and gay men. In L. D. Garnets & D. C. Kimmel (Eds.), *Psychological perspectives on lesbian and gay male experiences* (pp. 331–37). New York: Columbia University Press.

Garnets, L. D., & Kimmel, D. C. (1993b). Introduction: Lesbian and gay male dimensions in the psychological study of human diversity. In L. D. Garnets & D. C. Kimmel (Eds.), *Psychological perspectives on lesbian and gay male experiences* (pp. 1–51). New York: Columbia University Press.

Garnett, G. P., & Anderson, R. M. (1993). Contact tracing and the estimation of sexual mixing patterns: The epidemiology of gonococcal infections. *Sexually Transmitted Diseases*, 20, 181–91.

Garnett, G. P., & Anderson, R. M. (1996). Sexually transmitted diseases and sexual behavior: Insights from mathematical models. *Journal of Infectious Diseases*, 174 (suppl. 2), S150–S161.

Geary, D. C., Rumsey, M., Bow-Thomas, C. C., & Hoard, M. K. (1995). Sexual jealousy as a facultative trait: Evidence from the pattern of sex differences in adults from China and the United States. *Ethology and Sociobiology*, 16, 355–83.

Geertz, C. (1992). The bazaar economy: Information and search in peasant marketing. In M. Granovetter & R. Swedberg (Eds.), *The sociology of economic life*. Boulder, CO: Westview.

Gelles, R. J. (1974). *The violent home: A study of physical aggression between husbands and wives*. Newbury Park, CA: Sage.

Gilkes, C. T. (1995). The storm and the light: Church, family, work, and social crisis in the African-American experience. In N. Ammerman & W. C. Roof (Eds.), *Work, family, and religion in contemporary society* (pp. 177–98). New York: Routledge.

Gilmartin, K. (1996). We weren't bar people: Middle-class lesbian identities and cultural spaces. *GLC*, 3, 1–51.

Gilson, A. B. (1995). *Eros breaking free: Interpreting sexual theo-ethics*. Cleveland: Pilgrim.

Glick, P., & Lin, S. (1986). Recent changes in divorce and remarriage. *Journal of Marriage and the Family*, 48, 737–47.

Glock, C. (1993). The churches and social change in twentieth-century America. *Annals of the American Academy of Political and Social Science*, 527, 67–83.

Goffman, E. (1977). The arrangement between the sexes. *Theory and Society*, 4, 310–31.

Goldscheider, F., & Waite, L. J. (1991). *New families, no families? The transformation of the American home*. Berkeley and Los Angeles: University of California Press.

Granovetter, M. (1985). Economic action and social structure: The problem of embeddedness. *American Journal of Sociology*, 91, 481–510.

Gray, E. R., & Thumma, S. L. (1997). The gospel hour: Liminality, identity, and religion in a gay bar. In P. E. Becker & N. L. Eiseland (Eds.), *Contemporary American religion: An ethnographic reader* (pp. 79–98). Walnut Creek, CA: Alta Mira.

Greeley, A. M. (1989). *Religious change in America*. Cambridge, MA: Harvard University Press.

Greeley, A. M. (1994). *Sex: The Catholic experience*. Allen, TX: Thomas More.

Grossbard, A. (1978). Towards a marriage between economics and anthropology. *American Economic Review*, 68, 33–37.

Grossbard, A. (1980). The economics of polygamy. *Research in Population Economics*, 2, 231–50.

Gusfield, J. R. (1981). *The culture of public problems: Drinking-driving and the symbolic order*. Chicago: University of Chicago Press.

Gutman, H. G. (1976). *The black family in slavery and freedom, 1750–1925*. New York: Pantheon.

Guttentag, M., & Secord, P. F. (1983). *Too many women: The sex ratio question*. Beverly Hills, CA: Sage.

Hannan, M. T., & Freeman, J. (1977). Population ecology of organizations. *American Journal of Sociology*, 82, 929–64.

Hansen, G. L. (1985). Perceived threats and marital jealousy. *Social Psychology Quarterly*, 48, 262–68.

Hartman, A. (1994). Social work practice. In F. G. Reamer (Ed.), *The foundations of social work knowledge* (pp. 13–50). New York: Columbia University Press.

Hartman, K. (1996). *Congregations in conflict: The battle over homosexuality*. New Brunswick, NJ: Rutgers University Press.

Haveman, H. A., & Rao, H. (1997). Structuring a theory of moral sentiments: Institutional and organizational coevolution in the early thrift industry. *American Journal of Sociology*, 102, 1606–51.

Heckman, J. (1976). The common structure of statistical models of truncation, sample selection, and limited dependent variables and a simple estimator for such models. *Annals of Economic and Social Measurement*, 5, 475–92.

Heckman, J. (1979). Sample selection bias as a specification error. *Econometrica*, 45, 153–61.

Hengehold, L. (2000). Remapping the event: Institutional discourses and the trauma of rape. *Signs*, 26 (1), 189–214.

Herdt, G. (1992a). Coming out as a rite of passage: A Chicago study. In G. Herdt (Ed.), *Gay culture in America: Essays from the field* (pp. 29–67). Boston: Beacon.

Herdt, G. (Ed.). (1992b). *Gay culture in America: Essays from the field*. Boston: Beacon.

Herek, G. M., & Capitanio, J. (1995). Black heterosexuals' attitudes toward lesbians and gay men in the United States. *Journal of Sex Research*, 32, 95–105.

Hertel, B. R. (1995). Work, family, and faith. In N. Ammerman & N. C. Roof (Eds.), *Work, family, and religion in contemporary society*. New York: Routledge.

Hertel, B. R., & Hughes, M. (1987). Religious affiliation and support for "pro-family" issues in the United States. *Social Forces, 65*, 858–82.

Hilton, N. Z., Harris, G. T., & Rice, M. E. (2000). The functions of aggression by male teenagers. *Journal of Personality and Social Psychology, 79*, 988–94.

Hochschild, A. R. (1983). *The managed heart: Commercialization of human feeling*. Berkeley and Los Angeles: University of California Press.

Hondagneu-Sotelo, P. (1994). *Gendered transitions: Mexican experiences of immigration*. Berkeley and Los Angeles: University of California Press.

Horowitz, R. (1983). *Honor and the American dream: Culture and identity in a Chicano community*. New Brunswick, NJ: Rutgers University Press.

Horwitz, A., White, H. R., & Howell-White, S. (1996). Becoming married and mental health: A longitudinal study of a cohort of young adults. *Journal of Marriage and the Family, 58*, 895–908.

House, J. S., Landis, K. R., & Umberson, D. (1988). Social relationships and health. *Science, 241*, 540–45.

Hout, M., & Greeley, A. (1987). The center doesn't hold: Church attendance in the United States, 1940–1984. *American Sociological Review, 52*, 325–45.

Houts, R., Robins, E., & Huston, T. L. (1996). Compatibility and the development of premarital relationships. *Journal of Marriage and the Family, 58*, 7–20.

Huang, G., & Tausig, M. (1990). Network range in personal networks. *Social Networks, 12*, 261–68.

Hubert, M., Bajos, N., & Sandfort, T. (Eds.). (1998). *Sexual behaviour and HIV/AIDS in Europe: Comparisons of national surveys*. London: UCL.

Hunter, J. D. (1991). *Culture wars*. New York: Basic.

Hupka, R. B., & Bank, A. L. (1996). Sex differences in jealousy: Evolution or social construction? *Cross-Cultural Research, 30*, 24–59.

Hurtig, J. (1996). Pilsen: Parishes and churches in a Mexican-American neighborhood. In L. Livezey (Ed.), *Religious organizations and structural change in metropolitan Chicago: The research report of the Religion in Urban America Program* (pp. 139–74). Chicago: University of Illinois at Chicago Publication Services.

Huston, T. L., & Robins, E. (1982). Conceptual and methodological issues in studying close relationships. *Journal of Marriage and the Family, 44*, 901–25.

Icard, L. (1986). Black gay men and conflicting social identities: Sexual orientation versus racial identity. *Journal of Social Work and Human Sexuality, 4*, 83–93.

Jackson, J. J. (1983). Contemporary relationships between black families and black churches in the United States: A speculative inquiry. In W. V. D'Antonio & J. Aldous (Eds.), *Families and religion* (pp. 191–220). Beverly Hills, CA: Sage.

Jaynes, G. D., & Williams, R. M. (1989). *A common destiny: Blacks and American society*. Washington, D.C.: National Academy Press.

Jepperson, R. L. (1991). Institutions, institutional effects, and institutionalism. In W. W. Powell & P. J. DiMaggio (Eds.), *The new institutionalism in organizational analysis* (pp. 143–63). Chicago: University of Chicago Press.

Johnson, D. K. (1997). The kids of fairytown: Gay male culture on Chicago's Near

North Side in the 1930s. In B. Beemyn (Ed.), *Creating a place for ourselves* (pp. 97–118). New York: Routledge.

Johnson, M. P. (1973). Commitment: A conceptual structure and empirical applications. *Sociological Quarterly,* 14, 395–406.

Johnson, M. P. (1995). Patriarchal terrorism and common couple violence: Two forms of violence against women. *Journal of Marriage and the Family,* 57, 283–94.

Johnson, M., & Milardo, R. (1984). Network interference in pair relationships: A social psychological recasting of Slater's theory of social regression. *Journal of Marriage and the Family,* 46, 893–99.

Jones, L. N. (1993). Timeless priorities in changing contexts: African Americans and denominationalism. In J. W. Carroll & W. C. Roof (Eds.), *Beyond establishment: Protestant identity in a post-Protestant age* (pp. 228–47). Louisville: Westminster/John Knox.

Joyner, K., & Laumann, E. O. (2001). Teenage sex and the Sexual Revolution. In E. O. Laumann & R. T. Michael (Eds.), *Sex, Love, and Health in American: Private Choices and Public Consequences* (pp. 41–71). Chicago: University of Chicago Press.

Judson, F. N., & Paalman, M. (1991). Behavioral interventions in developed countries. In J. N. Wasserheit, S. O. Aral, K. K. Holmes, & P. J. Hitchcock (Eds.), *Research issues in human behavior and sexually transmitted diseases in the AIDS era* (pp. 296–304). Washington, DC: American Society for Microbiology.

Kalmijn, M. (1991a). Shifting boundaries: Trends in religious and educational homogamy. *American Sociological Review,* 56, 786–800.

Kalmijn, M. (1991b). Status homogamy in the United States. *American Journal of Sociology,* 97, 496–523.

Kalmijn, M. (1994). Assortative mating by cultural and economic occupational status. *American Journal of Sociology,* 100, 422–52.

Kalmijn, M. (1998). Intermarriage and homogamy: Causes, patterns, trends. *Annual Review of Sociology,* 24, 395–421.

Kalmijn, M., & Flap, H. (2001). Assortative meeting and mating: Unintended consequences of organized settings for partner choices. *Social Forces,* 79 (4), 1289–1312.

Kanazawa, S., & Still, M. C. (1999). Why monogamy? *Social Forces,* 78, 25–50.

Kang, J., & Mahay, J. (2001). Space, race, and community in sexual partnering: Implications for STD transmission. Paper presented at the annual meeting of the Population Association of America, Washington, DC, 29 March.

Kanter, R. M. (1968). Commitment and social organization: A study of commitment mechanisms in utopian communities. *American Sociological Review,* 33, 499–517.

Kanter, R. M. (1972). *Commitment and community: Communes and utopias in sociological perspective.* Cambridge, MA: Harvard University Press.

Keelan, J. P., Dion, K. L., & Dion, K. K. (1994). Attachment style and heterosexual relationships among young adults: A short-term panel study. *Journal of Social and Personal Relationships,* 11, 201–14.

Kendall, C. (1994). The construction of risk in AIDS control programs. In R. G.

Parker & J. H. Gagnon (Eds.), *Conceiving sexuality: Approaches to sex research in postmodern world* (pp. 249–58). New York: Routledge.

Kennedy, E. L., & Davis, M. D. (1997). I could hardly wait to get back to that bar: Lesbian bar culture in Buffalo in the 1930s and 1940s. In B. Beemyn (Ed.), *Creating a place for ourselves* (pp. 27–72). New York: Routledge.

Kerckhoff, A. C. (1974). The social context of interpersonal attraction. In T. L. Huston (Eds.), *Foundations of interpersonal attraction* (pp. 61–78). New York: Academic.

King, C. E., & Christensen, A. (1983). The relationship events scale: A Guttman scaling of progress in courtship. *Journal of Marriage and the Family, 45*, 671–78.

King, K., Balswick, J., & Robinson, I. E. (1977). The continuing premarital Sexual Revolution among college females. *Journal of Marriage and the Family, 39*, 455–59.

Kinkaid, D. L. (2000). Social networks, ideation, and contraceptive behavior in Bangladesh: A longitudinal analysis. *Social Science and Medicine, 50*, 215–31.

Kinsey, A. C., Pomeroy, W. B., & Martin, C. E. (1948). *Sexual behavior in the human male.* Philadelphia: Saunders.

Kinsey, A. C., Pomeroy, W. B., Martin, C. E., & Gebhard, P. H. (1953). *Sexual behavior in the human female.* Philadelphia: Saunders.

Klemmack, S. H., & Klemmack, D. L. (1976). The social definition of rape. In M. J. Walker & S. L. Brodsky (Eds.), *Sexual assault* (pp. 135–47). Lexington, MA: D. C. Heath.

Klinkenberg, D., & Rose, S. (1994). Dating scripts of gay men and lesbians. *Journal of Homosexuality, 26*, 23–35.

Knoke, D., & Laumann, E. O. (1982). The social organization of national policy domains: An exploration of some structural hypotheses. In P. V. Marsden & N. Lin (Eds.), *Social structure and network analysis* (pp. 255–70). Beverly Hills, CA: Sage.

Knopp, L. (1995). Sexuality and urban space: A framework for analysis. In D. Bell & G. Valentine (Eds.), *Mapping desire* (pp. 149–64). New York: Routledge.

Kollock, P. (1994). The emergence of exchange structures: An experimental study of uncertainty, commitment, and trust. *American Journal of Sociology, 100*, 313–45.

Kollock, P., Blumstein, P., & Schwartz, P. (1994). The judgment of equity in intimate relationships. *Social Psychology Quarterly, 57*, 340–51.

Koo, H., Suchindran, C. M., & Griffith, J. (1984). The effects of children on divorce and remarriage: A multivariate analysis of life table probabilities. *Population Studies, 38*, 451–71.

Koss, M. P. (1988). Hidden rape: Sexual aggression and victimization in the national sample of students in higher education. In M. A. Pirog-Good & J. E. Stets (Eds.)., *Violence in dating relationships: Emerging social issues* (pp. 145–68). New York: Praeger.

Koss, M., Dinero, T., Seibel, C., & Cox, S. (1988). Stranger and acquaintance rape: Are there differences in the victims' experiences? *Psychology of Women Quarterly, 12*, 1–24.

Koss, M. P., Gidycz, C. A., & Wisniewski, N. (1987). The scope of rape: Incidence and prevalence of sexual aggression and victimization in a national sample of higher education students. *Journal of Consulting and Clinical Psychology, 55* (2), 162.

Krane, M. (1977). A definition of dyadic boundaries and an empirical study of boundary establishment in courtship. *International Journal of Sociology of the Family*, 7, 107–23.

Kreiger, S. (1982). Lesbian identity and community: Recent social science literature. *Signs*, 8, 91–108.

Krulewitz, J. E., & Payne, E. J. (1981). Attributions about rape: Effects of rapist force, observer sex, and sex role attitudes. *Journal of Applied Social Psychology*, 8, 291–305.

Kurth, S. B. (1970). Friendship and friendly relations. In G. J. McCall (Ed.), *Social relationships* (pp. 136–70). Chicago: Aldine.

Kurz, D. (1989). Social science perspectives on wife abuse: Current debates and future directions. *Gender and Society*, 3, 489–505.

Lamont, M. (1999). Introduction: Beyond taking culture seriously. In M. Lamont (Ed.), *The cultural territories of race: Black and white boundaries* (pp. ix–xx). Chicago: University of Chicago Press.

Lancaster, R. (1988). Subject honor and object shame: The construction of male homosexuality and stigma in Nicaragua. *Ethnology*, 28, 111–26.

Laudarji, I. B., & Murphy, L. G. (1996). The urban ministry of West Side churches. In L. W. Livezey (Ed.), *Religious organizations and structural change in metropolitan Chicago: The research report of the Religion in Urban American Program* (pp. 107–38). Chicago: University of Illinois at Chicago Publication Services.

Laumann, E. O. (1966). *Prestige and association in an urban community*. New York: Bobbs-Merrill.

Laumann, E. O. (1973). *Bonds of pluralism: The form and substance of urban social networks*. New York: Wiley.

Laumann, E. O., & Gagnon, J. H. (1994). A sociological perspective on sexual action. In R. G. Parker & J. H. Gagnon (Eds.), *Conceiving sexuality: Approaches to sex in the post-modern world* (pp. 118–213). New York: Routledge.

Laumann, E. O., Gagnon, J. H., Michael, R. T., & Michaels, S. (1994). *The social organization of sexuality: Sexual practices in the United States*. Chicago: University of Chicago Press.

Laumann, E. O., Mahay, J., & Youm, Y. (2002). Sex, intimacy, and family life in the United States. Paper presented at the International Sociological Association XV World Congress of Sociology, Brisbane, 11 July.

Laumann, E. O., & Michael, R. T. (Eds.). (2001). *Sex, love, and health in American: Private choices and public policies*. Chicago: University of Chicago Press.

Laumann, E. O., & Youm, Y. (1999). Race/ethnic group differences in the prevalence of sexually transmitted diseases in the United States: A network explanation. *Sexually Transmitted Diseases*, 26, 250–61.

Lauria, M., & Knopp, L. (1985). Toward an analysis of the role of gay communities in the urban renaissance. *Urban Geography*, 6, 152–69.

Lawler, E. J. (1992). Affective attachments to nested groups: A choice-process theory. *American Sociological Review*, 57, 327–39.

Lawler, E. J., & Yoon, J. (1993). Power and the emergence of commitment behavior in negotiated exchange. *American Sociological Review*, 58, 465–81.

Lawler, E. J., & Yoon, J. (1996). Commitment in exchange relations: Test of a theory of relational cohesion. *American Sociological Review,* 61, 89–108.

Lennon, M. C., & Rosenfield, S. (1994). Relative fairness and the division of housework: The importance of options. *American Journal of Sociology,* 100, 506–31.

Lerman, R. I. (1989). Employment opportunities of young men and family formation. *Papers and Proceedings of the American Economic Association,* 79, 62–66.

Leslie, L. A., Huston, T., & Johnson, M. (1986). Parental reactions to dating relationships: Do they make a difference? *Journal of Marriage and the Family,* 48, 57–66.

Levine, M. P. (1992). The life and death of gay clones. In G. Herdt (Ed.), *Gay culture in America: Essays from the field* (pp. 68–86). Boston: Beacon.

Lewis, R. (1973). Social reaction and the formation of dyads: An interactionist approach to mate selection. *Sociometry,* 36, 409–18.

Lichter, D., LeClere, F., & McLaughlin, D. (1991). Local marriage markets and the marital behavior of black and white women. *American Journal of Sociology,* 96, 843–67.

Lichter, D., McLaughlin, D. K., Kephart, G., & Landry, D. J. (1992). Race and the retreat from marriage: A shortage of marriageable men? *American Sociological Review,* 57, 781–99.

Liefbroer, A., Gerritsen, L., & Gierveld, J. D. (1994). The influence of intentions and life course factors on union formation behavior of young adults. *Journal of Marriage and the Family,* 56, 193–201.

Lincoln, C. E., & Mamiya, L. H. (1990). *The black church in the African American experience.* Durham, NC: Duke University Press.

Lloyd, K., & South, S. (1996). Contextual influences on young men's transition to first marriage. *Social Forces,* 74 (3), 1097–1119.

Lloyd, S. A., Cate, R. M., & Henton, J. M. (1984). Predicting premarital relationship stability: A methodological refinement. *Journal of Marriage and the Family,* 46, 71–76.

Loiacano, D. K. (1989). Gay identity issues among black Americans: Racism, homophobia, and the need for validation. *Journal of Counseling and Development,* 68, 21–25.

Lorde, A. (1984). *Sister outsider.* Trumansberg, NY: Crossing.

Lupton, D. (1999). *Risk.* New York: Routledge.

Madriz, E. (1997). *Nothing bad happens to good girls: Fear of crime in women's lives.* Berkeley and Los Angeles: University of California Press.

Magana, J. R., & Carrier, J. M. (1991). Mexican and Mexican American male sexual behavior and spread of AIDS in California. *Journal of Sex Research,* 28, 425–41.

Mahay, J., Laumann, E. O., & Michaels, S. (2001). Race, gender, and class in sexual scripts. In E. O. Laumann & R. T. Michael (Eds.), *Sex, love, and health in America: Private choices and public policies* (pp. 197–238). Chicago: University of Chicago Press.

Mann, M. (1986). *The sources of social power: A history of power from the beginning to A.D. 1760.* Vol. 1. New York: Cambridge University Press.

Manning, W., & Smock, P. (1995). Why marry? Race and the transition to marriage among cohabitors. *Demography*, 32, 509–20.

Mare, R. (1991). Five decades of educational assortative mating. *American Sociological Review*, 56, 15–32.

Mare, R., & Winship, C. (1991). Socioeconomic change and the decline of marriage for blacks and whites. In C. Jencks & P. Peterson (Eds.), *The urban underclass* (pp. 175–202). Washington, DC: Urban Institute.

Marín, B. V. (1996). Cultural issues in HIV prevention for Latinos: Should we try to change gender roles? In S. Oskamp & S. C. Thompson (Eds.), *Understanding and preventing HIV risk behavior: Safer sex and drug use* (pp. 157–76). Thousand Oaks, CA: Sage.

Markova, I., & Wilkie, P. (1987). Representations, concepts, and social change: The phenomenon of AIDS. *Journal for the Theory of Social Behavior*, 17, 398–409.

Marks, N. (1996). Flying solo at midlife: Gender, marital status, and psychological well-being. *Journal of Marriage and the Family*, 58, 917–32.

Marks, N., & Lambert, J. D. (1998). Marital status continuity and change among young and midlife adults. *Journal of Family Issues*, 19, 652–86.

Marler, P. L., & Hadaway, C. K. (1993). New church development and denominational growth (1950–1988): Symptom or cause? In D. A. Roozen & C. K. Hadaway (Eds.), *Church growth and denominational growth* (pp. 47–86). Nashville: Abingdon.

Marsden, P. V. (1987). Core discussion networks of Americans. *American Sociological Review*, 52, 122–31.

Marsden, P. V. (1988). Homogeneity in confiding relations. *Social Networks*, 10, 57–76.

Martin, D. (1981). *Battered wives.* Volcano, CA; Volcano.

Massey, D. S., & Denton, N. A. (1993). *American apartheid: Segregation and the making of the underclass.* Cambridge, MA: Harvard University Press.

Mastekaasa, A. (1994). The subjective well-being of the previously married: The importance of unmarried cohabitation and time since widowhood or divorce. *Social Forces*, 73, 665–92.

McCall, G. J., McCall, M. M., Denzin, N. K., Suttles, G. D., & Kurth, S. B. (1970). *Social relationships.* Chicago: Aldine.

McCall, G. J., & Simmons, J. L. (1978). *Identities and interactions: An examination of human associations in everyday life.* New York: Free Press.

McLanahan, S. S., & Casper, L. (1995). Growing diversity and inequality in the American family. In R. Farley (Ed.), *State of the Union: America in the 1990s* (pp. 1–45). New York: Sage.

McLanahan, S., & Sandefur, G. (1994). *Growing up with a single parent: What hurts, what helps.* Cambridge, MA: Harvard University Press.

McLaughlin, D. K., & Lichter, D. T. (1997). Poverty and the marital behavior of young women. *Journal of Marriage and the Family*, 59 (3), 582–95.

McLaughlin, D. K., Lichter, D. T., & Johnston, G. M. (1993). Some women marry young: Transitions to first marriage in metropolitan and nonmetropolitan areas. *Journal of Marriage and the Family*, 55, 827–38.

McMullen, M. (1994). Religious polities as institutions. *Social Forces,* 73, 709–28.

McPherson, J. M. (1982). Hypernetwork sampling: Duality and differentiation among voluntary organizations. *Social Networks,* 3, 225–49.

McPherson, M. (1983). An ecology of affiliation. *American Sociological Review* 48, 519–32.

McRoberts, O. M. (2003). *Streets of glory: Church and community in a black urban neighborhood.* Chicago: University of Chicago Press.

Michael, R. T., Gagnon, J. H., Laumann, E. O., & Kolata, G. B. (1994). *Sex in America: A definitive survey.* New York: Little, Brown.

Michael, R. T., & Tuman, N. B. (1985). Entry into marriage and parenthood by young men and women: The influence of family background. *Demography,* 2, 515–44.

Miller, A. S. (1996). The influence of religious affiliation on the clustering of social attitudes. *Review of Religious Research,* 37, 219–32.

Mirowsky, J., & Ross, C. (1989). *Social causes of psychological distress.* New York: Aldine de Gruyter.

Monti, J. (1995). *Arguing about sex: The rhetoric of Christian sexual morality.* Albany: State University of New York Press.

Moore, G. (1990). Structural determinants of men's and women's personal networks. *American Sociological Review,* 55, 726–35.

Morgan, S. P., & Waite, L. J. (1987). Parenthood and the attitudes of young adults. *American Sociological Review,* 52, 541–47.

Morris, C. (1990). AIDS: Does the church care? *Sojourners,* 19, 19–21.

Morris, M., & Kretzschmar, M. (1995). Concurrent partnerships and transmission dynamics in networks. *Social Networks,* 17, 299–318.

Morris, M., Zavisca, J., & Dean, L. (1995). Social and sexual networks: Their role in the spread of HIV/AIDS among young gay men. *AIDS Education and Prevention,* 7 (suppl.), S24–S35.

Mortensen, D. T. (1988). Matching: Finding a partner for life or otherwise? *American Journal of Sociology,* 94 (suppl.), S215–S240.

Mott, F., & Moore, S. (1983). The tempo of remarriage among young American women. *Journal of Marriage and the Family,* 45, 427–36.

Mowday, R., Porter, L., & Steers, R. (1982). *Employee-organization linkages: The psychology of commitment, absenteeism, and turnover.* New York: Academic.

Murray, S. O. (1996). *American gay.* Chicago: University of Chicago Press.

Nannini, D. K., & Meyers, L. S. (2000). Jealousy in sexual and emotional infidelity: An alternative to the evolutionary explanation. *Journal of Sex Research,* 37, 117–22.

Nathanson, C. A. (1991). *Dangerous passages.* Philadelphia: Temple University Press.

Newman, J. C., Des Jarlais, D. C., Turner, C. F., Gribble, J., Cooley, P., and Paone, D. (2002). The differential effects of face-to-face and computer interview modes. *American Journal of Public Health,* 92, 294–97.

Newton, E. (1993). Just one of the boys: Lesbians in Cherry Grove, 1960–1988. In H. Abelove, M. A. Barale, & D. V. Halpern (Eds.), *The lesbian and gay studies reader* (pp. 528–41). New York: Routledge.

O'Flaherty, K., & Eells, L. W. (1988). Courtship behavior of the remarried. *Journal of Marriage and the Family, 50,* 499–506.

Oppenheimer, V. K. (1988). A theory of marriage timing. *American Journal of Sociology, 94,* 563–91.

Oppenheimer, V. K. (1994). Women's rising employment and the future of the family in industrial societies. *Population and Development Review, 20,* 293–342.

Oppenheimer, V. K., Kalmijn, M., & Lim, N. (1997). Men's career development and marriage timing during a period of rising inequality. *Demography, 34,* 331–41.

Oppenheimer, V. K., & Lew, V. (1995). Marriage formation in the 1980s: How important was women's economic independence? In K. Mason & A. Jensen (Eds.), *Gender and family change in industrialized countries* (pp. 105–38). Oxford: Clarendon.

Oropesa, R. S., Lichter, D. T., & Anderson, R. N. (1994). Marriage markets and the paradox of Mexican American nuptiality. *Journal of Marriage and the Family, 56,* 889–907.

Ostrow, D. G., Beltran, E., & Joseph, J. (1994). Sexual behavior research on a cohort of gay men, 1984–1990: Can we predict how men will respond to interventions? *Archives of Sexual Behavior, 23,* 531–52.

Parish, W. L., Laumann, E. O., Cohen, M. S., Pan, S., Zheng, H., Hoffman, I., Wang, T., & Ng, K. (2003). Population-based study of chlamydial infection in China: A hidden epidemic. *Journal of the American Medical Association, 289* (10), 1265–73.

Park, R. E. ([1929] 1967). The city as a social laboratory. In R. H. Turner (Ed.), *Robert E. Park on social control and collective behavior* (pp. 3–18). Chicago: University of Chicago Press.

Parker, R. G., & Carballo, M. (1990). Qualitative research on homosexual behavior and bisexual behavior relevant to HIV/AIDS. *Journal of Sex Research, 27,* 497–525.

Parks, M. R., Stan, C. M., & Eggert, L. L. (1983). Romantic involvement and social network involvement. *Social Psychology Quarterly, 46,* 116–31.

Parsons, T. (1951). *The social system.* New York: Free Press.

Parsons, T. (1968). On the concept of value-commitments. *Sociological Inquiry, 38,* 135–60.

Peach, C. (1974). Homogamy, propinquity, and segregation: A re-evaluation. *American Sociological Review, 39:* 636–641.

Peters, J. H. (1976). Comparison of mate selection and marriage in the first and second marriage in a selected sample of the remarried. *Journal of Comparative Family Studies, 7,* 483–91.

Peterson, J. L. (1992). Black men and their same-sex desires and behaviors. In G. Herdt (Ed.), *Gay culture in America: Essays from the field* (pp. 147–64). Boston: Beacon.

Pines, A. M., & Friedman, A. (1998). Gender differences in romantic jealousy. *Journal of Social Psychology, 138,* 54–71.

Podolny, J. M. (1993). A status-based model of market competition. *American Journal of Sociology, 98,* 829–72.

Pollack, R. A. (2000). Theorizing marriage. In L. J. Waite, C. Bachrach, M. Hindin, E. Thomson, & A. Thornton (Eds.), *The ties that bind: Perspectives on marriage and cohabitation* (pp. 111–25). New York: Aldine de Gruyter.

Pollak, R. A. (1985). A transaction cost approach to families and households. *Journal of Economic Literature,* 23, 581–608.

Ponse, B. (1978). *Identity in the lesbian world.* Westport, CT: Greenwood.

Potterat, J. J., Rothenberg, R. B., Woodhouse, D. E., Muth, J. B., Pratts, C. I., & Fogle, J. S., II. (1985). Gonorrhea as a social disease. *Sexually Transmitted Diseases,* 12, 25–32.

Potterat, J. J., Rothenberg, R. B., & Muth, S. Q. (1999). Network structural dynamics and infectious disease propagation. *International Journal of STD and AIDS,* 10, 182–85.

Powell, W. W., & DiMaggio, P. J. (Eds.). (1991). *The new institutionalism in organizational analysis.* Chicago: University of Chicago Press.

Puente, T., & Quintanilla, T. (1997, April 13). Bringing it together. *Chicago Tribune,* 13 April, sec. I, p. 1.

Putnam, R. (2000). *Bowling alone.* New York: Simon & Schuster.

Qian, Z. (1998). Changes in assortative mating: The impact of age and education, 1970–1990. *Demography,* 35, 279–92.

Raley, R. K. (2000). Recent trends and differentials in marriage and cohabitation: The United States. In L. J. Waite, C. Bachrach, M. Hindin, E. Thomson, & A. Thornton (Eds.), *The ties that bind: Perspectives on marriage and cohabitation* (pp. 19–39). New York: Aldine de Gruyter.

Ramsoy, N. R. (1966). Assortative mating and the structure of cities. *American Sociological Review,* 31, 773–86.

Reckless, W. C. ([1926] 1982). The distribution of commercialized vice in the city: A sociological analysis. In G. A. Theodorson (Ed.), *Urban patterns: Studies in human ecology* (pp. 55–60). University Park: Pennsylvania State University Press.

Reid, P. N. (1992). The social function and social morality of social work: A utilitarian perspective. In P. N. Reid & P. R. Popple (Eds.), *The moral purposes of social work* (pp. 34–50). New York: Nelson-Hall.

Reiss, I. L. (1986). *Journey into sexuality: An exploratory voyage.* Englewood Cliffs, NJ: Prentice-Hall.

Reiss, I. L., Anderson, R. E., & Sponaugle, G. C. (1980). A multivariate model of determinants of extramarital permissiveness. *Journal of Marriage and the Family,* 42, 395–411.

Renzetti, C. M. (1992). *Violent betrayal: Partner abuse in lesbian relationships.* Newbury Park, CA: Sage.

Robinson, I., & Jedlicka, D. (1982). Change in sexual attitudes and behavior of college students from 1965 to 1980: A research note. *Journal of Marriage and the Family,* 44, 237–40.

Robinson, I., Ziss, K., Ganza, B., & Katz, S. (1991). Twenty years of the Sexual Revolution, 1965–1985. *Journal of Marriage and the Family,* 53, 216–20.

Robinson, S. L. (1996). Trust and breach of the psychological contract. *Administrative Science Quarterly,* 41, 574–99.

Rochefort, D. A., & Cobb, R. W. (Eds.). (1994). *The politics of problem definition.* Lawrence: University of Kansas Press.

Rodgers, R., & Conrad, L. (1986). Courtship for remarriage: Influences on family reorganization after divorce. *Journal of Marriage and the Family,* 48, 767–75.

Rogers, W. C., & Thornton, A. (1985). Changing patterns of first marriage in the United States. *Demography,* 22, 256–79.

Roof, W. C. (1993). *A generation of seekers: The spiritual journeys of the baby boom generation.* San Francisco: Harper.

Roof, W. C., & McKinney, W. (1985). Denominational religion and the new religious pluralism. *Annals of the American Academy of Political and Social Science,* 480, 24–38.

Roof, W. C., & McKinney, W. (1987). American mainline religion. New Brunswick, NJ: Rutgers University Press.

Rosenberg, D., Moseley, K., Kahn, R., Kissinger, P., Rice, J., Kendall, C., Coughlin, S., & Farley, T. A. (1999). Networks of persons with syphilis and at risk for syphilis in Louisiana: Evidence of core transmitters. *Sexually Transmitted Diseases,* 26 (2), 108–14.

Ross, C. E. (1995). Reconceptualizing marital status as a continuum of social attachment. *Journal of Marriage and the Family,* 52, 129–40.

Rothenberg, R. B., & Potterat, J. J. (1988). Temporal and social aspects of gonorrhea transmission: The force of infectivity. *Sexually Transmitted Diseases,* 15, 88–92.

Rothenberg, R. B., Potterat, J. J., & Woodhouse, D. E. (1996). Personal risk taking and the spread of disease: Beyond core groups. *Journal of Infectious Diseases,* 174 (suppl.), S144–S149.

Rothenberg, R. B., Sterk, C., Toomey, K. E., Potterat, J. J., Johnson, D., Schrader, M., & Hatch, S. (1998). Using social network and ethnographic tools to evaluate syphilis transmission. *Sexually Transmitted Diseases,* 25, 154–60.

Rothenberg, T. (1995). And she told two friends: Lesbians creating urban space. In D. Bell & G. Valentine (Eds.), *Mapping desire* (pp. 165–81). New York: Routledge.

Roy, M. (Ed.). (1976). *Battered women: A psychosocial study of domestic violence.* New York: Van Nostrand Reinhold.

Rubin, G. S. (1999). Thinking sex: Notes for a radical theory of the politics of sexuality. In R. Parker & P. Aggleton (Eds.), *Culture, society, and sexuality: A reader* (pp. 143–78). London: UCL.

Rusbult, C. E., Johnson, D. J., & Morrow, G. D. (1986). Predicting satisfaction and commitment in adult romantic involvements: An assessment of generalizability of the investment model. *Social Psychology Quarterly,* 49, 81–89.

Sacher, J., & Fine, M. (1996). Predicting relationship status and satisfaction after six months among dating couples. *Journal of Marriage and the Family,* 58, 21–32.

Sadownick, D. (1996). *Sex between men: An intimate history of the sex lives of gay men postwar to the present.* San Francisco: Harper San Francisco.

Sampson, R. J. (2002). Studying modern Chicago. *City and Community,* 1, 45–48.

Sandefur, R. L., & Laumann, E. O. (1998). A paradigm for social capital. *Rationality and Society,* 10, 481–501.

Scanzoni, J. K. P., Teachman, J., & Thompson, L. (1989). *The sexual bond: Rethinking families and close relationships.* Newbury Park, CA: Sage.

Scharfe, E., & Bartholomew, K. (1994). Reliability and stability of adult attachment patterns. *Personal Relationships, 1,* 23–43.

Schein, E. H. (1991). What is culture? In P. J. Frost, L. F. Moore, M. R. Louis, C. C. Lundberg, & J. Martin (Eds.), *Reframing organizational culture* (pp. 243–53). Newbury Park, CA: Sage.

Schneider, A., & Ingram, H. (1993). Social construction of target populations: Implications for politics and policy. *American Political Science Review, 87,* 334–47.

Schoen, R., & Wooldredge, J. (1989). Marriage choices in North Carolina and Virginia, 1969–71 and 1979–81. *Journal of Marriage and the Family, 51,* 465–81.

Schroeder, K., & Mahay, J. (2000). The sexually partitioned city: Ethnicity, geography, and sexuality in the city of Chicago. Paper presented at the annual meeting of the Population Association of America, City, 24 March.

Schwartz, P., & Gillmore, M. R. (1990). Sociological perspectives on human sexuality. In K. K. Holmes, S. Lemon, W. Stamm, & W. Cates Jr. (Eds.), *Sexually transmitted diseases* (2d ed., pp. 45–54). New York: McGraw-Hill.

Scott, D. (1994). Jungle fever? Black gay identity politics, white dick, and the utopian bedroom. *GLQ, 1,* 299–321.

Scott, J. F. (1965). The American college sorority: Its role in class and ethnic endogamy. *American Sociological Review, 30,* 514–27.

Seidman, S. (1989). Constructing sex as a domain of pleasure and self-expression: Sexual ideology in the sixties. *Theory, Culture, and Society, 6,* 293–315.

Seidman, S. (1999). Contesting the moral boundaries of eros. In N. J. Smelser & J. Alexander (Eds.), *Diversity and its discontents* (pp. 167–89). Princeton, NJ: Princeton University Press.

Senchak, M., & Leonard, K. E. (1992). Attachment styles and marital adjustments among newlywed couples. *Journal of Social and Personal Relationships, 9,* 51–64.

Shaver, P. R., & Brennan, K. A. (1992). Attachment styles and the big five personality traits: Their connections with each other and with romantic relationship outcomes. *Personality and Social Psychology Bulletin, 18,* 536–45.

Sherkat, D. E., & Ellison, C. G. (1995). Sociology and the scientific study of religion. *Social Forces, 73,* 1255–66.

Sherkat, D. E., & Ellison, C. G. (1997). The cognitive structure of a moral crusade: Conservative Protestantism and opposition to pornography. *Social Forces, 75,* 957–82.

Shilts, R. (1987). *And the band played on: Politics, people, and the AIDS epidemic.* New York: St. Martin's.

Simmel, G. ([1903] 1971). The metropolis and mental life. In D. N. Levine & M. Janowitz (Eds.), *Georg Simmel on individuality and social forms.* Chicago: University of Chicago Press.

Simon, H. (1957). *Administrative behavior* (2d ed.). New York: Macmillan.

Simon, W., & Gagnon, J. H. (1987). A sexual scripts approach. In J. Greer & W. T. O'Donohue (Eds.), *Theories of human sexuality* (pp. 363–83). New York: Plenum.

Simon, W., & Gagnon, J. H. (1998). Homosexuality: The formulation of a socio-
    logical perspective. In P. M. Nardi & B. E. Schneider (Eds.), *Social perspectives in
    lesbian and gay studies: A reader* (pp. 59–67). London: Routledge.

Slater, P. E. (1963). On social regression. *American Sociological Review,* 28, 339–65.

Smelser, N. J. (1998). The rational and the ambivalent in the social sciences. *Ameri-
    can Sociological Review,* 63, 1–16.

Smith, C. (1998). *American evangelicalism: Embattled and thriving.* Chicago: University
    of Chicago Press.

Smith, K. R., Zick, C. D., & Duncan, G. (1991). Remarriage patterns among re-
    cent widows and widowers. *Demography,* 28 (3), 361–74.

Smits, J., Ultee, W., & Lammers, J. (1998). Educational homogamy in 65 countries:
    An explanation of differences in openness using country-level explanatory vari-
    ables. *American Sociological Review,* 63, 264–85.

Smock, P. (1990). Remarriage patterns of black and white women: Reassessing the
    role of educational attainment. *Demography,* 27, 467–73.

Smock, P., & Manning, W. (1997). Cohabiting partners' economic circumstances
    and marriage. *Demography,* 34 (3), 331–41.

South, S. J. (1986). Sex ratios, economic power, and women's roles: A theoretical
    extension and empirical test. *Journal of Marriage and the Family,* 50, 19–31.

South, S. J. (1991). Sociodemographic differentials in mate selection preferences.
    *Journal of Marriage and the Family,* 53, 928–40.

South, S. J. (1992). For love or money? Sociodemographic determinants of the ex-
    pected benefits from marriage. In S. South & S. E. Tonay (Eds.), *The changing
    American family: Sociological and demographic perspectives* (pp. 171–94). Boulder,
    CO: Westview.

South, S. J. (1993). Racial and ethnic differences in the desire to marry. *Journal of
    Marriage and the Family,* 55, 357–70.

South, S. J., & Lloyd, K. M. (1992). Marriage opportunities and family formations:
    Further implications of imbalanced sex ratios. *Journal of Marriage and the Family,*
    54, 440–51.

South, S. J., & Lloyd, K. M. (1995). Spousal alternatives and marital dissolution.
    *American Sociological Review,* 60, 21–35.

South, S. J., & Mesner, S. F. (1988). The sex ratio and women's involvement in
    crime: A cross-national analysis. *Sociological Quarterly,* 28, 171–88.

Spanier, G., & Glick, P. (1980). Mate selection differentials between whites and
    blacks in the United States. *Social Forces,* 58, 707–25.

Sparling, P. F., & Aral, S. O. (1991). The importance of an interdisciplinary ap-
    proach to prevention of sexually transmitted diseases. In J. N. Wasserheit, S. O.
    Aral, K. K. Holmes, & P. J. Hitchcock (Eds.), *Research issues in human behavior
    and sexually transmitted diseases in the AIDS era* (pp. 10–11). Washington, DC:
    American Society for Microbiology.

Sprecher, S. (2001). Equity and social exchange in dating couples: Associations with
    satisfaction, commitment, and stability. *Journal of Marriage and the Family,* 63,
    599–613.

Sprecher, S., & Felmlee, D. (1992). The influence of parents and friends on the quality and stability of romantic relationships: A three-wave longitudinal investigation. *Journal of Marriage and the Family*, 54, 888–900.

Sprecher, S., & McKinney, K. (1993). *Sexualities*. Newbury Park, CA: Sage.

Sprecher, S., McKinney, K., & Orbuch, T. L. (1987). Has the double standard disappeared? An experimental test. *Social Psychology Quarterly*, 50, 24–31.

Stearns, P. N. (1989). *Jealousy: The evolution of an emotion in American history*. New York: New York University Press.

Stets, J. E., & Pirog-Good, M. A. (1987). Violence in dating relationships. *Social Psychology Quarterly*, 50, 237–46.

Stokes, J. P., Vanable, P. A., & McKirnan, D. J. (1996). Ethnic differences in sexual behavior, condom use, and psychosocial variables among black and white men who have sex with men. *Journal of Sex Research*, 33, 373–81.

Stolzenberg, R. M., Blair-Loy, M., & Waite, L. J. (1995). Religious participation in early adulthood: Age and family life cycle effects on church membership. *American Sociological Review*, 60, 84–103.

Stolzenberg, R. M., & Relles, D. (1990). Theory testing in a world of constrained research design: The significance of Heckman's censored sampling bias correction for nonexperimental research. *Sociological Methods and Research*, 18, 395–415.

Stolzenberg, R. M., & Relles, D. (1997). Tools for intuition about sample bias and its correction. *American Sociological Review*, 62, 494–507.

Stone, D. A. (1989). Casual stories and the formation of policy agendas. *Political Science Quarterly*, 104, 281–300.

Straus, M. A. (1971). Some social antecedents of physical punishment: A linkage theory interpretation. *Journal of Marriage and the Family*, 33, 658–63.

Straus, M. A. (1979). Measuring intrafamily conflict and violence: The Conflict Tactics (CT) scales. *Journal of Marriage and the Family*, 41, 75–88.

Sudman, S., & Bradburn, N. M. (1982). *Asking questions: A practical guide to questionnaire design*. San Francisco: Jossey-Bass.

Surra, C. A., & Gray, C. R. (2000). A typology of processes of commitment to marriage: Why do partners commit to problematic relationships? In L. J. Waite, C. Bachrach, M. Hindin, E. Thomson, & A. Thornton (Eds.), *The ties that bind: Perspectives on marriage and cohabitation* (pp. 253–80). New York: Aldine de Gruyter.

Sweeney, M. (1997). Remarriage of women and men after divorce: The role of socioeconomic prospects. *Journal of Family Issues*, 18, 479–502.

Swidler, A. (1980). Love and adulthood in American culture. In N. J. Smelser & E. H. Erikson (Eds.), *Themes of work and love in adulthood* (pp. 120–47). Cambridge, MA: Harvard University Press.

Swidler, A. (2001). *Talk of love*. Chicago: University of Chicago Press.

Swidler, A. (2002). Saving the self: Endowment vs. depletion in American institutions. In R. Madsen, W. M. Sullivan, A. Swidler, & S. M. Tipton (Eds.), *Meaning and modernity: Religion, polity, and self* (pp. 41–55). Berkeley and Los Angeles: University of California Press.

Tanfer, K., & Schoon, J. J. (1992). Premarital sexual careers and partner change. *Archives of Sexual Behavior,* 21, 45–68.

Taylor, R. J., Chatters, L. M., Tucker, M. B., & Lewis, E. (1990). Developments in research on black families: A decade review. *Journal of Marriage and the Family,* 52, 993–1014.

Teachman, J., & Heckert, A. (1985). The impact of age and children on remarriage. *Journal of Family Issues,* 6, 185–203.

Thomas, S. B., & Quinn, S. C. (1991). The Tuskegee syphilis study, 1932–1972: Implications for HIV education and AIDS risk education programs in the black community. *American Journal of Public Health,* 81 (11), 1498–1504.

Thomson, E., & Collela, U. (1992). Cohabitation and marital stability: Quality or commitment? *Journal of Marriage and the Family,* 54, 259–67.

Thompson, L., & Walker, A. J. (1982). The dyad as the unit of analysis: Conceptual and methodological issues. *Journal of Marriage and the Family* (44), 889–900.

Thornton, A. (1989). Changing attitudes toward family issues in the United States. *Journal of Marriage and the Family,* 51, 873–93.

Thornton, A., Alwin, D. F., & Camburn, D. (1987). The influence of the family on premarital sexual attitudes and behavior. *Demography,* 24, 323–40.

Thornton, A., Axinn, W., & Teachman, J. (1995). The influence of school enroll-ment and accumulation on cohabitation and marriage in early adulthood. *American Sociological Review,* 60, 762–74.

Thornton, A., & Camburn, D. (1987). Religious participation and adolescent sex-ual behavior and attitudes. *Journal of Marriage and the Family,* 51, 641–53.

Thornton, A., & Freedman, D. (1982). Changing attitude toward marriage and single life. *Family Planning Perspective,* 14, 297–303.

Thorpe, R. (1997). A house where queers go: African-American lesbian nightlife in Detroit, 1940–1975. In E. Lewin (Ed.), *Inventing lesbian cultures in America* (pp. 40–61). Boston: Beacon.

Tourangeau, R., Rips, L. J., & Rasinski, K. (2000). *The psychology of survey response.* Cambridge: Cambridge University Press.

Treas, J. (1993). Money in the bank: Transaction costs and the economic organiza-tion of marriage. *American Sociological Review,* 58, 723–34.

Treas, J., & Giesen, D. (2000). Sexual infidelity among married and cohabiting Americans. *Journal of Marriage and the Family,* 62, 48–60.

Treichler, P. (1999). AIDS, homophobia, and biomedical discourse: An epidemic of signification. In R. Parker & P. Aggleton (Eds.), *Culture, society, and sexuality: A reader* (pp. 357–86). New York: UCL.

Trent, K., & South, S. (1992). Sociodemographic status, parental background, childhood family structure, and attitudes toward family formation. *Journal of Marriage and the Family,* 54, 427–39.

Tucker, M. B. (1987). The black male shortage in Los Angeles. *Sociology and Social Research,* 71, 221–27.

Tucker, M. B., & Mitchell-Kernan, C. (1995). *The decline in marriage among African Americans: Causes, consequences, and policy implications.* New York: Sage.

Turner, J. H. (1999). Toward a general sociological theory of emotions. *Journal for the Theory of Social Behaviour, 29*, 133–62.

Turner, J. H. (2000). *On the origins of human emotion: A sociological inquiry into the nature of human affect.* Stanford, CA: Stanford University Press.

U.S. Bureau of the Census. (1998). Marital status of persons 15 years and over, by age, sex, race, Hispanic origin, metropolitan residence, and region: March 1998. *Current Population Reports, 20*, 1–9.

Van Campenhoudt, L., Cohen, M., Guizzardi, G., & Hausser, D. (Eds.). (1997). *Sexual interactions and HIV risk: New conceptual perspectives in European research.* London: Taylor & Francis.

Van Haitsma, M. (1999). Methods summary and overview for CHSLS. University of Chicago. Typescript.

Vaughan, D. (1986). *Uncoupling: Turning points in intimate relationships.* New York: Oxford University Press.

Vetere, V. A. (1983). The role of friendship in the development and maintenance of lesbian love relationships. *Journal of Homosexuality, 8*, 51–65.

Waite, L. J. (1995). Does marriage matter? *Demography, 32*, 483–507.

Waite, L. J. (2000). Trends in men's and women's well-being in marriage. In L. J. Waite, C. Bachrach, M. Hindin, E. Thomson, & A. Thornton (Eds.), *The ties that bind: Perspectives on marriage and cohabitation* (pp. 368–92). New York: Aldine de Gruyter.

Waite, L. J., & Gallagher, M. (2000). *The case for marriage: Why married people are happier, healthier, and better off financially.* New York: Doubleday.

Waite, L. J., & Hughes, M. E. (1999). At risk on the cusp of old age: Living arrangements and functional status among black, white, and Hispanic adults. *Journal of Gerontology, 54B*, S136–S144.

Waite, L. J., & Joyner, K. (2001). Emotional satisfaction and physical pleasure in sexual unions: Time horizon, sexual behavior, and sexual exclusivity. *Journal of Marriage and the Family, 63*, 247–64.

Waite, L. J., & Spitze, G. D. (1981). Young women's transition to marriage. *Demography, 18*, 681–94.

Walker, L. E. (1984). *The battered woman syndrome.* New York: Springer.

Waller, M. R. (1999). Meanings and motives in new family stories: The separation of reproduction and marriage among low-income black and white parents. In M. Lamont (Ed.), *The cultural territories of race: Black and white boundaries* (pp. 182–218). Chicago: University of Chicago Press.

Warner, R. S. (1994). The place of the congregation in the contemporary American religious configuration. In J. P. Wind & J. W. Lewis (Eds.), *American congregations* (vol. 2, pp. 54–99). Chicago: University of Chicago Press.

Wasserheit, J., & Aral, S. O. (1996). The dynamic topology of sexually transmitted disease epidemics: Implications for prevention strategies. *Journal of Infectious Diseases, 174* (suppl.), S201–S213.

Wasserman, S., & Faust, K. (1994). *Social network analysis: Methods and applications.* Cambridge: Cambridge University Press.

Watney, S. (1999). Safer sex as community practice. In R. Parker & P Aggelton (Eds.), *Culture, society, and sexuality: A reader* (pp. 405–15). New York: UCL.

Weeks, J. (1996). The construction of homosexuality. In S. Seidman (Ed.), *Queer theory/sociology* (pp. 41–63). Cambridge, MA: Blackwell.

Weeks, J. (2000). *Making sexual history.* Cambridge: Polity.

Wellman, B., Wong, R. Y., Tindall, D., & Nazer, N. (1996). A decade of network change: Turnover, persistence, and stability in personal communities. *Social Networks,* 19, 27–50.

West, C., & Zimmerman, D. (1987). Doing gender. *Gender and Society,* 1, 125–51.

Westoff, C. F., & Ryder, N. B. (1977). *The Contraceptive Revolution.* Princeton, NJ: Princeton University Press.

Weston, K. (1995). Get thee to a big city: Sexual imaginary and the great gay migration. *GLC,* 2, 253–77.

White, G. L., & Mullen, P. E. (1989). *Jealousy: Theory, research, and clinical strategies.* New York: Guilford.

White, H. (1981). Where do markets come from? *American Journal of Sociology,* 87, 517–47.

Whyte, M. K. (1990). The second time around. In *Dating, mating, and marriage* (pp. 219–40). New York: Aldine de Gruyter.

Williams, J. E., & Holmes, K. A. (1981). *The second assault: Rape and public attitudes.* Westport, CT: Greenwood.

Williamson, O. E. (1981). The economics of organization: The transaction cost approach. *American Journal of Sociology,* 87, 548–77.

Williamson, O. E. (1985). *The economic institutions of capitalism.* New York: Free Press.

Willis, R. J. (1999). A theory of out-of-wedlock childbearing. *Journal of Political Economy,* 107, S33–S64.

Wilson, B. F., & Clarke, S. C. (1992). Remarriages: A demographic profile. *Journal of Family Issues,* 13, 123–41.

Wilson, M. I., & Daly, M. (1993). An evolutionary psychological perspective on male sexual proprietariness and violence against wives. *Violence and Victims,* 8, 271–94.

Wilson, W. J. (1987). *The truly disadvantaged: The inner city, the underclass, and public policy.* Chicago: University of Chicago Press.

Wilson, W. J. (1996). *When work disappears.* New York: Vintage.

Wilson, W. J., & Neckerman, K. M. (1986). Poverty and family structure: The widening gap between evidence and public policy issues. In S. H. Danziger & D. H. Weinberg (Eds.), *Fighting poverty: What works and what doesn't* (pp. 232–59). Cambridge, MA: Harvard University Press.

Winship, C., & Mare, R. (1992). Models for selection bias. *Annual Review of Sociology,* 18, 327–50.

Wirth, L. ([1938] 1956). Urbanism as a way of life. In E. W. Marvick & J. A. J. Reiss (Eds.), *Community life and social policy: Selected papers by Louis Wirth* (pp. 110–32). Chicago: University of Chicago Press.

Wolf, D. G. (1979). *The lesbian community.* Berkeley and Los Angeles: University of California Press.

Wright, R. (1994). *The moral animal: The new science of evolutionary psychology.* New York: Pantheon.

Wuthnow, R. (1988). *The restructuring of American religion.* Princeton, NJ: Princeton University Press.

Wuthnow, R. (1998). *Loose connections: Joining together in America's fragmented communities.* Cambridge, MA: Harvard University Press.

Ybarra, L. (1983). Empirical and theoretical developments in the study of Chicano families. In A. Valdez, A. Camarillo, & T. Almaguer (Eds.), *State of Chicano research on family, labor, and migration: Proceedings of the First Stanford Symposium on Chicano Research and Public Policy* (pp. 91–110). Stanford, CA: Stanford University, Center for Chicano Research.

Youm, Y. (2000). Trust in U.S. families: Its effects on the formation and dynamics of families. Ph.D. diss., University of Chicago.

Youm, Y. (2001). Family formation: Why are African Americans less likely to marry? Paper presented at the annual meeting of the American Sociological Association, Anaheim, CA, 19 August.

Youm, Y. & Laumann, E. O. (2001). Social network effects on the transmission of sexually transmitted diseases. Paper presented at the Sunbelt XXI International Social Network conference, Budapest, 27 April.

Youm, Y., & Laumann, E. O. (2002). Social network effects on the transmission of sexually transmitted diseses. *Sexually Transmitted Diseases,* 29 (11), 689–97.

Youm, Y., & Laumann, E. O. (2003). The effect of structural embeddedness on the division of household labor: A game-theoretic model with a network approach. *Rationality and Society,* 15 (2), 243–80.

Young, L. A. (Ed.). (1997). *Rational choice theory and religion.* New York: Routledge.

Zammuner, V. L., & Fischer, A. H. (1995). The social regulation of emotion in jealousy situations: A comparison between Italy and the Netherlands. *Journal of Cross-Cultural Psychology,* 26, 189–208.

Zinn, M. B. (1979). Political familism: Toward sex role equity in Chicano families. *Aztlan,* 8, 13–26.

Zucker, L. (Ed.). (1988). *Institutional patterns and organizations.* Cambridge, MA: Ballinger.

# Contributors

**Stephen Ellingson**
is assistant professor of sociology and
director of the Lilly Program for
Congregational Ministry at Pacific
Lutheran Theological Seminary.

**Edward O. Laumann**
is the George Herbert Mead
Distinguished Service Professor
at the University of Chicago and
in the College.

**Zohar Lechtman**
is a doctoral candidate in sociology
at the University of Chicago.

**Jenna Mahay**
is a postdoctoral fellow in the
NIA-sponsored Chicago Center
on Demography and Economics
of Aging.

**Anthony Paik**
is assistant professor of sociology at
the University of Iowa.

**Kirby Schroeder**
is a doctoral candidate in sociology
at the University of Chicago.

**Nelson Tebbe**
is acting assistant professor
of lawyering at New York
University School of Law
and a doctoral candidate.

**Jennifer Tello Buntin**
is a doctoral candidate in sociology
at the Univesity of Chicago.

**Martha Van Haitsma**
is co-director of the Survey Lab
at the University of Chicago.

**Yoosik Youm**
is assistant professor of sociology at the
University of Illinois at Chicago.

# Author Index

# Subject Index

*Page numbers in italics refer to figures and tables.*

abortion: black church and, 330, 332; Catholic teachings on, 294, 332; CHSLS respondents on, *60, 62;* Westside neighborhood attitude toward, 63

abstinence-only approach, 302, 303

acquaintances. *See* friendship networks

acquaintance with current neighbors, 269, *276,* 277, 278, 279

Active Proud Black Lesbians and Gays, 119

adultery. *See* extramarital sex

African American gay men: community attitude toward homosexuality, 100, 102, 112, 121–22, 330n, 331; hiding their gay identity, 330n; as outside boundaries of "acceptable blackness," 102; private sex marketplaces of, 111, 112; racism experienced in broader gay community, 103, 111; in Southtown neighborhood, 112; support groups for, 113

African American lesbians: community attitude toward homosexuality, 100, 102, 112, 121–22, 330n, 331; complexity of sexual relationships of, 166; identifying with race more than sexuality, 120, 122; lesbian sex mar-

kets for, 117–22; as outside boundaries of "acceptable blackness," 102; racism experienced in broader gay community, 103, 119; supports groups for, 119

African Americans: on AIDS, 299, 300; on bisexuality, 112; Catholicism among, 333n; census data of 1990, *53;* CHSLS focusing on, 43; and class, 44; "don't ask, don't tell" policy in, 100, 121–22; family formation and high rate of concurrency in, 89; greater likelihood of STD infection among, 272; on homosexuality, 100, 102, 112, 121–22, 330n, 331; intimate-partner violence among, 207–8, 209, 209n, *212, 232–33,* 235, 236, 237, 258–60; median age at first marriage increasing, 128; polygamy among, 177, 179, 184, 187; racial gap in marriage, 30–31, *171,* 171–72, 179, 184, 191; sex ratio imbalance in, 171–72, 184; sexual jealousy among, 207–8, 213, 221, 223; sexual-matching patterns in, *178,* 178–79, *180;* social networks and marriage rates of, 30–31; in Southtown neighborhood, 57; structural embeddedness among,

lesbians (*continued*)
    seminating information to, 19;
    Southtown neighborhood residents
    on, 120, 121; Westside neighbor-
    hood residents on, 120–21. *See also*
    African American lesbians; Hispanic
    lesbians; lesbian sex markets
lesbian sex markets: brief history of
    American, 97–99; in Chicago, 115–
    22; in Erlinda neighborhood, 119; as
    relational, 94, 97–98, 115, 123; in
    Shoreland neighborhood, 115–16,
    116n, 119; in Westside neighborhood,
    119; for white women, 115–17; for
    women of color, 117–22; women's
    softball leagues in, 21, 98, 116
Leticia, 226–27, 262
liberation theology, 338, 339, 341, 342
lifestyles, risks associated with, 288, 307
local brokers, defined, 17
long-term polygamy: among African
    American men, 184; of CHSLS re-
    spondents, 175–79, 176; and family
    formation, 358; by gender, 178; as
    hybrid strategy, 170; by race, 178,
    180; women choosing, 183–84
love: American myth of, 355; love con-
    quers all myth, 357–58
Lutherans, 315n, 321

machismo: among rural Mexican immi-
    grants, 5; and "culture of silence"
    about sexuality, 290; in Hispanic sex-
    ual culture, 22, 294; and intimate-
    partner violence, 256, 294; and public
    gay identity, 357; in Puerto Rican
    men, 255, 295; and same-sex rela-
    tionships, 100, 113; and STDs, 295
mainline Protestantism, 140; Lutherans,
    315n, 321; membership decline in,
    313n; in Shoreland neighborhood, 55,
    110, 320–28, 346, 353; social-justice
    issues facing, 323. *See also* Episcopal
    Church; United Church of Christ
"make or buy" decisions, 166
male homosexuality. *See* gay men

male same-sex markets. *See* gay male
    sex markets
markets: as socially constructed, 12. *See
    also* marriage market; sex markets
marriage: age and likelihood of, 155,
    156; black church focusing on, 331;
    in Christian view of sexuality, 311,
    314; Cox proportional hazard model
    of, 191, 192; decline of, 31; disinvest-
    ment in, 352; event-history analysis
    of, 190–92; forced sex perpetrated
    by spouse, 242; as implicit long-term
    contracts, 16; increase in age at, 34,
    127, 128; individual and social bene-
    fits of, 156; marital status by race and
    gender in Chicago, 178; monogamy
    and, 179, 182; multinomial logit
    analysis of sexual-matching patterns,
    189–90; polygamy as alternative to,
    172–73, 182–85, 183; proportion of
    never-married men older than
    thirty-five, 181; racial gap in, 30–31,
    171, 171–72, 179, 184, 191; relation
    to sex, 167–68, 173, 358; sexual-
    matching strategies and, 174, 179–
    84, 181; Shoreland neighborhood re-
    ligious leaders on, 320; social net-
    works and, 30–31, 173–75; structural
    embeddedness and, 185–87, 191;
    transaction-cost perspective on, 169;
    two beliefs that facilitate, 174. *See
    also* divorce; extramarital sex; mar-
    riage market; remarriage
marriage, gay. *See* same-sex union cer-
    emonies
marriage market: defined, 11; economic
    approach to, 11–12; opportunities in
    sex markets as constraints on, 172–
    73; social structure affecting, 12
master-status categories, 7, 9
masturbation, 321
"meat markets," 10
mediated sexual marketplaces, 18
men: age and process of partnering,
    145–53; attractiveness increasing
    with age, 132; in commercial sex